WRONG WAY

WRONG WAY

HOW PRIVATISATION & ECONOMIC REFORM BACKFIRED

EDITED BY DAMIEN CAHILL & PHILLIP TONER

IN CONJUNCTION WITH BLACK INC.

Published by La Trobe University Press in conjunction with Black Inc.
Level 1, 221 Drummond Street
Carlton VIC 3053, Australia
enquiries@blackincbooks.com
www.blackincbooks.com
www.latrobeuniversitypress.com.au

9781760640385 (paperback)
9781743820605 (ebook)

A catalogue record for this book is available from the National Library of Australia

Cover design by Kim Ferguson
Text design and typesetting by Tristan Main
Maps by Alan Laver

CONTENTS

PART TWO: PRIVATISATION AND DEREGULATION

PART THREE: MACRO-ECONOMIC DIMENSIONS

INTRODUCTION: SITUATING PRIVATISATION AND ECONOMIC REFORM

DAMIEN CAHILL AND PHILLIP TONER

Why This Book and Why Now?

Since the early 1980s, Australia and its economy have been radically transformed by the processes of privatisation, deregulation and marketisation; free trade agreements; and new approaches to macro-economic policy focused on balancing budgets, reducing rates of income and corporate tax, constraining organised labour and targeting inflation. Markets have become the preferred means of delivering public amenities, and a general aversion to direct government service provision sits alongside rhetorical fidelity to 'slimming the state'. Going by the euphemistic terms 'economic reform' and 'microeconomic reform' to its adherents – and, variously, 'economic rationalism', 'neoliberalism' or 'market fundamentalism' to its detractors – the commitment to such processes has come to form a political consensus across the major political parties, the senior ranks of the public service and the news media, especially the financial press.

More than sufficient time has elapsed since the general adoption of economic reform in Australia to make a mature assessment of actual policy outcomes against policy intentions. It is no longer credible to explain away the deleterious consequences of this process as 'transitional problems' or as the result of imperfect implementation. Through a series of detailed case studies commissioned from leading Australian experts, *Wrong Way* critically analyses the effects of privatisation, contracting out and economic reform. Its key findings are that not only have processes of reform failed to deliver many of the benefits promised by their advocates, they have also imposed a raft of economic and social costs on the Australian community.

While voices of dissent have been present throughout the long history of this project, more recently the wisdom of a dogmatic attachment to economic reform has been questioned even among some of its hitherto strongest supporters. When Rod Sims, head of the Australian Competition and Consumer Commission (ACCC) and historically a staunch advocate of economic reform, argued in 2016 that privatisation had increased prices, stifled productivity and created the conditions for unaccountable oligopolies, it was clear that a shift in the climate of opinion was afoot (Hatch 2016). Similarly, former head of the Business Council of Australia (BCA) Tony Shepherd who, as chair of the Abbott government's National Commission of Audit, has been a strong advocate for smaller government, recently lamented the loss of expertise and policy formulation competence in government due to job losses and an excessive reliance on external consultants (Donaldson 2018).

Internationally, the Organisation for Economic Co-operation and Development (OECD) has been warning of the negative effects of stark income inequality on economic growth since 2008. Its 2015 report, *In It Together: Why Less Inequality Benefits All*, argues that inequality produced by neoliberal policies has dampened growth. The OECD has also revised its long-standing endorsement of labour market deregulation and is highlighting the adverse effects on labour markets of the surge in precarious employment. In a policy about-face, it now advocates collective bargaining, 'provided it is quite centralised or co-ordinated,' which it argues has positive effects on 'labour market resilience' (OECD 2017: 9). Similarly, the International Monetary Fund (IMF) – responsible for the imposition of neoliberal 'structural adjustment programs' across the Global South – has revised its support for fiscal 'austerity' and for the removal of controls on international capital flows (Ostry, Loungani and Furceri 2016).

The broader context underpinning this change of mind is the radically transformed economic environment since the 2008 global financial crisis. Anaemic growth, deflation, high unemployment, austerity, rising economic insecurity and increasing levels of wealth and income inequality have generated widespread disenchantment with mainstream politics, the neoliberal consensus, globalisation and even democracy itself. Many of the unexpected political turns of the last few years – the surge in support for Bernie Sanders and the election of Donald Trump in the United States; Jeremy Corbyn and the Brexit vote in the United Kingdom; the rise of nationalist parties in Western and Eastern Europe – are only comprehensible within this context. Neoliberalism might still be the dominant ideology, but it is nonetheless being challenged from the left, the right and the centre.

Most of the nineteen chapters in this book offer an empirical case study of the effects of economic reform within a specific industry. These include electricity (Quiggin); child care (Hill and Wade); aged care (Davidson); employment services (Olney and Gallet); the National Broadband Network (Ridge); prisons (Andrew and Baker); residential housing (Phibbs and Gurran); banking (Jones); private health insurance (Duckett); the Higher Education Contribution Scheme (Spies-Butcher and Bryant); and vocational education and training (Toner). Also included are chapters covering broad transformational policies that affect all industries, including free trade agreements (Ranald); liberalised foreign investment policy (Richardson); labour market deregulation (Stanford); and monetary policy (Beggs). Other chapters reflect on both the causes and consequences of these policies, including the loss of expertise within the public sector (Davies); the growth of income and wealth inequality under economic reform (Stilwell); the central role of computerised general equilibrium modelling in justifying economic reform, how its assumptions are contradicted by the facts of modern economies and why these assumptions exaggerate the benefits and minimise the cost of reform (Brain); and, finally why the concept of 'productivity' has been central to justifications of economic reform in the neoliberal era despite the flaws in its measurement and its disappointing record (Quiggin).

The sheer breadth of sectors, services, practices and policies covered in this collection is a clear testament to the scale of neoliberal ambition and its root-and-branch transformation of the Australian economy, Australian political culture and society.

Before Economic Reform

In order to appreciate how radical a shift in public policy the process of privatisation and economic reform was, a brief reflection on the *status quo ante* is needed. Economic histories and political textbooks prior to the 1990s described the post–World War II period in Australia as a 'mixed economy,' with private enterprise dominating output, employment and investment, but with the state directly producing a much greater share of goods and services than is the case today (Butlin et. al. 1982). Wages were set through centralised wage fixing and union density was high. Private business was both more co-ordinated and more tightly regulated through such mechanisms as marketing boards that governed every conceivable agricultural and mining commodity. Among other large enterprises, the Commonwealth government provided the monopoly telecommunications service (Telecom), the major airline (Qantas), the postal service, shipping services and Australia's largest bank (the Commonwealth Bank). Individual states owned banks, insurance companies and a range of monopoly utilities, including electricity, transport and water corporations. Government business enterprises and utilities were controlled by government but generally managed at arm's length through institutions such as statutory authorities. Established by acts of parliament and overseen by boards, these statutory authorities were ultimately responsible to a government minister. While they could raise capital on open markets and largely invest independently of direct government control, importantly their founding legislation typically set multiple objectives: in addition to delivering services efficiently, they were required to facilitate the development of other industries, promote regional development and train professionals and tradespeople, usually in excess of their own direct needs (Toner 1998).

In part, the arrangement of the mixed economy was a pragmatic one: it responded to the relatively small scale of already extant capitalist enterprises, which thus required large public investments to adequately supply essential services and foster demand. It was also a partly ideological arrangement, a form of nation-building, and a commitment to avoid another major depression. The nation-building project was also driven by the major strategic impetus drawn from World War II, including the aims of increasing the population, promoting industrialisation and developing Australia's scientific and technological base.

It is important to keep some critical perspective here to avoid the erroneous perception that this was a halcyon era. For example, female labour force participation was discouraged and the tariff system, while successful in promoting a diversified industrial base, became ossified. Successive Australian governments failed to adapt to changing global economic conditions with, for example, more sophisticated industrial policies focused on innovation, and making state support conditional on firms achieving efficiency and export targets.

Nevertheless, there were and are sound reasons for state ownership of natural monopolies: to establish universal delivery of essential services at reasonable prices; to retain a capacity to regulate and mediate the relationship between capital and labour and implement intelligent industry policy in technologically strategic industries. In their respective chapters, both John Quiggin and Michael Beggs note that productivity and macroeconomic performance during the postwar boom right up until the mid-1970s was exceptional compared to the period of economic reform that was to come.

The Process of Economic Reform in Australia

Many histories of economic reform in Australia adopt a triumphalist posture. They portray this process as, at first, a victory of reason over discredited ideas and rent-seeking interests and, second, as an inevitable accommodation to a globalising world economy (see for example Parkinson 2014). Former head of the Productivity Commission Gary Banks (2005: 2) was even moved to use a biblical analogy, describing the period prior to reform as 'paradise lost', and the period after reform as paradise 'regained' (albeit avoiding the sin of pride by stipulating only 'partly' regained). This book charts a different course.

While there are antecedents in earlier government interventions, most notably the Whitlam government's 1973 tariff cut, economic reform in Australia became a state logic from the early 1980s onwards, under successive federal Labor and conservative governments. The key activities constituting this logic were: floating the Australian dollar; deregulation of financial and labour markets; a commitment to free trade realised by dismantling the century old tariff system and prioritising the interests of finance capital and agribusiness over manufacturing capital; the corporatisation or privatisation of profitable, publicly owned businesses; and the institutionalisation of neoliberal governance through the Council of Australian Governments (COAG) and the National Competition Policy (NCP), a set of provisions introduced in the 1990s with the aim of promoting micro-economic reform. There was also massive state subsidisation of private markets for services such as education, welfare, superannuation and health insurance.

Each major stage of economic reform was heralded by a torrent of reviews, inquiries and assessments.[1] Each of these repeated the claim that privatising profitable government business enterprises and contracting out remaining taxpayer-funded government services would improve:

- 'Transparency' in price setting and in the quality and quantity of services offered (in contrast to the multiple and sometimes contradictory objectives imposed on public providers);
- 'Accountability' through competition between providers;
- Choice for consumers;
- 'Efficiency' and 'effectiveness' through the creation of incentives to better align management interests with those of owners and consumers;
- Risk management; and
- Economic performance through the restriction of the scope of state activity.

The claim frequently made by conservative British prime minister Margaret Thatcher that 'there is no alternative' ('TINA') to neoliberalism became the accepted wisdom of political and business elites. For its proponents, so-called economic reform was founded upon rational, objective economic analysis and would make people's lives fundamentally better. As is characteristic of ideological movements, adherents explained away negative developments as the results of incorrect implementation, political interference and electoral backlash to 'reform fatigue' – in sum, 'transitional problems'. Historically then, economic reform has been relatively impervious to criticism and to evidence querying its success (Quiggin 2002).

Explaining the Persistence of Neoliberalism in Australia

In *Wrong Way* we explain the unreasonable persistence of neoliberalism in Australia and other advanced economies as the effect of powerful intellectual *ideas*, the *economic interests* served by these ideas, and the *institutions* formed to implement neoliberal public policy. Despite long-standing reservations and apparently self-defeating outcomes, neoliberalism has remained ascendant through the mutual reinforcement of these three elements.

Ideas

Part economic theory, part political philosophy, neoliberalism has many intellectual sources. Some elements are internally contradictory, but like all abstractions simultaneously offering a critique of existing society and the promise of a better life, it exercises a powerful influence over believers.

The origin of the neoliberal movement – if not of neoliberal ideas themselves – is generally traced to 1947, when a small group of intellectuals, mainly economists, met in Mont Pèlerin, Switzerland, to discuss what they viewed to be the growing collectivist threat posed by the rise of Keynesian forms of economic planning in Britain, the United States and Europe (Burgin 2012; Cahill and Konings 2017). In the context of the expanding size of government and the welfare state after World War II, the Mont Pèlerin group argued that social democratic forms of economic management were akin to fascism and that the state should reduce its scope and devolve most remaining functions to the private sector. Clearly this swam against the tide of the times.

However, the movement received a major impetus due to the onset of stagflation (simultaneously low economic growth, high unemployment and high inflation) from the mid-1970s. This instigated a questioning of conventional Keynesian macro-economic management as the three defining features of stagflation, neoliberals claimed, were incompatible with and not explained by Keynesian theory (this claim is incorrect; see Krugman 2009). In addition, relatively stable postwar relations between capital and labour in advanced economies broke down as workers used strikes to defend their living standards in response to stagflation. Further instability was created by currency crises, growing trade and debt imbalances across developed nations caused in part by massive increases in the price of oil in the early 1970s, and the globalisation of production and finance that had been underway since the 1960s. By 1973 the postwar Bretton Woods system of capital controls and fixed exchange rates had collapsed.

Policymakers across the globe responded in broadly similar ways to the resulting economic crisis. These policies included removing restrictions on international capital flows; floating exchange rates; expanding free trade agreements; deregulating labour markets; and reducing the role of the state in the economy by privatising profitable government enterprises and contracting out remaining government services. Control of monetary policy was removed from government and placed in the hands of independent agencies, like the Reserve Bank of Australia (RBA). These neoliberal policies were intended to increase the role of market forces in the national and international economy and expressed a fundamental hostility to the state as an ineffective, inefficient and self-interested institution.

Where did these ideas come from? During the 1970s, Keynesian ideas were supplanted by a resurgence of pre-Keynesian orthodox or neoclassical economics, and new ideas about how markets operate and how macro-economic analysis should be conducted. Under such views, traditional countercyclical fiscal and monetary policies are by definition ineffective. Government economic stimuli simply 'crowd out' or substitute for private spending, only boosting inflation and not output. Monetary policy would now be focused solely on targeting and controlling inflation. Furthermore, it was assumed that labour and capital would be fully employed once subject to market forces. State ownership came to be understood as inherently inefficient, and government services were viewed as failing to meet consumer needs.

In Australia, neoclassical or orthodox economics provided a key rationale among local neoliberal advocates. In universities and the public sector, orthodox economists were deeply attracted to an abstract understanding of the economy as a self-regulating mechanism that operates according to precise mathematical laws that can be analysed using systems of simultaneous equations and calculus. Given a prodigious array of improbable assumptions regarding the nature of markets and participants within them, these techniques can demonstrate that markets generate optimal outcomes in terms of efficient and effective resource use for producers and consumers. Quite literally, these techniques show that, when largely unfettered by government, markets deliver, to paraphrase Voltaire, the best possible outcomes in the best of all possible worlds.

The ultimate expression of this orthodoxy is the 'general equilibrium model', a mathematical model of an entire economy. Applying such a model became feasible because of rising computing power precisely at the time of the neoliberal take-off in the early 1970s. These models are used extensively in universities and government economic departments, especially in the Productivity Commission and its antecedents, to 'prove' that large gains are to be made from implementing neoliberal economic policies of capital and labour market deregulation, free trade, privatisation and contracting out. However, these results depend on a priori assumptions about markets and behaviour that are either unfalsifiable or 'directly contradicted by observation' (Kaldor 1972: 1238). In his contribution to the collection, Peter Brain describes the 'unscientific' character of these economic models, how they justify deregulation, inequality and unemployment. He also provides an alternative model (see Chapter 16).

A related intellectual strain underpinning neoliberalism is public choice theory, according to which voters, politicians and bureaucrats alike are driven by the same self-interested motivations that are presumed to dominate regular economic behaviour (Buchanan 2003). From Adam Smith's *The Wealth of Nations* (1776) to the present, orthodox economists have relied on the paradoxical assertion that the pursuit of individual self-interest gets transformed through healthy market competition into both private and public gain. Bakers and candlestick makers supply just the right quantity of their goods at the lowest price – not out of goodwill but to maximise their own profit. But public choice theory suggests that self-interest on the part of politicians and bureaucrats produces contrary outcomes – private gain and public loss. Democracy generates coalitions of special interests that seek to use government coercive tax and regulatory power to direct economic 'rents' to them by imposing financial burdens on others; politicians prosper only by pandering to powerful lobby groups, and bureaucrats are motivated by empire building and career progression achieved by assisting politicians meet the needs of special interests (Stigler 1971).[2] For public choice 'government failure' is worse than 'market failure'. Solutions to the former include transferring democratic decision-making on economic policy to 'independent' entities (like shifting monetary policy to the Reserve Bank), a radical reduction in the size of the state and the devolution of state functions to markets.

In Australia the neoliberal conviction about the inherently oppressive nature of the state and the idealisation of the market as a source of efficiency, effectiveness and liberty became the explicit and implicit public policy benchmark for assessing public sector performance and radically reimagining the role and functions of the state. This created an inherent bias against public sector investment, ownership and delivery. Notwithstanding potential contradictions between the different strands of neoliberal thought, in practice it provided a malleable and highly effective intellectual framework that came to be accepted as policy common sense.

Neoliberal public policy justifications were often crude in the extreme, shorn of the multitude of assumptions that marked sophisticated neoclassical analysis. Indeed, advanced orthodox economic analysis had not only established over the last century that highly restrictive and positively 'otherworldly' conditions were required to generate idealised market outcomes, it had also shown that modern economies are dominated by oligopoly and monopoly markets that operate under completely opposite conditions. At a more rarefied level, leading neoclassical theorists had concluded the whole neoclassical conceptual apparatus of rationality, optimality and equilibrium was unsound even on its own terms.[3] In sum, neoliberal economic arguments are often a simplistic parody of sophisticated orthodoxy.

The disappointing outcomes of economic reform detailed in this book flow directly from this failure to understand the actual economics of modern economies in general, and the economic effects of government activities being privatised and contracted out in particular. For example, asymmetric information between producers and consumers makes the assumption of rational choice problematic. In addition, many government services contracted out have complex and even contradictory objectives, such as employment services which seek to promote equity in the labour market by encouraging the participation of educationally disadvantaged and/or disabled people in training and employment, but also are required to achieve labour market efficiency by addressing skill shortages. The latter may be more efficiently achieved by targeting educationally advantaged and able people for training. It is also complex to specify accurately what activities will best achieve these objectives. These difficulties make it impossible for governments and consumers to efficiently contract out, choose competing suppliers and objectively monitor performance. Contributing to all of this is an ever expanding but malfunctioning regulatory apparatus governing each contracted out and privatised activity.

Interests

The rolling economic crises of the 1970s sowed fertile soil for neoliberal ideas. By this time, neoliberals had established the organisations to disseminate their ideas. Large businesses, especially those in the finance industry, and those subject to increased government regulation due to the expansion of environmental controls on industrial pollution and consumer product safety (like cigarettes), funded a global network of think tanks, including the Heritage Foundation in the United States, the Institute of Economic Affairs in the United Kingdom, the Centre for Independent Studies and the Institute of Public Affairs in Australia. Acting as 'second-hand dealers in ideas' these agencies condense more complex intellectual arguments into readily digestible opinion pieces and policy backgrounders infused with emotionally potent rhetoric aimed at shifting political debate towards the neoliberal worldview (Hayek 1949: 372).

At the broadest level, business has benefitted from policies to deregulate labour markets and reduce union bargaining power. Jim Stanford's analysis of neoliberal labour market policy charts these effects in detail (see Chapter 9). Specific industries, such as banking and finance, which gained from financial deregulation and the removal of capital controls, also benefitted greatly from neoliberal policies. Evan Jones' argues that financial deregulation encouraged the 'antisocial character' of banks (see Chapter 10), while Peter Phibbs and Nicole Gurran argue that financial deregulation was a powerful driver in the creation of 'housing' as a distinct asset class and driver of booming house prices (see Chapter 11). Mining and large agribusiness benefitted from the removal of tariffs on imported inputs and export controls on mineral resources, as well as the ending of price and quantity controls on domestic agriculture (statutory marketing boards for agricultural commodities were a common means of regulating competition and strongly supported by small farmers and the old Country Party that later became the more neoliberal oriented National Party). These were just some of the obvious economic interests that gained from the promotion of neoliberal economic policies at the outset of the reform process.

As the process matured it created new and large interests. The managers and major shareholders of privatised government business across the banking, electricity, telecommunications and insurance sectors experienced a massive transfer of wealth from the public to themselves. Major consulting, accounting and law firms now earn large fees advising government on privatisations and public-private partnerships (PPPs). The massive growth of state subsidised quasi-markets benefitted specific industries such as private health insurance firms. Stephen Duckett critically assesses the case for government subsidising private health insurance (see Chapter 2). Contracting out of high-level information and communications technology (ICT) and policymaking capacities by government created large new markets, especially for major multinational corporations. Paul Davies highlights the loss of engineering expertise in the public sector with government becoming a 'dumb buyer' of ICT and infrastructure (see Chapter 6). Contracting out also produced a whole new class of 'entrepreneurs', many of whom became exceedingly wealthy.[4] Sue Olney and Wilma Gallet highlight the perverse incentives created for private employment services in what were formerly publicly delivered activities (see Chapter 7). Toner charts the rapid rise of the publicly funded but privately delivered training market, and uses orthodox economic analysis to explain widespread quality diminution and malfeasance in this market (see Chapter 3). Some politicians and senior bureaucrats supporting privatisation and contracting out have regularly been rewarded with well-remunerated advisory or even board positions post-retirement in these firms or their industry associations.

Dependent on the continued flow of either profitable government businesses to privatise, or government contracts and subsidies, these new industries established industry associations to advocate for further reform. Examples include the Australian Council for Private Education and Training (ACPET), 'a strong voice to promote the choice and diversity that the private sector offers and influence the legislation, regulations, compliance requirements and policies which affect the business environment in which they operate' (ACPET 2017). Infrastructure Partnerships Australia (IPA), established in 2005, with both private and public sector members, advocates *inter alia* for the expansion of PPPs and privatisation. For example, according to the IPA 'there is greater scope for involving the private sector in the delivery of prison services and infrastructure. International and domestic research shows that private prisons generally deliver superior outcomes on cost and provide a quality of service at least as good as (and often better than) the public sector' (IPA 2009). Jane Andrew and Max Baker in their examination of the costs of prison reform and privatisation in Victoria conclude otherwise (Chapter 4). The IPA board includes key financiers and investors in infrastructure, like Macquarie Bank and Morgan Stanley, major legal firms with construction expertise, the federal Department of Communications, the New South Wales Treasury, the New South Wales Department of Planning and the Victorian Treasury.

Institutions

Leading institutionalist economist Douglas North provides perhaps the most widely accepted and succinct definition of institutions and their economic function:

> Institutions are the humanly devised constraints that structure political, economic and social interaction. They consist of both informal constraints (sanctions, taboos, customs, traditions, and codes of conduct), and formal rules (constitutions, laws, property rights) … Institutions provide the incentive structure of an economy; as that structure evolves, it shapes the direction of economic change towards growth, stagnation, or decline. (1991: 97).

During the 1980s and 1990s neoliberalism became embedded in the Australian public service through rules of conduct, constraints on the scope of acceptable advice, and incentives to recruit and promote people who shared the broad neoliberal worldview. A migration of senior executives from the key economic departments of Treasury and Finance to other departments from the 1980s onwards led to the creation of a diaspora of policymakers sympathetic to the neoliberal worldview. These other departments included the centre of government policy formation, the Department of Prime Minister and Cabinet, and the key spending departments of Health, Education and Social Security. Neoliberalism was also cemented federally through organisations such as COAG, and the greatly expanded policy role granted to the chief advocate of neoliberalism within government, the Productivity Commission. State governments created similar institutions to promote and enforce the new orthodoxy. Combined, these institutional changes imparted a self-sustaining dynamic to the reproduction of neoliberal practices and ideas. Michael Pusey's *Economic Rationalism in Canberra: A Nation-Building State Changes Its Mind* (1991) charted the radical shift in political and economic opinion in the upper echelons of the federal public service and development of collective neoliberal 'groupthink'. Pusey (1991: 6) identified exposure to neoclassical economics as the prime cause of this shift in thinking within the upper echelons of the public service: 'a passage through an economics curriculum in their early twenties is the single factor that most strongly sets these young forty-plus captains of a nation-building state against its historical mission'.

The combination of neoliberal ideas, powerful interests and institutionally embedded practices created a potent ensemble of social and economic forces that imparted an inexorable momentum to economic reform.

Evaluating Economic Reform

How then to evaluate four decades of economic reform? The most commonly made case for economic reform is Australia's strong macro-economic performance. Since the 1991 recession, the Australian economy has experienced over a quarter century of uninterrupted economic growth. Identifying the determinants of this growth is a fraught endeavour as it is difficult to isolate precisely the relevant variables and their complex interactions. But other factors are also important in explaining this growth – many of which have little direct or casual connection with economic reform in Australia. Some of these include a relatively benign international economy (excluding the global financial crisis) and strong deflationary forces in the world economy over thirty years; the incredible rise in demand for Australian commodities from a rapidly growing Chinese economy; the global diffusion of new technologies and production techniques, and the huge expansion in female workforce participation and general workforce educational attainment that occurred in Australia over this period. Nonetheless, it seems reasonable to suggest that key elements of economic reform facilitated this expansion, including large inflows of foreign investment and a floating dollar, which helped mitigate inflation during the recent mining boom.

However, against this are the large costs of economic reform set out in this book. These include, for example, the reduction in quality and waste caused by malfeasance in the vocational education and training (VET) market; cost pressures on households and business following privatisation of the electricity sector; losses suffered by business and households from financial planning scandals and an increasingly oligopolistic banking industry; the economic burden of growing income and wealth inequality; waste caused by government becoming a 'dumb buyer' of infrastructure and ICT services; and the great financial burden on households of rapid home price rises caused primarily by financial deregulation leading to massive growth in lending and household debt. Also by many conventional measures, the Keynesian era boom from the late 1940s until the early 1970s compares more than favourably with the more recent period of sustained growth. In the former, average rates of economic growth and productivity were higher, unemployment was consistently lower, government budget surpluses were common, and there was less economic inequality and lower rates of household debt. Some of these points are taken up in John Quiggin's consideration of the 'lost golden age' story of productivity (see Chapter 15) and Michael Beggs' analysis of monetary policy, inflation and employment (see Chapter 14). Certainly, the recent boom compares more favourably with the period from the 1970s until the early 1980s, but that time was marked by global economic crisis, so, if we're using it as the benchmark for economic performance, the bar is being set rather too low.

A central neoliberal aim was to reduce the role of government in the economy. By many measures this has not occurred. Economic reform has not created a system of free markets, but a labyrinthine new architecture of regulations, contracts and subsidies. That the role of the state has been transformed but continues to remain central should be no surprise. The neoliberal dream was that the state could be reduced to Adam Smith's 'three duties of the sovereign': the provision of defence, the protection of property and person, and the creation and maintenance of infrastructure (and that even some of these could be privately funded or contracted out!). Modern complex economies not only require these but also that the state contribute to the reproduction of the family, skilled labour, the promotion of innovation and social cohesion against the constant revolutionary changes to the means of production and social relations effected by capitalism.

Beyond Economic Reform

All chapters in this book conclude either with guidance to reform 'economic reform' in specific industries subject to privatisation or contracting out, or by suggesting new approaches to economic policy.

While the scope of this book is certainly comprehensive, it has far from exhausted neoliberalism's reach in Australia. Potential topics for further investigation include, for example: privatisation of airports and ports; the abandoning of industry policy; failure in the LNG gas market; the private superannuation industry; PPP's for infrastructure delivery; water pricing and regulation of the Murray-Darling Basin and delegating certification of new building work to private for-profit firms. Nonetheless, the chapters collected here are an attempt to bring evidence to bear on what has often been a highly divided policy discussion. *Wrong Way* is driven by the need to seize the opportunity presented by the evident failure of the neoliberal agenda and the growing opposition to it and to carve out a new meaning for 'economic reform'.

Endnotes

1 Some of the key documents include: *National Competition Policy: Report* (1993); *National Commission of Audit* (1996); *The Benefits of Microeconomic Reform* (1998); *National Commission of Audit: Towards Responsible Government* (2013); *The Australian Government Competition Policy Review* (2015).

2 George Stigler, a leading neoclassical economist and market advocate, argued for the inevitability of 'regulatory capture' of government by special interests and the impossibility of regulation in the public interest. 'Until the basic logic of political

life is developed, reformers will be ill-equipped to use the state for their reforms, and victims of the pervasive use of the state's support of special groups will be helpless to protect themselves'. (Stigler 1971: 18). However, the efficacy of regulation was a key presumption of Australian neoliberal policymakers! They relied as much on the vast array of new regulatory regimes established to monitor and control the new markets they created as the discipline of the market to ensure the goals of privatisation and contracting out were met. (See Black 2013 for a thorough critique of Stigler's arguments.) The failure of privatisation and contracting out in the industries covered in this book is as much due to regulatory failure as it is to policymakers not understanding the 'markets' they created. Regulatory failure has flowed from this misunderstanding.

3 Over thirty years ago, leading general equilibrium theorists Hugo F. Sonnenschein, Rolf Mantel and Gérard Debreu proved that a 'stable' and 'unique' equilibrium in a general equilibrium system is impossible. According to Ackerman (2002: 135), 'The guaranteed optimality of market outcomes and laissez-faire policies died with general equilibrium'.

4 Large for-profit vocational training firms listed on the local stock exchange have received billions in taxpayer-funded subsidies. These firms have very high rates of profit so that 'every dollar of public subsidy paid results in thirty cents of profit for distribution to the company's shareholders' (Yu and Oliver 2015).

REFERENCES

Ackerman, F. (2002) 'Still dead after all these years: Interpreting the failure of general equilibrium theory', *Journal of Economic Methodology*, 9 (2): 119–139.

Australian Council for Private Education and Training website, 'About ACPET Membership'. www.acpet.edu.au/join/about-membership

Banks, G. (2005) 'Structural reform Australian-style: Lessons for others?' Presentation to the IMF, World Bank and OECD, Australian Government Productivity Commission, May 2005.

Black, W.K. 'Discrediting regulation: from George Stigler to Tyson's fraud-free carbon tax fantasy', *New Economic Perspectives*, 8 July 2013.

Buchanan, J.M. (2003) *Public Choice: The Origins and Development of a Research Program*. Virginia: Center for Study of Public Choice, George Mason University.

Burgin, A. (2012) *The Great Persuasion: Reinventing Free Markets Since the Depression*. Cambridge: Harvard University Press.

Butlin, N.G., Barnard, A. and Pincus, J.J. (1982) *Government and Capitalism: Public and Private Choice in Twentieth-Century Australia*. Sydney, Allen & Unwin.

Cahill, D. and Konings, M. (2017) *Neoliberalism*. Cambridge, Polity Books.

Donaldson, D. (2018) 'Tony Shepherd: Public service capability run down "too far"', *The Mandarin*, 1 February 2018.

Hatch, P. (2016) 'Privatisation has damaged the economy, says ACCC chief', *The Sydney Morning Herald*, 26 July 2016.

Hayek, F.A. (1949) 'The intellectuals and socialism', *The Intellectuals: A Controversial Portrait*. Illinois, The Free Press, 1960: 371–384.

Infrastructure Partnerships Australia (2009) *Submission to the NSW Upper House Inquiry on the Privatisation of Prisons and Prison-related Services*, March.

——(2017) *Our Board*, http://infrastructure.org.au/our-board/

Kaldor, N. (1972) 'The irrelevance of equilibrium economics', *Economic Journal*, LXXXII: 1237–1255.

Krugman P. (2009) 'The stagflation myth', *The New York Times*, 3 June 2009.

North, D.C. (1991) 'Institutions', *The Journal of Economic Perspectives*, 5 (1): 97–112.

OECD (2015) *In It Together: Why Less Inequality Benefits All*, 21 May.

——(2017) 'Editorial and Executive Summary', *OECD Employment Outlook 2017*. OECD Publishing, Paris.

Ostry, J., Prakash, L. and Davide, F. (2016) 'Neoliberalism: Oversold?' *IMF Finance & Development*, 53 (2), June 2016: 38–41.

Parkinson, M. (2014) *Reflections on Australia's Era of Economic Reform*, Canberra, Treasury, Commonwealth of Australia, 5 December 2014.

Pusey, M. (1991) *Economic Rationalism in Canberra: A Nation-Building State Changes Its Mind*. Cambridge, Cambridge University Press.

Quiggin, J. (2002) 'Economic Governance and Microeconomic Reform' in Stephen B. (ed.), *Economic Governance and Institutional Dynamics*. New York, Oxford University Press.

Stigler, G. (1971) 'The Theory of Economic Regulation', *The Bell Journal of Economics and Management Science*, 2 (1): 3–21.

Toner, P. (1998) 'Trends in NSW Government Apprenticeship intake: Causes and Implications', *Australian Bulletin of Labour*, 24 (2), June: 141–157.

Yu, S. and Oliver, D. (2015) *The Capture of Public Wealth by the For-Profit Vet Sector*. Workplace Research Centre, Sydney University.

PART ONE

THE CONTRACT STATE

CHAPTER 1

THE 'RADICAL MARKETISATION' OF EARLY CHILDHOOD EDUCATION AND CARE IN AUSTRALIA

ELIZABETH HILL AND MATT WADE

Over the past four decades, a large and sophisticated market in early childhood education and care (ECEC) has emerged in Australia.[1] The sector now caters for more than 1.2 million children, almost one-third of those aged 0 to 12 years (SCRGSP 2017).[2] ECEC services in Australia have always been provided in the private market, initially by local councils, not-for-profit and community-based organisations, and other small providers (Brennan 1998). However, reforms since the 1980s have underpinned a 'radical marketisation' of the sector (Newberry and Brennan 2007: 228) and by 2017 for-profit companies provided nearly half of all ECEC services (see Figure 1). Government policy has shifted from supply-side finance in the form of operational subsidies and capital grants, to demand-side support in the form of direct subsidies to parents. As the for-profit market has matured, ECEC services have become a new asset class attracting increasing investment from a range of large corporations, including some listed on the Australian Stock Exchange. This radical transformation has been delivered by policies introduced by both Labor and Liberal–National governments. The policy aim has been to deliver a sustainable sector that provides affordable, accessible and high-quality ECEC services for families. But, in the analysis that follows, we show that radical marketisation has had mixed success in delivering these policy goals.

Figure 1. Commonwealth-approved ECEC services by provider management type.[3]

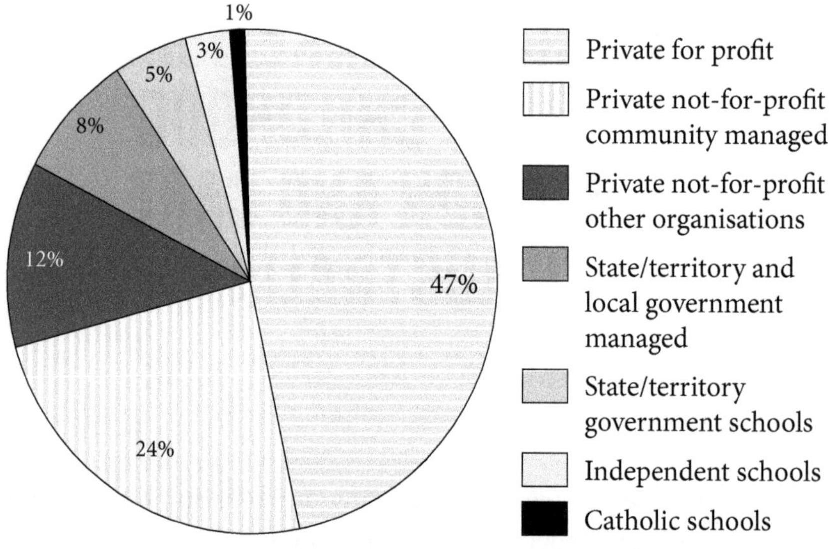

Source: ACEQA 2017

1970s: Mainstreaming ECEC

Until the early 1970s almost all centre-based ECEC was provided by a combination of philanthropic organisations and small private not-for-profit businesses. Commonwealth financial support for ECEC services was first provided in 1972, when the Whitlam Labor government passed the *Child Care Act*. Under this new legislation $6.5 million was allocated to non-profit ECEC organisations catering for the children of employed and ill parents. The funding was delivered directly to service providers in the form of capital grants, recurrent grants to pay for qualified staff and to support children with special needs, and grants for research on ECEC. Only centres that delivered eight hours of service per day, forty-eight weeks per year were eligible for funding. In 1974, Commonwealth funding was extended to all ECEC services, not just those catering for vulnerable families. This included an expanded group of ECEC services per day, including preschools, family daycare, outside school hours care and playgroups.[4] These changes reflected the Whitlam government's commitment to women's equality and participation in paid work. The expanded eligibility criteria increased the number of ECEC places available to Australian families (Brennan 1998).

1980s and 1990s: The Shift to Demand-Side Financing

The increased participation of women in the workforce throughout the 1980s, combined with the commitment of the Labor government led by Bob Hawke to reducing child poverty, produced renewed political pressure to expand ECEC services. In 1984, the Hawke government introduced a new system of fee relief and needs-based planning for child care places, called Child Care Assistance (Brennan 1998). The new system radically reorganised the government's approach from a supply-side to a demand-side funding model: operational subsidies that were formally linked to staffing costs and designed to meet the total cost of service provision were replaced with a per capita subsidy for each enrolled child. This single change saw funding stripped out of the ECEC sector. The shortfall was, in part, compensated by parent fees, which in turn were subject to a means-tested system of fee relief (McIntosh and Phillips 2002). This new demand-side financing model kept a check on the government's ECEC expenditure. At the outset, Child Care Assistance was only available to not-for-profit providers, formally maintaining Labor's commitment to a publicly funded not-for-profit ECEC sector. However, this radical reorganisation of the funding model laid the foundation for increased marketisation (Meagher and Wilson 2015: 52).

In 1990, the Hawke Labor government extended government fee relief to parents using *for-profit* ECEC services. This was a compromise decision brokered by Minister for Community Services and Health Neal Blewett after years of internal party debate about the level and aim of public funding of ECEC (Brennan 1998: 186).[5] Extending the new demand-driven funding model to the private for-profit sector increased the supply of child care places and aimed to limit public expenditure. But it also effectively dismantled the planned approach to Commonwealth support for expanded ECEC (Brennan 1998: 194). Efforts to secure a minimal standard of service from ECEC centres receiving Commonwealth funding was implemented with the introduction of a quality improvement and accreditation scheme in 1994.

The evolution of the ECEC funding framework in the 1990s reflected the application of National Competition Policy (NCP) to human services and the prioritisation of Commonwealth support for *users* rather than *providers* of services. The NCP preferred model was easily applied to the existing private structure of ECEC services, as was evident in the 1996 Economic Planning and Advisory Commission (EPAC) report, *Future Child Care Provision in Australia.* This report had been commissioned by the government led by Paul Keating but was finalised under Prime Minister John Howard. The EPAC report framed parents explicitly as 'consumers' who would exercise 'choice' in the ECEC marketplace (Brennan 1998: 208–212). By the time the Howard government came to power in March 1996, the Commonwealth's ECEC policy framework provided for extensive for-profit provision of services with limited planning.

Within two decades, ECEC policy settings had made a wholesale shift: from the Whitlam government's supply-side funding for community-based, non-profit ECEC services focused on disadvantaged children and social justice, to a marketised approach that relied on for-profit providers backed by Commonwealth subsidies. These user-pays services were delivered to customers from all social backgrounds, who, in turn, were eligible for a means-tested public subsidy. The demand-driven model of the 1990s attracted for-profit companies into the ECEC sector and delivered a rapid increase in the number of ECEC places available (Brennan 1998). However, the reliance on for-profit ECEC providers exposed the sector to new forms of vulnerability and risk.

2000s: The Emergence of Corporate Child Care

In the early 2000s Prime Minister John Howard frequently described the struggle of parents to balance their work and family responsibilities as "the barbecue stopper of Australian society" (Howard 2002). In response to rising childcare costs his government expanded public subsidies. This included the introduction of a capped Child Care Tax Rebate (CCTR) for out-of-pocket child care costs. This rebate, introduced in 2004, complemented the Commonwealth's main form of child care subsidy, the Child Care Benefit.

Rapid expansion in the sector, underpinned by large and growing public subsidies made investment in ECEC an attractive business proposition. As early as 1994, business journalist Adele Ferguson wrote that:

> Generous federal government funding of child care, a variety of government financial assistance schemes for parents, tax loopholes and even exemption in some areas from fringe benefits tax are underwriting the success of this 1990s phenomenon ... For many property owners and developers, including foreign residents, the flood of government money is a life saver, and possibly a licence to get rich.

By the 2000s a number of large companies had entered the ECEC market, exposing children, parents and government to new forms of business risk.

Ferguson's critical assessment of the risks embedded in the policy framework is highlighted in the story of the rise and fall of Eddie and Le Neve Groves' company, ABC Learning. In 1988 the Groves' opened their first ECEC centre in suburban Brisbane. Throughout the 1990s they deployed an 'opco-propco'[6] business model backed by debt and 'innovative' accounting practices, becoming not only Australia's but the world's largest publicly listed ECEC operator (Newberry and Brennan 2013; Kruger 2009). ABC Learning was listed on the Australian Stock Exchange in 2001 and became a star performer when its share price rose more than 300 per cent in the first five years. In 2004–05, ABC Learning's profits were over $50 million and by 2005–06 its market capitalisation reached $2.6 billion (Rush and Downie 2006). In 2006, Eddie Groves topped Australia's Young Rich List, with personal wealth of $260 million. At its peak, ABC Learning provided approximately 20 per cent of all long daycare places in Australia (Rush and Downie 2006). But the imperative to drive strong investment returns saw the Groves overreach, and in 2007 their ECEC empire began to crumble. The company went into voluntarily liquidation in 2008[7], and the Rudd Labor government was forced to spend $56 million keeping the 678 centres run by ABC Learning open[8] while a buyer was found. The government then provided a $15 million concessional loan to the GoodStart Early Learning consortium, which eventually acquired the company.[9]

Not all for-profit providers are large corporations using sophisticated accounting and management techniques to boost market share and profits. However, systemic reliance on for-profit providers can expose Australian families and government to significant risks. The collapse of ABC Learning shows how a guaranteed cash flow provided by government subsidies can create perverse incentives for private providers to adopt risky business practices.[10]

The demise of ABC Learning also showed how the Commonwealth ultimately bore the risk of corporate failure in the sector. The political and economic cost of an essential service like ECEC suddenly being withdrawn due to the collapse of a major provider was untenable, and, in the case of ABC Learning, the Rudd Labor government had little choice but to provide the funds to keep the centres open while an alternative arrangement was found. Not only was the Commonwealth spending billions on childcare subsidies, it was effectively the sector's insurer of last resort.

The Contemporary ECEC Sector

The ABC Learning debacle did not provoke any change in the Commonwealth's demand-side funding model, nor the controversial opco-propco investment model, which continues to be used by large commercial investors. The expansion of public subsidies to services provided by for-profit providers has underwritten the development of commercial ECEC as 'a true property investment class' (Colliers 2016a: 3). Investment houses now laud the sector as a profitable, blue-chip investment, with reported total revenue of $12.4 billion and profits of $992 million in 2016–17 (IBISWorld 2017). Reports of acquisitions and leasing arrangements in the ECEC sector regularly appear in the financial press and global consulting firms and industry groups spruik the 'strong investment fundamentals' of the sector (Colliers 2016a: 8). Alongside demographic trends and strong female workforce participation rates, Commonwealth industry assistance is highlighted in these reports as a key investment fundamental:

> Australia has in recent years experienced a surge in demand of child care services and as the costs of these services has increased, so too has government support … the government's continued

> financial support, acting as the main driver for growth, has transformed this sector into an investment grade asset class.' (Colliers 2016b: 1)

The property and land assets associated with ECEC services are especially appealing to some investors. Companies are attracted by the long-term leases (fifteen to twenty years is the new standard) in the sector and the value of the land on which centres are built. Rising property values have consolidated the shift in the structure of provider type away from a majority of community-based not-for-profits towards publicly listed commercial companies and Australian real estate investment trusts (AREITs) (Colliers 2016b: 4).[11]

The appeal of ECEC to new institutional corporate players, such as G8 Education Limited,[12] Arena REIT, Folkestone Education Trust, and Affinity Education Group, has contributed to a steady process of market consolidation in what has traditionally been a highly fragmented sector. While only 1 per cent of providers operate 25 or more services, these large corporations provide a third of all Commonwealth-approved services, with medium-sized providers delivering a further 29 per cent (ACEQA 2017). In 2016–17, the four largest ECEC companies accounted for approximately 20 per cent of total revenue in the sector (IBISWorld 2017:18). It is clear from the investment industry literature that these large corporations derive greatest returns from an investment profile that delivers economies of scale. This suggests the acquisition of smaller rivals by large corporations through aggressive strategies aimed at enhancing market share can be expected to continue (IBISWorld 2017: 18). A director of auction house Burgess Rawson describes child care centres as the company's 'most sought after asset class' for which they have a clearance rate of 'over 95 per cent' (Tan 2017).[13] The involvement of big investment firms in the Australian ECEC sector draws attention to an anomaly in Australia's education system: while for-profit providers are prohibited from running schools, and most tertiary students attend publicly owned campuses where government policy regulates student fees, parents using ECEC services are highly exposed to private-sector risk, and children – most of whom are aged less than five – are exposed to market forces. In a variety of ways, this has compromised the sustainability, accessibility, affordability and quality of ECEC services in Australia in recent years.

Has Radical Marketisation Delivered?

Since the late 1990s, persistent public concern about the cost and availability of high-quality ECEC has been a challenge for successive governments. Various attempts to expand provision while keeping the cost to parents down have seen expenditure on ECEC as a share of government outlays grow sharply, especially during the past decade (see Figure 2). ECEC assistance ballooned from 0.8 per cent of total Australian government expenditure in the mid-2000s to around 1.7 per cent by 2014–15 (Productivity Commission 2014: 10). Ongoing attempts by federal governments to address problems with affordability have seen increasing amounts of public funding spent on ECEC.

Figure 2. Government expenditure on child care fee assistance, 2011–2021.[14]

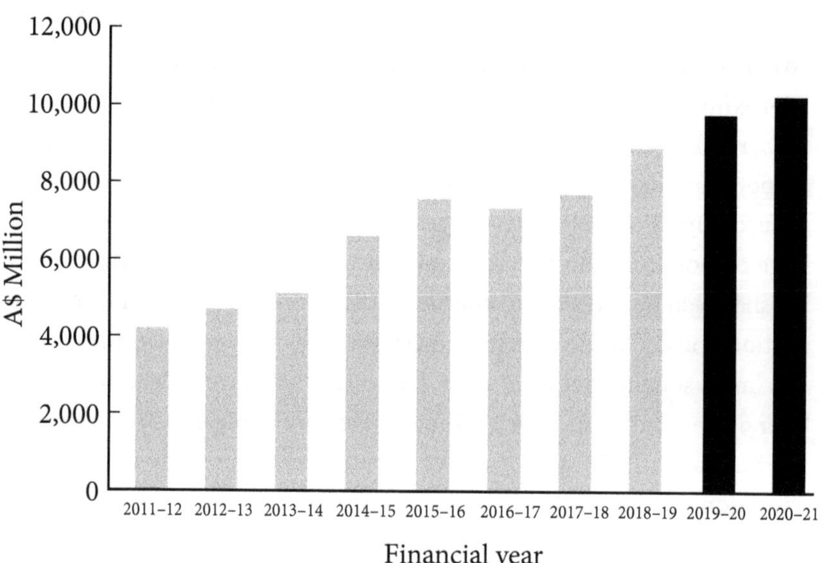

Source: Table 3.1: Top 20 programs by expenses, Commonwealth Budget Papers for years 2011 to 2017. Data for 2013–14, 2017–18 and 2018–19 are estimates. Data for 2019–20 and 2020–2021 are projections.

The new *Jobs for Families* Child Care Package, implemented in July 2018, includes far-reaching changes to the funding model for ECEC and an injection of an additional $3.5 billion over five years. The main reforms are to streamline the current Child Care Benefit (CCB) and Child Care Rebate (CCR) into a single Child Care Subsidy (CCS), and to introduce an hourly benchmark rate for each form of care (long daycare, family daycare, outside school hours care, etc.). Low-income families who meet a work activity test (or are exempt from it) are eligible for a public subsidy equal to 85 per cent of the benchmark fee. Higher-income families receive a much lower level of subsidy. The new CCS is expected to benefit most families earning up to $170,000.[15] Commonwealth budget papers for 2017–18 show the new package will make child care fee assistance the federal government's fourteenth-largest program by expenditure. At $7.55 billion, child care fee assistance in 2017–18 will be higher than army capabilities, government schools national support and naval capabilities (Department of Treasury 2017). The forward estimates show that by 2020–21 child care fee assistance will top $10 billion and rank as the twelfth-largest federal government program by expenditure (Department of Treasury 2017: 6–12). The extent to which the new funding model improves ECEC accessibility and affordability for households is yet to be determined.

Price

Rising public subsidies for child care have had a growing impact on the federal budget, raising the question of their long-term sustainability. But there has also been debate about the inflationary impact the demand-side policy approach of successive governments has had on prices in the sector. The 2014 AMP.NATSEM study concluded that 'child care subsidies certainly improve affordability, but they also likely contribute to higher child care prices' (Phillips 2014: 5).

Australia's modern marketised child care sector has been marked by rapid price inflation. The media frequently draws attention to high child care costs, stoking broader voter concern about the rising cost of living. There are reports of long daycare centres in the vicinity of Sydney's central business district charging up to $200 per day per child (Scarr 2017), which equates to annual fees of $48,000 per annum for a child in care five days per week for a standard 48-week working year. The popular focus on cost has made the affordability of child care a perennial topic of debate in Australian politics.

Public perceptions of rising child care costs are reflected in official price data. Analysis of the child care component of the consumer price index (CPI) by AMP.NATSEM (Phillips 2014: 6) found the gross cost of child care rose by almost 10 per cent per annum between 2003 and 2013, more than three times the average annual increase of the CPI in that period. The study estimated that 'the almost 10 per cent annual increase translates into a 150 per cent price hike in ten years, rising from around $30 per day in 2003 to $75 per day in 2013'. Of the eighty-seven expenditure categories monitored by the Australian Bureau of Statistics (ABS), in the five years prior to March 2014 the price growth in child care was only eclipsed by utilities and tobacco.

While federal subsidies have helped offset the direct cost of child care for Australian families there is strong evidence that the share of income committed to child care by households that use child care has grown significantly during the past two decades. Data from the Household, Income and Labour Dynamics in Australia (HILDA) Survey provide a unique insight into how much household 'out-of-pocket' costs of child care have changed. Each wave of the HILDA Survey since 2001 has asked households who use child care to report their usual weekly expenditure for each child 'after any regular child care benefit you may receive has been deducted'. This data series covers the period when Australia's modern privatised child care sector expanded rapidly amid growing demand for child care services.

The 12th Annual Statistical Report of the HILDA Survey (2017) shows large increases in household expenditure on child care for children aged under five in the decade to 2015. In 2002 and 2003, the median weekly expenditure on child care by those families was $93 for couple families and $56 for single-parent families. But by 2014 and 2015, the corresponding medians had climbed to $162 and $114, which translate to real increases of 74 per cent and 104 per cent respectively.

It is not just the real cost of child care than has grown since the early 2000s. The HILDA data suggests that the *share* of income devoted to child care by families paying for long daycare services for 0–5 year olds also increased markedly between 2002–03 and 2014–15. This was true for households across the income distribution. However, the impact was not uniform, with households in the bottom two-thirds of the income distribution facing a much higher increase in share of income spent on child care than households in the top third (HILDA 2017: 24, see Table 1). Disproportionate increases across the tercile groups mean that by 2015 the median percent of household income spent on child care by the wealthiest third of households was less than that spent by the poorest third of households – 7 per cent compared to 8.5 per cent. In 2002, poorer households paid a smaller share of household income on child care than wealthier households. By 2015, this had been reversed, with poorer households paying a larger share of household income than their wealthier counterparts.

Table 1: Median proportion of household income spent on child care (0–5 years) by tercile of the income distribution (%), 2002–2015.

	Bottom third	Middle third	Top third
2002 to 2003	5.7	5.8	6.4
2004 to 2005	4.9	6.9	6.8
2006 to 2007	6.6	6.8	7.4
2008 to 2009	6.2	7.1	7.9
2010 to 2011	6.9	7.2	6.9
2012 to 2013	8.6	8.2	7.4
2014 to 2015	8.5	8.1	7

Source: HILDA 2017: 24

There is an expectation that the new *Jobs for Families* Child Care Package will reduce the inflationary pressures that were a feature of the previous funding model. However, in a demand-side funding model price inflation remains a risk.

Access and Availability

Most Australian children now participate in some type of formal ECEC, at least in the year immediately prior to full-time schooling (Productivity

Commission 2014: 93).[16] But despite significant sectoral growth, access to child care remains controversial. The Productivity Commission (2014: 9) concluded in 2014 that accessing child care and early childhood learning is a challenge for many families: 'A number of parents struggle to find ECEC services that meet their needs and enable them to increase their work commitments or they make substantial adjustments to work hours to accommodate available care and/or school hours'. The Commission drew particular attention to supply constraints on outside school hours care and the effect this has on many parents who are therefore unable to work longer than the school day (Productivity Commission 2014: 7).

HILDA data shows that the availability of child care has been a persistent problem for families with young children, especially since 2009 (HILDA 2017). It revealed that about 70 per cent of parents who used, or considered using, child care between 2002 and 2015 experienced difficulties with availability of child care (HILDA 2017: 26). ABS data has also highlighted a widespread need for additional formal care. In June 2014, there were 248,600 children whose parent(s) reported a need for additional formal child care. Almost half (49 per cent) of these required long daycare. The majority (67 per cent) said that one to two additional days a week of child care was required (ABS 2015). According to the HILDA survey, parents cite 'availability' as the most common difficulty associated with child care (above both 'cost' and 'quality'), identified by 82 per cent of households with children aged 0–4 who have used or thought about using child care.

Quality

The quality of ECEC service provision is not uniform between for-profit and not-for-profit centres. As early as 1989, ABS data showed that commercial, for-profit centres employed fewer qualified staff, fewer ancillary staff and four times as many staff under eighteen years as not-for-profit centres (Brennan 1998: 202). Variability in the quality of ECEC services was also identified between corporate child care centres and community-based or independent private child care centres in the mid-2000s (Rush 2006: 2007).[17] Concerns about variable standards across the sector led to the introduction of the National Quality Framework (NQF) in 2012. This applies to all Commonwealth-supported ECEC services. Seven quality areas, eighteen standards and fifty-eight elements make up the National Quality Standard (NQS) of the framework. Each quarter the Australian Children's Education and Care Quality Authority (ACEQA) reports on the quality ratings in approved services. Data shows that the NQS has supported quality improvements across all provider types in the sector: in 2017, 91 per cent of all approved services received a quality rating from ACEQA, with 73 per cent of these deemed to be 'meeting' 'or above' the National Quality Standard (ACEQA 2017). However, quality ratings vary for different provider types, with 41 per cent of private not-for-profit community-managed services rated as exceeding the NQS compared with only 19 per cent of private for-profit providers[18] (see Figure 3).

Figure 3. Commonwealth approved ECEC services with a quality rating by provider management type and overall quality rating level.

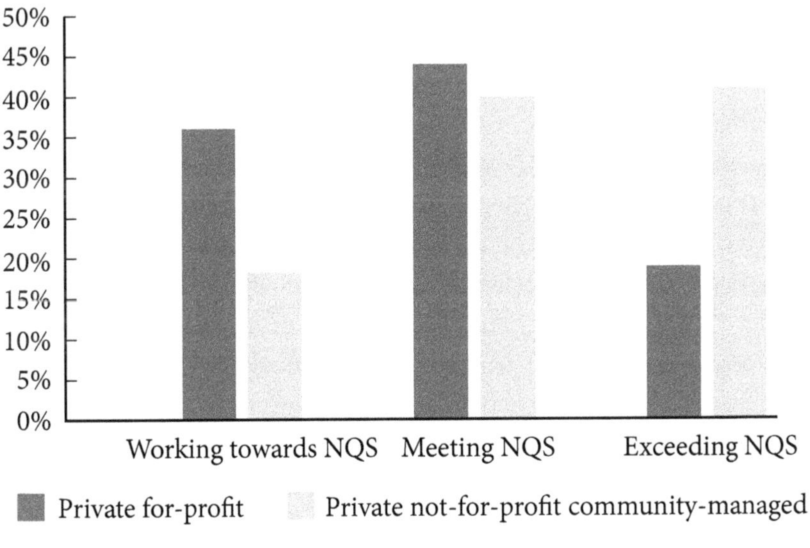

Source: ACEQA 2017

Under the NQF all those who work with children in the sector must have, or be enrolled in, a Certificate III qualification in ECEC. Regulations regarding the number of university-trained teachers employed in child care facilities have also boosted the professional expertise available to children and the quality of education available. These measures have improved the working environment for ECEC staff and created new career pathways for employees. Nevertheless, ECEC workers remain among the lowest paid workers in the Australian economy, leading to problems with retention of the workforce (Irvine et al 2016). Low pay is the most commonly cited reason for why workers leave the sector (Department of Education 2013: 34). High staff turnover poses a significant challenge to the quality of ECEC provided to children. As a feminised industry, the work done by ECEC workers has historically been undervalued, and the current demand-side funding model makes it difficult for providers to increase wages.[19]

The Impact of Radical Marketisation in ECEC

Commonwealth support for ECEC is set to reach a record $10 billion in 2020–21. But have the reforms of the past four decades delivered sustainable, accessible, affordable and high-quality ECEC services that meet the needs of Australian children and their parents?

The demand-side funding model and reliance on private for-profit providers has dramatically increased the total number of ECEC places available to parents. However, ECEC is still in short supply in many locations and parents continue to report major problems with access and affordability. The perennial mismatch between consumer demand and the supply of services point to widespread market failure associated with the demand-side funding model. Despite growing government expenditure on ECEC services, child care remains the biggest barrier to female workforce participation in Australia (ABS 2017). This should be a concern given the Australian government's official commitment to increasing women's workforce participation by 25 per cent by 2025 (Commonwealth of Australia, 2017).

There is also evidence that the marketised funding model is failing many vulnerable children. The 2015 Australian Early Development Census (AEDC), a three-yearly national assessment of childhood development at the time children start school, shows the proportion of under-fives that were vulnerable in two or more of the report's five key indicators increased from 10.8 per cent in 2012 to 11.1 per cent in 2015. This raises important questions about the accessibility and quality of

ECEC services available to Australia's most vulnerable children. And there are concerns that access for vulnerable children is set to worsen under the new Child Care package in which the number of subsidised hours of ECEC available to disadvantaged households has been halved[21] and more stringent work activity testing threatens to reduce access to subsidised services for households in which parents have casual or flexible working patterns (Brennan and Adamson 2016). While the majority of families are expected to benefit from the newest funding model, tighter work activity testing is likely to reinforce current socio-economic inequalities and risk limiting access to ECEC for the children most likely to benefit. Ensuring equality of access to all Australian children remains a challenge in the demand-driven marketised ECEC system.

The evolution of federal government policy over the past four decades has created a major new private for-profit industry in ECEC. Whether the profit-maximising behaviour of corporate providers can be consistent with the goal of providing high-quality care and education for very young children is open to question. Quality indicators for the sector show that lower quality services are more likely to be delivered in large-scale for-profit centres than in not-for-profit community services. Furthermore, the costly taxpayer-funded bailout required following the collapse of ABC Learning in 2008–09 showed how vulnerable the federal government is to private-sector risk in ECEC. In recent years the sector has attracted significant investment from very large corporations; it remains to be seen how these powerful new players will influence policy and practice in the industry.

Despite these and other problems highlighted by the radical marketisation of ECEC in this chapter, the Productivity Commission's 2017 draft report on the Reforms to Human Services Inquiry cited ECEC as a 'well established market' that demonstrates 'the value that user choice and competition can have in human services' (61). The perceived success of ECEC is pointed to as the rationale for introducing the market discipline of enhanced competition and user choice in other human services, including social housing, end-of-life care and public hospitals. But high prices, lack of affordability, limited accessibility and growing demands on the federal budget suggest that the current ECEC policy framework would be better framed as a cautionary tale for governments as they deliberate on future financing and delivery models of essential human services – particularly those for vulnerable populations.

Endnotes

1 This includes long daycare, family daycare, preschool/kindergartens and outside school hours care (OSHC).

2 This is the number of children in Commonwealth-approved ECEC places. This number has increased threefold, from 398,930 in 1998 to 1,220,549 in 2016 (SCRGSP 2002, Table 14A.9 and SCRGSP 2017 Table 3A.18). The proportion of children in Commonwealth-approved ECEC places has risen from 23.2 per cent in 2006 to 31 per cent in 2016 (SCRGSP 2017, Table 3A.18).

3 This includes long daycare, family daycare, outside school hours care, preschool/ kindergartens. Only approved ECEC services are eligible for government funding (ACEQA 2017).

4 Preschools are typically run on a half-day or short-day basis for children just prior to starting formal school; family daycare services are provided in a home-based setting for a small number of children; outside school hours care is for school-age children who need care before the school day begins and once it ends, during school holidays, etc; playgroups are community-organised short hours services.

5 Since the late 1980s Senator Peter Walsh had been concerned about the large and growing budgetary commitments to ECEC. Walsh viewed public funding of ECEC as an expensive and unnecessary form of middle-class welfare that provided high-quality ECEC for a select few. Blewett was a strong supporter of publicly funded ECEC, arguing that it was a public good that promoted economic and social justice. At the height of the debate there was a real risk that Commonwealth funding might be cut altogether. The compromise deal brokered by Blewett reflects these circumstances. For a detailed account of the debate within the ALP, see Brennan 1998: 184–188.

6 An opco-propco business model is premised on the separation of the operational side of a business (opco) from the property side (propco), with complex leasing and exchange agreements linking the two. For a detailed analysis of the ABC Learning opco-propco model, see Newberry and Brennan 2013.

7 Goodstart Early Learning is a not-for-profit company established by the Brotherhood of St Laurence, Mission Australia, The Benevolent Society and Social Ventures Australia in 2009 (Bita 2009).

8 Down from 800 centres in 2006.

9 To be repaid over seven years at the government's cost of finance, see Bita 2009.

10 In 2005–06 it was estimated that ABC Learning received $206 million in Commonwealth government subsidies via the CCB (Rush and Downie 2006).

11 An Australian real estate investment trust (AREIT) is a unitised portfolio of property assets that is listed on the stock exchange. AREIT is the new name given

to what were called 'listed property trusts' prior to 2008.

12 G8 is Australia's largest listed ECEC company, operating 511 centres in 2016, or 6.2 per cent of centres (Colliers 2016b: 4)

13 Ray White Commercial NSW reports more than $200 million of child care assets changed hands in 2016, $120 million of which were in the NSW child care market, 80 per cent of which was located in metropolitan Sydney (Cummins 2017).

14 Child Care Fee Assistance includes the Child Care Benefit and the Child Care Rebate. From 1 July, 2018 the Child Care Benefit and Child Care Rebate was replaced by the Child Care Subsidy. Top 20 programs by expenses, Commonwealth Budget Papers for years 2011 to 2017. Table 3.1. Data for 2013–14, 2017–18 and 2018–19 are estimates. Data for, 2019–20 and 2020–2021 are projections.

15 Although the stringent work activity test that is part of the new package is expected to make government supported ECEC difficult to access for those with insecure work and unpredictable hours of work such as those working in casual employment (Brennan and Adamson 2016:2–3).

16 The ABS classifies 'children' as aged 0 to 11, while the Productivity Commission includes 12-year-olds in its definition.

17 The criteria for measuring quality in the study included: time to develop relationships with individual children; programming to accommodate children's individual needs and interests; the variety of equipment provided; the quality and quantity of the food provided; staff-to-child ratios (Rush 2006 and 2007).

18 The quality ratings for different provider types are shaped by the type of services provided. ACEQUA data shows that 58 per cent of preschools/kindergartens have achieved a quality ranking 'exceeding NQS', whereas only 17 per cent of OSHC and 30 per cent of long daycare centres have achieved this high rating (ACEQA 2017: 14). Long daycare is disproportionately represented in the for-profit sector.

19 Given the structure of the financing model, it is likely government would have to provide additional funds specifically earmarked for the ECEC workforce to improve wages. In 2012 the Gillard Labor government provided an additional $2 billion to increase social and community service workers' wages.

20 Prior to July 2018, all children had access to twenty-four hours per week of subsidised ECEC, regardless of parents' workforce participation.

References

Australian Bureau of Statistics (2015) *Childhood Education and Care, Australia, June 2014, Cat. No. 4402.0*, 23 April.

——(2017) *Barriers and Incentives to Labour Force Participation, Australia, July 2016 to June 2017, Cat. No. 6239.0*, 11 December.

Australian Children's Education and Care Quality Authority (2017) *NQF Snapshot Q2 2017: A Quarterly Report from the Australian Children's Education and Care Quality Authority*, August.

Australian Early Development Census (2015), *2015 AEDC National Report: A Snapshot of Early Childhood Development in Australia*. Canberra, Commonwealth of Australia.

Bita, N. (2009) 'Charity takeover of ABC Learning', *The Australian*, 10 December.

Brennan, D. (1998) *The Politics of Australian Child Care: Philanthropy, Feminism and Beyond*. Melbourne, Cambridge University Press.

Brennan, D. and Adamson, E. (2016) *Family Assistance Legislation Amendment (Jobs for Families Child Care Package) Bill 2015*, Submission to Senate Education and Employment Committee, January 2016. Canberra, Parliament of Australia.

Colliers (2016a) *Child Care: Australia's Burgeoning Real Estate Investment Class*, Colliers International, June. Sydney, Colliers.

——— (2016b) 'Child care in Australia', *Child Care White Paper: An Industry Review*, May 2016. Sydney, Colliers International.

Commonwealth of Australia (2017) *Towards 2025: A Strategy to Boost Australian Women's Workforce Participation*, Department of the Prime Minister and Cabinet. Canberra, Commonwealth of Australia.

Cummins, C. (2017) 'Numbers adding up for child care', *Sydney Morning Herald*, 17 May.

Department of Education (2014) 2013 *National Early Childhood Education and Care Workforce Census*, The Social Research Centre, May.

Department of Treasury (2017) *Commonwealth Government Budget 2017–18*, Budget Paper No. 1. Canberra, Australian Government.

Economic Planning Advisory Commission (1996) *Future Child Care Provision in Australia, Task Force Final Report*, November. Canberra, Australian Government Publishing Services.

Ferguson, A. (1994) 'The industries set for success', *Business Review Weekly*, 25 July: 50.

Howard, J. (2002) Transcript of the Prime Minister The Hon. John Howard MP address to Qld Liberal Party State Convention, 7 September 2002, PM Transcripts, Department of the Prime Minister and Cabinet, transcript 12990.

IBISWorld (2017) *Child Care Services – Australia Market Research Report*, Industry Report Q8710, March.

Irvine, S., Sumsion, J., Lunn, J. and Thorpe, K. (2016) 'One in five early childhood educators plan to leave the profession', *The Conversation*, 23 June.

Kruger, C. (2009) 'Lessons to be learnt from ABC Learning's collapse', *The Sydney Morning Herald*, 2 January.

McIntosh, G. and Phillips, J. (2002) *Commonwealth Support for Child Care*. Canberra, Parliament of Australia.

Meagher, G. and Wilson, S. (2015) 'The politics of market encroachment: policymaker rationales and voter responses' in Meagher, G. and Goodwin, S. (eds), *Markets, Rights and Power in Australian Social Policy*. Sydney, Sydney University Press.

Melbourne Institute (2017) *Household Income and Labour Dynamics in Australia Survey: Selected Findings From Waves 1 to 15*, Melbourne Institute Applied Economic and Social Research. Parkville, University of Melbourne.

Newberry, S. and Brennan, D. (2013) 'The marketisation of early childhood education and care (ECEC) in Australia: A structured response', *Financial Accountability and Management*, 20 (3): 227–245.

Phillips, B. (2014) 'Child care: affordability in Australia', *AMP.NATSEM Income and Wealth Report*, 35, June 2014.

Productivity Commission (2014) *Childcare and Early Childhood Learning*, Productivity Commission Inquiry Report, 1 (73), October. Canberra, Australian Government.

——(2017) *Introducing Competition and Informed User Choice into Human Services: Reforms to Human Services*, Draft Report, June. Canberra, Australian Government.

Rush, E. (2006) Child Care Quality in Australia, TAI Discussion Paper No. 84, April. Canberra, The Australia Institute.

——(2007) 'Employees' views on quality' in Hill, E., Pocock, B. and Elliot, A. (eds), *Kids Count: Better Early Childhood Education and Care in Australia*. Sydney, Sydney University Press.

Rush, E. and Downie, C. (2006) *ABC Learning Centres: a case study of Australia's largest child care corporation*, TAI Discussion Paper no. 87, June. Canberra, The Australia Institute.

Scarr, L. (2017) 'Families face crippling childcare costs as rebate cap hits', News.com.au, 16 February.

Steering Committee for the Review of Government Service Provision (2017) *Report on Government Services 2017, Volume B: Child Care, Education and Training*. Canberra, Productivity Commission.

Steering Committee for the Review of Commonwealth/State Service Provision (2002) *Report on Government Services 2002*, AusInfo. Canberra, Productivity Commission.

Tan, S-L. (2017) 'Child care asset yield at a record low,' *Australian Financial Review*, 17 May.

CHAPTER 2

COERCING, SUBSIDISING AND ENCOURAGING: TWO DECADES OF SUPPORT FOR PRIVATE HEALTH INSURANCE

STEPHEN DUCKETT

The financing of health care in Australia has been contested terrain for seventy years, particularly since the mid-1960s. From then, right through to the early 1990s, the first round of contests revolved around the fight to implement, reimplement and preserve universal health insurance. The second round, which remains in play, is about the extent of public funding – direct or indirect – for private health insurance. In this chapter, I briefly describe the first contest to establish the context for a closer analysis of the second contest.

Whitlam to Wooldridge: The Battle for Universal Health Insurance

Table 1 opposite summarises the policy choices and values that underpinned health policy from the 1950s to the mid-1990s.

During the late 1960s, a resurgent Labor party under Gough Whitlam transformed the debate about health care in Australia. In a bold announcement in 1968, Whitlam proposed a Canadian-type universal health insurance scheme to replace the ramshackle private scheme supported by the then Liberal government (see Whitlam 1968). The new scheme was greeted bitterly by private health insurers, the Australian Medical Association (AMA), the Liberal Party and its coalition partners, the

Table 1: Choices in health policy in Australia, 1949–1996

Political period	Overarching policies	Key attributes and slogans
1949–1972 Liberal and Country Party	• Support for private health insurance for both hospital and medical care	• Emphasis on individual self-reliance • Selective and residual policies • 'Private practice, publicly supported' (Fox 1963) • Patching up and propping up private health insurance
1972–1975 Labor Party (Whitlam)	• Introduction of Medibank	• 'Universal health insurance' • Mutualisation/risk sharing across the whole population • Emphasis on equity and universalism
1975–1983 Liberal and Country Party (Fraser)	• Dismantling of Medibank • End of universality, reintroduction of means tests	• Promise to 'maintain Medibank' • Mutualisation through private health insurance • Segmented/targeting of subsidies
1983–1996 Labor Party (Hawke; Keating)	• Reintroduction of Medibank (and universality) under new name, Medicare	• Mutualisation/risk sharing across the whole population • Emphasis on equity and universalism • Slow reduction in government subsidies of private health care • Aberrant 1994 budget, which proposed a co-payment for general practice

Source: Adapted from Duckett (2008)

Country (now National) Party, but was eventually legislated in a joint sitting of parliament in 1974, and implemented under the title 'Medibank' in 1975, just months before the government was dismissed (Scotton 1978; Scotton and Macdonald 1993).

Despite promising to 'Maintain Medibank' in the 1975 election campaign, the newly elected Fraser government proceeded to transform Medibank beyond all recognition through a series of incremental changes over the course of its term. These favoured a system with private health insurance at its centre (Duckett 1979, 1980; Scotton 1980).

In 1984, the re-elected Labor government restored universality under the new name of Medicare (Duckett 2003). A key task of the new government was to stabilise policy and differentiate itself from the Liberals who, in election after election, promised to return to a private health insurance–centric system. During this period, private health insurance lobbyists continuously campaigned for Medicare to be dismantled (their preferred option) or, failing that, for private health insurance to be subsidised. Regarding the latter point, lobbyists argued that people who took out private insurance were 'taking a load off' the public system and deserved to be rewarded. Labor did not succumb to this lobbying; the government response was an attempt to shift responsibility back to industry through proposals for industry reform (Gath 1999).

In the early 1990s, the Liberals began to rethink their policy position on health care and eventually realised that a continued opposition to Medicare was to their electoral detriment. Persuaded by shadow minister for health Michael Wooldridge, a doctor who had written an MBA thesis on health policy during the Fraser years (Wooldridge 1991), the Liberals eventually accepted the principle of universality and promised to keep Medicare – a promise maintained during the Howard years. Although vestiges of opposition to universality remain – and the rhetoric of Medicare as a 'safety net' occasionally re-emerges – Dr Wooldridge deserves credit for leading a redirection of Liberal health policy away from its narrow focus on opposition to Medicare.

The Howard Years: 'Private Insurance is in Our DNA'

Healthcare battles since the mid-1990s have been quite different from the previous era. By that time, Medicare had become an accepted part of the landscape, with policy on the conservative side of politics now focusing on supporting private insurance rather than opposing public, universal insurance (see Table 2).

Table 2: Choices in health policy in Australia, since 1996

Political period	Policy choices	Key attributes/slogans
1996–2007 Liberal–National Coalition (Howard)	• Extensive financial and policy support for private health insurance and private delivery • Targeting of financial support for medical services	• 'Run for cover' • Carrots and sticks to encourage private health insurance • 'Best friend Medicare ever had'
2001–2013 Labor (Rudd/Gillard/Rudd)	• Limiting growth in rebate subsidies	• Health reform within context of Medicare
2013– Liberal–National Coalition (Abbott/Turnbull)	• Continued support for private health insurance • 2014 Budget attempted co-payments • Industry reform	• Medicare is 'unsustainable'

Source: Author's analysis

Although the Liberal Party now eschewed the destruction of Medicare, a signal policy victory for private health insurance lobbyists towards the end of the Hawke–Keating period was the creation of a public climate in which it was felt that people who took out private health insurance deserved to be rewarded for their actions, preferably by a subsidy. One of the early acts of the new Howard government was to introduce such a subsidy. This was the first step in a series of policies designed to encourage – or, indeed, coerce – people to take out private health insurance. The estimated cost of the first scheme – known as the Private Health Insurance Incentive Scheme (PHIIS) – was about $600 million per annum, about one-tenth the cost of subsidies in 2017. This scheme and all the subsequent ones left Medicare untouched – in line with the pre-election commitment – but the emphasis of policy under the Liberal–National government remained one in which private health insurance was critically important.

Health minister Dr Michael Wooldridge's first reading speech introducing the PHIIS revealed the ideological commitment to private health insurance. Wooldridge asserted that the bill was:

> the centrepiece of the government's strategy to rescue Medicare from collapsing under the weight of demand for publicly funded hospital and medical services. The Scheme does so by recognising the value of the private sector as an indispensable complement to the public sector, and acknowledges that, by making the fullest use of the sum of our hospital resources, we will be able to ensure that Australians have reasonable access to the full range of public and private services. (House of Representatives, 1996)

Explicit here is the view that the best way to support the public sector (vividly described as 'collapsing under the weight of demand'), is to support the private sector, and that investment in private health insurance will reduce the demand for public hospitals, and will presumably reduce public hospital waiting lists. Even at the time this was seen to be a false premise (Duckett and Jackson 2000), for reasons discussed below.

The first reading speech for the PHIIS went on to talk about a 'necessary balance between the use of the public and private health systems', and used apocalyptic language ('ongoing and increasingly precipitous decline'; 'arrest the catastrophic decline') to describe the decline in health insurance that had ostensibly occurred. This doomsday scenario was concocted through a selective use of statistics, highlighting the decline in insurance for public hospital care – a product that had become irrelevant with the introduction of Medicare – rather than the quite modest decline in insurance coverage rates for private hospital care (see Figure 1).

The minister concluded his speech:

> These incentives will provide the injection of funds, and public confidence, into a private health system which for too long has been neglected, while our public hospitals are straining at the seams to cope with demand … The Private Health Insurance Incentives Scheme and the related measures being introduced today, highlight

> the government's absolute determination to turn this around, to make the most of our existing health care assets, both public and private, and to ensure that Australia and Australians can look forward confidently to assured quality health care, with the maximum of individual choice. (House of Representatives, 1996)

Again we can see the preoccupations that characterised health policy during the Howard years: an emphasis on building up private care, coupled with the rhetoric of individual choice.

Assessed against its own objectives, the new scheme was a failure: private health insurance coverage continued to decline. The next few years saw a bewildering array of new schemes, including a dramatic increase and expansion of the health insurance subsidy – up to 30 per cent of the cost of premiums.

One 'stick' or coercion component of the carrot-and-stick combination that characterised the Howard government's policies was a surcharge on taxable income for middle- to high-income earners. Initially, in 1997, the levy was struck at 1 per cent of taxable income payable by people with incomes above the specified threshold who did not have hospital insurance. The levy has since evolved and now has three rates with differing income thresholds up to a maximum of 1.5 per cent for people with incomes above $140,000. People on those incomes can purchase products costing less than they would otherwise pay in tax, making private health insurance effectively free for that group.

The introduction of these surcharge arrangements was accompanied by a rhetoric asserting that people who could afford private health insurance should not be using public hospitals – with the implicit assumption being that public hospitals were a residual 'safety net' service for the poor rather than a universal service. Again, this had little impact on insurance coverage (Butler 2001; Hall et al. 1999; Robson and Paolucci 2012).

In 2000, the government introduced 'lifetime cover', another coercive measure, whereby people who did not take out insurance before the age of thirty would face higher premiums thereafter (a loading of 2 per cent for each year they joined after thirty, up to a maximum loading of 70 per cent on the base premium). This new policy was accompanied by a 'run for cover' advertising campaign to get people to join before the loadings came into effect (Ellis and Savage 2008). The campaign showed people with private insurance on trolleys being rushed past patients waiting for public hospital care. The new lifetime cover, which traded on people's fear of the future – specifically, the fear that if they did not take out health insurance it would become much more expensive to do so in the future – led to a significant increase in private insurance coverage, the majority of which were policies with excess or co-payment requirements (see Figure 1).

Figure 1. Introduction of the private health insurance rebate had almost no impact on coverage.

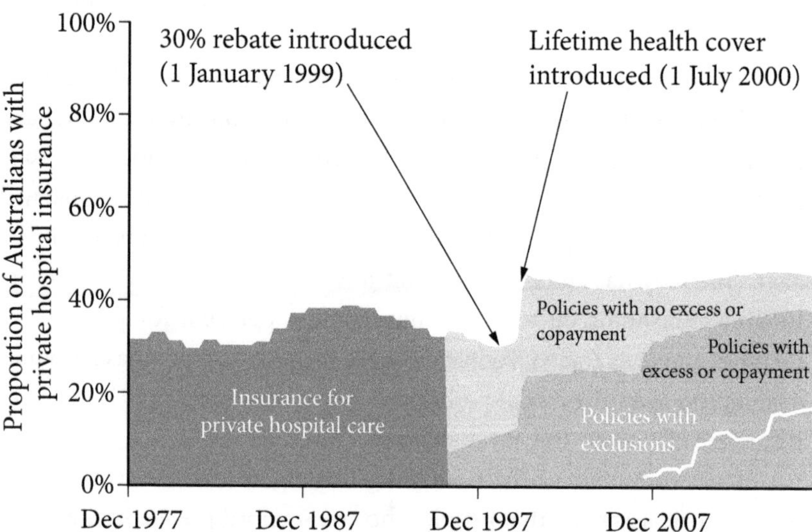

Source: Author's analysis.[1]

Evaluation of the Policies of the Howard Years

Importantly, for all the talk about the new policies' potential to reduce demand on public hospitals, there was virtually no shift in public and private shares of hospital admissions over the ensuing years (Moorin and Holman 2006).

Today there are a huge variety of private health insurance products, offering apparent choice to consumers around the cost of up-front payments in the event of hospitalisation (for example, the contributor might be required to pay the first $500, which is an example of a deductible cost, co-payment or excess cost), and whether the policy will cover all exigencies (whether maternity care or mental health care will be covered, which is an example of a common exclusion). The higher the required up-front payment for a hospital admission ('deductible') and the greater the exclusions, the lower the premium.

However, as behavioural economics literature makes clear, people can be overwhelmed by choices, and so an expansion of options does not necessarily lead to a better fit between a person's economic interests and the choice/s they make (Angner 2016; Schram and Sonnemans 2011). The complexity of health insurances on offer compounds the problem; consumers make clearly irrational choices, like selecting a product with a higher deductible when an equivalent product with a lower deductible is available for the same price (Bhargava et al. 2017; Frank and Lamiraud 2009; Sinaiko and Hirth 2011).

Most of the increases in coverage following the introduction of lifetime cover occurred in products with deductibles, which implies that new private health insurance holders hoped not to use their products, perhaps intending to use public hospitals should the need arise. Further, increases in premiums, and the slow growth of personal incomes, is leading many people to drop their level of cover, switching from 'full coverage' to products with deductibles and exclusions. The vast majority (88 per cent) of health insurance policies now have some form of deductible and there has also been a steady increase in the proportion of policies with exclusions: now, about 40 per cent of the insured population have products that do not cover hospital admissions for all types of conditions (see Figure 1).

Economic research suggests that rebates are a very expensive way to boost private health insurance coverage for two reasons. First, a proportion of rebate expenditure will be wasted on people whose behaviour will not change – the 40 per cent of the population who already had insurance. Spending on these people represents a dead weight loss, creating little 'additionality' (McEldowney 1997). Second, it takes a very large change in private health insurance premiums to alter an individual's decision on whether to take out private health insurance (Cheng 2013). This finding appears to have held true in Australia: when the value of the rebate was changed for older and wealthier Australians in 2005 and 2014 respectively, the level of private health insurance coverage did not appear to respond (Kettlewell et al. 2018).

A key justification for the rebate – both the original PHIIS and all the subsequent rebate initiatives – was that increased support for private hospital care would take pressure off public hospitals. If this were true, then one would expect that more private activity would be associated with shorter public waiting lists. However, as I have shown previously (Duckett 2005), a more logical reality applies: shorter public hospital waiting times are associated with a greater proportion of public activity rather than a greater proportion of private activity. This still holds true (see Figure 2).

Figure 2. Public hospital waiting times are shorter when the public hospital share of activity is greater, 2014–15.

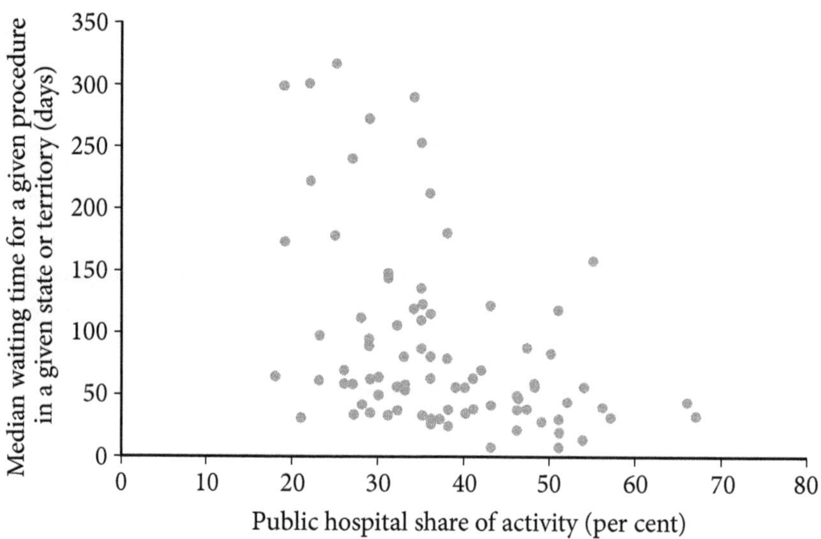

Source: Author's analysis[2]

Longer waits and relatively more private hospital activity might occur for a number of reasons: people might seek private care to avoid long waits; surgeon time is limited and if that time is spent in private care, there is less time to provide for public hospital care; or, surgeons may create longer waiting times to increase the demand for private care, which for them is more remunerative. Whatever the reason, policies directed at increasing public hospital provision and the public hospital share of work are more likely to reduce public hospital waiting times than indirect and expensive policies aimed at supporting private hospital care. Expanding the private hospital share is therefore not a good way of improving public hospital waiting times and does not provide a justification for the private health insurance rebate.

The failure of carrots and sticks to have an impact on demand for Australia's public hospitals is not surprising. First, few private hospitals provide emergency care, so public-to-private hospital diversion is essentially limited to elective care. Second, some elective procedures are only performed in public hospitals because they may require specialised equipment or skills, and some patients may be at higher risk post-surgery, and thus require the more extensive support available in public hospitals. Third, thresholds to admit patients to private hospitals might be lower than for public hospitals. Those patients admitted to private hospitals for procedures that may not be clinically necessary or that confer limited benefit might never have been admitted to a public hospital – and so, no demand would be shifted. Fourth, some of the people who take out health insurance in response to a subsidy will be relatively healthy and so would have created very little demand on the public system previously; thus, there would be little impact on public hospital demand in the process of their shifting. Finally, the products people take out because of fear or coercion appear to be simple 'placeholders' to avoid the tax surcharge or to keep options open for the future; these are characterised by seeking out the cheapest options, which are those with deductibles and exclusions. These people may expect their present needs to still be met by admission to public rather than private hospitals.

Despite their limited benefit, rebates have been expensive. In 2016–17, the Commonwealth government spent $6 billion – or 9 per cent of all

Commonwealth healthcare spending – on private health insurance rebates. The subsidy for private care is even larger than this because Medicare pays a rebate against the cost of medical bills for private hospital care (75 per cent of schedule fee), amounting to a further $3 billion in 2016–17; and private hospitals 'cream skim': they select healthier patients to treat, and transfer patients with complications to public hospitals (Cheng et al. 2015). Total Commonwealth government support for health insurance, private hospitals and private practice in private hospitals is thus larger than the net value of all other industry assistance (estimated at $9.1 billion; see Productivity Commission, 2017).

During the period that Tony Abbott was health minister, from 2003 to 2007, the government increased subsidies for doctors who bulk-billed, leading to an increase in bulk-billing rates (which had been in decline). Abbott used this experience to claim that the Liberals 'were the best friends Medicare ever had' (Elliot 2006), conveniently disregarding the party's decades of opposition to universality and bulk-billing. The 2014 Budget, introduced during Abbott's term as prime minister, proposed a co-payment for general practice visits, further undermining that claim. As this chapter shows, the Abbottism more consistent with both the Liberal Party's track record and its ideology was the claim about Liberal governments that 'private insurance is in our DNA' (Dunlevy 2012).

The Labor Years

The Rudd government elected in 2007 had an ambitious reform agenda. It established a National Health and Hospitals Reform Commission (NHHRC) – of which I was a member – with very broad terms of reference. The Commission was independent but was chaired by a person employed by a major private health insurer and included a former Liberal state health minister. It squibbed the issue of private health insurance, aiming rather 'to see the overall balance of spending through taxation, private health insurance, and out-of-pocket contribution maintained over the next decade' (NHHRC 2009).

The political reality is that almost 50 per cent of the population now has private health insurance. This forms an important proportion of the electorate. Despite a large expenditure on the rebate, Labor has not attempted to abolish it; rather, its approach has been to reduce its value over time through means testing and capping subsidy growth so that it remains in line with general inflation rather than the higher rate of growth in private health insurance outlays. Current rebates are shown in Table 3.

TABLE 3: PRIVATE HEALTH INSURANCE REBATE ENTITLEMENT BY INCOME THRESHOLD 2017–18

Status	Income thresholds			
	Base	Tier 1	Tier 2	Tier 3
Single	$90,000 or less	$90,001 – $105,000	$105,001 – $140,000	$140,001 or more
Family	$180,000 or less	$180,001 – $210,000	$210,001 – $280,000	$280,001 or more
Age				
Under 65	25.934%	17.289%	8.644%	0%
65 to 69	30.256%	21.612%	12.966%	0%
70 plus	34.579%	25.934%	17.289%	0%

Source: ATO 2018

The significant reduction from the Liberal government policy of 30 per cent rebate that occurred under Labor for those under 65 is clear.

The Abbott–Turnbull years

Prior to the 2013 election, then Opposition leader Abbott promised to reverse Labor's policy of limiting support for private health insurance. This reversal has not occurred, possibly because there is little electoral advantage for the Liberals and, conversely, the impact on the budget is large.

This period saw the full privatisation of the government-owned private insurer, Medibank, which was listed on the stock exchange in November 2014. Medibank had been corporatised in 1998, and was required to return annual dividends to Treasury (Buckmaster and Davidson 2006).

Medibank's privatisation meant that the two largest private health insurers, with a combined market share of 52 per cent of hospital policies, both operate as for-profits in Australia. (BUPA Australia is a subsidiary of a UK not-for-profit, but repatriates surpluses to the UK.)

Slow wages growth and the rising cost of essential services has placed pressure on private health insurers. Membership growth has stalled and there is a rise in the take-up of products with deductions and exclusions. When consumers use these products, they are often faced with unexpectedly large out-of-pocket costs, which increases dissatisfaction with private health insurance. In an unusual attack on private health insurers by a Liberal minister, the then health minister Sussan Ley described these products as 'junk policies' (Gardner 2015) and established a Private Health Ministerial Advisory Committee to attempt to improve standardisation and customer information. The confusing array of products on the market today means that private health insurance has turned full circle, back to pre-Medicare days, when the market was described as 'unnecessarily complex and beyond the comprehension of many' (Committee of Enquiry into Health Insurance 1969). In late 2017, the government announced policies to increase consumer information about private health insurance products and to relax some regulations, such as allowing funds to discount premiums for people under thirty. These changes are unlikely to have much impact on the take-up of insurance (Duckett 2017).

Future Policies

Introducing the health insurance rebate in 1999 did not achieve its stated objective: it led to almost no increase in coverage. A significant increase in health insurance membership occurred with the introduction of lifetime cover. Removing or phasing down the rebate, while keeping lifetime cover and penalties on higher-income earners who do not have health insurance, may have a limited effect on membership. It may also have a limited impact on the level of coverage, given the changes in the types of products purchased that have already occurred.

Although a moderate decline in insurance coverage and consequential marginal increased demand for public hospital admissions could be absorbed by the public sector, a dramatic shift would be disruptive and could impede access. Predicting the impact of phasing down the rebate is difficult. On the one hand, given constrained wage growth, current policyholders may be more sensitive to an effective price increase in the cost of insurance now, compared to when the rebate was introduced. If the price sensitivity ('price elasticity') of private insurance demand is higher now, reducing the rebate might accelerate the rise of junk policies or lead people to drop their coverage altogether. On the other hand, the increased proportion of private health insurance policies with high deductibles and extensive exclusions into which people were effectively coerced – the so-called 'junk policies' – may not lead to any change in demand for public hospital admissions, weakening any economic case to subsidise prviate health insurance (Frech and Hopkins 2004).

Whether private health insurance should be subsidised is a separate issue. Whatever future policies are on the extent of private health insurance subsidies, there is need for caution in managing the transition. Impacts on both public hospitals and on family budgets need to be properly assessed in new policy design.

Government spending on the private health insurance rebate could be slowed by further tightening inflation adjustments (for example, using an index which has a slower growth rate), limiting the rebate to those with lower incomes (for example, the Base group) or changing the rebate percentage for Tier 1 and 2, or just for Tier 2 contributors. The separate rates for older Australians should be withdrawn because the principle of community rating, where risks are pooled across the whole community so there are no differential premiums based on a person's individual health risk, provides sufficient protection for older Australians (Daley et al. 2016). Currently, rebates are provided for both hospital and general (extras) insurance. But extras insurance has no relationship to public hospital use, so differential rebates could be applied to these products, or the rebate could be eliminated altogether, with potentially minimal impact on public hospitals.

Many people may feel 'forced' into private insurance because of the Medicare levy surcharge, a stick that makes private health insurance virtually free for middle- to high-income earners. If this stick were abolished, there would likely be a drop in private health insurance, including among people who are not subject to the surcharge. Such a change would force private health insurers to become more competitive and respond better to public dissatisfaction.

If elected, Labor has foreshadowed that it will cap growth in private health insurance for two years and institute a Productivity Commission review of the industry (Karp 2018; Sivey 2018). Such a review, with wide terms of reference, could allow a broader range of options to be considered, including phasing out community rating (Vaithianathan 2004). Again, more disruptive change may force the industry to be more competitive.

Conclusion

The private health insurance rebate was introduced with an ideological purpose: to strengthen private health insurance, which in turn strengthens private health care. It was dressed up as a move to reduce demand for public hospital care but there is no evidence that it was successful in this aim.

As health minister in the Howard government, Tony Abbott claimed that support for private health insurance was in the Liberals' DNA. This historically accurate representation of the Liberal position, in both government and Opposition, may be due to their general support for markets; individualised (that is, market-based) freedom (in this case the capacity to choose one's own doctor); providing opportunities for large corporates in the health sector, or the interpenetration of the Liberal Party membership and donor base with private practice and private hospitals. These factors, or some combination thereof, were at play during the Fraser years (Duckett 1979; 1980; 1984).

Although the Liberals can rightly claim that their private health insurance policies have done nothing to overtly undermine universality, underwriting the private sector comes with its costs for the public sector, not only in terms of the opportunity cost – the more than $6 billion of annual government outlays on the rebate. For example, the hours spent by a surgeon who works in the private sector are not available to the public sector (Cheng et al. 2013). As the remuneration per hour is higher in the private sector, the effects of this adverse substitution are exacerbated.

Despite its manifold weaknesses and consumer unrest, private health insurance policy seems now to have reached stability. For the Liberals, the cost of further increasing subsidies is expensive and, in a time of large deficits, unlikely to gain Budget support, despite an ideological predisposition. Also, voters expect the Liberals to support private health insurance – as 'it is in their DNA' – so there may be no electoral gain from investing further in that area. Labor seems to have been content to rely on a policy that has slowed growth in costs, and future policies will probably be incremental – a slow chipping away, rather than a dramatic reduction in the subsidy. Subject to the outcome of any review of private health insurance if Labor is elected, private health insurance policy looks to enshrine wasteful expenditure – a subsidy to the industry of more than $10 billion each year through the private health insurance rebate and the Medicare in-hospital rebate – which is larger than the current subsidies to agriculture, mining and manufacturing combined. It will also continue to coerce consumers to reluctantly take out private health insurance policies because of fear of the future and tax penalties.

Endnotes

1 There is no published information on insurance for private hospital care (called 'Supplementary insurance' prior to 1977). There is a discontinuity in the series in 1996, as data on insurance for private hospital care was decomposed into information about different products.

2 The observations are median waiting times for more common procedures in the larger states. The figure shows that the greater the proportion of activity in the public sector in larger specialties in larger states, the shorter the median waiting times Conversely, a larger private proportionate share is associated with longer public waiting.

References

Angner, E. (2016) *A Course in Behavioral Economics*. London and New York, Palgrave Macmillan.

ATO (2018) Income thresholds and rates for the private health insurance rebate, 29 June.

Bhargava, S., Loewenstein, G. and Sydnor, J. (2017) 'Choose to lose: health plan choices from a menu with dominated options', *Quarterly Journal of Economics*, 132 (3): 1319–1372.

Buckmaster, L. and Davidson, J. (2006) 'The proposed sale of Medibank Private: historical, legal and policy perspectives', Research Brief, 2, Department of Parliamentary Services. Canberra, Parliament of Australia.

Butler, J.R.G. (2001) *Policy Change and Private Health Insurance: Did the Cheapest Policy Do the Trick?* National Centre for Epidemiology and Population Health. Canberra, Australian National University.

Cheng, T.C. (2013) *Does Reducing Rebates for Private Health Insurance Generate Cost Savings?* Melbourne Institute of Applied Economic and Social Research. Carlton, University of Melbourne.

Cheng, T.C., Guyonne, K. and Anthonty, S. (2013) 'Public private or both?: analysing factors influencing the labour supply of medical specialists', Working Paper. Melbourne, Melbourne Institute.

Cheng, T.C., Haisken-DeNew, J.P. and Yong, J. (2015) 'Cream skimming and hospital transfers in a mixed public-private system', *Social Science & Medicine*, 132: 156–164.

Committee of Enquiry into Health Insurance (1969) 'Report (Chair: Justice John Nimmo)'. Canberra, Australian Government Printer.

Daley, J., Coates, B. and Young, W. (2016) *Age of Entitlement: Age-Based Tax Breaks.* Melbourne, Grattan Institute.

Duckett, S. (1979) 'Chopping and changing Medibank part 1: implementation of a new policy', *Australian Journal of Social Issues*, 14: 230–243.

——(1980) 'Chopping and changing Medibank part 2: an interpretation of the policy making process', *Australian Journal of Social Issues*, 15: 79–91.

——(1984) 'Structural interests and Australian health policy', *Social Science & Medicine*, 18 (11): 959–966.

——(2003) 'Making a difference in health care' in Ryan, S. and Bramston, T. (eds), *The Hawke Government: A Critical Perspective*: 215–224. North Melbourne, Pluto Press.

——(2005) 'Private care and public waiting', *Australian Health Review*, 29 (1): 87–93.

——(2008) 'The continuing contest of values in the Australian healthcare system' in den Exter, A. (ed.), *Access to Health Care: Solidarity and Justice.* Rotterdam, Erasmus University Press.

——(2017) 'Changes to lure young people into private health insurance won't slow increase in premiums', *The Conversation*, 13 October.

Duckett, S. and Jackson, T. (2000) 'The new health insurance rebate: an inefficient way of assisting public hospitals', *Medical Journal of Australia*, 172 (9): 439–444.

Dunlevy, S. (2012) 'Tony Abbott to axe health insurance means test "as soon as we can"', *The Australian*, 15 February.

Elliot, A. (2006) '"The best friend Medicare ever had"? Policy narratives and changes in Coalition health policy', *Health Sociology Review*, 15 (2): 132–143.

Ellis, R. and Savage, E. (2008) 'Run for cover now or later? The impact of premiums, threats and deadlines on private health insurance in Australia', *International Journal of Health Care Finance and Economics*, 8 (4): 257–277.

Fox, T. (1963) 'The Antipodes: private practice publicly supported', *The Lancet*, 281 (7286): 875–879.

Frank, R.G. and Lamiraud, K. (2009) 'Choice, price competition and complexity in markets for health insurance', *Journal of Economic Behavior & Organization*, 71 (2): 550–562.

Frech, H. E. and S. Hopkins (2004). 'Why subsidise private health insurance?' *Australian Economic Review*, 37 (3): 243–256.

Gardner, J. (2015), 'Health Minister Sussan Ley attacks "junk" private health insurance', *The Sydney Morning Herald*, 28 October.

Gath, S. (1999) 'Enhanced consumer rights in private health care: have the "Lawrence Amendments" delivered?', *Journal of Law and Medicine*, 6: 241–252.

Hall, J., De Abreu Lourenco, R. and Viney, R. (1999) 'Carrots and sticks – the fall and fall of private health insurance in Australia', *Health Economics*, 8 (8): 653–660.

House of Representatives (1996) *Hansard*, Canberra, Australian Government, 13 December.

Karp, P. (2018) 'Labor promises to cap health insurance premium rises at 2 per cent for two years', *The Guardian*, 4 February.

Kettlewell, N., Stavrunova, O. and Yerokhin, O. (2018) 'Premium subsidies and demand for private health insurance: results from a regression discontinuity design', *Applied Economics Letters*, 25 (2): 96–101.

McEldowney, J.J. (1997) 'Policy Evaluation and the Concepts of Deadweight and Additionality: A Commentary', *Evaluation Evaluation*, 3 (2): 175–188.

Moorin, R.E. and Holman, C.D.J (2006) 'Does federal health care policy influence switching between the public and private sectors in individuals?', *Health Policy*, 79 (2–3): 284–295.

National Health and Hospitals Reform Commission (2009) *A Healthier Future For All Australians – Final Report of the National Health and Hospitals Reform Commission.* Canberra, Australian Government.

Productivity Commission (2017) 'Trade and Assistance Review, 2015–16', (Canberra: Productivity Commission).

Rhema, V. (2004) 'A Critique of the Private Health Insurance Regulations', *Australian Economic Review* 37 (3): 257–270.

Robson, A. and Paolucci, F. (2012) 'Private health insurance incentives in Australia: the effects of recent changes to price carrots and income sticks', *Geneva Papers on Risk and Insurance: Issues and Practice*, 37 (4): 725–744.

Schram, A. and Sonnemans, J. (2011) 'How individuals choose health insurance: an experimental analysis', *European Economic Review*, 55 (6): 799–819.

Scotton, R.B. (1978) 'Health services and the public sector' in Scotton, R.B. and Ferber, H. (eds), *Public Expenditures and Social Policy in Australia, Volume 1: The Whitlam Years, 1972–75*. Melbourne, Longman Cheshire.

——(1980) 'Health insurance: Medibank and after' in Scotton, R.B. and Ferber, H. (eds), *Public Expenditures and Social Policy in Australia, Volume 1: The Whitlam Years, 1972–75*. Melbourne, Longman Cheshire.

Scotton, R.B. and Macdonald, C.R. (1993) The Making of Medibank, no. 76, School of Health Services Management. Sydney, University of NSW.

Sinaiko, A.D. and Hirth, R.A. (2011) 'Consumers, health insurance and dominated choices', *Journal of Health Economics*, 30 (2): 450–457.

Sivey, P. (2018) 'Labor's 2 per cent cap on private health insurance premium rises won't fix affordability', *The Conversation*, 8 February.

Whitlam, E.G. (1968) 'The alternative national health programme', *Australian Journal of Social Issues*, 3 (4): 33–50.

Wooldridge, M.R.L. (1991) 'Health policy in the Fraser years – 1975–83', Department of Administrative Studies, Faculty of Economics and Politics, MBA thesis. Melbourne, Monash University.

——(1997) 'Private Health Insurance Incentives Bill 1997', *Senate Hansard*, 27 Feburary.

CHAPTER 3

A TALE OF MANDARINS AND LEMONS: CREATING THE MARKET FOR VOCATIONAL EDUCATION AND TRAINING

PHILLIP TONER

The creation of a 'training market' for public and privately funded vocational education and training (VET) is one of the most transparent failures of neoliberal public policy over the last three decades. There is a direct line connecting the early neoliberal economic arguments and pedagogy formulated by VET mandarins – those who designed and managed the VET system in the early 1990s – to its subsequent implementation. The VET market is an exemplar of the great damage inflicted when a naïve, idealised neoliberal conception of how markets work becomes the basis for public policy. Serious quality problems in the VET market arose from a misconceived analysis of both the economics of the private training market, and from the actual level of demand for quality training in large parts of the labour market. Further, the pedagogical system known as competency based training (CBT), instituted to develop competition between registered training organisations (RTOs) and flexibility in all aspects of training content and delivery has actually led to diminished quality of training and malfeasance among many RTOs, employers and students.

Why VET Matters

The fundamental objectives of publicly funded VET are to improve economic efficiency by redressing market impediments to private investment in VET, and to improve social equity by boosting the participation of disadvantaged groups in education and work (Productivity Commission 2011: 295). The failure of VET to achieve these objectives, due to declining quality, matters deeply. In 2016, there were 1.3 million students enrolled in the government-funded VET system, amounting to 7.8 per cent of the population aged between 15 and 64 years (NCVER 2017a: i).[1]

The effects of poor-quality VET delivery include a reduction in labour productivity; lower mobility of workers across occupations, industries and locations; lower employment when qualifications do not meet industry demand; losses to the taxpayer; monetary and emotional costs to students participating in poor quality training, including cancellation of their qualifications by the regulator; higher search costs on potential users seeking to avoid adverse selection of VET providers; and an adverse perception of quality that can reduce student and employer engagement with VET training. The central role of tradespeople and technicians in innovation (Toner 2011a) is undermined when the capacity of the VET system to maintain its technological currency is reduced (Toner 2005). The scale of public and private investment in VET is such that even a small improvement in the allocation of resources and funding would result in significant economic and social gains.

Creating the Training Market

Origins of the Training Market

Milton Friedman, one of the chief advocates of neoliberalism, first outlined the arguments for separating the role of government as a direct producer of educational services and VET from its role in financing education and training. His core argument was that making public training funds contestable through a voucher system would better meet the needs of students and employers, lower costs and improve pedagogical innovation (Friedman 1955). However, it was not until the early years of the Thatcher government in the UK during the 1980s that a fully integrated neoliberal training market was implemented. This market involved four key elements: competition between public and private providers through contracting out publicly funded VET; the establishment of a VET quality regulator; a new pedagogy known as competency-based training; and a new national system of qualifications (National Vocational Qualifications) based on CBT principles (Bates 2002). Following these 'reforms' the English VET system has been widely recognised as the worst among advanced European nations, a source of persistent skill shortages, low worker productivity and the failure to integrate disadvantaged groups (Leitch 2006).

Historically, the intellectual centre of gravity among education mandarins in Australia was the UK, and this was reinforced by the rise of neoliberal public policy in Australia. The UK VET model was quickly replicated in Australia during the 1990s.[2] The Productivity Commission (2011) provides the most exhaustive recent statement of the orthodox economic case for contracting out public VET.[3] In short, the assumption was that a training market would improve technical efficiency by creating incentives for public and private training providers to minimise costs. It would also impose efficiency in the allocation of training resources by more closely tying training provision to user demand. It would lift dynamic efficiency by promoting innovation in service delivery (Deveson 1990: 9). A core objective for the training market was to enable customised training tailored to the needs of an individual student and employer through flexibility in training content, delivery and assessment. The redesigned training system was to be an essential complement to the broader push for labour market deregulation and flexibility (Dawkins 1989).[4]

However, the introduction of the training market into Australia was based neither on evidence regarding the performance and efficiency of the *status quo ante*, nor on a detailed analysis of the economics of the training market. Rather, its introduction relied solely on the kind of *a priori* reasoning that is the foundation of neoclassical economics: that allocating public training funds through a market-based system and introducing competition between providers would by definition create a better system. To be blunt: the revolution in VET funding, content and assessment the mandarins advocated was public policy based on arm-waving generalities and ideology.

Implementing the Training Market

Since the early 1990s Australian governments have incrementally instituted a training market by increasing the share of public funds diverted from the public provider, mainly TAFE, to private registered training organisations (RTOs). From a few early pilot programmes the training market emerged officially with the introduction in 1998 of User Choice policy, in which 'the flow of public funds to individual training providers ... reflects the choice of individual training provider made by the client' (Selby-Smith 1998: 7). Under User Choice all public funding for off-the-job apprenticeships and traineeships was 'contestable'. In 2008 Australian governments moved to make all public VET funds contestable (COAG 2008). However, it is worth noting the enthusiasm with which the individual states embraced the new policy varied considerably.

Technical and further education institutions (TAFE) and other public providers continue to receive direct funding, although an increasing proportion is subject to competition between providers. The share of total VET funds allocated on a competitive basis has increased markedly from 25.3 per cent in 2001 to 44.2 per cent in 2015 (Productivity Commission 2017: Table 5A.10). Numerous mechanisms have been used to allocate public training funds, including tendering for the delivery of courses nominated by government, and 'entitlement' funding, whereby specified courses are subsidised but students and/or employers are free to chose an RTO and a voucher system where courses and providers are decided solely by students. Various systems have also been used for pricing publicly funded training including: competitive prices for tendered qualifications; research into the 'efficient cost' of delivery for different qualifications to fix prices, with students able to choose their preferred RTO in some jurisdictions; prices determined by the nominal (anticipated) hours of delivery for a given qualification; and uncapped pricing, which was most prominently used under the former VET Fee-Help scheme.

In addition to contestability, or making public training funds open to competition between providers, key to the implementation of the training market were two complementary changes to pedagogy in 1999 – the introduction of training packages and CBT. Training packages and the NQF provided national, as opposed to state-based, courses and qualifications.

Consistent with the goal of 'flexibility' and meeting the needs of industry, the skills and knowledge content in training packages is expressed broadly, to enable the customisation of training to the needs of individual students and firms.[5]

It is important to note that from the beginning of the training market private RTOs were given status equivalent with TAFE in their ability to deliver training based on training packages, assess students and issue qualifications and receive public funding for this training, as well as deliver fully privately funded training. RTOs are registered with the Australian Skills Quality Authority (ASQA), the national regulator, to deliver a specific range of courses at given levels of qualification, typically between the levels of Certificate I and Diploma, but even including degrees. This equivalent status gave private RTOs access to an essential and economically valuable commodity: qualifications that are frequently a precondition for work in many occupations.

At the beginning of the training market–era almost all publicly funded VET was delivered by TAFE colleges, and other public institutions such as agricultural colleges. Not-for-profit adult and community education (ACE) providers were also important in the system. In 1996, 98 per cent of students receiving publicly funded VET were in TAFE (83 per cent) or not-for-profit community education providers (15 per cent), but by 2016 this had fallen to 49 per cent and 6 per cent respectively (NCVER 2016a: Table 11).[6] The number of students in for-profit or other RTOs receiving government funds increased from just 23,000, or 2 per cent of students, in 1996 to 575,000, or 45 per cent of publicly funded VET students, in 2016 (NCVER 2017c unpublished data).

There was a corresponding shift in the distribution of government funds. In 2015, a total of $4 billion, or 42 per cent of total operating expenses for publicly funded VET, went to non-TAFE providers (NCVER 2016b: 6).[7] Contestability also resulted in a huge increase in the number of RTOs registered to deliver publicly funded VET, from around 400 in 1995, to 1931 in 2016, with the majority of these being private providers (Korbel and Misko 2017: 13; NCVER 2017a: 5).

Advocates for contestability suggest that the radical transformation in the supply of VET over the last three decades simply reflects the considered preferences of students and employers, who, empowered under the training market to exercise choice, have selected the optimum RTO to meet their demand for high-quality skills. Further, advocates suggest contestability has improved training quality. These claims are highly disputed.

A Trial Run for the Training Market

At first, the training market was implemented incrementally. Two early and highly instructive examples of its implementation were traineeships and the international VET student market. Their relevance as case studies lies in the scale of outright rorting under private provision and the causes of this malfeasance, which persist under the current system.

Traineeships

Traineeships were introduced in 1985. Like traditional apprenticeships, they combine work and formal off-the-job vocational training in a specific occupation. Unlike apprenticeships, the great majority of traineeships are in low-paying and mostly low-skilled service occupations.[8]

It was not until the early 1990s that traineeships experienced a major surge in numbers following an extension of employer subsidies from apprenticeships to traineeships, the introduction of a so-called 'training wage' (a lower wage for trainees compared to non-trainee workers in equivalent jobs), and the introduction of 'fully on-the-job' traineeship training, allowing employers to have training occur in the workplace rather than off the job. The number of trainees surged from 12,000 in 1990 to 300,000 in 2012, a 25-fold increase (NCVER 2017a: Table 1). Consequently, 'quality concerns … emerged as traineeship numbers took off' (Knight 2012: 20).

The reasons employers are attracted to the traineeship system are self-evident; the reasons for a worker to enter a traineeship are less clear. The prime motivation cited by trainees was to get a job. Cully and Curtain (2001a: ix) found that, in contrast to traditional apprentices, 'many trainees had, at best, only a tenuous connection to the training aspect of their [traineeship]'. For these people, undertaking a traineeship offers

> a path out of unemployment into the secondary labour market or an artificial barrier into a higher paying job, while for others it offers better prospects with their current employer or a different employer, some of whom do not require completion of the qualification to be persuaded of the person's competence. (Cully and Curtain 2001b: 212–213)

The key point is that entry into what were previously unregulated, low-skilled jobs, mostly for those disadvantaged in the labour market, now required participation by both the trainee and employer in a formal system of regulated training. These reasons for employer and worker participation in traineeships did not prove conducive to a demand for or a supply of quality training. The ballooning cost of subsidies and concern about the quality of training and job outcomes eventually led government to tighten subsidy eligibility, causing trainee numbers to plummet by close to two-thirds from 2012 to 2016 (Hargreaves, Stanwich and Skujins 2016).

Skilled Migration Program and Private RTOs

Under the Australian Skilled Migration program eligibility to attain permanent residency is based on a points system, with priority offered to foreign nationals possessing qualifications and experience in an occupation listed on the national skills shortage list. Additional points are granted to potential migrants holding a relevant qualification from a domestic RTO or university. Until recently, the range of occupations on the list was wide, including many VET occupations such as cooks and hairdressers (Birrell, Healy and Kinnaird 2007). VET proved a very attractive pathway to Permanent Residency (PR). The number of overseas students in private VET colleges increased from 11,000 in 2000 to 192,300 in 2009, a 16.5-fold increase (Productivity Commission 2011: Table B.21).

Following a series of scandals involving regulators' concerns about quality, the poor treatment of students, and closure of private colleges leaving students stranded, the federal government instituted a review of the migration system. The Baird Review (2010) revealed that the link between PR and VET was the prime driver of foreign-student participation in training. 'This link has resulted in some providers and their agents being interested in 'selling" a migration outcome to respond to the demand from some students to "buy" a migration outcome' (Baird 2010: 6–7). The report also revealed that the quality of training was of marginal interest to many students. A low-quality training market flourished due to the joint interests of students and RTOs: 'In some cases students appear to collude with these people [RTOs] for mutual gain. In such cases this usually results in poor education outcomes.' The Review issued this prescient warning: 'The issues international education is facing right now are likely to be future issues for the whole education sector. It would be naive of us to think otherwise' (Baird 2010: 7; 5).

These two early examples – traineeships and the skilled migration program – stimulated the entry of many private providers and encouraged RTOs, students and employers to game the system, setting a template for future behaviour. They also illustrate the difficulty of regulating a large market with multiple participants, low barriers to entry for RTOs, and perverse incentives on both the supply and demand sides of VET, which leads participants to collude in diminished quality. These are themes to which this chapter will return.

Scale of the Quality Problem

There is no official data permitting an estimate of the scale of the quality problem in the training market. For example, there are no rankings of the relative performance of RTOs against the variety of standards that apply which would enable students to make informed selections among providers.[9] However, there are several indicators that show the problem is significant.[10]

Regulatory Audits

To date, private providers have been the locus of regulatory concerns regarding the quality of VET provision. Since its inception, the training market has been regulated by different agencies at state and national levels; but, since 2011, the principal regulator has been ASQA. ASQA undertakes regular audits of all RTOs and over the four years from 2012–13 to 2015–16 conducted approximately 1500 to 1200 RTO audits each year (ASQA 2016a: 48). The outcome of two different RTO audits are reported: an initial audit after an RTO has been operating for 12 to 18 months; and a final audit of any RTO not initially found to be compliant and given 20 working days to rectify the problem with advice from ASQA. From the 2011–12 financial year to 2015–16 the average level of initial RTO compliance against national standards was just 22 per cent. In other words, on initial audit, only one in every five RTOs was found to be compliant. After rectification, the average level of compliance was only 76 per cent: only three in four RTOs on average were compliant. ASQA expressed particular concern about the high level of non-compliance with standards that 'relate to meeting the needs of industry and learners and ensuring the quality of training and assessment' (ASQA 2016a: 55). ASQA does not report what happens to the nearly one-quarter of audited RTOs that fail to pass the final audit.

Regulator Reviews

In addition to audits, the regulator undertakes investigations 'where systemic risks are identified' (ASQA 2017a). To date, ASQA has identified systemic risks in training for aged and community care in Australia, childcare, construction, security and equine industries. In addition, strategic reviews were carried out into RTO marketing to students, minimum prescribed VET teaching qualifications, and duration of training. On the latter, the ASQA 'found that the long-term quality of Australia's VET sector is at risk unless the issue of unduly short training is definitively addressed' (ASQA 2017b). That systemic risk exists on a matter so fundamental as the duration of training and volume of learning more than three decades into the life of the training market speaks eloquently to the scale of the quality problem and the difficulty of finding regulatory solutions to these problems.

In addition, the NSW Independent Commission Against Corruption (ICAC) undertook several damming reviews into VET provision in New South Wales over the first half of the 2000s. Using its extraordinarily powerful investigatory powers, it revealed extensive low-quality training and corruption across several sectors. The ICAC ceased its investigations not because it had exhausted the scope of malfeasance but simply because it believed it had expended sufficient resources to illuminate the scale of the problems and expected government to remedy them.

The Market for Low-Quality Training

A central assumption of the mandarins who designed the training market was that it was in the enlightened self-interest of students to choose high-quality RTOs. For many students this assumption proved to be wrong. I address these market dynamics shortly, but for now, let's examine one estimate of the scale of student demand for low-quality training.

In a recent report for NSW TAFE, Boston Consulting (2015) provided a market segmentation analysis of the priority students give to quality in the selection of a provider against other factors that may influence their choice, including price, length of time to achieve a qualification, location, and mode of delivery and assessment (online versus classroom-based). The purpose was to show where TAFE stood in a market as 'providers are defining their competitive advantage by identifying and tailoring their offerings to specific customer segments' (Boston Consulting 2015: 54). The key point revealed by the analysis was that between 40 and 55 per cent of the student market are willing to trade quality for lowest price and convenience. For these students a 'primary concern is obtaining a qualification, rather than necessarily the quality of that qualification' and 'price is very important ... [they are] willing to trade quality for it' and/or they 'have limited agency ... [or are] highly susceptible to aggressive recruitment strategies.'

Employer Associations

Major employer associations, including the Australian Industry Group (AiG) and Australian Chamber of Commerce and Industry, that were key advocates of the present system, now argue that there are fundamental problems with the design of the training market. Their judgement is that the market has reduced the quality of provision; created a disconnect between student choice and industry skills needs; and that reputational damage to the training system has reduced the incentive of employers and workers to acquire VET qualifications (Mitchell 2012: 34–35; 38–39). They expressed similar disquiet in a recent federal parliamentary inquiry into private RTOs (Commonwealth of Australia 2015). The AiG stated that it 'has experienced disquiet from employers concerning inadequate time in the delivery of courses by providers, inadequate assessment of competence and poor quality training outcomes.'

The Housing Industry Association (HIA), another early key supporter of the training market, finds the system of training and assessment for apprentices in the construction industry to be fundamentally unfit for purpose. In many industries the acquisition of qualifications is linked to increments in award-wage levels, given the former is intended to signal a certain level of worker competence and productivity. According to the HIA, such wage setting 'requires a comprehensive, well-structured framework within which the competencies of apprentices can be accurately assessed: such a system does not currently operate' (HIA 2015: 4; 3; 18).

It is important to note that, nonetheless, like the VET mandarins, employer associations continue to support the current system. The reasons for the persistence of this commitment, despite their critical judgements on actual outcomes, are taken up in the conclusion to this chapter.

Causes of Failure

Specific economic and pedagogical conditions in the training market help to explain the scale and scope of poor quality and malfeasance.

Economic Factors

An efficient market assumes a 'sovereign consumer' or that buyers are adequately, if not perfectly, informed. This assumption in turn relies on the condition that information about the VET market is valid, accessible and obtainable at low cost. It also assumed that consumers can process information to make informed decisions and that it is in the enlightened self-interest of consumers to choose a high-quality producer. For many students these assumptions are invalid.

First, there are no reliable official indicators of RTO quality. Toner (2011b) outlines the profound methodological issues in developing quality metrics for VET, given its diverse objectives and the extensive statistical adjustments required to construct valid comparisons of RTOs.[11] Practical problems of scale prohibit the development of useful metrics, as there are well over 4000 RTOs (1931 of which deliver publicly funded VET) delivering over 2000 different national training package qualifications and 943 nationally recognised accredited courses (Korbel and Misko 2016: 13).

Developing valid quality indicators for each qualification at each RTO would be impossible.

Second, RTOs can engage in obfuscation by misinforming potential students as to the quality of training and its labour market outcomes.[12]

Third, a large proportion of VET students have low levels of education, limited literacy, numeracy and problem-solving capacity.[13] This is not unexpected given the increased participation of disadvantaged groups is an explicit objective of publicly funded VET. The limited information processing ability of many VET students also calls into question the efficacy of constant demand by government and the VET regulator to improve student choice of RTO by increasing the volume and quality of information about RTO performance.

Finally, for a large proportion of the market, improving the quality of information is irrelevant, as many VET participants are in fact indifferent to the quality of training. This is explained below.

There are well-defined and carefully documented conditions creating 'perverse incentives' for students and/or employers not to demand quality training, and for providers to thus supply such low-quality training. This applied to traineeships and overseas VET students in particular, but indifference to VET quality is widespread.

One condition is when a student has limited intrinsic motivation to undertake training but participation is government-mandated to, for example, maintain welfare payments.[14] Some people obligated to train will put less effort into study and seek out providers that are prepared to accept minimal effort.

Mandated training also occurs with 'occupational licensing', a legislated requirement to attain a VET qualification to work in a specific occupation. Three joint conditions give rise to indifference to the quality of training. First, students view the mandated training as an unnecessary bureaucratic impost, often because they already have extensive work experience in the same or similar occupation, and there may be no wage increment for them upon attaining the qualification. Second, employers are also indifferent to the quality of training because they experience recruitment difficulties and are keen to quickly expand the size of the 'qualified' labour pool. ASQA (2017a) found these conditions applied in three industries – childcare, aged care and the security industry – subject to review because of rising alarm about training quality. Third, both ASQA and the NSW ICAC found collusion to reduce quality when there is high employer demand for qualified labour and students want a licence to work but lack the literacy and numeracy proficiency to attain it legitimately.[15]

A broader perspective on the potential scale of perverse incentives is provided by NCVER surveys of employers' 'reasons for using the VET system'.[16]

A key assumption in the creation of the training market over the last three decades is that competition would boost quality. At least in many fields of teaching, this has not happened. A central reason for this is that entry by RTOs into the training market requires minimal investment in buildings and equipment and there are inadequate standards for teacher qualifications and teaching resources. These low barriers to entry and exit by RTOs can be exploited by opportunistic providers. The scale of entry and exit by RTOs into and out of the training market is large. In the five years to 2015, the annual combined rate of RTO exit and entry was 13 per cent (Korbel and Misko 2016: 15). At this rate, the total stock of RTOs would, in theory, turn over every 7.6 years.

The public funding system also reduces the incentive of private providers to invest due to the relatively limited duration of some government training contracts (which can be as short as one semester), and uncertainty over continuity of funding in a competitive market (Allen Consulting Group 2011: 10). Also, government funding of training in the competitive market does not make explicit allowance for capital costs.[17]

Low barriers to entry and exit greatly reduce the risk of business failure due, say, to an inability to attract or retain students, or adverse action by regulators against an opportunistic provider. Under these conditions, even where some providers seek to act ethically, the force of competition can drive them from the market if ethical provision results in higher costs (ASQA 2017a). The problem of low barriers to entry is now widely acknowledged, but a solution within the private training market remains elusive.

Given these conditions, the decision to engage in malfeasance and quality diminution by an RTO is essentially strategic, determined, in large part, by the answers to the following questions: what are the rewards for opportunistic behaviour? Will these rewards more than cover the cost of entry and exit? And what is the probability of successful adverse action by a regulator? This understanding of malfeasance is consistent with the neoclassical theory of crime deterrence (Becker 1968) and recent more sophisticated models, which emphasise the ability of a corporate malefactor to limit detection by controlling the flow of information and delaying sanctions through legal appeals (Shapira and Zignales 2017).

Market Structure

In the total VET market, covering the privately and publicly funded VET system, there are around 4 million students and over 4000 RTOs, but 42 per cent of providers had fewer than 100 students enrolled in 2014 (Korbel and Misko 2016: 19). This market structure of VET providers is not conducive to efficient regulation and is indicative of very low barriers to entry and exit (Korbel and Misko 2016: 23).

Reduced Government Funding

Due to a combination of contestability and government funding restraint, resources for VET teaching have fallen perilously. By one standard measure, real (inflation-adjusted) government recurrent funding for VET fell by 39 per cent between 2005 and 2014. It is disingenuous of the Commission (2017: 5.34) to suggest that 'low or decreasing unit costs can indicate efficient delivery of VET services' without considering that such a large reduction in resourcing can have the opposite effect (Productivity Commission 2017: 5.34).

Previous research indicates underinvestment in TAFE is a chronic problem and this has reduced the capacity of the system to keep up to date with new technologies and maintain the currency of teacher skills and knowledge (Toner 2005). This declining capacity is likely to have worsened in the last decade.

A large reduction in real government funding per hour of teaching will arguably restrict the scope for investment by ethical RTOs to improve the quality of their teaching and reinforce incentives by other RTOs to maintain profitability through quality diminution.

A Market- or State-Controlled System?

A key objective in introducing the training market was to make the system more responsive to the needs of industry, employers and individual students. If the publicly funded system was actually driven by the needs of the labour market then overall enrolments would on average grow steadily by around 2 per cent per year, in line with annual growth in the labour force. But this is not the case, as annual student enrolments are quite volatile (see Figure 1). For example, from 2010 to 2012 they increased by 20 per cent but then fell by 22 per cent between 2013 and 2015. The average annual number of enrolments over the period 1997 to 2016 was 1.3 million students, so large shifts in the absolute number of students were required to elicit these proportional changes.

These fluctuations are overwhelmingly driven not by the needs of the labour market, but by changes in government policy to overall funding, the opening and closure of specific training programs, and change to rules governing student eligibility for government funding. For example, between 2012 and 2015 the number of trainees fell by 50 per cent, from 300,000 to 150,000, as government tightened eligibility rules to rein in ballooning employer subsidies and training costs and because of concerns that many traineeships were not in occupations subject to skill shortages (NCVER 2017d: Table 1). In 1999, 24,500 students enrolled in VET Fee-Help; by 2015 this had grown to 582,000; and, due to outrageous rorting of the system and a subsequent tightening of the rules, in 2016 this had fallen to 429,000 (Department of Education and Training 2016b). Further large reductions are anticipated.

These huge swings in student numbers induced by government fiat have major implications for quality in the system. First, large fluctuations make rational planning and resourcing difficult for ethical providers. Second, great uncertainty over the anticipated level of student demand reinforces the short-term investment horizon of for-profit RTOs, and reduces the incentive to invest in equipment and staff and increases incentives for opportunism by RTOs. Finally, huge swings in enrolments expose the tenuous connection to the labour market of many publicly funded courses. The sensitivity of annual student enrolments to changes in the level of government training subsidies suggests that, at least for many students and employers, the perceived benefits of participating in training are marginal. An implication of this is that students and employers who are only marginally attached, or indifferently committed, to training will be undemanding of high-quality service.

Figure 1. Annual change in government-funded VET students in Australia

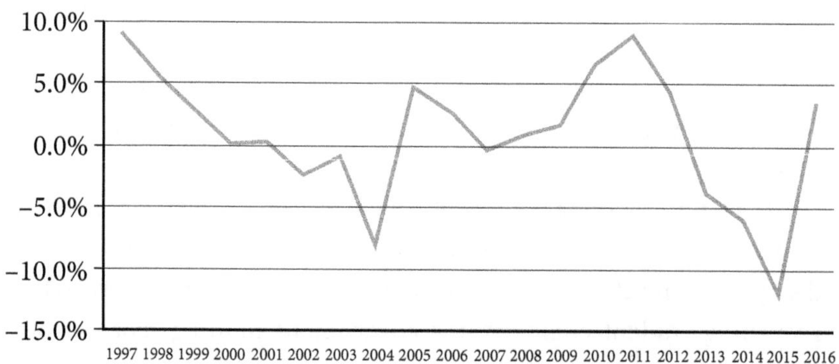

Source: Derived from NCVER 2017d: Table 10

Pedagogy

CBT and Training Packages

The pedagogical system used to facilitate the training market is a central cause of quality diminution. Competency-based training was gradually applied to different industry sectors from the early 1990, but from 1999 all nationally accredited VET training has been in the form of training packages based on CBT principles. Put simply, training packages are developed by representative bodies in major industries and set out the training content and assessment methods for qualifications covering most occupations in each industry. Educationists have been critical of training packages and CBT from the outset, arguing that they are focused on training for, and assessment of, discrete tasks with inadequate recognition of underpinning knowledge; that they are too oriented to the needs of an individual workplace (as opposed to an ideal type of occupation); that the content of training packages is developed by industry representatives with little if any consultation with TAFE teachers; and that the assessment methods and standards to assess student competence are too vague (Cornford 2000; Guthrie 2009; Wheelahan 2016).

Imprecision in training packages is central to RTO quality diminution. Loose specification adversely affects virtually every aspect of training, including volume of learning, assessment, performance standards, duration of training, student entry standards, teacher qualifications and learning resources. This ambiguity results in low validity and reliability of assessments and difficulties for VET regulators enforcing imprecise standards. Expressed less formally, it can result in 'tick and flick' training. Critically, to ensure flexibility in adapting training packages to client needs, the organisations that produce them do not produce textbooks or learning materials. The task of converting high-level statements of training content into teaching lessons for each client is left to decentralised RTOs. From the beginning of the training market, innumerable independent reviews, parliamentary inquiries and regulator reports have sought tighter specification in training packages.

Imprecision in the volume and assessment of learning flows directly from an elemental flaw in the original design of the training market, one which persists to this day. This flaw is the tension between the principles of 'flexibility' and 'standardisation' that underpin the system (Toner 2014). Flexibility in all aspects of VET was sought to allow the customisation of training to the needs of individuals, workplaces and industries. Standardisation was applied to create national as opposed to state-based qualifications and regulation, but was not applied to form prescriptive and detailed content and assessment methods. At key moments in the formation of the training market, when the principles of standardisation and flexibility have conflicted, priority has been given to the former. An identical argument was later made by Bowman and McKenna (2016), who focused on the 'dynamic tension, built into the system, to achieve both national consistency and sufficient flexibility to ensure that training meets specific local, industry and learner needs.'

Giving priority to flexibility created fundamental ambiguity as to whose needs VET is intended to serve. Is it the individual, the employer or industry?[18] Arguably each entity has differing perspectives on the content and assessment of training. Meeting these diverse interests requires a degree of 'elasticity' in the system that is incompatible with prescriptive standards.[19]

These sources of ambiguity can be exploited by RTOs, employers and students to collectively lower the costs involved in, respectively, granting a qualification, receiving a qualification, and increasing the pool of qualified labour.

Limits to VET Regulation

Aside from problems with the efficacy of regulation caused by the sheer number of RTOs and qualifications and loose specification of standards, there are other limits to the effectiveness of regulation. These include constrained regulatory resources and the need for regulators to adhere to principles of natural justice and administrative law – which in turn can lead to protracted enforcement action (Department of Education and Training 2016c: 25). Limits are also imposed by the legislated requirement for ASQA (2016b: 4) 'to achieve a reasonable balance between the responsibility to deliver protection to the community and the burden imposed by external intervention'.

Conclusion

Why has a system so widely recognised as deeply flawed persisted for more than three decades and proven so resistant to change? There are a number of reasons. Ideological commitment among the economic mandarins to the market and to contracting out public services remains potent. The Productivity Commission (2016), for example, recommitted its support to the training market subject to vaguely specified improvements in 'stewardship'. But a successful ideology always has strong material foundations. The traditional rationale for taxpayer support of VET training is to overcome employer reluctance to invest in industry-level or general skills as opposed to firm-specific skills. Employers cannot ensure workers remain with the firm to recoup the cost of providing their employees with skills that are transferable across industries and firms. However, the degree of customisation permitted under the training market enables employers to have taxpayers fund their firm-specific training. The AiG note that 'employers and individual students, wherever possible, need to have training delivery and outcomes shaped to meet their organisational and individual needs. There is considerable flexibility built into the application of qualifications to meet employers' or individuals' needs' (Commonwealth of Australia 2015).

Aside from private RTOs, global capital markets, such as private equity, have in the last decades seen education, including VET, as an important new asset class (Shubber 2017). The private training market is big business – public spending generates billions in revenue each year and high profit rates (Yu and Oliver 2015). The attitude of highly influential and politically well-connected capital markets to VET is neatly summed up in this quote from an investment adviser:

> Education is a beautiful business when it works. Fat fees, hefty annual increases, recurring income and high switching costs are just a few traits of high-performing education providers. Investors who have understood the sector's potential have done exceptionally well. (Featherstone 2014)

As noted earlier, the training market was introduced without any robust evidence the former publicly delivered system was inadequate or that the proposed new model could be efficiently and effectively implemented. After three decades of revolutionary change, it is clear the training market is incapable of delivering the quantity and quality of essential intermediate-level skills the economy needs to help firms compete and implement ever-accelerating technical change. This incapacity of the domestic training system has resulted in chronic skills shortages that are filled by greater dependence of employers on migration. This creates a vicious cycle of reduced demand for and supply of domestically trained tradespeople and technicians. It also increases resentment against migrants and reduces support for migration within the population. Destruction of the former public VET system has also removed a traditional support for disadvantaged groups to enter employment and education and lowered social mobility. It has cemented the problem of a disengaged and disconnected welfare-dependent underclass.

Despite the significant interests imparting inertia to the training market, reality has a way of aggressively butting up against ill-conceived ideologies. The problems identified above are being increasingly acknowledged. For example, both the Business Council of Australia (2017) and Innovation and Science Australia (2017) have identified the critical function of the VET system in the Australian innovation system and lamented the declining ability of the system to achieve this function.

There are moves in some Australian states to 'wind back the clock' and identify TAFE as the nominally preferred provider. Some states are acting unilaterally to remove poor-quality RTOs and courses by restricting their eligibility for funding. At a national level there are incremental moves by the mandarins to tighten standards around, for example, duration, volume of learning, moderation of assessment, teacher qualifications and student course entry requirements. Ironically, this emulates those features of the earlier TAFE system the training market was intended to eradicate. This can be viewed as either policy 'tension' or incoherency. Arguably, gradual improvement is occurring in a deeply flawed system. Against this must be set the loss of what is by now two generations of experienced TAFE teachers, and a large depreciation in the stock of technological capital. Investment is required in people, buildings and equipment, plus the reinvention of centralised curriculum development centres with a capacity to write textbooks, develop learning resources and maintain the currency of teacher knowledge. The scale of reinvestment required is large.

The training market has followed the classic trajectory of neoliberal public policy: ebullient expectations quickly followed by disappointment leading to incessant and expensive – though largely futile – bureaucratic tinkering resulting in intensified regulation and altered incentives. The waste of public and private funds caused by the training market over three decades is difficult to estimate but, even on conservative assumptions, must be many billions. The time remaining to effect a rescue of the public VET system is rapidly diminishing.

Endnotes

1 The total VET system, comprised of government-funded and fee-for-service domestic and international students, is much larger, with 4 million students enrolled in 2016, or 42 per cent of the population aged 15 to 64. The sector is comprised of 4036 RTOs, of which 77 per cent are for-profit private and they account for 59 per cent of total students (NCVER 2017b: 6–8). Nearly half of all subject enrolments were government-funded (NCVER 2017b: Table 11).

2 There are many excellent histories of the training market, including, for example, Ryan (2011).

3 Toner (2011b) provides a comprehensive rebuttal of these arguments.

4 The byzantine process of negotiation between unions, employers and political parties required to introduce the training market, and the eventual disenchantment of some unions with the new market is described in Brown (2006), Ewer et al (1991) and Hampson (2002).

5 Prior to the introduction of training packages, detailed and uniform curricula, textbooks, learning materials, assessment methods and standards were produced by specialist professional TAFE teachers in well-resourced, centralised curriculum development centres. An explicit goal of the system was uniformity and consistency in training content and assessment for each occupation within each state. Uniformity was also promoted through moderation of marking standards, and was bolstered by the long average tenures of TAFE teachers, and agreement between teachers and industry that the prime objective of training was to impart skills and knowledge for a 'representative' trade occupation in a given industry. Skills and knowledge were to be of sufficient breadth and depth to facilitate transferability of the occupation across firms in a given industry. The preference among employers for trade workers with broad skills was due to the average small size of firms, which tended to lack the scale required to deploy specialised labour. Unions liked transferable, as opposed to firm-specific, skills due to the bargaining power it gave their members (Curtain 1987). In summary, TAFE served both the occupation and the industry. Imparting high-quality transferable skills that facilitated entry to skilled occupations was implicitly assumed to serve the interests of the student. In the current system the focus of teaching is on the needs of the individual workplace, which has raised concerns regarding the transferability of these skills across firms. It was this uniformity and absence of provider choice that were particular targets of training market advocates.

6 The 1996 data includes both publicly funded and fee-for-service students attending VET.

7 In 2003, funding of non-TAFE RTOs accounted for 7 per cent of total national VET operating expenditure. By 2015, it was 22 per cent (NCVER 2016b). The non-TAFE share of students in 2015 was substantially greater than the share of public funding. The difference is mostly accounted for by the now defunct VET Fee-Help (VFH) scheme, a student loan scheme similar to HECS. VFH funds going to non-TAFE providers is not included in conventional VET finance reporting, though recently released data enables an adjustment to be made (NCVER 2016b: 4). In 2015, \$2.46 billion of VFH loans were accounted for by non-TAFE RTOs in addition to the \$1.54 billion identified in

the standard VET finance system. Thus, in 2015, a total of $4 billion, or 42 per cent of total operating expenses for publicly funded VET, went to non-TAFE providers (NCVER 2016b: 6). This is close to the non-TAFE share of total students.

8 Like so much of the local system, traineeships were an adaptation of UK initiatives: the Youth Training System and later Modern Apprenticeships. These are now abandoned or have been revised due to quality problems (Ryan and Unwin 2001).

9 These national standards cover all aspects of the VET system (ASQA 2016b: 12), but, as this chapter argues, there are fundamental flaws in the design of these standards. Further, we argue that the assumption that better supply of information by itself will lift quality is flawed, as it fails, for example, to take into account the 'perverse incentives' driving participation of many students and employers in training.

10 There are many more indicators but space precludes using them. For example, a review of VET Fee Help found 'serious concerns over the quality, probity and conduct of some providers, low completion rates and unethical practices' (Department of Education and Training 2016a: 5).

11 The Productivity Commission (2011: xlvi) has found that 'there are no unequivocal indicators of teaching quality in VET.'

12 The federal Department of Education and Training review of VET Fee-Help (2016b: 24) found that 'an essential challenge to the scheme has been dealing with uninformed, poorly informed or misinformed consumers who may not understand their options or the implication of these options. Critical to understanding this is the scale and breadth of unethical practices undertaken by some providers and brokers employed to attract and enrol students.'

13 Standardised international tests of adult literacy, numeracy and problem-solving reveal significant educational disadvantage among many VET students. Between 50 and 77 per cent of all persons with a Certificate I to IV are classified within the lowest two levels of the five-level scale used (derived from ABS 2008: Table 10). Level three is the 'minimum required for individuals to meet the complex demands of everyday life and work in the emerging knowledge-based economy' (Australian Bureau of Statistics 2008: 5).

14 The Department of Education and Training (2016a: 21) review of VFH concluded that low demand for quality by some students was caused by 'income support payments such as Newstart Allowance, Youth Allowance and the Work for the Dole programme [which] require recipients to apply for jobs, train or study to remain eligible for support. In these instances, people enrol in a VET course … to meet their obligations.'

15 The ICAC concluded that the scale of fraudulent training provision in licensed occupations threatened both public safety and survival of legitimate training providers for these licensed occupations. These occupations included safety induction and heavy plant operation in the construction industry; building contractor and building certifier for residential building and security guards. (These ICAC studies are summarised in Toner 2014.)

16 In 2015, 36.6 per cent of all employers, excluding employers with apprentices and trainees, had jobs that 'required a vocational qualification' (NCVER 2015: Table 1). Of this group 62 per cent of employers stated that the qualification was needed to

'provide the skills required for the job'. This is closely followed in importance by 'legislative, regulatory or licensing requirements' (52.1 per cent), and 'to meet and maintain professional or industry standards' (27.9 per cent). The next most important reason was 'to improve the quality of goods and services provided' (3.6 per cent, NCVER 2015: Table 10). In other words, some form of compulsion was a dominant reason for requiring workers to have VET qualifications. What is unknown is what proportion of this large potential pool of firms colludes with employees and/or RTOs to reduce the burden of mandated training.

17 Government could redress these disincentives to investment in physical and human teaching capital by increasing the duration of contracts, but this would contradict a key objective of contracting out, which is both to maximise competition between providers and to supply flexibility in meeting fluctuations in demand for training. There are also potentially massive administrative problems in making explicit allowance for capital costs such as estimating capital costs per course or qualification; accounting for and disposing of capital goods after exit of a private RTO; and ensuring an RTO receiving publicly funded capital did not use it to deliver privately funded training.

18 This ambiguity is reflected in the following official description of whose needs training packages are intended to serve from the Australian Industry Skills Committee (2016: 5–6). 'Training packages do not prescribe how an individual should be trained. RTOs use training packages to help design curriculum and/or learning and assessment methodologies that assist individuals to gain and/or demonstrate they have the skills and knowledge specified in training packages. Training is tailored to individual learner needs and can be contextualised to the specific circumstances of an employer and/or industry sector.'

19 The scale of training customisation is large. In a survey of employers, Smith et al. (2017: 24) found that 75 per cent of employers 'who used nationally recognised training said that this training was customised to the specific needs of their organisations, with 30.3 per cent saying that it was customised to a great extent.'

References

Allen Consulting Group (2011) *Competitive tendering and contestable funding in VET: approaches to supporting access and equity*, report to National VET Equity Advisory Council, Melbourne.

Australian Bureau of Statistics (2008) *Adult Literacy and Life Skills Survey, Summary Results Australia. Reissue*, Canberra, (Cat. No. 4102.0).

Australian Industry Skills Committee (2017) Industry Reference Committees. Operating Framework for the Development of Training Packages.

Australian Skills Quality Authority (2016a) *Annual Report 2015–16*, asqa.gov.au/publications/annual-reports.html

——(2016b) *Regulatory Risk Framework*, April, asqa.gov.au/sites/g/files/net2166/f/ASQA_Regulatory_Risk_Framework.pdf

——(2017a) *Strategic Reviews*, asqa.gov.au/about/strategic-reviews

——(2017b) *Course duration, 2017*, asqa.gov.au/about/strategic-reviews/course-duration-2017

Baird, B. (2010) 'Stronger, simpler, smarter ESOS: supporting international students', *Review of the Education Services for Overseas Students (ESOS) Act 2000*, Canberra, Commonwealth of Australia.

Bates, I. (2002) *The Competence and Outcomes Movement: The Landscape of Research, 1986–1996*, School of Education, VET Post 14 Research Group, Leeds, University of Leeds.

Becker, G.S. (1968) 'Crime and punishment: an economic approach', *Journal of Political Economy* 76 (2): 169–217.

Birrell, B., Healy, E. and Kinnaird, B. (2007) 'Cooks galore and hairdressers aplenty', *People and Place*, 15 (1): 30–44.

Boston Consulting (2015) *The NSW Vocational Education and Training Market and TAFE NSW's Competitive Position Within It.* Available at: psa.asn.au/wp-content/uploads/2013/01/TAFE-NSW-Public-Report-BCG-1.pdf

Bowman, K. and McKenna, S. (2016) 'The development of Australia's national training system: a dynamic tension between consistency and flexibility', NCVER, Adelaide.

Brown, T. (2006) 'From union inspired to industry led: how Australian Labour's training reform experiment turned sour', *Journal of Industrial Relations*, 48 (4): 491–505.

Business Council of Australia (2017) *Future-Proof. Protecting Australians Through Education and Skills*, October, bca.com.au/publications/future-proof-protecting-australians-through-education-and-skills

Commonwealth of Australia (2015) *Getting Our Money's Worth: The Operation, Regulation and Funding of Private Vocational Education and Training (VET) Providers in Australia.* Canberra, Commonwealth of Australia, 15 October.

Cornford, I. (2000) 'Competency-Based Training: Evidence of a Failed Policy in Training Reform', *Australian Journal of Education* 44 (2): 135–154.

Council of Australian Governments (2008) *Meeting 29 November 2008 attachment B productivity agenda.* http://www.coag.gov.au/node/294#Attachments 9

Cully, M. and Curtain, R. (2001a) *Reasons For New Apprentices' Non-Completions*, National Centre for Vocational Education Research.

——(2001b) 'New apprenticeships: an unheralded labour market program', *Australian Bulletin of Labour*, 27 (3), September: 204–215.

Curtain, R. (1987) 'Skill formation and the enterprise', *Labour and Industry*, 1 (1): 8–38.

Dawkins J. (1989) *Improving Australia's Training System*, Australian Government Publishing Service, Canberra

Department of Education and Training (2016a) *Redesigning VET FEE-HELP Discussion Paper*, Canberra, Commonwealth of Australia.

——(2016b) *2016 VET FEE-HELP Statistical Report*, Canberra, Commonwealth of Australia.

——(2016c) *Quality Assessment in Vocational Education and Training – Discussion Paper*, Canberra, Commonwealth of Australia.

Deveson, I. (1990) *Training costs of award restructuring: report of the Training Costs Review Committee*, Volume 1, Canberra.

Ewer, P. et al. (1991) *Politics and the Accord.* Sydney, Pluto Press.

Featherstone, T. (2014) 'Top-Performing Education Stocks', *The Bull*, 17 March.

Friedman, M. (1955) 'The role of government in education' in Solo, R.A. (ed.) *Economics and the Public Interest.* New Brunswick, Rutgers University Press: 127–134.

Guthrie, H. (2009) *Competence and Competency Based Training: What the Literature Says.* Adelaide, National Centre for Vocational Education Research.

Hampson, I. (2002) 'Training Reform: Back to Square One?', *Economic and Labour Relations Review* 13 (1): 149–174.

Hargreaves, J., Stanwick, J. and Skujins, P. (2016) *The Changing Nature of Apprenticeships: 1996–2016.* Adelaide, National Centre for Vocational Education Research.

Housing Industry Association (2015) *Inquiry into Vocational Education and Training in New South Wales,* Submission No. 216, 14 August. Sydney, Parliament of New South Wales.

Innovation and Science Australia (2017) *Australia 2030: Prosperity Through Innovation.* Canberra, Commonwealth of Australia.

Knight, B. (2012) *Evolution of Apprenticeships and Traineeships in Australia: An Unfinished History.* Adelaide, National Centre for Vocational Education Research.

Korbel, P. and Misko, J. (2016) *VET Provider Market Structures: History, Growth and Change.* Adelaide, National Centre for Vocational Education Research.

Leitch, S. (2006) *Prosperity for All in the Global Economy: World Class Skills.* London, HM Treasury.

Mitchell, J. (2012) *From Unease to Alarm: Escalating Concerns About the Model of 'VET Reform' and Cutbacks to TAFE.* Highgate, John Mitchell and Associates.

National Centre for Vocational Education Research (2015) *Australian Vocational Education and Training Statistics: Employers' Use and Views of the VET System 2015.* Adelaide, National Centre for Vocational Education Research.

——(2016a) *Historical Time Series of Apprenticeships and Traineeships in Australia from 1963 to 2016.* Adelaide, National Centre for Vocational Education Research.

——(2016b) *Australian Vocational Education and Training Statistics: Financial Information 2015.* Adelaide, National Centre for Vocational Education Research.

——(2017a) *Australian Vocational Education and Training Statistics: Government-Funded Students and Courses 2016.* Adelaide, National Centre for Vocational Education Research.

——(2017b), *Australian Vocational Education and Training Statistics: Total VET Students and Courses 2016.* Adelaide, National Centre for Vocational Education Research.

——(2017c) *Government-Funded Students and Courses: VET Students 2003–2016*, unpublished data. Adelaide, National Centre for Vocational Education Research.

——(2017d) *Historical Time Series of Government-Funded Vocational Education and Training in Australia, from 1981*. Adelaide, National Centre for Vocational Education Research.

Productivity Commission (2011) *Vocational Education and Training Workforce Research Report*, Canberra.

——(2011b) *Vocational Education and Training Workforce*, Draft Research Report. 2010: A Response by Phillip Toner.

——(2011) V*ocational Education and Training Workforce Research Report*, Canberra.

——(2016) *Introducing Competition and Informed User Choice into Human Services: Identifying Sectors for Reform, Study Report*. Canberra.

——(2017) 'Chapter 5, Vocational Education and Training', *Report on Government Services 2016, Volume B*. Canberra, Australian Government Productivity Commission.

Selby-Smith, J. (1998) *User Choice*. Adelaide, National Centre for Vocational Education Research.

Shubber, K. (2017) 'Learndirect faces collapse after failing to suppress Ofsted report', *Financial Times*, 15 August.

Smith, E., Smith, A., Tuck, J. and Callan, V. (2017) *Continuity and Change: Employers' Training Practices and Partnerships with Training Providers*. Adelaide, National Centre for Vocational Education Research. Ryan, P. and Unwin, L. (2001) 'Apprenticeship in the British "Training Market"', *National Institute Economic Review*, 178 (1): 99–114.

Ryan, R. (2011) *How VET Responds: A Historical Policy Perspective*. Adelaide, National Centre for Vocational Education Research.

Toner, P. (2005) *Keeping Up with Technology: A Pilot Study of TAFE and the Manufacturing Sector*. Adelaide, National Centre for Vocational Education Research.

——(2011) *Workforce Skills and Innovation: An Overview of Major Themes in the Literature*, Directorate for Science, Technology and Industry Working Paper. Paris, OECD.

——(2011b) *Draft Research Report November 2010: A Response*. Canberra, Vocational Education and Training Workforce Productivity Commission.

——(2014) 'Contracting out publicly funded vocational education: a transaction cost critique', *The Economic and Labour Relations Review* 2014, 25 (2): 222–239.

Shapira, R. and Zingales, L. (2017), *Is Pollution Value Maximizing? The Dupont Case*, NBER Working Paper No. w23866. Cambridge, Harvard Law School Forum on Corporate Governance and Regulation.

Wheelahan, L. (2016) 'Patching bits won't fix vocational education in Australia – a new model is needed', *International Journal of Training Research*, 14 (3): 180–196.

Yu, S. and Oliver, D. (2015) *The Capture of Public Wealth by the For-Profit Vet Sector*. Workplace Research Centre, Sydney University.

CHAPTER 4

THE REAL COST OF PRISON REFORM: THE CASE OF PRIVATISATION IN VICTORIA

JANE ANDREW AND MAX BAKER

A problem looms large in Australia. Despite stable crime rates across the country (Goh and Holmes 2017), the prison population in many states has grown 35 per cent in the last ten years (Russell and Baldry 2017), and prisons are now operating at 111.4 per cent of capacity (Productivity Commission 2017: Figure 8.8). As a result, our prisons are overflowing with inmates, who all need to be housed, clothed, fed and rehabilitated. As might be expected, the rate of increase in prisoner population has not been met with an equivalent increase in prison infrastructure – producing a sector that is stretched beyond capacity and struggling to meet its most basic functions (Rubinsztein-Dunlop 2014). In 2016 alone, the Australian adult prison population grew by 8 per cent (ABS 2016), intensifying problems in the sector, including the deterioration of prison buildings, the diminution of rehabilitative programs, increased workplace stress for prison officers, a reduction in the delivery of appropriate health care, and a growing culture of idleness within jails (Jewkes, Crewe and Bennett 2016). Incidents of self-harm have risen, cells designed for one inmate are now being used for three, and the waiting time to see a doctor can be as long as a month. Some have argued that our growing reliance on prisons to quarantine 'social dysfunction' from mainstream society represents a shift from social to penal forms of poverty management (Wacquant 2009: 203;

2010; 2014), making prisons the 'frontline criminal justice strategy' (Brown 2015: 1).

Our growing reliance on prisons has produced complex policy dilemmas for state governments, who are charged with providing prison services that are sufficiently resourced to facilitate the rehabilitation of incarcerated people (Mackay 2015). Given that prisons cost approximately $3.7 billion annually (Productivity Commission 2017: Table 8A:2), the community expects the state to ensure prisoners are held securely, that activities within prisons are undertaken effectively and that employees experience a safe workplace. While a tough approach to crime has tended to appeal to voters, a costly and ineffective prison system does not.

As a response, a number of state governments have contracted some of their prison services to the private sector in the hope that these providers will contain costs and optimise service delivery outcomes. Over the last thirty years, five states – Queensland, New South Wales, South Australia, Western Australia and Victoria – have used private contractors in some form to deliver prison services. Private prisons now incarcerate 18.7 per cent of the prison population in Australia (Productivity Commission 2017: Table 8A.4), which is the highest rate of private incarceration per capita of any country in the world (Mason 2013: 1–2). Of the 101 prisons in Australia, private contractors operate nine facilities in five different states: two prisons in Queensland, two in New South Wales, one in South Australia, two in Victoria and two in Western Australia. These prisons are now responsible for almost 7000 Australian prisoners (Productivity Commission 2017: Table 8A.4).

The use of competitive or market-based service delivery models has followed international trends in public service delivery that have seen services sold off, contracted out, or delivered through varied forms of partnerships (Peck and Theodore 2007; Springer 2010). Within debates about public service privatisation, accounting has played an important role in the production of market logics, helping to normalise notions of 'efficiency' and 'costs' in policymaking circles (Andrew and Cahill 2009; Lapsley 1999). While researchers increasingly acknowledge the socially constructed nature of accounting information, in wider circles it is often taken to present neutral, unbiased and factual representations of the material world, thus making it politically potent. Accounting has not only offered 'a language to judge policy in terms of costs' but also 'pre-orders what we see as possible and desirable', or even what is considered commonsense for policymakers (Andrew and Cahill 2017: 14). Given this, policy discussions have become dominated by discussions of efficiency, effectiveness and value for money, displacing discussions of social outcomes to the margins of these debates. This privileging of costs in debates about corrective services in Australia has had the effect of occluding other important aspects of the justice system, such as prisoner health, recidivism and social outcomes (Andrew 2007; Andrew and Cahill 2009).

While the implications of privatised corrections are diverse, in this chapter we explore the impact prison privatisation has had on the costs of service delivery in Victoria from 1996 ,when the state's first private prison opened, through to 2017 when the most recent prison opened at Ravenhall. We first consider the logics that have governed prison reform in Victoria, paying attention to the role accounting information has played in framing these debates. We then discuss the costs of privatising prisons, including a discussion of the costs of contracting, the relative costs of private prisons in comparison to public ones, and the many costs that continue to be borne by the state even though they arise as a direct result of privatisation. Finally, we argue that good policy would consider the total cost of commitment, which would include hidden costs and the costs of failure. To do this, costs would need to be reframed so that they can incorporate the social dimensions of incarceration, not just the financial aspects.

Victorian Private Prisons

Victoria is interesting for a number of reasons: it is the only state in Australia to utilise BOOT (Build Own Operate and Transfer) contracts; more prisoners are incarcerated in private facilities than any other state in the country (approximately 30 per cent); and one private prison was returned to public management because of significant contractual breaches and performance issues. Taken together, the experiences of Victoria mean it offers a unique case study to explore the ways in which experiments with privatisation survive disappointments and failures and are reshaped to ensure ongoing market-oriented reforms can withstand what we see as empirically rich, evidence-based criticisms.

Victoria's experimentation with privatisation between 1994 and 2000 was informed by the Department of Treasury's infrastructure investment policy (Stockdale 1994), which promoted a flow of private-sector capital and investment into public sector activities to stimulate growth and efficiency, deliver cost savings to the community and meet the government policy objective of risk transfer to the private sector (Auditor-General of Victoria 1999: 4.23). In Victoria's case, this sent a clear message that successful bidders would be assessed on their ability to minimise costs and take on the risks associated with prisons (Love et al. 2000).

Victoria's first private prison, Deer Park Metropolitan Women's Correctional Centre (now known as the Dame Phyllis Frost Centre), began operation in 1996. It was contracted to Corrections Corporation Australia, the Australian subsidiary of Corrections Corporation America. The initial contract period ran for twenty years but it could be extended for up to ten more years if both parties agreed (Auditor-General of Victoria 1999: 73). The year after Deer Park opened, two other private prisons began their operations. The medium-security Fulham Prison contracted to the GEO Group Australia, a local subsidiary of American company The GEO Group Inc., opened in 1997, and the high-security and remand prison at Port Phillip, contracted to the British multinational security services company G4S, opened later that same year. Port Phillip and Fulham continue to be operated by these companies, and are currently the two largest prisons in Victoria. At present, Victoria is about to open the largest prison in the country at Ravenhall, and this will be managed by the GEO Group.

Initial Costs and Yearly Contract Fees

When all three private prisons were constructed, the contractors received a twenty-year commitment from the government, each containing an estimated future cost in total fees which greatly exceeded any net present value calculation based on the stated yearly fee. The agreed yearly fees consisted of

Table 1: Victorian private prisons

Prison	Time operating	Number of prisoners	Security	Contractor
Deer Park	1996–2000	260	Minimum, medium, maximum	CCA
Fulham	1997–ongoing	777	Minimum, medium	GEO Group
Port Phillip	1997–ongoing	1000+	Medium, maximum	G4S
Ravenhall	2017–ongoing	1000+	Medium, maximum	GEO Group

Table 2: Private prison costs and total commitment in 1996 and 1997

Prison	Initial Cost	Total time commitment	Yearly fee	Total $ commitment	PLF
Deer Park	$21m (1996)	20 years	$5.2m	$607m	$689k
Fulham	$54m (1997)	20 years	$22m	NA	NA
Port Phillip	$54m (1997)	20 years	$15.9m	NA	$946k

Table 3: Private prison costs and total commitment in 2017

Prison	Initial Cost	Total time commitment	Total Yearly fee	Total $ commitment
Ravenhall	$668.6m	28 years	$219.12[1]	$5,478m[2]
Fulham	See Table 2	20 years	$72.55m[3]	$1,451m
Port Phillip	See Table 2	20 years	$155.65m[4]	$3,113m

two components: a larger prison 'operations fee' and a smaller fee for education and training, healthcare, prison industries and other programs. Each contract also included a performance-linked fee (PLF) paid annually and in arrears, of which 35 to 40 per cent was linked to achieving accommodation-related targets and the remainder was linked to prison service targets (English and Walker 2004: 67). The table opposite summarises the financial costs and commitment made by the government to private prison providers within Victoria within two main periods of contract negotiations.

In the first period of negotiation (1996–97), it is important to introduce some context in relation to the initial costs, which amounted to $129 million in total. This outlay to private contractors to build and house Victoria's 6522 prisoners was more than half the state's total outlay on school upgrades, at $210 million in 1996 for its 900,000 school students. It is also worth noting that these contracts are fixed and difficult to renegotiate once in place. The initial contractual terms across all three prisons have remained in place for twenty years, and have only recently been renegotiated. In many ways, the renegotiation appeared to favour the private provider. Many of the costs associated with running a private prison market are not properly outsourced and are attributed to both private and public prisons across the sector (Andrew, Baker and Roberts 2016).

In the more recent period of contract negotiation, the decision was made to extend the Fulham contract and was justified by comparing the private prison to a public sector comparator: it was claimed that the prison cost $161 per prisoner per day while state-run medium-security prisons cost $182 per prisoner per day (Department of Justice 2016b). The decision to continue using a private operator to run Fulham has been justified using what is called a 'hypothetical, risk-adjusted' (Department of Justice 2016b) public sector comparator. However, the calculation of the comparator allows considerable leeway for estimates and assumptions that favour the private sector. Likewise, the extension contract for Port Phillip was negotiated at $3113 million over its twenty-year lifespan, which is the equivalent to $155.7 million in fees paid yearly to the contractor. Again, the Department of Justice chose to use a public-sector comparator to justify the extension. The assessment determined that while taxpayers were committed to outlaying $3 billion to a private contractor over the next twenty years, they were actually saving $219 million compared to the hypothetical state-run prison (Department of Justice 2016b). While both Fulham and Port Phillip contract extensions use a public sector comparator, the Department of Justice disclosed different types of information to justify each decision, making it difficult to independently interrogate the assumptions and estimates made, or to adequately assess the financial advantages of continued privatisation.

More recently, the Victorian government contracted the GEO Group to build and manage their newest prison at Ravenhall (see Table 1). The construction of Ravenhall Prison in Melbourne's western suburbs, adjacent to Dame Phyllis Frost women's prison (previously Deer Park), was completed in 2017, and they received their first medium-security prisoners in late 2017. It has a current capacity of 1000 beds, but will be able to expand to a maximum of 1300 in anticipation of future growth in prisoner numbers. The state government has announced that Ravenhall will cost a total of $2.5 billion for a 28-year contract, including design and construction as well as operating costs. This claim is questionable as it is based on 'discounted' rather than real (or nominal) fee payments. If the cost of Ravenhall is calculated in the same way as Port Phillip and Fulham (using nominal payment) its total cost of commitment would be much closer to $5.5 billion, which means the prison is likely to cost approximately $219 million a year in fees to the GEO Consortium. The tender was not open to a bid from the public sector, so, again, private bids for the contract were tested in relation to a hypothetical public comparator to see if they offered better value for money. However, it is not clear how the cost of the public sector comparator was established – the summary document contains no formula for the calculation beyond a breakdown of costs into services and facilities.

Operating Costs

In order to measure and compare prison operating costs, most jurisdictions in Australia have tended to calculate the cost per prisoner per day (Andrew and Cahill 2009). While this calculation is problematic, if taken on face value prison privatisation in Victoria does not appear to have translated into lower costs per prisoner per day. As of 2015–16, 28.8 per cent of prisoners in Victoria were held in private facilities, compared to the national average of 18.7 per cent. This means that Victoria holds the largest percentage of its inmates in private prisons when compared to other jurisdictions (Productivity Commission 2017: Table 8A.4). However, the cost of incarceration in Victoria is $289.83 per prisoner per day, which is significantly higher than the national average of $209.96, making Victoria's costs the third highest in Australia after Tasmania and the Australian Capital Territory, neither of which have privately managed prisons (Productivity Commission 2017: Table 8A.19). These costs have been steadily growing by 15 per cent per annum from 2011–12, when the amount was $252.58.

While these figures do not account for state-specific variables, they are significant because they indicate that a much higher use of private prisons has not translated into obvious cost efficiency. Moreover, at the aggregate level there appears to be a lack of evidence to support privatisation on the basis of cost. By way of example, the budget for custodial services has doubled in the last ten years from $408 million in 2005–06 (Department of Treasury Victoria 2007) to $813 million[5] in 2015–2016 (Productivity Commission 2017: Table 8A33), a growth of 6 per cent above inflation.

While there is little academic research on the effects of economic reforms on the prison sector, Sands and Hodge (2014) studied the historical impact of privatisation on the average annual cost of incarcerating prisoners in Victoria. They found that although privatisation initially lowered the average cost of incarceration in the Victorian custodial system, these gains were lost over time.

Unfortunately, detail around the costs associated with the private provision of prison services in Victoria continues to remain a black box. While it is possible to determine the initial costs of the projects, there is no publicly available evidence that would allow observers to compare these costs to the costs associated with public-sector provision. Despite this, Victoria has continued with further privatisation and the claims it will deliver better value for money (Minister for Corrections 2015).

Equally concerning is the existence of *other* costs not included in traditional accounting analysis, which we call 'failure' and 'hidden' costs. In the case of Victoria, these other costs have been excluded from privatisation debates despite their relevance to the broader impact of privatisation.

The Cost of Failure

Victoria's initial experiment with prison privatisation was far from smooth. In 1999, Peter Kirby undertook an investigation into the performance of private operators, releasing the 'Kirby Report' (2000) the following year. In it, he identified several problems, including limited provision of health services, inadequate prison programs, insufficient staff training, and the fragmentation of service delivery in private prisons (Kirby 2000: 4–5).

The report foreshadowed a series of problems at Deer Park, including two deaths in custody, assaults on staff and prisoners, and arson. Corrections Victoria was forced to step in and take over the prison in 2000 (Department of Justice 2000). A subsequent inquiry suggested these failures could be attributed to poor leadership, a lack of staff training, staff shortages, budget constraints, and poor design of the facilities (Department of Justice 2000: 3). The subsequent decision to return Deer Park to public ownership and control came at a huge cost to Victorian taxpayers. The agreement required the government 'to purchase the Centre's buildings, infrastructure and chattels' at the cost of approximately $21 million (Legislative Council of NSW, General Purpose Standing Committee 3, 2009: 209), $2 million of which was purely the legal cost of administering the takeover. The public takeover of Deer Park, combined with the outcomes of the Kirby Report, motivated the department to make changes in risk assessment requirements and to limit the role of contractors (English 2007). It is questionable whether these measures have acted as sufficient safeguards for future contractor failure or improved accountability (Hodge and Sands 2014). Despite the experience of Deer Park in Victoria, the costs associated with failure remain outside the scope of much of the policy debates on prisons.

More recently, the Victorian government released a 'project summary' outlining information related to the extension of the contracts at Fulham and Port Phillip. Among other things, this included an assessment of risk 'in order to achieve the best value for money by allocating risks to the party best able to manage them' (Department of Justice and Regulation and Department of Treasury and Finance 2016a: 16). The assessment categorises risks into those associated with operations, the site, changes to law, force majeure and insurance, but provides little detail about the rationale for determining why some risks are considered as shared between the government and the contractor, and why some are considered the sole responsibility of the contractor. For example, the risk associated with the 'performance standard' of the prison is considered fully transferable to the contractor; while in a technical sense this may hold true, if the contractor fails to provide services to the specified standard, the risks would ultimately be shared. If we imagine a prison that is not offering sufficient vocational programs, or has a lack of health services, then the prisoners themselves are at a disadvantage and, in the case of the lack of rehabilitative work, the consequences are likely to be borne by the state more broadly when the person is released. While it may be true to say that the state can insist on improvements based on the terms of the contract, and that the contractor can incur abatements, this offers only a very narrow assessment of these risks and it produces the impression that they can, in fact, be wholly transferred.

Hidden Costs

Over the last decade, the contracting process for prisons in Victoria has become more complex. Ravenhall's contract alone consists of forty detailed schedules. The creation and monitoring of these contracts involves significant costs and expertise and, in the case of Victoria, the creation of a separate 'Contract Administrator'. As a result, privatisation has required major departmental retooling to provide adequate oversight of outsourced services. To assist in managing the complex legal side of privatisation, the Victorian government engages a variety of consultants to support their contract creation and negotiation with private operators and to oversee the delivery of contractual commitments. However, these consulting services introduce a new set of tensions, because consultants are motivated to 'gain future contracts, which encourages them to say what they think governments want to hear in preference to what they ought to hear' (Mulgan 2017). These consulting services often go unreported in the debate over privatisation, despite the state's growing reliance on them. To highlight the significance of these costs, in Table 2 we have listed the advisory services used to secure and administer the newly signed Ravenhall contract.[6]

TABLE 2: ADVISORY SERVICES ASSOCIATED WITH RAVENHALL CONTRACT

Services	Cost ($)
Strategic public-private partnership procurement adviser Ravenhall prison project	433,400
Ravenhall prison project	148,500
Commercial lead Ravenhall prison project	797,696
Technical lead	1,224,760
Procurement adviser services	245,000
Procurement adviser services	150,000
Security adviser	803,194
Facilities management adviser	440,728
Engineering services adviser	1,306,485
Design adviser	1,990,000
Cost consultant	377,630
Probity adviser	144,182
Commercial and financial adviser	1,030,700
Legal adviser	1,186,975
Project director Ravenhall prison project	1,699,500
Interim commercial and legal adviser	149,591
Interim commercial lead	215,000
Prisoner reintegration system business analysis	127,187
Total	12,470,528

As the Victorian government 'contracted out' prison services, they were forced to 'contract in' a range of professional services. While the costs of these services were reported, they were not included in the overall cost of the contracts, despite having been incurred for no reason other than to facilitate further privatisation within the sector. Many of the professional services outlined above were required because the government did not have the professional skills 'in house' to ensure contract optimisation, both at the point of negotiation and during implementation. In other words, agencies lack the capacity to assess whether the contracts they agree to give the government and taxpayer adequate value for money (Mulgan 2017). This reliance on private sector expertise to create and assess contracts underlying the delivery of core government services represents a reduction of the state's capacity to hold private prison operators accountable for excess costs and to inhibit opportunistic behaviour.

Invariably, contracts leave space for interpretation, providing the contractor with some scope to deliver on the legal requirements within the contract, while creating opportunities to charge additional fees for work outside the specified conditions. Changes in sentencing patterns or changes in community standards create opportunities for private providers to impose greater costs on the state. One such example is the management of prisoners on remand. As the conditions for parole tightened in response to high-profile cases of violent behaviour while on bail, such as the Jill Meagher case in Victoria in 2012, the state has had to manage growing numbers of prisoners awaiting sentencing. In these circumstances, private providers can negotiate to provide additional services at a premium, knowing the state has no option but to accommodate people on remand.

Taken together, these costs – those disclosed in the contract, those associated with failure, and those hidden beyond the core parameters of the cost case – are both substantial and opaque. This needs to enter the discussion on economic reforms in Victoria in order to produce a more informed dialogue about the role of the state, the relative importance of cost and the nature of those costs within core activities.

Broadening the Meaning of 'Cost' for Future Reforms

Victoria has the highest proportion of inmates held in private prisons of any state in Australia, and is currently in the process of bringing online the largest privately built and managed prison in Australian history. Despite claims that prison privatisation delivers value for money, the merits of privatisation remain difficult to assess. To highlight the limitations of economic reforms in the prison sector, we must acknowledge the specific cost of delivering Victorian prison infrastructure, the additional risks associated should these prison operators fail, and the hidden costs.

While it may be impossible to determine the 'true' costs of Victoria's private prisons, we have outlined the significant construction costs and long-term fee commitments associated with privatisation in Victoria. Despite the state's investment in private prison provision, the operational costs of Victoria's private prisons have grown over the last twenty years, outstripping other states in Australia. In addition to disclosed costs, the state does not appear to have a robust approach to risk, particularly in regards to the risk of service failure. There are many hidden costs associated with the process of privatisation, and these appear to be borne entirely by the state. Moreover, the growing complexity around the process of contracting out correctional services has exposed a dearth of expertise in government, which has resulted in the contracting in of professional services – such as contract negotiators, and probity advisers.

By shining an empirical spotlight on costs, we run the risk of implying that they should be the central or most important aspect of these discussions. Cost is clearly an important factor, and has been a key driver in the reform of the prison sector. But it is a poor proxy for good policy. Critical research in the sector argues that a focus on the financial costs limits the debate, diminishing the discussion of more substantial concerns, such as the goals of incarceration, prisoner health and wellbeing, the over-representation of Indigenous people in jail, the use of prisons to house people with mental health issues or drug and alcohol dependencies, appropriate mechanisms for effective rehabilitation, and the working conditions of prison officers (Andrew 2007; Andrew, Baker and Roberts 2016). While this chapter suggests that prison privatisation has not delivered on its promised cost savings to Victorian taxpayers, we also believe that assessments focused purely on value for money provide insufficient grounds upon which to formulate prison policy.

The Victorian government the state has continued to pursue further privatisation. Not only does this run counter to the financial evidence within the policy framework, there is much beyond cost that drives privatisation. Even so, other political and ideological drivers have remained buried in the public debates about cost effectiveness, value for money and performance improvement. Given prison privatisation in Victoria represents long-term contractually-bound commitments to often foreign-owned for-profit operators, the reforms mean that the state is locked in to long-term fiscal and policy commitments for running its justice system. To remain cost-effective private prisons need to be used, encouraging the state to guarantee a supply of prisoners to prisons, thus fortifying imprisonment as the primary mechanism used to respond to antisocial and criminal behaviours. Private prison contracts also mean the state lacks the flexibility to experiment with other forms of policy in the criminal justice space, because to do so would be to undo much of the desired budgetary gains that drove initial reforms. In addition, if costs are to offer a useful evidence base for economic reforms in the prison sector, the reforms must include an assessment of the total cost of commitment.

Endnotes

1 Calculated as nominal value of $5478 million paid evenly over twenty-five periods (Department of Justice and Regulation and Department of Treasury and Finance 2015). Amount also includes a PLF of up to $2 million per year.

2 Calculated at a future value of $2529 million based on the 5.55 per cent annual rate and even monthly payments (Department of Justice and Regulation and Department of Treasury and Finance 2015).

3 Calculated at $1451 million nominal cash flows distributed evenly over twenty years (Department of Justice and Regulation and Department of Treasury and Finance 2016a).

4 Calculated at $3113 million nominal cash flows distributed evenly over twenty years (Department of Justice and Regulation and Department of Treasury and Finance 2016b).

5 This list was compiled from a search for Ravenhall prison services on www.tenders.vic.gov.au/tenders/contract/list.do on 11 September 2017

6 This list was compiled from a search for Ravenhall prison services on www.tenders.vic.gov.au/tenders/contract/list.do on 11 September 2017.

References

Andrew, J. (2007) 'Prisons, the profit motive and other challenges to accountability', *Critical Perspectives on Accounting*, 18 (8): 877–904.

Andrew, J., Baker, M. and Roberts, P. (2016) *Prison Privatisation in Australia: The State of the Nation*. Sydney, The University of Sydney.

Andrew, J., and Cahill, D. (2009) 'Value for money neo-liberalism in New South Wales Prisons', *Australian Accounting Review*, 19 (2): 144–152.

Andrew, J., and Cahill, D. (2017) 'Rationalising and resisting neoliberalism: the uneven geography of costs', *Critical Perspectives on Accounting*, 45 (Supplement C): 12–28.

Auditor-General of Victoria (1999) *Victoria's Prison System Community Protection and Prisoner Welfare*, Special Report No. 60. Melbourne, Victorian State Government.

Australian Bureau of Statistics (2016) 4517.0 – *Prisoners in Australia*, 2016, 8 December.

Brown, W. (2015) *Undoing the Demos*. Brooklyn, Zone Books.

Department of Justice and Regulation, and Department of Treasury and Finance (2015) *Ravenhall Project Summary*. Melbourne, Victorian State Government.

——(2016a) *Project Summary Partnerships Victoria Fulham Correctional Centre Contract Extension*. Melbourne, Victorian State Government.

——(2016b) *Project Summary: Partnerships Victoria Port Phillip Prison Contract Extension*. Melbourne, Victorian State Government.

Department of Justice (2000) *Correctional Services Commissioner's Report on Metropolitan Women's Correctional Centre's Compliance with its Contractional Obligations and Prison Services Agreement*, Office of the Correctional Services Commissioner, September. Melbourne, Victorian State Government.

Department of Treasury Victoria (2007) *Financial reports for the State of Victoria 2006–2007*. Melbourne, Victorian State Government.

English, L.M. (2007) 'Performance audit of Australian public private partnerships: legitimising government policies or providing independent oversight?' *Financial Accountability and Management*, 23 (3): 313–336.

English, L., and Walker, R. G. (2004) 'Risk weighting and accounting choices in public–private partnerships: case study of a failed prison contract', *Australian Accounting Review*, 14 (33): 62–77.

Goh, D., and Holmes, J. (2017) 'Crime hits a new low', NSW Bureau of Crime Statistics, 3 April.

Jewkes, Y., Crewe, B., and Bennett, J. (2016) *Handbook on Prisons*. New York, Routledge.

Kirby, P. (2000) *Report on the Independent Investigation into the Management and Operation of Victoria's Private Prisons*. Melbourne.

Lapsley, I. (1999) 'Accounting and the new public management: instruments of substantive efficiency or a rationalising modernity?' *Financial Accountability and Management*, 15 (3–4): 201–207.

Legislative Council of NSW, General Purpose Standing Committee 3 (2009) *Inquiry into the Privatisation of Prisons and Prison-Related Services: Final Report*. Sydney, NSW Parliament.

Love, P., Wood, E., Picken, B.M. and Confoy, B. (2000) 'The privatisation of correctional facilities in Australia', *Facilities*, 18 (1/2): 56–65.

Mackay, A. (2015) 'Overcrowding in Australian prisons: the human rights implications', *Precedent*, 37 (128).

Mason, C. (2013) *International Growth Trends in Prison Privatization*, The Sentencing Project, 20 August.

Minister for Corrections (2015) 'Work begins on Victoria's newest prison', *Delivering for All Victorians*, 12 February.

Mulgan, R. (2017) 'Outsourcing failures exposes weakness in both government and business', *The Canberra Times*, 2 May.

Peck, J., and Theodore, N. (2007) 'Variegated Capitalism', *Progress in Human Geography*, 31 (6): 731–772.

Productivity Commission (2017) *Report on Government Services*, 7 February. Canberra, Australian Government.

Rubinsztein-Dunlop, S. (2014) 'Australia's prison system overcrowded to bursting point with more than 33,000 people in jail', *ABC News*, 3 July.

Russell, S., and Baldry, E. (2017) 'In charts: how Australia's prisoner population is booming', *ABC News*, 28 July.

Sands, V.J. and Hodge, G.A. (2014) 'The Victorian Government's prison privatisation project (1992–2010): The pathway to efficiency? A longitudinal analysis', *Journal of Contemporary Issues in Business and Government* 20 (1): 7–26.

Springer, S. (2010) 'Neoliberalism and geography: expansions, variegations, formations', *Geography Compass* 4 (8): 1025–1038.

Stockdale, A.R. (1994) *Infrastructure Investment Policy for Victoria*. Melbourne, Department of the Treasury.

Wacquant, L. (2009) *Prisons of Poverty*, vol. 23. Minneapolis, University of Minnesota Press.

——(2010) 'Class, race and hyperincarceration in revanchist America', *Daedalus*, 139 (3): 74–90.

——(2014). 'Class, race and hyperincarceration in revanchist America', *Socialism and Democracy*, 28 (3): 35–56.

CHAPTER 5

THE MARKETISATION OF AGED CARE IN AUSTRALIA

BOB DAVIDSON

Over the last quarter century, there have been major changes to the provision of aged care services in most developed countries, including Australia. These changes can be seen, for example, in the levels, sources and distribution of funding, the nature of demand for care, and the supply of care, in terms of both its forms and who provides it. These changes have emerged primarily from two major reform processes that have unfolded throughout the period. As with society more broadly, there has been micro-economic policy change, which in this case has been effected via the marketisation of publicly funded aged care services. Alongside this, there have been changes in the philosophy, goals and practice of what is considered to be good care for older people, a process that has been driven by professional and clinical considerations. While the two reform processes arose largely independently of each other, they have become intertwined through the impact of the economic changes on both aged care service systems and the actual services in a range of ways, as this chapter will note.

The main focus of this chapter, however, is the first of these processes, marketisation, here defined as the introduction or extension of market mechanisms and non-government bodies to functions and activities formerly funded and delivered by government agencies. The chapter notes the ageing of the population and developments in aged care practice that have been central to producing the context in which marketisation has occurred. It then examines the drivers of the marketisation of aged care in Australia, the history of its implementation, the outcomes of the process, and some alternatives to current policy.[1] Importantly, the story of aged care in Australia over the last quarter century is also a valuable case study of the experience of the marketisation of human services more broadly, illustrating the rationales, mechanisms, dynamics, players and private interests that come into play.

The Context of the Marketisation of Aged Care

As in most developed countries, the population of Australia has been ageing for some years, a process that is projected to accelerate from 2020 onwards, and continue until the middle of the twenty-first century. Alongside this, there are other demographic and societal changes that continue to affect the number and composition of people who provide care, both paid and unpaid, including the greater participation of women in the workforce, lower birth-rates, smaller households and migration (Productivity Commission 2008; Australian Treasury 2010). Together, these developments will generate significant pressures on the aged care system over the coming decades, substantially increasing the demand for and cost of care and limiting the growth of the supply of people who can provide that care. In turn, these developments have a range of major long-term implications for governments, most fundamentally requiring them to address the fiscal implications of the growth in demand, and to establish the conditions to ensure an adequate supply of quality care. Changes to aged care services have thus been necessary – but that did not necessarily require extensive marketisation.

Most aged care is 'informal' care, which is unpaid and provided by family or friends. For older people without access to informal care or with high care needs, there are two major types of 'formal' (paid) care: residential care and home care. While the large majority of older people receiving paid care in Australia receive home care, the unit cost and total cost of residential care are much higher (Productivity Commission 2011). For both fiscal and quality-of-life reasons, government policy is aimed at increasing home care in order to enable older people to stay at home as long as possible, rather than go into residential care.

There has also been continuing development of a wider range of care services, supports, and activities in both major forms of paid care, including specialised services (for example, for dementia), more personalised services to respond to individual needs, and a focus on the enablement of older people to maximise their independence and activity.

The Drivers of Marketisation

The most fundamental driver of the marketisation of aged care in Australia over the last thirty years has been the broader neoliberal transformation of the economy and society in that period, with its core messages of the power and superiority of markets, and the desirability of reducing the role of the state. Within this broader ideology, governments have developed a particular rationale for the marketisation of human services in general, as well as more specific rationales for each human service. For example, there are common elements in the arguments used to justify the marketisation of aged care and higher education, but there are also distinct arguments used for each sector.

The public rationale for the marketisation of aged care services presented by governments has been primarily based on two elements. First, it has been presented as essential in ensuring the financial and operational sustainability of services in the face of demographic and societal changes. Second, it has been promoted as an essential element in improving the services, in terms of their effectiveness (quality, diversity and responsiveness), equity, and efficiency, and by enhancing choice and control for service users, the transparency of decision-making, and the accountability of providers and government. Behind this public rationale, however, there have been a number of other powerful drivers of marketisation that explain not just its widespread adoption but why it continues to be extended, even as the limits and problems of markets in human services are increasingly revealed. The pro-market ideology and philosophies of powerful entities in government and business have been a central factor in shaping the culture, mindset and language of stakeholders and the wider public on this issue. Debate about marketisation is typically conducted in a context where untested assumptions about the desirability of markets and the benefits of for-profit providers are default positions for government, while the public is encouraged to regard human services such as aged care as simply another commodity to be purchased, rather than as an essential service that is their right as citizens.

Marketisation has also often been co-opted as a smokescreen or Trojan horse to enable decision-makers to introduce changes they believe to be essential but politically contentious. The presumed virtues of competition and choice have been used to progress hidden or opaque political agendas to reduce the power of unions, reduce total government expenditure, transfer costs to users and reduce government responsibility for higher-risk activities.

Marketisation also creates many private interests, including large organisations whose primary aim is to gain access to public funds that can provide a large and stable source of revenue, and whose substantial economic and political power enables them to influence government in changing the design and management of human services programs and markets in ways that benefit them (Gingrich 2011). This factor becomes increasingly important as marketisation takes hold within a sector, accelerating its expansion, although this is often a subtle and opaque process (Murray and Fritjers 2017).

The Implementation and Limits of Marketisation

The marketisation of human services has taken many forms across different locations and types of services. While each specific case is unique to some extent, there are also common features across human services more broadly that provide valuable lessons for policymakers. This section presents some of the key considerations about the marketisation of human services in general, before describing how marketisation has unfolded in aged care in Australia.

There are four core mechanisms by which the marketisation of human services is implemented or extended: *contestability*, enabling the potential for new entrants; *competition* between providers (where providers may be chosen by government, users, or a combination of both); *choice*, whereby service users (or their families) are able to determine the services they receive and who provides them; and *co-payments* by users in addition to a government subsidy. The differences between human service markets essentially arise from differences in how these mechanisms are applied in each case.

While there are sound social and economic reasons for using each of these mechanisms to some extent in most human services, there are limits to the extent to which market mechanisms can be used in the provision of any human service limits. These limits emerge naturally from inherent features of both markets and human services. In summary, these limits exist for the following reasons:

(a) Virtually all markets, including in the broader economy, are imperfect to some extent;

(b) Human services have a number of common distinctive characteristics that, taken together, distinguish them from other 'products' (goods and other services);[2]

(c) These distinctive characteristics create issues for the provision of human services *irrespective of markets*, including problems commonly ascribed to markets and/or for-profit-providers (FPOs);[3]

(d) Flowing directly and inevitably from (c), government has to play a major role in most human services if the quantity and quality of these services are to be maintained at the level demanded by a modern developed nation. In particular, government must be both a major source of purchasing power and a regulator of the entry and behaviour of providers; hence, most markets for these services are 'managed markets' (also known as quasi-markets), which operate in some fundamentally different ways from conventional markets (Le Grand and Bartlett 1993, Davidson 2015); and

(e) Notwithstanding the point in (c) above, the distinctive characteristics of human services are also a source of significant and intrinsic market failure such that when human services are provided via markets, the above problems arising from the general failure of markets and the inherent problems of providing these services are exacerbated.

The combined effect of these factors is that market mechanisms are most effective in human services when used in a limited and strategic way, and the excessive use of one or more of them generates a range of problems, as discussed later.[4]

One important implication of these factors is that regulation is critical for the effective marketisation of human services, given the extensive asymmetries of information and the limited capacity of many 'consumers'. The approach most commonly proposed is to increase the regulation of the actual services – that is, the regulation of the *behaviour* of providers – but historical experience suggests that once the regulation of the *entry* of providers is relaxed and a sector is opened up to many providers, especially large corporate FPOs, the regulation of services not only has limited effect, but can be used by powerful incumbents to entrench and extend their privileges. Economic theory points to the problems that can emerge from high barriers to entry, but to obtain a 'second-best' market situation (Lipsey and Lancaster 1956), especially in human services where major public funding and many vulnerable people are involved, there needs to be tight control of the entry of new providers, with a particular focus on their demonstrated capability and commitment (Davidson 2017).

The marketisation of aged care in Australia is no simple story, with many confounding variables in any attempt to determine its true drivers and effects. For example, the 'product' is very diverse, and marketisation has unfolded alongside other major developments. Path dependency, or the power of established institutions and past policies to shape and limit future policies (Liebowitz and Margolis 1995), is important. Marketisation did not begin in the 1990s with a clean slate of total government provision, but rather there had been a significant presence of non-profit organisations (NPOs) and FPOs in residential care and NPOs in home care since the 1950s. Indeed, government had already intervened to reverse the growth of FPO nursing homes in the 1970s (Sax 1985). Moreover, at different points since the early 1990s there has been a range of goals and mechanisms for the marketisation of aged care in Australia.

We can identify three major stages in the modern marketisation of aged care in Australia. The first stage, from the early 1990s until 1996, saw the introduction of competitive processes for the allocation of funds, and the opening of government-funded home care to FPOs. During this period, the major goals of marketisation were to establish a more consistent and planned basis for administering aged care funding, to extend new forms of home care services as quickly as possible, and to make funding more explicitly contestable The second stage, from 1996 to 2011, began with the election of the Howard government, which sought to make the sector more dependent on market forces and the 'user pays' principle. The ultimate changes to policy were less significant than the rhetoric suggested, but over time there was a gradual and controlled extension of market mechanisms and new government-funded services, a key goal of which was to increase the diversity of providers and services.

The third – and current – stage of marketisation was triggered by the Productivity Commission's inquiry into aged care (2011), and the subsequent Gillard government's 'Living Longer Living Better' package (Department of Health 2012). Since then there have been continuing changes to funding and regulation aimed at moving towards a 'consumer-driven competitive market', and at transferring part of the financial burden from government to users. A key development that has evolved during the current stage has been to change the basis on which providers are chosen and funding is distributed under each of the major programs. Under the system in place since the early 1990s, governments used competitive processes to assess and shortlist the best providers in each locality from which service users could then choose; since 2012, there has been a staged movement from this system to a 'demand-based' model, giving users more freedom to choose providers, and making provider revenue more dependent on the decisions of users. In 2016 the *Aged Care Roadmap* (Aged Care Sector Committee 2016) was released, signalling an intention to further marketise aged care. This document argued the need for 'attitude shifts' by users, and proposed 'increased competition, supported by an agile and proportionate regulatory framework' with 'financing arrangements where the market determines price, those that can contribute to their care do, and government acts as the safety net and contributes when there is insufficient market response' (Aged Care Sector Committee 2016).

An important development in aged care over the last quarter-century has been the growing power of large non-government providers, both non-profit and for-profit. The substantial growth and consolidation of larger non-profit charity and religious providers has occurred at the expense of smaller community-based ones. While the strength of the large NPOs and the nature of the funding system has limited the extent to which FPOs have increased their overall market share in both residential and home care, there has been a significant change in the composition of the FPOs over time, from a multitude of small, commonly single-facility, family-owned organisations, towards the greater presence of large corporations. Marketisation has led to a stronger focus by providers on commercial objectives – lower costs, financial viability, growth, profit – at the expense of social objectives, as shown in the mission drift by NPOs large and small (Weisbrod 2004), and the greater presence of large FPOs that are legally obliged to maximise shareholder returns. Importantly, policy and regulation are now also substantially influenced, if not captured, by larger providers, both NPO and FPO. Not only are policy and advisory forums dominated by these providers and by consumer groups sympathetic to market mantras, but representatives of providers sit on regulatory bodies.

The Outcomes of Marketisation

This section considers the outcomes of marketisation in relation to the three major public goals of the process outlined earlier in the chapter.

Reducing the Long-Term Cost of Aged Care for Government

While the continuing growth in the number of older people and the increasing diversity of funded services has meant that the total cost to the public purse of aged care has continued to rise, substantial costs have been transferred to users through means tests and a range of co-payments. Unfortunately, one effect of that has been to reduce access to and/or the quality of care for a number of people.

One mechanism by which marketisation is claimed to reduce pressure on future government expenditure is by improving the allocative and productive efficiency of the service system and of individual providers. The unit cost of delivering services appears to have been reduced under the influence of marketisation, but there is little robust evidence as to the extent to which that reflects a better use of resources or simply lower quality services as has clearly been the case with some providers. While there have been various measures that constitute genuine improvements in efficiency with no loss of quality (for example, through the use of technology or better organisation of staff time), it is not at all clear that marketisation has driven these improvements. There are also a number of significant efficiency costs arising from competition, such as the transition costs of ownership changes and users changing providers; the potential inefficiencies from excess supply under the differentiated competition market model now characteristic of the sector; and dynamic efficiency costs such as the uncertainty of future revenue leading to reduced investment by providers (Davidson 2015: 98).

One counterproductive effect of marketisation on resources has been the generation of significant 'leakages of the service dollar' on costs that are only present because of markets. These leakages come in many forms, including through multiple and large transaction costs (for example, from tender processes), the many 'satellite functions' generated by marketisation (for example, marketing, IT systems for individual payments; private care advisers; etc.), and the large profits extracted by some providers (Stewart Brown 2011).

Establishing the Conditions to Ensure Supply Over the Longer Term

A key plan of the government strategy to ensure the future supply of aged care services has been to encourage more providers to enter the market, an approach that in part has involved reducing the barriers to entry based on standards. While new providers have entered, marketisation has also led to many takeovers and mergers, with the result that in total there are now fewer providers of residential aged care than at the turn of the century. Moreover, an increase in the number of provider organisations is unlikely, by itself, to increase the supply of services. The real need is for action to ensure the supply of key *inputs*, notably labour (in both residential and home care) and financial capital (for investment in building residential care facilities). However, uncertainty about both of these inputs means that the future supply of sufficient quality care for the ageing population over the next thirty years is far from secure.

The government estimates that the aged care workforce needs to grow 'from around 360,000 currently to almost one million by 2050' (Wyatt 2017) in order to meet projected demand. Drawing on the work of Folbre (2006), a 'high road' approach would aim to make the aged care sector a more attractive place to work through measures such as supporting improved wages, training and qualifications; setting mandatory minimum staffing levels; raising the status of care work; and promoting positive work environments and career paths for staff. While there is evidence that competition has led to some providers improving the quality and training of staff, the commercial pressures generated by marketisation have led others to take a 'low road' approach, based on less skilled staff, more casual staff, minimum wages and little training. Similarly, marketisation has produced a situation such that the sector is now almost totally dependent on non-government bodies – particularly large corporations – for financial capital, the continuing flow of which will likely remain dependent on such bodies being able to extract large profits. In a relatively low-risk industry that is heavily underpinned by public funding and has a guaranteed clientele for decades to come, this is an inefficient use of available funds.

Improving Services

Despite a range of concerns about aged care (see below) and regular media horror stories about the sector, the aged care system in Australia remains fundamentally sound in terms of its basic quality, and the access to care available to large numbers of older people. Indeed, judged against the key service objectives set out earlier, aged care may be better than it was a quarter century ago. However, while it is possible to identify a number of positive outcomes of marketisation (for example, some new service options and higher quality services for some older people), there is strong evidence that the overall improvements in the sector have primarily resulted from other factors, especially the professionally driven reform of aged care practice; the industry structure and norms shaped by earlier policies that are now threatened by increasing marketisation; and various non-market-based structural and administrative changes to government programs.

There are also various aspects of aged care services where the overall effects of marketisation are mixed or uncertain, We have seen above that this is the case in regards to efficiency. Another such aspect concerns choice and control. While the rhetoric of marketisation is that it gives service users more choice and control over the services they receive and who provides them – and this has in fact been the case for substantial numbers of people – marketisation has led to a general diminution of the rights of users as *citizens*, which have increasingly been replaced by their 'rights' as 'consumers' or 'customers'. The result is that many older people, especially those with less financial and cultural capital, no longer receive as much advice and assistance from government agencies or from socially focused providers, and their choice and control has been reduced.

Beyond these mixed results, there are a number of other more clearly negative effects of marketisation on the quality, equity and accessibility of services for many users that have developed in the wake of processes such as fiscal restraint, the additional financial burden on users and their families, and the greater focus by providers on commercial objectives. Marketisation has reduced equity, intensifying the duality of services, especially in residential care, with higher-quality care in more expensive facilities, and poorer care further down the price ladder. It has also encouraged more providers to give priority to more affluent or lower cost users (cream-skimming) so as to improve their financial bottom line, while the demise of government providers means that there is now no guarantee of a provider-of-last-resort. In those cases where providers have reduced the quality of their care, this is revealed by aspects such as less qualified and experienced staff, lower staff numbers, a greater reliance on casual labour, lower quality facilities and meals in residential care, and instances of neglect and abuse arising from systemic deficiencies.

Marketisation has reduced the stability and continuity of aged care services. Contrary to the predictions of pure neoclassical theory that markets will reach a competitive equilibrium, an implicit goal of markets, built as they are on competition and innovation, is *instability*, with all of these processes predicated on a continual struggle between suppliers ever-seeking to change their products to be more appealing to buyers than their competitors. This instability is reflected, for example, in the frequency with which the ownership and internal organisation of residential facilities change. Overall, marketisation has led to less financial and service quality accountability by providers to both government and users, despite more detailed requirements for some aspects. Far from the enhanced transparency promised by the advocates of marketisation, the concept of commercial-in-confidence has increasingly come to dominate over other considerations, leading to a reduction in the financial and operational data that is publicly available.

The Way Forward

A central argument of this chapter is that while reform of aged care services has been necessary, and that some limited and strategic use of market mechanisms was a desirable element in that reform, government policy has been misguided in some important respects. In some cases, change has gone in the right direction but too far; in others, it has gone the wrong way. The remainder of this chapter presents some alternative policies and approaches that point to an ideal greenfield arrangement while also keeping in mind what can realistically be achieved in the context of the current industry and realpolitick given the major movement to markets since 2012.

On the demand side, ideally the eligibility and entitlements of service users should be determined independently of providers, funding should follow the choice and decisions of service users, and there should be some level of co-payment that varies according to the financial means of the user. These settings are now largely in place. However, policy has commonly overestimated the capacity of most service users and their families to function as effective 'consumers', as would the rational, fully informed *homo economicus* of neoliberal theory. There has been insufficient recognition of both the limited personal agency of many users, the major information asymmetries that are at the heart of the distinctiveness of human services, and the many limitations inherent in human service markets (Davidson 2015). Current policy emphasises the need for better information, a desirable step, but one that by itself cannot overcome these inherent limits and the resulting potential power of providers in a marketised environment.

However, the most concerning aspects of current policy are on the supply side. The current policy to increase the decentralisation of delivery and to expand the diversity of providers and services is desirable, but in other ways policy has moved further away from some of the essential features of a well-functioning aged care system – in particular, the need for rigorous control of the entry of new providers. Given the now substantial presence of large profit-focused corporations and smaller FPOs, many with no prior experience in aged care, we may now have passed the point beyond which effective control of entry can be restored. In this context, the regulation of actual services becomes even more important, with a need for additional mandatory requirements on key matters like staff-to-user ratios in nursing homes. One feasible step would be to review the composition of funding, regulatory and advisory bodies to ensure they are not dominated by narrow sectional interests, but rather reflect the user and public interests that the system is supposed to serve.

Notwithstanding the thrust of much of this chapter about the limits of human service markets and greater information, policy in regard to these markets is likely to be more effective where it strengthens the operation of the market. This especially applies with regard to the regulation of provider behaviour and ensuring better information for those who pay for and use the services. Even in the absence of mandatory requirements on key matters, providers should be required to make detailed information on their service capability, use of resources, finances and performance publicly available. Requiring greater transparency in these and other ways would recognise that the concept of commercial-in-confidence should have limited relevance when substantial public funds and the welfare of vulnerable people are at stake, especially when there are multiple organisations capable of providing these services. It would also be an essential step towards ensuring that consumers have access to essential data in a competitive market where 'consumer choice is at the heart of services' (Harper et al 2014), which the government now claims is its key goal. Shining a spotlight on the service and financial behaviour of providers should reduce their capacity to extract large profits, rein in potential abuse in their behaviour, and desirably lead to poorer providers withdrawing from the industry.

A central issue in ensuring the supply of aged care in the future will be to meet the demand for labour. In this respect, policy should support 'high road' measures aimed at improving the status, training, wages and conditions of workers so that the sector becomes one that can attract and retain quality staff.

There are two powerful messages from the story of aged care in Australia. The first is that however carefully and gradually marketisation is introduced, it brings with it a number of problems and costs. The second is that eventually powerful private interests, both NPO and FPO, come to substantially determine what happens in the sector. Marketisation has led to some positive outcomes, but overall it has not achieved its own ostensible goals, and, in a number of ways has been counterproductive. It has turned aged care into a lucrative business for large providers, often at the expense of users and public funds. Overall, it may be better than it was a quarter century ago, but the improvements are likely to have resulted substantially from factors other than marketisation. Extending marketisation further, as is current policy, will exacerbate the current problems. Yet short of a major crisis in the sector returning to a more socially driven sector would seem very difficult now.[5] Tight regulation of the entry of providers is fundamental to effective marketisation, but it is now almost certainly too late to turn back the tide of large FPOs, or to stem the mission drift of many NPOs, or to restore strong government competitors to the field.

Aged care in Australia provides a powerful example of how, once the regulation of the entry of providers is relaxed in a human services sector, the problematic features of marketisation emerge inexorably over time. Contrary to the rhetoric, the power of larger providers relative to that of the users and buyers of human services increases under marketisation. In such a context, the regulation of providers becomes even more important, but no amount of the regulation of provider behaviour will lead effectively to optimum service standards. Nonetheless, there are measures that involve working through the market that could generate better outcomes in the current environment, especially by requiring all providers to open up their operations and finances to greater public scrutiny.

Endnotes

1 A more detailed discussion of the processes and outcomes of the marketisation of human services can be found in Davidson 2012, 2015 and 2016. Fine and Davidson (2018) outline the wider context of these changes in relation to global forces and care services more broadly.

2 These characteristics are a direct result of the greater likelihood and relative immutability of certain critical limits of most human services in relation to demand (limited personal agency and financial capacity of many users), supply (limited capacity to increase productivity) and the final product (limited measurability, observability and homogeneity) (see Davidson 2015: 47–63).

3 For example, even monopoly government providers cannot observe or measure much of the work done by staff working with service users; are limited in how much they can reduce unit cost and increase productivity without harming quality; and are subject to budget pressures that may lead them to 'cream skim' (give priority to less costly or more affluent users).

4 These problems can be seen in other human services such as child care (see Chapter 1), employment services (see Chapter 7) and higher education (See Chapter 13). The most extreme example in Australia has been the debacle in recent years in the vocational education and training services (VETS) sector, as discussed in Chapter 3.

5 Alternatively, change might flow from a crisis for the nation more broadly (for example, war or depression), where the public accepts the need to redress the imbalance between public and private power that inevitably comes from a prolonged period of excessive reliance on 'the market'.

References

Aged Care Sector Committee (2016) *Aged Care Roadmap*, Department of Health, March. Canberra, Australian Government.

Australian Treasury (2010) *The 2010 Intergenerational Report: Australia to 2050 – Future Challenges*, January. Canberra, Australian Government.

Davidson, B. (2012) 'Contestability in human services markets', *Journal of Australian Political Economy*, 68, Summer 2011–12: 213–239.

——(2015) 'Contestability in human services and its impact on service providers – a case study of community aged care in New South Wales', PhD thesis, Social Policy Research Centre, Faculty of Arts and Social Science, September. Sydney, University of New South Wales.

——(2016) 'Marketisation and human services providers: an industry study' in Lee, F.S. and Cronin, B. (eds), *Handbook of Research Methods and Applications in Heterodox Economics*, Chapter 19. Cheltenham, Edward Elgar.

——(2017) 'Optimum Contestability in Human Services: An Alternative to Letting a Hundred Feral Cats Bloom', paper presented to the Australian Conference of Economists, 21 July.

Department of Health (2012) *Living Longer Living Better: Aged Care Reform Package*, April. Canberra, Australian Government.

Fine, M. and Davidson, B. (2018) 'The Marketization of Care: Global challenges and national response in Australia', *Current Sociology*, 66 (4): 503–516.

Folbre, N. (2006) 'Demanding quality: worker/consumer coalitions and "high road" strategies in the care sector', *Politics and Society*, 34: 11–31.

Gingrich, J.R. (2011) *Making Markets in the Welfare State: The Politics of Varying Market Reforms*, Cambridge, Cambridge University Press.

Harper, I., Anderson, P., McCluskey, S. and O'Bryan, M. (2014) *The Australian Government Competition Policy Review, Draft Report*, September. Canberra, Australian Treasury.

Le Grand, J. and Bartlett, W. (eds) (1993) *Quasi Markets and Social Policy*. London, Macmillan.

Liebowitz, S.J. and Margolis, S.E. (1995) 'Path dependence, lock-in, and history', *Journal of Law, Economics, and Organization*, 11 (1), April: 205–226.

Lipsey, R.G. and Lancaster, K. (1956) 'The general theory of the second best', *Review of Economic Studies*, 24 (1): 11–32.

Murray, C.K. and Fritjers, P. (2017) *Game of Mates: How Favours Bleed a Nation*. Currumbin, Publicious.

Productivity Commission (2008) *Trends in Aged Care Services: Some Implications*, Productivity Commission, September. Canberra, Australian Government.

Productivity Commission (2011) *Caring for Older Australians*, Inquiry Report, Productivity Commission, August. Canberra, Australian Government.

Sax, S. (1985) *A Strife of Interests: Politics and Policies in Australian Health Services*. Sydney, George Allen & Unwin.

Stewart Brown Business Solutions (2011) *Aged Care Financial Performance Survey for Year Ended 30 June 2010*, Submission 842 to Productivity Commission Inquiry into Caring for Older Australians, March.

Weisbrod, B.A. (2004) 'The pitfalls of profits', *Stanford Social Innovation Review*, 2 (3): 40–47.

Wyatt, K. (2017) 'New aged care workforce taskforce to focus on safety and quality', Minister for Aged Care, media release, 1 November.

CHAPTER 6

THE LOSS OF PUBLIC SECTOR ENGINEERING COMPETENCE

PAUL DAVIES

The way that large publicly funded infrastructure projects are designed, financed, delivered and evaluated to meet public need in Australia has changed fundamentally in recent decades. Two-thirds of the value of total engineering construction activity is now being carried out by the private sector, an inversion of the how this work was distributed during the 1980s and '90s (ABS 2017). This change is a result of policies that have included government agencies and public sector asset owners reducing their direct engineering workforce and increasing the use of privately contracted constructors and consultants during all project phases. The privatisation of major public utilities is also a factor. There is a consensus that these developments have created a range of problems, inhibiting the efficiency, effectiveness and accountability of infrastructure delivery (Australian Senate 2012). An increased demand for public infrastructure due to population growth, the depreciation of assets, and the impact of the mining construction boom over the last decade have exacerbated the consequences of these problems.

The registered trade union for professional engineers, Professionals Australia (formerly Association of Professional Engineers, Scientists and Managers Australia, or APESMA), advocates and organises to deal with the consequences of these changes: not only do they threaten jobs and employment security, they undermine the professional and ethical foundations upon which good engineering practice is based. There is, we argue, a strong alignment between good engineering decision-making and the public interest. Good engineering decisions, for example, aim to deliver a high benefit-to-cost ratio through the application of technical expertise at all project phases. As the engineering workforce is made less stable, and as governments lose engineering capability, the ability of engineers and, in turn, government to make the best decisions is compromised.

This chapter discusses the causes of declining employment of engineers in the public sector. It sets out the adverse effects of this decline on public sector purchasing, accountability and infrastructure planning. It also describes how falling public sector employment of engineers is exacerbating a general trend towards increased instability in engineering employment. Finally, it provides a sketch of measures to efficiently remedy these problems by reforming government procurement practices as a means to improve workforce development and re-establish public sector engineering capability.

Causes of the Decline in Public Sector Engineering Competence

Neoliberal policies of outsourcing, including the privatisation of major public utilities such as electricity, transport and water, an increased reliance on public-private partnerships (PPPs), and reduced infrastructure spending have together resulted in a dramatic fall in public sector employment of engineers. As I will explain, this loss of public sector engineering talent was not compensated by an equivalent rise in employment in large private firms; rather, there has been a deterioration in the quality of engineering employment across the board.

A 2012 Senate inquiry into engineering skills shortages found that government departments have incrementally reduced in-house engineering expertise:

> It is a matter of historical record that, during the 1980s and 1990s, the public sector began to outsource infrastructure and other engineering work to private industry. Government public utility, infrastructure and other departments offered redundancies to engineers and public companies were privatised. Engineering

> positions in the public sector dried up, and cadetship programs were cut (Australian Senate 2012: par. 2.10).

According to Engineers Australia (Yates 2000: 11) another key driver of reduced engineering capability is the neoliberal belief system known as 'managerialism' (Yates 2000). Managerialism in the engineering context is predicated on the 'view in the bureaucracy that you do not need to have technical expertise to manage a technical function'; according to APESMA's evidence given to the 1995 parliamentary inquiry, *Public Business in the Public Interest: An Inquiry Into Commercialisation in the Commonwealth Public Sector* (Section 2.2) 'managerialism implies that generalists are capable of managing engineering contracts. The resulting reduction in the number of engineers employed by the public sector due to these reforms has been so significant that the engineering profession has coined the term *de-engineering* to describe it.' Engineers Australia (2016a: 1) found that only twenty years ago, governments collectively employed over 100,000 engineers across Australia; today this figure is less than 20,000, only one-fifth of what it was two decades ago.

Over the past decade a consensus has been established regarding the critical loss of public sector engineering capability. Public sector engineering jobs have been cut and restructured to decrease engineering skill requirements, while the private sector engineering workforce has become increasingly unstable, creating capability and workforce development problems across the profession. This has led to increasing uncertainty and scepticism about public and private project value and utility, eroding public confidence in investment decision-making. These costs are manifest in major projects across Australia, amounting to billions of dollars.

Consult Australia cites a study of public sector employment share from 1984 to 2005. During this period the percentage of electricity, gas and water supply industry employees in the public sector dropped from 95.9 per cent to 54.7 per cent. In the construction industry this dropped from 12.2 per cent to 0.5 per cent in 2005. Five years after the 2012 Senate inquiry, 82 per cent of respondents to a Professionals Australia survey confirmed that the problem of degraded asset-owner engineering capability persists (Professionals Australia 2017a).

Effects of the Decline

Public Sector as an Uninformed Purchaser

Of trends in the employment of public sector engineers, the Senate inquiry noted:

> The first and most obvious implication of this is that government departments, having shed their engineering staff, now lack any real in-house engineering expertise. Mr Ian Marler, Vice Chairman, Consulting Surveyors National, elaborated on the difficulties that arise when government departments lose their engineers with surveying skills, using a New South Wales example: '[If] you took the Institution of Surveyors in New South Wales: many years ago it probably had 80 per cent government and 20 per cent private. I would say that almost the reverse would apply today. There has been a gradual transition as more and more government departments shed staff. That raises the other complexity, too, in that if you are tendering for government work, whether you have competent people within government able to assess the tenders and all of those sorts of things. It has that downside. But I would guess that it has been that 80/20 back to 20/80' (Australian Senate 2012: par. 2.11).

Similarly, Engineers Australia (2016b: 2) commented that 'engineering structures in all levels of government have been radically downsized over the past two decades in favour of outsourced resources, to the point where the public sector's ability to manage engineering contracts and capacity to adequately assess the engineering competencies of contractors and subcontractors has been severely compromised. The consequences manifest themselves in higher costs and in a growing list of failures chronicled by auditors-general.'

The downsizing of the public sector engineering workforce affects all phases of infrastructure development. At the earliest stages of a project, the relative degradation of asset-owner capacity affects the ability to develop, evaluate and promote public-sector-produced infrastructure concepts and options. Consequently, decision-makers are more likely to rely upon, expect or favour unsolicited tenders or 'market-led solutions' to address – or purport to address – public infrastructure needs. Without public sector–led options one can imagine how governments, keen to be seen to be active, can be persuaded to adopt infrastructure proposals packaged and marketed by private-sector interests. The potential of this situation to compromise government is obvious. However, instead of rebuilding capacity to enable governments to develop their own project options and, by implication, assist in the assessment of tenders from the private sector (unsolicited or otherwise), the recent trend has been for Australian governments to issue guidelines to help the private sector make more attractive propositions to ministers. Interestingly, engineering considerations are not mentioned at all in the NSW Guidelines for Unsolicited Proposals (NSW Government 2017). Examples of completed NSW unsolicited projects include the Crown gambling venue at Barangaroo, toll roads, and the conversion of hospital accommodation for nurses into university student accommodation.

Is it in the public interest to leave substantive decision-making about what infrastructure projects will be built to commercial interests, with little if any real input from technical engineering specialists employed by asset owners and public sector agencies? There are suggestions that in New South Wales ministers have hindered public transport agencies from developing transport (rail) options so that commercial interests in the road sector have opportunities to build toll roads. Is this an unintended consequence of degraded asset-owner technical and engineering capability, or a desired outcome?

Beyond the project concept development stage, a traditional public interest perspective favours a separation of interests and functions during scoping and construction. Asset owners, on behalf of the public, need sufficient levels of capability to direct public spending on construction. They need to: establish effective operational and legal relationships with contractors; understand project scope in detail; understand labour and material requirements and supply issues; understand and manage regulatory matters, community and environmental disruption; and, to direct, inform and manage contractual and legal arrangements, including the anticipation of and preparation for possible disputes and litigation. Such capability would ensure value for money and operate as a bulwark against profiteering and other types of malpractice.[1]

The 2012 Senate inquiry found insufficient public sector engineering capability, especially in project scoping is responsible for waste, and results in delays and disputes. In short, public sector engineering shortfalls have made infrastructure investment riskier while costs have increased and project delivery times have blown out.

More evidence of this situation was revealed in the Building the Education Revolution Implementation Taskforce Final Report (BER Taskforce), which identified only the Queensland state government as 'an informed buyer of capital works projects' (2011: 53). The Taskforce stated, 'there is a correlation between states' capacity to leverage existing public works capacity and their overall value for money outcomes' (53). The report specifically outlined a decline in engineering capacity in the public sector and, referring to some state government initiatives to rebuild road agency engineering capacity, argued that this 'may therefore be an indication that a significant level of in-house expertise is beneficial in ensuring that governments get value for money over the life of an asset' (58). The Western Australian state government's work towards increasing its informed purchaser capability through the establishment of the Centre for Excellence and Innovation in Infrastructure Delivery in 2007, in order to 'improve collaboration, share knowledge and drive reform across a broad spectrum of activities associated with public works, infrastructure delivery and strategic asset management' (CEIID website) also appears to represent a tacit agreement with this analysis.

An Australian National Engineering Taskforce (ANET)[2] and Professionals Australia survey series also provides evidence about structural changes in the engineering workforce and associated effects on project cost and delivery. More than 80 per cent of respondents, surveyed across the private and public sectors, agreed that a shortage of engineers in government/asset-owner organisations contributes to higher project costs. The most common claim is that asset owners are effectively uniformed purchasers and that the consequences can be more than just increased waste, as this comment from a survey respondent summarises:

> Part of my job is to check design and I'm picking up fatal flaws in the plans, flaws that can kill people – this is mistakes mostly done

> by consultants but managed by in-house project managers that don't have the background knowledge to do that type of work ... We get project overruns because drawings etc. are at such a standard you're paying for significant contract 'variations' or 'stuff ups'.

Nearly 80 per cent of respondents saw this situation as unsustainable, with the long-term consequences being 'if we become an uninformed purchaser and the project manager doesn't recognise this, then we'll start building things that could have some fatal flaws in it – plus we won't have the people that even recognise the flaws.' Respondents claimed that lower standards result in degraded assets and higher long-term costs due to more maintenance requirements and shorter asset life.

In Sydney alone, which is currently host to the biggest transport infrastructure spend in the nation's history, the price of the Westconnex road project has blown out from $12 to $17 billion in just five years and the road is still more than five years away from the planned completion date. This project is worthy of particular attention due to the corporate structures established for its construction, which created unprecedented walls of secrecy to prevent even parliamentary scrutiny of contracts and performance. What could be the public policy rationale for a system which removes contracting, technical and engineering decision-making from public scrutiny?

Accountability and corruption issues are a direct consequence of this loss of internal competence in the public sector. There have been numerous cases of dubious practice in Australia's infrastructure construction sector. The Lane Cove tunnel in New South Wales, the Sydney Cross City Tunnel, and in Brisbane the Airport Link and RiverCity Motorway were all subject to various forms of overpricing due to inflated traffic forecasts or other forms of misleading and deceptive conduct.

Even when corporate behaviour and engineering work are not so degraded as to warrant legal action, it is not uncommon for projects to be delivered at such low-quality levels that costly reworking and operational adjustments become necessary. The South West Rail Link in Sydney was delivered on schedule in 2016, but it was in such poor shape that trains were forced to travel well below normal speed limits for many months while expensive repair work was carried out by the network owner, Sydney Trains, a public sector agency. The line was built by the John Holland Group, and the contract was managed by Transport for NSW under a new model for engaging contractors called the authorised engineering organisation (AEO) model. In essence, this is a form of self-regulation where government outsources its engineering assurance responsibilities. Just prior to the handover to Sydney Trains, reports by government engineers reviewing the line identified major construction faults, which had somehow passed the outsourced engineering authorisation. Reworking by public sector asset owners has been an all too prevalent problem affecting; for example, Sydney's rail station upgrade program and road reconstruction in South East Queensland following flooding in 2010 and 2011. Further examples are too numerous to list.

Described in these reports, surveys and inquiries are the shape, causes and consequences of a structural change in the way public investment is used to deliver community infrastructure. The evidence shows that these changes have been counterproductive to public interest, inefficient and wasteful. One could be excused for thinking that these issues appear to have been addressed through tinkering with contracting models and project-approval mechanisms. Construction contracting models, such as both the design and construct (D&C) model and the alliancing model, are the most common forms used during the construction phase, and there are numerous studies that purport to show the relative effectiveness of these contract forms in controlling cost and performance for different types of projects or project phases. However, as the 2012 Senate Inquiry found, contract management is no substitute for technical skill and capacity, and these models, including their refinements, have produced no significant improvements in reducing waste and avoiding risk in infrastructure delivery.

There is ample anecdotal evidence that, in practice, commercial parties to construction contracts routinely seek to exercise their power to vary contracts and shift cost. It is argued by some that this is simply a matter of commercial necessity since the preference of asset owners and governments is for the lowest price, and this means that successful bids are only ever (initially) marginally commercially viable. As respondents to an ANET and Professionals Australia survey series (2016) put it, the situation 'leads to contractors building more risk into their tenders, increasing project costs, or increased contractual claims during delivery'; 'We tend to be held to ransom by big construction managers which increases cost and ultimately government outgoings.' Again at the crux of this is the phenomenon of public sector asset owners being uniformed purchasers.

Adverse Effect on the Engineering Workforce

The dramatic fall in public sector employment and increased contracting out is having a knock-on effect in the private sector. Many private firms traditionally recruited experienced public sector engineers but no longer have a ready source of supply (Senate Inquiry 2012: para 2.12). State and local government public works departments and utilities once took on graduate engineers, providing them with several years experience, before they would move on to private firms. This important function of the public sector has diminished substantially.

In both the public and private sector there is evidence that participation in conventional engineering workforce development practices, such as structured on-the-job learning programs like cadetships has declined and industry investment in student development has decreased. Organisers of Professionals Australia's student and graduate programs for engineers report a steady decline in cadetship opportunities as well as ongoing difficulties with students finding workplace placements to satisfy degree requirements. This is particularly troubling as it is widely understood that workforce capability suffers from the poor alignment and integration of formal education and training with workplace-based learning. This decline in the training capacity of the engineering industry generally is in part a function of the growth of employment in smaller engineering consulting firms who are either too specialised to provide the necessary breadth of training experience, or too focused on running their business to provide adequate on-the-job supervision.

*

The decline of the public sector share of total engineering employment has also contributed to the problem of a loss of permanent employment as a higher proportion of the engineering workforce shifts to the private sector and become contract workers. There are also reduced career paths due to an increased share of employment in small, specialised engineering firms. These circumstances, combined with the fact that 'infrastructure development in Australia has been characterised by boom/bust cycles for decades' results in an:

> increasing intermittency of engineering work … [which] is incompatible with the aspirations and commitments of career development and modern lifestyles … The shift of engineering employment from public sector employment to private sector has meant more contract positions replacing ongoing salaried employment … Engineers have career ambitions like everyone else and opportunities for career development in engineering are limited and are diminishing over time. Instead, engineers have pursued lateral career moves into other areas of work (Kaspura 2017: 19–20).

These changes have contributed to increased instability in the engineering workforce generally. The erosion of the public sector engineering workforce capacity exacerbates the effects of overall workforce volatility resulting from cyclical private sector engineering activity. Findings of serious workforce capability problems in a 2009 engineering workforce survey (ANET Engineers Survey 2010) were the catalyst for the development of a research and reform agenda undertaken by ANET. These findings included:

- 60.6 per cent of respondents identified an engineering skills shortage in their work section; More than half of the survey comments identified a specific discipline or area that was in short supply;
- 40.2 per cent of respondents felt that their organisation did not have the right skills mix to meet current or future needs; and
- 54.3 per cent of respondents identified a loss of capability in their workplace.

Findings of a more recent survey in this series included persistently low levels of female participation (12 per cent), and increased levels of immigration through temporary and permanent migration that persisted well after the peak of the mining construction boom, and at rates significantly higher than annual domestic graduations (Kaspura 2017).

This survey also found that female engineers reported average earnings of 89 per cent of their male counterparts, that 13.1 per cent of the female workforce dropped out between the 20 to 29, and 30 to 39 age brackets, compared with a drop of only 1.4 per cent for the male workforce in these age brackets (Professionals Australia 2017b). While the situation described by this survey indicates aspects of a possible skills shortage in 2009, there is now evidence of significant unemployment and under-employment of engineers at an aggregate workforce level (Department of Employment 2017).

How to Reverse the Decline

A notable effort to lead structural reform of the engineering workforce is the Australian National Engineering Taskforce (ANET). It identified project scoping and procurement, workforce supply and demand by sector and discipline, migration, female participation, recruitment and retention strategies, VET and higher education as key topic areas for research projects and industry engagement throughout the period from 2009 to 2012. The main findings and recommendations of this work, anticipating those of the 2012 Senate inquiry, were that:

- Governments should use purchasing power to drive workforce development, to ensure industry provide more cadetships and workplace learning opportunities (Senate Inquiry 2012: par 5.46),[3] and to ensure public sector engineering capability is built and sustained at appropriate levels;
- Procurement practices be reformed to ensure value for money, and that all projects be subject to comprehensive public interest based performance evaluations (based on accepted auditing office principles);
- Engineering should be regulated as a registered profession; and
- An engineering workforce development council be established to address issues of market failure.

Suffice to say, engineering workforce problems are complex and will not be addressed simply by efforts to increase supply, whether through uncapped university places or increased immigration.

Unfortunately, the erosion of public sector capacity to plan, buy, develop, operate, and maintain community assets continues. Public sector–wide job cuts and agency restructures are now routine, often with no apparent connection to the demand for government services, including community infrastructure needs. At the time of writing the NSW government has announced an arbitrary 15 per cent staffing cut to its peak transport agency. Meanwhile, government transport infrastructure spending in New South Wales is at record high levels, with major road, rail and light rail projects still more than five years from completion. These projects include Australia's first automated and driverless metro rail network. With billions of dollars already known to have been wasted on these projects due to incorrect or poor scoping and purchasing, it would be reasonable to ask how further cuts to asset-owner resources are likely to affect the value and utility of the transport projects for which the NSW government is responsible.

The cost of infrastructure building failure is routinely reported in the mainstream media, usually by news of revised budgets, increased project charges, costs and delays. Although the consequences are reported and always worn by the public, there appears to be little political will to implement solutions (see Grattan Institute 2018). Solutions are not guaranteed of course, but improving the ability of the public sector to assess project needs and to evaluate purchasing options is hardly a radical demand. When governments cannot buy rail fleet of the correct size to fit existing rail lines and platforms (O'Sullivan 2016), or when they fail to plan for metropolitan light rail lines with compatible gauges (O'Sullivan 2017), it is not difficult to identify a problem and formulate efficient and effective remedies. We may not yet be at the stage where government has lost complete control of its spending decision capability and where political gift-giving replaces effective accountability, good administration and public sector technical expertise, but there is reason to question whether we have the ability and the right policies to avoid arriving at that point in the future. Government procurement needs to be reformed so that public interest standards for community infrastructure are delivered. This can be done in a way that will rebuild the ability of asset owners to properly scope projects and to control project delivery. It can be done to drive engineering workforce development generally, to improve the participation of women, to reduce unemployment and to ensure immigration is used to fill genuine gaps. A reform agenda to these ends has been developed through ANET.

Effective reform will rebuild confidence in government decision-making about public infrastructure. However, beyond the lack of political will and leadership, the challenge to implementing such reforms appears to be the ideological orthodoxy of treasury officials and other policy-makers who promote the notion of a small (and increasingly smaller) public sector and the related idea that lowest-price contracting is always for the best. The ironic, perverse or perhaps intentional outcomes of the consequent policy settings are as enumerated above: increased project capital costs, undermined reliability of public assets and degraded workforce capability. Engineering integrity and the ethical foundations of the profession as a public good are directly threatened. The benefits of reforms that effectively deal with these consequences will not only restore public interest engineering but create a practical alignment of public resources and effort with community infrastructure need.

ENDNOTES

1 Issues of corporate corruption in the construction and consulting sectors, involving companies very active in Australian infrastructure, and the alleged failure of governments to effective intervene are discussed by Carmen Lawrence (2017).

2 ANET was formed in 2009 and is a collaboration of unions, professional associations and peak-employer and education-sector groups undertaking a research and reform agenda on the engineering workforce and broader issues confronting the industry.

3 'The committee believes that cadetships, graduate positions and workforce training are crucial measures to address the skills shortage. The committee believes that governments can use their purchasing power to encourage industry to meet its training obligations. The recommendations made by Roads Australia and General Electric appear to have some merit, although the particulars of any incentive program attached to requests for tender processes will need to be looked at closely by government'. (Senate Inquiry 2012: par. 5.46).

REFERENCES

Australian Bureau of Statistics (2017) *Engineering Construction Activity Australia, 2017*, Cat. No. 8762.0. Canberra, Australian Government.

ANET Engineers Survey 2010, 2012. Professionals Australia, 2016.

Australian National Engineering Taskforce Engineers (2010) *Australian National Engineering Taskforce Engineers Survey*, March.

Australian Senate (2012) *The Shortage of Engineering and Related Employment Skills*, Senate Education, Employment and Workplace Relations References Committee, Australian Senate, July 2012. Canberra, Australian Government.

Building the Education Revolution Implementation Taskforce (2011) *Building the Education Revolution Implementation Taskforce: Final Report*. Canberra, Commonwealth of Australia.

Centre for Excellence and Innovation in Infrastructure Delivery (2012). www.ceiid.wa.gov.au Last accessed 23 April 2012

Department of Employment (2017) 'Labour Market Research – Engineering', Labour Market Research and Analysis Branch, Department of Employment. Canberra, Australian Government.

Engineers Australia (2016a) *Response to Supplementary Question: NSW Inquiry into the Procurement of Government Infrastructure Projects*, June. Barton, Engineers Australia.

——(2016b) *Procurement of Government Infrastructure Projects*, February. Barton, Engineers Australia.

Grattan Institute (2018), 'Transport and Cities', *Grattan Institute*, https://grattan.edu.au/home/transport-and-cities/

Kaspura, A. (2017) *The Engineering Profession: A Statistical Overview*, Thirteenth Edition, 21 Mar. Barton, Engineers Australia.

Lawrence, C. (2017) 'Corporate corruption and government failure to act: who's running this country', *The Guardian*, 2 February.

NSW Government (2017) 'Unsolicited Proposals', *NSW Government*, 23 February.

O'Sullivan, M. (2017) 'Why Sydney's new light rail trams won't carry passengers on inner west line', *The Sydney Morning Herald*, 26 July.

Parliament of the Commonwealth of Australia (1995) *Public Business in the Public Interest: An Inquiry into Commercialisation in the Commonwealth Public Sector, 78/1995*, Joint Committee of Public Accounts, 5 November. Canberra, Australian Government Publishing Services.

Professionals Australia (2017a) *Independent Contractors Report 2017*, www.professionalsaustralia.org.au/contractors-consultants/wp-content/uploads/sites/42/2014/07/2017-Contractor-Hourly-Rates-for-Engineers.pdf

——(2017b) *Stemming the Tide: Addressing the Attrition of Women from the STEM Workforce*, www.professionalsaustralia.org.au/professional-women/wp-content/uploads/sites/48/2014/03/Stemming-the-Tide-publication-web-version.pdf

Yates, A. (2000) *Government as an Informed Buyer: Recognising Technical Expertise as a Crucial Factor in the Success of Engineering Contracts*. Barton, Engineers Australia.

CHAPTER 7

MARKETS, MUTUAL OBLIGATION AND MARGINALISATION: THE EVOLUTION OF EMPLOYMENT SERVICES IN AUSTRALIA

SUE OLNEY AND WILMA GALLET

Australia's fully privatised employment services system comprises a range of organisations contracted by the federal government to help jobseekers move from welfare to work with direct assistance and support or referral to specialist services. Through more than two decades of reform in this arena, most jobseekers facing multiple and complex barriers to work have remained on the margins, or outside, of the labour market. In this chapter, we examine how Australia has reformed employment services, the rationale for such reform, and the consequences. In light of changes in the nature and conditions of work, we argue that to realise the full potential of Australia's human capital, and to contain the cost of particular groups of citizens being excluded from or opting out of the labour market, the time has come to rethink the concept of mutual obligation and the 'work first', outcomes-based funding model for employment services.

The Evolution of Employment Services

Since Federation, Australia has embraced the idea that the best form of welfare is a job. The proposition that work is central to meeting social and welfare needs was enshrined in H.B. Higgins' ruling in the landmark Australian labour law case of *Harvester* in 1907, which defined a 'fair and reasonable wage' and set a benchmark for Australian labour law (Mendes 2003). Castles (1985) coined the phrase a 'wage earner's welfare state' to underline the fact that in Australia, social protection developed more through a system of wage regulation, complemented by the pension and benefit safety net, than through a comprehensive, contributory welfare state. Policy encouraged individuals to look after their own health and welfare needs rather than looking to government for support and help to find work, and 'Australians came to believe all of their needs could be met by the labour market' (Bessant et al 2005: 91). However, the Great Depression of 1929–39, when a third of the Australian labour force relied on charities and jobs on public works projects to survive, highlighted a need for state intervention to protect citizens from the precariousness of the market. A profound shift in policy occurred with the 1945 White Paper *Full Employment in Australia*, which declared that 'full employment is a fundamental aim of the Commonwealth Government' (Commonwealth of Australia 1945).

The Commonwealth Employment Service (CES) was established in 1946 under the *Re-establishment and Employment Act 1945* as part of the postwar reconstruction (Harris 2001) and it played a key role in assisting returned soldiers to find work. In its first three decades, the CES focused on providing job placement assistance to people who were temporarily between jobs ('frictional unemployment') in a labour market that boasted full employment in the postwar economic boom.

However, unemployment increased in the 1970s. Following the 1981–82 recession, rapidly rising long-term unemployment emerged as a serious social and economic concern in member countries of the Organisation for Economic Co-operation and Development (OECD) (Langmore and Quiggin 1994). Policymakers were keen to develop strategies to re-engage long-term unemployed people in the labour market to reduce the risk they would become disconnected from mainstream social and economic life (OECD 1990). 'The Active Society' policy framework, developed by the OECD (OECD 1988) and adopted by several member countries, assumed that high rates of unemployment were likely to continue and that jobseekers needed to be supported – or *activated* – to develop skills, remain job-ready and maintain a pro-work ethic under those conditions. The concept of activation was operationalised in Australia through the Active Employment Strategy in 1988, which involved the integration of income support and labour market training programs (Cass 1988).

During the 1990s, faced with growing worldwide unease about the perverse social and economic effects of welfare dependency, the Australian Government embarked on reframing and redefining unemployment benefits from a rights-based entitlement to a conditional social protection (Mead 1992: 3). The 1994 *Working Nation* White Paper on employment and growth introduced extensive reforms to labour market assistance arrangements. It called for a concerted national effort to move unemployed Australians into work – a 'Job Compact' between the government, employment services and recipients of income support – stressing that they should not be 'left to drift' (Keating 1994a: 9). While acknowledging that economic growth alone was failing to move those who had been unemployed for twelve months or more into work, and that those people needed help and support from government and industry to find jobs, *Working Nation* also suggested that an overly generous social security system and a lax CES were contributing to persistent unemployment and deterring the long-term unemployed from adapting to changing labour market conditions (O'Neill 1995: 3). The government embraced a neoliberal approach to designing and delivering employment services in line with the recommendations of the National Competition Policy Review commissioned in 1992 (Hilmer, Raymer and Taperall 1993). In keeping with the Active Society policy framework, *Working Nation* introduced 'reciprocal obligation' – the concept that governments have a responsibility to create jobs within the economy, and to provide training and skill development programs for unemployed people, who, in return, are obliged to participate in labour market programs and actively look for work (Keating 1994a). The sole stated aim of the ensuing *Employment Services Act 1994* was 'to promote full employment by providing employment services that are free of charge' (Australian Government 1994 sec 3(1)). Under the Act, anyone unemployed for eighteen months or more was to be intensively case managed to help them prepare and search for work, and required to accept any reasonable offer of at least twelve months employment in a job generated through state subsidies to employers. For those unable to gain employment in the open labour market, the Job Compact would provide a work experience opportunity of at least six months to help break the cycle of unemployment (Keating 1994a: 9; see Mike Beggs on the evolution of economic policy on unemployment in Chapter 14).

The Process of Reform

The model for employment assistance unveiled by the Keating government in 1994 set the scene for Australia's current employment services system. Employment assistance was to be provided by the CES, and a new public agency that contracted out these services to private providers (O'Neill 1999). Each jobseeker's income support was contingent on working with a case manager to prepare for and find work. The case manager's role involved identifying and assessing barriers to the jobseeker's employment, preparing a plan of assistance to address those barriers, organising activities such as training, counselling or volunteer work to help the jobseeker become 'work ready', providing job-search assistance, monitoring progress towards work readiness, and reporting breaches of these activity requirements (Keating 1994b: 128). Success was measured in employment outcomes. The fundamental features of the Keating model have endured in Australia's employment services system through a succession of reforms as the environment around it has shifted. Arguably, the system has failed to respond to the most significant challenge over that time – a persistently high unemployment rate in the intervening decades.

Australia's employment services were fully outsourced through a competitive public tender process in 1998 and have undergone three major reforms since: *Job Network* (1998–2009), *Job Services Australia* (2009–15) and *jobactive* (2015–20). The Request for Tender under Job Network set a floor price for services and outcomes, and contracts were awarded on the basis of price and links to jobseekers and employers. By 2015, the price of employment services was fixed by government, with payment contingent on outcomes and contracts awarded on the basis of demonstrated expertise and complex statistical analysis of past performance (Department of Employment 2015a). Employment services providers – a mix of for-profit and not-for-profit organisations – are contracted to provide every person receiving unemployment benefits with assistance and support, either directly or through referral to specialist services, to help them move from welfare to work. Each person of working age seeking income support from government is assessed to identify issues keeping them out of the workforce, and streamed for different levels of assistance to overcome vocational and non-vocational barriers to work based on their level of need. The bulk of income for employment services providers is generated through job outcomes. While there are tiered incentives to focus on moving hard-to-place jobseekers into work, evidence suggests that jobseekers who need time and high levels of effort and investment to compete in the mainstream labour market with a low probability of success are relegated to the sidelines of the employment services system. They are referred to programs and services in order to meet the activity requirements for income support, but make no real progress towards employment (Considine, Lewis and O'Sullivan 2011).

The number of organisations contracted to deliver employment services dropped from a high of 306 in 1998 to 44 in 2015, with contracts increasingly held by large, experienced providers, but still evenly split between for-profit and not-for-profit organisations (Thomas 2007). In the early days of this quasi-market, government ministers openly stated that they did not want the new regime to become a 'hamstrung bureaucracy' (Vanstone 1996). And yet, while the number of providers diminished substantially over time, the bureaucratic and compliance requirements of the employment services system has increased significantly for both providers and jobseekers.

The nature of work available, where it exists, and conditions of employment have changed dramatically since employment services were first outsourced in the 1990s. Employers are increasingly seeking qualified, highly skilled, portable, contingent and 'work ready' workers, while employment opportunities for unskilled workers are falling. Technological change is affecting how and where work is done (Sundararajan 2017), and increasing automation is expected to reduce employment in both unskilled and semi-skilled professions by 10 to 40 per cent in the foreseeable future (Chalmers and Quigley 2017). This estimate is considerably higher than the projections offered in the Australian government's 2015 quinquennial Intergenerational Report, which assumes a constant rate of unemployment of around 5 per cent over the period from 2015 to 2055 (Australian Government 2015: 47).

Furthermore, the gig economy and zero-hours contracts are blurring boundaries between self-employment and employee status. Unskilled and low-skilled work has become increasingly casualised, with low wages and limited prospects of career advancement, leaving young jobseekers particularly disadvantaged (ACTU 2012: 14). There has also been a rise in contingent, part-time or ad hoc employment in some skilled industries, including health, allied health and post-compulsory education (Coates et al 2009). While arguably these trends respond to workers' demand for flexibility, they cater more to those from highly skilled, dual-career households or those without dependents than workers in single-income families needing stable housing and education for children and a steady income stream to accumulate superannuation – the lack of which can generate significant long-term public costs.

Simultaneously, the ratio of jobseekers to advertised vacancies has increased and employers are more selective in recruiting staff than they would be in a tighter job market (Department of Employment 2014: 1). Many are reluctant to hire people who have been unemployed for a long time 'because of concerns about attitude, work ethic, reliability, motivation and consistency' (Department of Education 2012: 16) – concerns that are arguably attributable to the critical portrayal of the long-term unemployed in politics, policy and the media. Compounding these jobseekers' marginalisation, government data reveals low levels of employer awareness of and engagement with the employment services system, and dissatisfaction with the system among those who do interact with it (Department of Education 2012: 16), a message reinforced by business owners (Strong 2017). In 2017, over 800,000 Newstart and Youth Allowance recipients and over one million underemployed workers were competing to fill fewer than 200,000 job vacancies (Whiteford 2017; ABS 2017a; ABS 2017b). At the bottom of the pool of available labour, the long-term unemployed are effectively a 'workforce of last resort' for employers, competing for 'second tier' employment (Isaac 1989: 51). Many of those live in communities of concentrated disadvantage (Vinson 2007; McLachlan, Gilfallen and Gordon 2013).

Launching *A New System for Better Employment and Social Outcomes* in 2015, the final report into a review of Australia's welfare system, the Australian government asserted that 'activation works' while claiming that over the last decade Australia's welfare system had 'grown relentlessly and become unsustainable' (Department of Social Services 2015a: 62; 2015b). Insisting in the report that everyone who could work in any capacity should work to reduce pressure on the welfare system, the government committed to creating one million new jobs within five years and two million new jobs over the next decade (Department of Social Services 2015a: 9; 136). These commitments tacitly acknowledged that no amount of preparation, penalties or incentives can move jobseekers into work where no employment opportunities exist.

Yet history shows that creating jobs does not guarantee employment for marginalised jobseekers. Policy changes over the last decade have changed the characteristics of people receiving unemployment benefits. There are now people actively engaged in the employment services system with little or no capacity to work full-time or who are only able to work episodically due to ill health, disability or caring responsibilities (Department of Social Services 2015a: 51; 57). In 2012, more than three-quarters of the jobseekers streamed to receive the highest level of assistance from employment services providers had more than five barriers to work identified in their job capacity assessment reports (Parliament of Australia 2012). These barriers include lacking the skills and attributes valued by employers, as well as structural and personal barriers to work.

The 2012 OECD report *Activating Jobseekers: How Australia Does It* found that Australia's activation strategy for the unemployed – enforcing work-readiness and mutual obligation requirements – contributed to it having one of the highest employment rates in the OECD (OECD 2012). But given the shifting composition of claimant groups eligible for employment services support, it is difficult to calculate the impact of the strategy on long-term unemployment. Clearly, the current pool of jobseekers who have been actively seeking work for a year or more includes people who would have been economically inactive in the past. Yet what remains consistent over time is that there are people receiving publicly funded employment assistance who are deemed capable of working by the government and who have not secured employment after actively seeking work for fifty-two weeks or more. As Figure 1 shows, attempts to move these jobseekers into work through case management, referral to other services, job-search assistance, vocational training, work experience programs, intermediate labour market programs, incentives, sanctions, post-placement support and wage subsidies have not had a significant or lasting impact on long-term unemployment.

FIGURE 1. AUSTRALIAN UNEMPLOYMENT AND EMPLOYMENT SERVICES INTERVENTIONS, 1986–2015

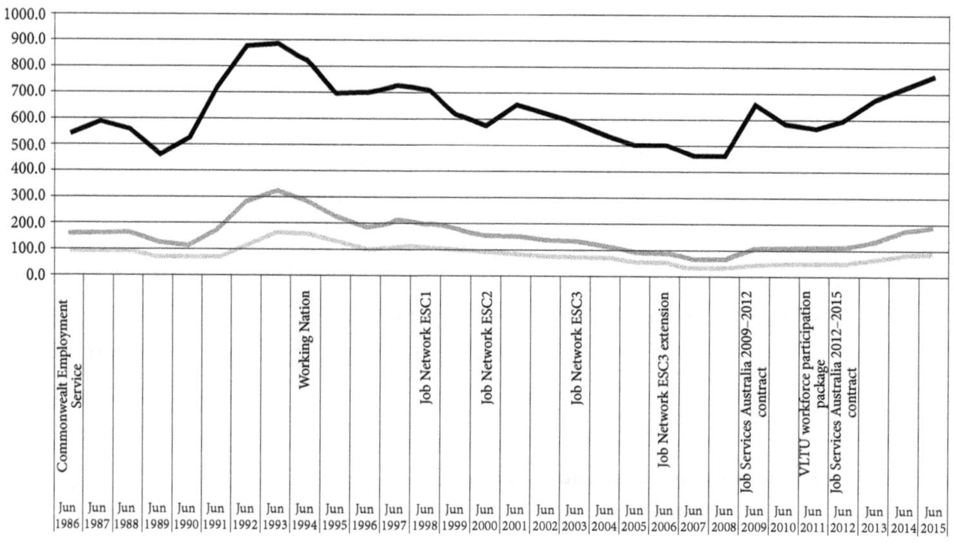

Source: ABS 2001; 2015

The Unintended Consequences of Reform

Against predictions and despite calibrated incentives, the prospects of the long-term unemployed moving from welfare to work have not improved over the course of two decades of radical institutional change underpinned by market-based instruments. Arguably, savings in the system have been achieved at the expense of jobseekers most in need of support to find a job, and the flow-on costs of their persistent unemployment ripple across government. Those costs are not factored into the employment services system's metrics, leaving the public value of the model open to debate (Moore 1995).

We argue that there are internal contradictions in the process of activating people facing multiple and complex barriers to work, stemming from neoliberal reforms and privatisation across the public sector, and that these contradictions exacerbate labour market disadvantage and marginalisation. For these jobseekers, the *process* of activation extends beyond the employment services system into multiple federal and state or territory government-funded services – health, education, housing and disability services – to address non-vocational barriers to work or gaps in skills. There is inadequate coordination and integration of these services. Poor employment outcomes for disadvantaged jobseekers suggest that there is limited understanding of the complexity of problems confronting marginalised jobseekers and no consensus on how to address these issues. Despite being the subject of ongoing, targeted employment assistance, the majority of long-term unemployed people and people at high risk of long-term unemployment in receipt of income support in Australia remain unemployed (Department of Education 2012: 8). Compounding their disadvantage, the marketisation of vocational education, for many, has resulted in training that is poorly matched to labour market needs and the burden of accumulated deferred debt under schemes such as VET Fee-Help (see Phillip Toner on vocational education and training in Chapter 3).

While employment services providers are clearly motivated by their contract to move jobseekers into work quickly, incentives for other actors to contribute to that goal are less clear. There is no requirement or incentive for service providers within or outside government to consider the consequences of their interaction with the long-term unemployed beyond their individual key performance indicators, and no overarching authority steering or coordinating their activity or capturing metadata on its impact. This is a significant weakness in the institutional architecture of activation and employment services. Both within government and under contract, every service provider interacting with the long-term unemployed and people at risk of long-term unemployment is working towards achieving key performance indicators tightly bound to the critical success factors of its own funding sources, and their efforts are not mutually reinforcing (Olney 2016).

Explaining the Gap Between Outcome and Intent

A fundamental weakness in the model appears to be framing long-term unemployment as an individual problem affecting people on the margins of society and the economy, and treating its causes and consequences across a fragmented service system. Market-based reforms are not a panacea for complex problems like long-term unemployment.

In outsourcing the delivery of employment services, the Australian government sought innovation, responsiveness, flexibility, understanding of the local environment and cost savings from a diverse range of providers who could shepherd the unemployed from welfare to work using their networks, skills and expertise, unencumbered by the constraints of government bureaucracy (Keating 1994b: 129; Maddock, Corden and Hunt 1998: 14). From the outset, contracts were awarded to a mix of for-profit and not-for-profit organisations, including faith-based organisations with strong track records of delivering state-funded assistance to welfare recipients (Gallet 2016). The government shied away from specifying processes to help people with multiple and significant labour market disadvantages because of the diversity of those jobseekers' motivations and barriers to work; instead, they adopted an outcomes-based funding model that offered providers financial and performance incentives to work with 'hard-to-place' jobseekers. But the 'black box' delivery model, and the market's inclination to maximise gain from contracts, has created particular problems for government as by-products of contracting out. Its response to providers exploiting weaknesses in the employment services contract by 'creaming' work-ready jobseekers that could generate fast income and 'parking' those harder to place was to increase regulation and oversight of the system. Over time, the innovation and flexibility sought from the market was tempered by explicit and complex rules and regulations on the part of government and organisational isomorphism among providers (Considine, Lewis and O'Sullivan 2015). On both sides, the focus on cost, compliance and outcomes sharpened.

Given the system's procurement and reporting framework, this effect is unsurprising. Employment assistance can increase the probability of someone finding work, but cannot guarantee it – an employment outcome can ultimately only be produced by a jobseeker and an employer. Yet achieving outcomes specified in the employment services contract not only generates income for providers, it positions them for success in future tenders for government business. That is a powerful incentive for providers to focus their efforts on activities most likely to help them meet their key performance indicators, and to minimise the cost of servicing the job-seekers least likely to generate income, regardless of the flow-on effects and costs they will engender elsewhere.

Policy Implications

The abiding foundations of reforms to Australia's employment services system are mutual obligation and outsourcing. Successive governments have followed these doctrines despite a lack of evidence that either has a significant or enduring positive impact on long-term unemployment. They continue to reform and adjust the welfare-to-work system through a complex mix of centralised and decentralised processes, markets, quasi-markets, sanctions and incentives designed to change the behaviour of unemployed people and the services they access. In theory, the market model of employment services promises responsiveness, flexibility and accountability at a local level. In practice, the incentives and metrics for the multiple services involved are not mutually reinforcing. The key strength of market-based approaches to delivering public services – calibration and interplay between providers' sources of revenue, sources of legitimacy, individual governance structures, the regulatory environment in which they operate and their relationships with their clients and other organisations – is lost or diluted in risk management and the pursuit of narrowly defined key performance indicators. The focus on producing value and reducing risk within narrow parameters and short time-frames are barriers both to defining the problem of labour market exclusion and finding the solution. In addition, given the changes to the labour market described earlier, entering and remaining in employment for low-skilled, disadvantaged job seekers is increasingly difficult.

Policy Alternatives

The problems discussed in this chapter underline the need for a new approach to active welfare. We offer two main policy alternatives: *system reform*, which encourages and rewards collective-action solutions and partnerships between Centrelink, employment services, complementary services, jobseekers and industry to improve the prospects of long-term unemployed people moving from welfare to work; and *welfare reform*, which frames income support as an investment in the health and wellbeing of individual, families and communities on the margins of the labour market and acknowledges that unemployment cannot always be solved by individual case management.

Address long-term unemployment with co-ordinated incentives

The first step is to reset the punitive aspects of mutual obligation. There is an inherent contradiction in the dual remit of employment service providers to support jobseekers into employment while monitoring them to ensure they fulfil the activity requirements for income support. These conflicting roles promote negative stereotypes that compromise the way in which employment assistance is viewed by jobseekers, caseworkers, employers and other services accessed by unemployed people. Shifting responsibility for activation and monitoring mutual obligation activity for people receiving income support to Centrelink would redress this issue and provide an opportunity to rebrand employment services as a connecting point for jobseekers and employers that is free of stigma. Removing the compulsory elements of jobseekers' interaction with employment services would reduce ongoing referrals of long-term unemployed people to activities that fulfil service providers' contractual obligations and maximise their profit but do little to enhance the employability of individual jobseekers – in turn, this would reduce the ongoing cost of employment services. Savings could be redirected to coordinating effort across all tiers of government to improve the prospects of long-term unemployed people finding work or creating their own employment, to helping people transition from unemployment to employment without fear of being worse off, and to working effectively with employers to anticipate and respond to labour market trends.

Acknowledge and address changes in the nature and availability of paid work

Continuing to treat long-term unemployment as an 'individual' problem in light of changing labour market conditions driven by economic policy, globalisation and technological change makes no sense. To realise citizens' full potential in an economy where the supply of labour exceeds demand, and to promote social cohesion, we must create opportunities for people excluded from the mainstream labour market to contribute to and participate fully in community and economic life without stigma.

We must acknowledge that there are rational disincentives for jobseekers with dependents to trade the surety of welfare and contingent access to subsidised necessities – housing, health services, transport and childcare – for precarious, transient, low-paid work. The burden of administering ongoing movement in and out of the welfare system is significant for government and for jobseekers, with high risk of adverse consequences. Many jobseekers now move in and out of employment or hold multiple short-term jobs concurrently, and this sits uneasily with an income support model founded on the premise that jobseekers will move into ongoing, full-time work. This was highlighted when the Australian government used an automated system of data-matching in 2016–17 to recover purported income support overpayments, checking tax office lump sum income records against fortnightly benefit payments, an approach that was subsequently found to be riddled with errors (Australian Senate 2017: 107). This reflects the broader problem of very high 'effective marginal tax rates' due to the interaction of the tax and welfare payments system, which can severely penalise jobseekers working even modest hours (Ingles and Plunkett 2016).

Responding to the complexity of new forms of work, several countries are piloting universal basic income systems as an alternative to the welfare state (*Futurism* 2017; Arthur 2016). Australia's welfare system is highly targeted and, as such, universal basic income is unlikely to gain local traction in the short term (Whiteford 2016). However, income support could be similarly framed as an investment in the health and wellbeing of individual, families and communities, and better designed to smooth transitions between welfare and work, rather than complicate them. The current 'work first', outcomes-based funding model and metrics for employment services dictates how providers interact with jobseekers, employers and other services, and compounds the difficulties experienced by 'hard-to-place' jobseekers. The pace of change in the nature and availability of work demands a new approach.

References

ACTU (2012) *Lives on Hold: Unlocking the Potential of Australia's Workforce*, Independent Inquiry into Insecure Work in Australia.

Arthur, D. (2016) *Basic Income: A Radical Idea Enters the Mainstream*, Research Paper, 18 November. Canberra, Parliament of Australia.

Australian Bureau of Statistics (2001) 'Table 14B_Apr86: Unemployed persons by duration of unemployment and sex – trend, seasonally adjusted, original (Apr 1986 – Mar 2001)', *6291.0.55.001 Labour Force, Australia, Detailed – Electronic Delivery.*

——(2015) 'Table 14B: Unemployed persons by duration of unemployment and sex – trend, seasonally adjusted, original', *6291.0.55.001 Labour Force, Australia, Detailed – Electronic Delivery.*

——(2017a) 'Table 24: Underutilised persons by age and sex, monthly', *6202.0 – Labour Force, Australia*, June 2017.

——(2017b) *6354.0 – Job Vacancies*, Australia, May 2017.

Australian Government (1994) *Employment Services Act (Cth)*. Canberra, Commonwealth of Australia.

——(2015) *2015 Intergenerational Report Australia in 2055*, Canberra, Commonwealth of Australia, 5 March.

Australian Senate (2017) *Report: Design, Scope, Cost–Benefit Analysis, Contracts Awarded and Implementation Associated with the Better Management of the Social Welfare System Initiative*, 21 June. Canberra, Parliament of Australia.

Bessant, J., Watts, R., Dalton, T. and Smyth, P. (2006) *Talking Policy: How Social Policy is Made*. Sydney, Allen & Unwin.

Cass, B. (1988) 'Unemployed in Australia', *Social Policy and Administration*, 22: 150–165.

Castles, F.G. (1985) The Working Class and Welfare: Reflections on the *Political Development of the Welfare State in Australia and New Zealand 1890–1980*. Sydney, Allen & Unwin.

Chalmers, J. and Quigley, M. (2017) *Changing Jobs: The Fair Go in the New Machine Age*. Carlton, Black Inc.

Commonwealth of Australia (1945) *Full Employment in Australia. Canberra*, Australian Government Printer.

Considine, M., Lewis, J.M. and O'Sullivan, S. (2011) 'Quasi-markets and service delivery flexibility following a decade of employment assistance reform in Australia', *Journal of Social Policy*, 40 (4): 811–833.

Considine, M., Lewis, J.M., O'Sullivan, S. and Sol, E. (2015) *Getting Welfare to Work: Street-Level Governance in Australia, the UK, and the Netherlands*. Oxford, Oxford University Press.

Coates, H., Dobson, I.R., Goedegebuure, L. and Meek, L. (2009) 'Australia's casual approach to its academic teaching workforce', *People and Place*, 17 (4): 47–54.

Department of Education, Employment and Workplace Relations (2012), *Employment Services – Building on Success Issues Paper*. Canberra, Australian Government.

Department of Employment (2014), *2014 Survey of Employers Who Have Recently Advertised*. Canberra, Commonwealth of Australia.

——(2015a) *Employment Services Procurement Information*. Canberra, Commonwealth of Australia.

Department of Social Services (2015a) *A New System for Better Employment and Social Outcomes – Report of the Reference Group on Welfare Reform to the Minister for Social Services*, February. Canberra, Commonwealth of Australia.

——(2015b) 'About the Review', *Review of Australia's Welfare System*, February. Canberra, Commonwealth of Australia.

Futurism (2017) Universal Basic Income Pilot Programs, https://futurism.com/images/universal-basic-income-ubi-pilot-programs-around-the-world

Gallet, W. (2016) 'Marketized employment services: the impact on Christian-based service providers and their clients', *International Journal of Public Sector Management*, 29 (5): 426–440.

Harris, P. (2001) 'From relief to mutual obligation: welfare rationalities and unemployment in 20th-century Australia', *Journal of Sociology*, 37 (1): 5–26.

Hilmer, F.G., Raymer, M. and Taperell, G. (1993) *National Competition Policy Review Report*. Canberra, Commonwealth of Australia.

Ingles, D. and Plunkett, D. (2016) *Effective Marginal Tax Rates TTPI, Policy Brief 1/2016*, Tax and Transfer Policy Institute, Crawford School of Public Policy. Canberra, Australian National University.

Isaac, J.E. (1989) 'The second tier and labour market flexibility', *Australian Economic Review*, 22 (1): 51–58.

Keating, P.J. (1994a) *Working Nation: The White Paper on Employment and Growth*. Canberra, Australian Government Publishing Service.

——(1994b) *Working Nation: Policies and Programs*. Canberra, Australian Government Publishing Service.

Langmore, J. and Quiggin, J. (1994) *Work for All: Full Employment in the Nineties*. Carlton, Melbourne University Press.

Maddock, L., Corden, S. and Hunt, T. (1998) 'Contracting out case management services for the unemployed in Australia', in OECD, *Contracting Out Government Services: Best Practice Guidelines and Case Studies No. 20*, Public Management Occasional Papers. Paris, OECD Publishing.

McLachlan, R., Gilfallan, G. and Gordon, J. (2013) *Deep and Persistent Disadvantage in Australia: Productivity Commission Staff Working Paper*, July 2013. Canberra, Australian Government.

Mead, L. (1992) *The New Politics of Poverty: The Nonworking Poor in America*, HarperCollins, New York.

Mendes, P. (2003) 'Teaching social policy to social work students: a critical reflection', *Australian Social Work*, 56: 220–234.

Moore, M.H. (1995) *Creating Public Value: Strategic Management in Government.* Cambridge, Harvard University Press.

Olney, S. (2016) *False Economy: New Public Management and the Welfare-to-Work Market in Australia.* Parkville, University of Melbourne.

O'Neill, S. (1995) *Working Nation: A Progress Report*, Current Issues Brief Number 32 1994/95, Parliamentary Research Service. Canberra, Commonwealth of Australia.

——(1999) *Changes to Employment Assistance: More or Less Effective*, Parliamentary Library, Research Paper 26, 29 June. Canberra, Parliament of Australia.

OECD (1988) *Employment Outlook 1988: Steps Towards an Active Society.* Paris, OECD Publishing.

——(1990) 'The path to full employment: structural adjustment for an active society', *Employment Outlook*: 7–12.

——(2012) *Activating Jobseekers: How Australia Does It. Paris*, OECD Publishing.

Parliament of Australia (2012) *Senate Standing Committee on Education Employment and Workplace Relations: Questions on Notice DEEWR Question No. EW1027_12.* Canberra, Australian Government.

Strong, P. (2017) *Change Management, Employment, the Economy and Local Communities – Bring Back the CES*, Council of Small Business of Australia, cosboa.org.au/blog/change-management-employment-the-economy-and-local-communities-bring-back-the-ces/

Sundararajan, A. (2017) 'The Future of Work', *Finance and Development*, 54 (2), June: 6–11.

Thomas, M. (2007) *A Review of Developments in the Job Network*, Parliamentary Library, Research Paper No. 15. Canberra, Parliament of Australia.

Vanstone, A. (1996) *Ministerial Statement, Reforming Employment Assistance, Helping Australians into Real Jobs.* Canberra, Australian Government Publishing Service.

Vinson, T. (2007) *Dropping Off the Edge: The Distribution of Disadvantage in Australia.* Curtin, Jesuit Social Services and Catholic Social Services Australia.

——2016 in Hartcher, P. (2016) 'What if everyone were given money for nothing?' *The Sydney Morning Herald*, 7 June.

Whiteford, P. (2017) 'Social security and welfare spending in Australia: assessing long-term trends part 2', *Austaxpolicy: Tax and Transfer Policy Blog*, 28 July, austaxpolicy.com/social-security-welfare-spending-australia-assessing-long-term-trends-part-2

PART TWO

PRIVATISATION AND DEREGULATION

CHAPTER 8

ELECTRICITY REFORM

JOHN QUIGGIN

Since the creation of the National Electricity Market (NEM) in the 1990s, electricity reform in Australia has been a comprehensive failure. None of its objectives of lower prices, greater system reliability or environmental sustainability have been met.

The core aim of policy should be a genuinely national electricity grid, with the goal of providing secure, affordable electricity to Australian households and businesses, while reducing and ultimately eliminating emissions of carbon dioxide (CO_2). The current NEM is not designed for this purpose and cannot achieve it. Rather, it is the product of a late twentieth-century ideological project, based on the hope that market incentives could outperform rational electricity supply system design and management. Nearly twenty years of unsatisfactory experience has proved that this is not the case, even for a traditional system based on coal-fired generation.

The Statutory Authority Model

The electricity supply industry in Australia developed in the late nineteenth century, with a mixture of public and private provision. However, private provision proved uniformly unsatisfactory. As a result, the industry was taken over by state governments. A notable example, discussed in Quiggin (2003), was the nationalisation of the privately owned Adelaide Electric

Supply Company by the conservative government in South Australia Under Sir Thomas Playford.

Public provision of electricity required innovative forms of governance. The term 'governance' is used to describe the processes by which institutions, including governments and corporations, are made accountable to those whom they are supposed to serve, such as citizens or shareholders. The expansion of government prior to the neoliberal era was also, in general, a period of improvements in governance, including innovations in organisational design and accountability.

One such innovation was the statutory authority, developed to provide public services without direct ministerial control. Statutory authorities were governed by a board of directors, typically constituted to represent what are now called 'stakeholder groups', including consumers, employees, community organisations and directors chosen for their professional expertise. It is notable that the statutory authority model flourished well before private corporations began to consider relationships with stakeholders as a necessary part of sustainable long-term governance.

The development of statutory authorities provided an organisational framework for the creation and provision of goods and services by government. Decision-making processes within statutory authorities were less rigid than in the traditional public service, since day-to-day decisions were the responsibility of the board, who ultimately remained responsible to governments. Statutory authorities in the electricity supply industry were constituted with the primary objective of delivering reliable supplies of electricity to the entire community at low cost. A variety of secondary social objectives, such as industry development, were also pursued. Statutory authorities were normally required to cover the full cost of provision through charges for electricity supply, including an amount sufficient to service the cost of capital, and with sufficient surplus to fund new investment.

Integration and Natural Monopoly

Although the structure of the electricity supply industry varied from state to state, the most common pattern was that of a single, vertically integrated monopoly, covering all aspects of the industry from electricity generation to retail functions such as connections and billing. This structure is consistent with the economic theory of 'natural monopoly'. A natural monopoly occurs when a good or service is most efficiently delivered by a single producer. Because it would be extremely costly for competing producers to build multiple network infrastructures of poles, wires, substations and so on to serve a single district, electricity transmission and distribution is a natural monopoly.

A natural monopoly may also arise when it is more cost-efficient for two different activities to be undertaken by a single firm – an 'economics of scope'. A clear example is the combination of electricity generation and retail functions. In the present market system, the wholesale price of electricity varies greatly over time, depending on demand. For example, prices in the NEM can vary from zero to a maximum of more than $14,000 per megawatt-hour (MWh). On the other hand, retail prices are generally fixed in advance. In a system where retail and generation firms are separated, both face substantial price risk. These risks may be hedged on financial markets, but hedging incurs a substantial cost that is ultimately passed on to consumers. On the other hand, when generation and retail are integrated within the same firms ('gentailers'), the risks wash out: high wholesale prices benefit the generation component of the firm but harm the retail component. Hence, the integration models makes good economic sense.

The economic benefits of integrating generation–retail and transmission–distribution activities are are less clear. They arise, for example, when it is necessary to choose between building new generating capacity in a given region, or when it is necessary to expand the transmission and distribution network to allow electricity generated elsewhere to be imported. More recently, a range of issues have emerged from the integration of intermittent renewable generation sources, such as solar photovoltaics, into electricity grids that were originaly designed for coal, which is characterised by a fixed supply of electricity. Accordingly there are challenge with the pricing systems associated with these integrations, These difficulties could be resolved directly in an integrated industry.

Criticisms

The main criticism of the statutory authority model was that it gave too much power to workers, and particularly to unions. This criticism was sometimes couched in the technical terminology of 'total factor productivity', and sometimes in the more explicitly anti-worker rhetoric of 'featherbedding'. Large reductions in employment in the 1980s and 1990s appeared to confirm the claim that previous employment levels had been too high.

The same criticism was applied to capital investment. The original statutory authorities had been dominated by engineers who were concerned above all with the reliability of supply. Critics argued that this had led to what they pejoratively referred to as 'gold plating' – that is, an overinvestment in redundant generating capacity and high-cost distribution networks.

In the early period of micro-economic reform, it appeared that such criticisms were valid. The deep recession of the early 1990s depressed the demand for electricity, resulting in spare capacity in most states. Interconnection through the national grid implied a lower need for redundant capacity in individual states, and therefore heightened the problem of oversupply. Privatised and corporatised enterprises responded by scaling back their investment programs and slashing their workforces.

With the benefit of hindsight, reading these criticisms is an exercise in irony. Many of the technical employees who were sacked in the name of reform were in fact eventually re-hired as (or replaced by) contractors, often at a higher cost to the public. The initial cutbacks in investment produced blackouts, which then demanded much more costly new investment. What was saved by dismissing workers responsible for keeping the lights on was entirely offset by increases in the number of managers and marketers with higher salaries, as well as the administrative staff needed to manage the multiplicity of retail operations. The flow-on costs to consumers and small business searching for and trying to negotiate lower retail electricity prices also needs to be considered.

On top of this there was the creation of a plethora of publicly funded regulatory bodies, most importantly: the Australian Energy Regulator, the Australian Electricity Market Operator and the Australian Energy Market Commission. State-level regulators continue to regulate electricity distribution in addition to the national regulators. The most recent entry to the field is the Energy Security Board (ESB), created by the Council of Australian Governments (COAG) in response to the obvious failure of existing bodies. The Turnbull government's current electricity policy is centred on the idea a 'National Energy Guarantee' (NEG). The NEG proposal is based on an eight-page document that was produced by the ESB within a period of weeks in response to a political imperative for urgency (Energy Security Board 2017). At the time of writing, nearly a year later, crucial aspects of the policy remain undefined.

Performance

CIGRE Australia's history of the Australian electricity industry (1996) shows a record of sustained and sometimes dramatic improvements to the extent, quality and cost efficiency of electricity supply under public ownership. During the decades after World War II, the publicly owned electricity supply industry was massively expanded, extending supply to the great majority of the Australian population and increasing generating capacity from around 3 GW in the early 1950s to 35 GW at the beginning of the reform period in 1990. Over the same period, real electricity prices fell by half, and, when the period of reform began, were among the lowest in the world. By 2017 Australian electricity prices were among the world's highest.

The National Electricity Market

As CIGRE Australia observes, 'despite the favourable comparative position disclosed by the statistics there emerged in the early 1990s a political consensus on the need for "reform" in the industry' (1996: 11). The NEM was implemented in the context of national competition policy (NCP) at a time when faith in competitive markets was at its peak. The design flaws that led to the failure of the NEM over the next twenty years were not anticipated.

The reforms of the 1990s were designed to change almost every aspect of the pre-reform institutional framework. It was hoped that the integrated, state-owned and bureaucratically run electricity monopolies would be replaced by a profit-oriented, privately-owned industry, operating in a competitive national market characterised by a clear separation between the activities of generation, transmission and distribution on the one hand, and retailing on the other. Consumers would be able to choose their supplier in a competitive retail market.

The National Grid

Because of Australia's geography, the establishment of separate electricity supply industries in each state was economically rational. Limited connections between Victoria and New South Wales were established as part of the Snowy Mountains Hydro-electric Scheme, which also created a new generator, the Snowy Mountains Hydro-electric Corporation. An interconnector between the Victorian and South Australian grids was added subsequently.

In physical terms, plans for the national grid involved the expansion of existing interstate links and the creation of a range of new links. The creation of a national grid is a necessary condition for the creation of a private national market, but it does not necessarily imply, a priori, that such a market will emerge. In a different policy environment, the decision to build a national grid could have been the precursor to the establishment of a unified national electricity supplier. More realistically, existing trade arrangements between the states could have formed the basis for the more frequent and extensive trading made possible by the national grid.

Following the agreement to construct a national grid in 1991, attention turned to the design of a NEM, modelled primarily on the system in place in the United Kingdom. Although it was already evident that the British model had serious flaws, it was hoped that Australia could learn from the British experience. The process of designing and implementing Australia's NEM was undertaken jointly by the National Grid Management Committee and COAG, and was part of the broader agenda of NCP (see Rann 1998 for a more detailed chronology).

At the system's core was the creation of a continuous-time auction market, whereby generators and users enter bids on a half-hourly basis. Each bid takes the form of a supply or demand schedule, indicating the agent's willingness to supply or demand electricity at given prices. These bids are combined to form aggregate demand and supply schedules. The intersection of the aggregate demand and supply schedules determines the dispatch price required to equate demand and supply for the given five-minute period. Because both available capacity and consumption demand tend to fluctuate, market clearing is undertaken at five-minute intervals. All bids made by generators that are less than or equal to the dispatch price are accepted and, conversely, all users with bids greater than or equal to the dispatch price have their demand met. These prices are averaged over a half-hour period to determine a spot price, which is the price ultimately received by generators and paid by purchasers. In addition to spot purchases, participants in the market may enter into long-term bilateral contracts or trade in a forward market. The Australian spot and forward markets were operated by a private, limited-liability company, the National Electricity Market Management Company (NEMMCO). The Australian Energy Market Operator (AEMO) replaced NEMMCO and related bodies in the gas industry in 2009.

Disaggregation

Before the reforms, the electricity industry was, in most cases, an integrated monopoly. A crucial element of the reforms was vertical and horizontal disintegration of the industry. Vertical disintegration was undertaken by separating the industry into the separate components of generation, transmission, distribution and retailing. Each of these components was horizontally disaggregated into separate firms to encourage competition.

The aggressive approach to horizontal disaggregation was consistent with the policy atmosphere of the early 1990s. It was also encouraged by a critical evaluation of the British electricity market. In their examination of the British market design, Green and Newbery (1992) had concluded that the market structure would allow for the extraction of substantial monopoly rents. The designers of the Australian NEM sought to avoid the anti-competitive features of the British market, and therefore encouraged the breakup of state electricity generation enterprises on horizontal as well as vertical lines.

Retail Contestability

Initially, electricity consumers were supplied by existing distribution enterprises, and at prices fixed by regulation. But the final stage of NEW implementation involved a gradual shift to retail 'contestability', where consumers would be able to choose a retailer for their electricity. That retailer would be responsible for purchasing wholesale electricity, paying the distributor for the use of their network and for services such as billing and metering. Distributors were allowed to continue to provide retail services, but were required to undertake elaborate 'ring fencing' exercises to ensure that their own particular retail services did not gain unfair advantages as a result of joint ownership.

Retail contestability was initially introduced only for large and medium-sized consumers. Because the NEM was introduced during a time of supply excess, prices in the wholesale electricity market were well below long-run average levels. These low wholesale prices were passed on to contestable customers in the former of cheaper electricity services, while retail consumers continued to pay the higher, fixed prices set roughly equal to long-run average cost. It was widely agreed that, when full retail contestability was introduced, ordinary consumers would enjoy the full benefits of such competition. However, in reality, the period of excess supply was short-lived. Even before the introduction of full retail contestability, wholesale prices had risen and there was considerable pressure to pass these cost increases on to households as well as to contestable customers.

The separation of retail and distribution was based partly on the belief that consumers would benefit from a choice between competing packages of electricity pricing and billing, and partly on a concern to limit the natural monopoly component of the industry, as far as this might be possible. However, for most households – and particularly in the absence of sophisticated metering – electricity is a simple commodity. Many householders would have preferred to continue buying their electricity directly from the distributor at stable prices, as they had done in the past. Despite the rhetoric of choice, this simple option had become unavailable, or, if it remained available, was subjected to steep price increases. Instead, consumers were faced with a new glut of new and confusing electricity service offers, often available only for a limited period after switching suppliers. The result was costly 'churn' between suppliers, as consumers sought to avoid constant price increases and retailers spent more and more money on their advertising and marketing budgets.

The organisation of the NEM and the retail electricity market also necessitated the creation of a wholesaling function in electricity. Since electricity is purchased in five-minute blocks in the market, while retail consumers face constant prices over periods of a month or a quarter, it became necessary that some market agent would serve the function of buying electricity at the spot price and supplying it in wholesale quantities at a stable wholesale price. This function is conceptually distinct from the retail activity of providing metering and billing services in return for a mark-up on the wholesale price. The joint provision of wholesale and retail services in the Australian NEM worked poorly, and retailers were eventually separated or acquired by generators.

Pool Markets and Price Risk

The core of the NEM was the creation of markets in which generators sold electricity to wholesalers and retailers, or directly to customers. Prices are highly variable, ranging from zero to a regulated maximum. Currently 2017–18 prices are set at $14,200/MWh.

The problem of price risk in the NEM is associated with the more general issue of prices as market signals. Prior to the NEM's introduction, state electricity enterprises normally set prices so as to recover the average cost of production as well as a return to capital invested in the enterprise. By contrast, in a competitive electricity market, generators are normally willing to supply electricity whenever the price exceeds the marginal cost of generation. However, in the short run, generating capacity is fixed. When there is excess capacity, the competitive equilibrium price will be equal to marginal cost for the marginal generator, and will normally be less than the long-run average cost of production. When generating capacity is fully used, the price will be determined by the amount customers are willing to pay for an additional unit of electricity. This amount is generally more than the long-run average cost of generation, and sometimes much more.

The pool price is therefore variable over time, with long periods in which prices are below average cost, and then these low prices are offset by brief peak-demand periods where prices are very high. However, if new investment is to be undertaken in the industry, the average price received over the long run must be equal to the average cost of generation including a return to capital invested in construction of new plants. Because investment will not take place while prices are consistently below the level required for profitability, price fluctuations will tend to cancel out in the medium term. Sustained periods of low prices will result in the cessation of new investment. Growth in demand and the ageing of existing plants will increase the frequency of peak-demand periods with their associated high prices.

Although price variations will tend to cancel out, this tendency does not fully eliminate risk. Under the pool system, the profitability of generators depends heavily on the relatively small number of periods of peak demand. A single hour in which the price is at the maximum of $14,200/MWh per megawatt-hour produces the same gross returns as an entire month during which the price is $20 per megawatt-hour. When fuel costs are taken into account, the disparity is even greater. Hence, the net return to generators over a given period may be significantly affected by the occurrence of a few more (or less) hot days than average. Such random shocks are eventually cancelled out, but only over periods of five to ten years or more.

Climate Policy

The agreement to construct a national grid in 1991 came shortly before the 1992 Earth Summit held in Rio de Janeiro, at which Australia signed the United Nations Framework Convention on Climate Change. Throughout the process of the design and implementation of the NEM, policymakers were aware – or should have been aware – that meeting the goals of stabilising the global climate would require radical changes in energy generation and use. Yet the NEM designers effectively ignored this, making no provisions for carbon pricing or renewable energy policies. This failure has remained unremedied for the past twenty-five years.

Instead, the NEM has continued to operate a design suited to the coal-based electricity industry of the 1990s. Climate-change policies including carbon pricing and renewable energy targets have been developed and implemented separate to the NEM. The failure to integrate climate policy and electricity market design has led to a series of increasingly desperate interventions, including the creation in August 2017 of the Energy Security Board and its proposal in October 2017 of a National Energy Guarantee and an Emissions Guarantee, on top of the NEM.

The Failure of the NEM

The national electricity objectives as stated in the *National Electricity (South Australia) Act 1996* are to promote efficient investment in, and efficient operation and use of, electricity services for the long-term interests of consumers of electricity with respect to:

> 1. Price, quality, safety, reliability, and security of supply of electricity; and
> 2. The reliability, safety and security of the national electricity system. (AEMC).

This objective has clearly not been met by the existing system. The main failures of the current system are:

> (a) Pricing. Electricity prices have risen greatly, reversing a long-term trend in their decline under the previous system of integrated, publicly owned electricity supply systems.
> (b) Reliability. The shift to market-based systems was followed by a series of supply failures, which necessitated costly investment in distribution networks at high cost to consumers.
> (c) Quality. Competition has led to substantial churn in retail markets, but customer satisfaction is poor – as poor as it is in the banking sector.
> (d) Efficient investment. The pricing system has not delivered coherent signals for investment. In particular, the existing system

has failed to cope with the entry of renewables.
(e) Efficient operation. Resources have been diverted from operational functions to management and marketing, resulting in higher costs and poorer service.

These failures are not incidental. They can be explained by fundamental, incurable flaws in the NEM model of pricing, regulation and incentives for investment. Marginal adjustments such as those currently proposed will prove inadequate. The only satisfactory option is a substantial shift away from a reliance on artificial markets, and the introduction of strategic and operational planning for the national grid.

Price Outcomes

In the early years of the NEM, retail prices fell modestly. This reflected both the long-term downward trend over the course of the twentieth century, and the fact that, at the commencement of the NEM, the industry had significant reserve capacity, which was mistakenly viewed as excess capacity. However, since 2005 prices have risen sharply in most states.

FIGURE 1. REAL AVERAGE RESIDENTIAL ELECTRICITY PRICES 2001–02 TO 2015–16

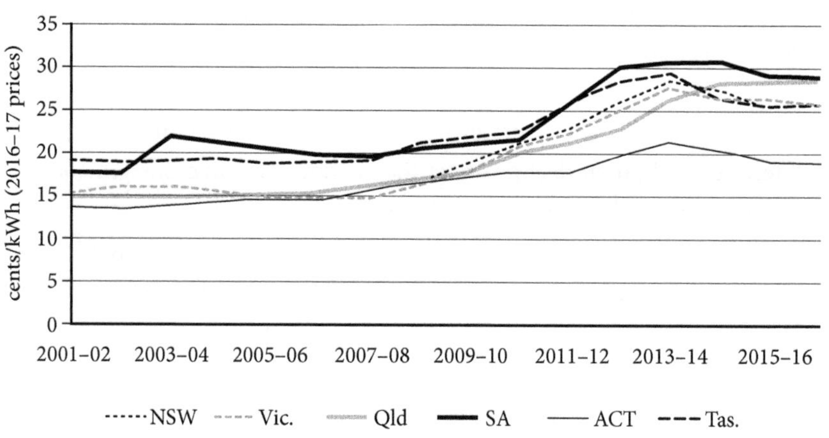

Source: Sadler 2017, The Australia Institute

Labour Costs and Productivity

One of the primary aims of the NEM reforms was to drive improvements in labour productivity. Efforts to reduce a perceived overstaffing and 'feather-bedding' were directed primarily at technical and trade workers, who experienced successive waves of redundancies. However, these reductions in employment have been more than offset by increases in the number of managers, sales workers and marketing professionals needed to operate in the new market framework.

A study of the electricity, gas and water industries by the Australia Institute found that the number of technical and trades workers employed in these industries had grown by less than the workforce as a whole between 1997 and 2012 (28 per cent, as opposed to 37 per cent). By contrast, the number of managers had more than doubled, HR and marketing professionals had more than tripled, and the number of sales workers had risen by 500 per cent. At the beginning of the reform period, technicians outnumbered managerial and retail staff; by the end, the reverse was true. According to the Institute's study, there was a manager for every thirteen workers in 1997, but by 2012 there was a manager for every nine.

The Failure of the Pricing Model

In a theoretically ideal competitive market, prices perform at least four distinct functions. First, they provide a signal to consumers about the social cost of the product they are consuming. Consumers will buy the product if – and only if – its value to them exceeds the price, which represents the value of the resources used to produce it. Second, and conversely, prices provide a signal to producers about the value of their product. Firms will produce more (or less) if the price is greater (or less than) than their cost of additional production. Third, prices provide a signal to firms about whether to invest in additional production capacity. If prices are high, and are expected to remain so for some time, the industry will attract new investment. If prices are low, there will be no new investment and existing capacity will be scrapped or allowed to run down. Fourth, and finally, competitive prices ensure that, in the long run, firms earn the market rate of return on the capital they have invested, no more and no less. The designers of electricity markets have attempted to reproduce all of these outcomes but have failed, cultivating instead several critical problems.

First, there are problems generic to network infrastructure industries. The physical network is a natural monopoly, which means the market is best served by a single set of wires or pipes. In the absence of regulation, a monopolist will charge prices that are too high, with the result that they will not perform their signalling functions properly. Consumers will get less than they should at a higher price, profits will be excessive and investment will be distorted. We didn't see such adverse outcomes under public ownership because profit maximisation was not an objective of the utility. These problems can be reduced, though not eliminated completely, by comprehensive price regulation. However, when privatised firms are regulated in this way, their primary incentive becomes to 'game' the system in order to secure higher returns. This often entails delaying investment or colluding to restrain supply, thereby raising wholesale prices.

A second problem is specific to the electricity industry. Because electricity can only be stored at high cost, using batteries or pumped storage, the cost of additional generation can fluctuate wildly. When all available generation capacity is in use, additional demand can only be met by measures such as 'load-shedding'. The Australian pool market price of power can rise to the regulated maximum, but even this is not high enough for the market to perform as it supposed to. On the other hand, on nights when demand is low the price can be zero or even negative, as operators prefer to keep their plants running than to shut them down and restart the next day. On the demand side, most consumers face fixed prices, and therefore take no account of the actual cost of the electricity consumed at any given time. Attempts to address this problem through 'smart meters' have so far had little, if any, success.

Private Rates of Return

Electricity networks are highly capital-intensive. As a result, the cost of electricity is predominantly determined by the capital value of the network and the rate of return earned by its owners. In the pre-reform era, public electricity enterprises funded their investment by issuing bonds, normally at a small premium to the government bond rate. In some cases, governments guaranteed these bonds. However, the primary reason for the low rate of return demanded for the bonds issued by public enterprises is that, under normal conditions, the risk of these investments is very low. By disaggregating the industry, the National Electricity Market created new sources of risk, most notably fluctuations in the pool price, which created risks for generators (who lost money when prices were low), and for retailers (who lost money when prices were high). Under the previous integrated system, such gains and losses netted out automatically. By contrast, the NEM required either a complex system of hedging markets or the integration of generators and retailers to form 'gentailers'. Neither has worked perfectly and the resulting costs have been passed on to consumers.

By contrast, the risk associated with the regulated monopoly components of the industry – transmission and distribution – have remained low. The standard method of regulation involved fixing allowable revenue based on an estimate of the efficient costs of operation.

Under national competition policy, regulators were required to set a rate of return derived from private enterprises. This normally involved setting a 'weighted average cost of capital', which was substantially higher than the true cost of capital for private firms, let alone the government bond rate that had previously formed the basis of electricity pricing.

The result of the requirement for excessive rates of return is that distributors have had a strong incentive to 'game' the system. Gaming the system is a two-step process: first, distributors make arguments that the required level of capital investment, to which the rate of return is applicable, is very high; then, to the extent that they can within a given regulatory period, they under-invest while claiming to have made gains in efficiency. The extent of gaming is illustrated by the fact that the market value of distribution assets is substantially greater than the value imputed by regulators (Thompson, MacDonald and Mouliakis 2016)

The Case for Renationalisation

The tragedy of this situation is that is all could have been avoided if we had seized the opportunity in the 1990s to build a unified national grid, with a single authority running transmission networks and the interconnectors between them. This would still facilitate competition in generation, but would abandon the idea of market incentives for the provision of network services.

Electricity networks are considered to be natural monopolies. Unlike other industries – where it makes sense for lots of businesses to compete with one another and drive costs lower – the cost and importance of supplying electricity means it make sense for one business to control the market. In light of this, this authority should not be a privatised firm or even a corporatised government enterprise. Instead, it should be a statutory authority with a primary mission of delivering energy security at low cost and managing a shift to decarbonisation.

An obvious question is whether re-nationalising the electricity network is politically feasible. While the political class on both sides views privatised infrastructure as an unchallengeable necessity, the general public has a different view. With only a handful of exceptions, voters have rejected privatisation whenever they have had a chance to do so (Quiggin 2014). The question of reversing past privatisations is more difficult, however, British polls show overwhelming public support for renationalisation, even though the electricity industry has been in private ownership for decades. Even a majority of conservative voters support public ownership (Dahlgreen 2017).

Among the many failures of micro-economic reform in Australia, the failure of the NEM has been the most spectacular. Not only have none of the promises of reform been delivered but the price increases reform has driven have been used as evidence to obstruct the shift to a decarbonised electricity supply. Though at this point, the best option would be a comprehensive nationalisation of grid management, distribution and supply (Quiggin 2017); the far more likely outcome is a series of piecemeal interventions, responding to the successive failures of the system. Unscrambling the egg of failed reform will be a complex and messy business. It will have to be done gradually, perhaps beginning with South Australia and Tasmania, the states worst affected by recent disasters. But there is no satisfactory alternative.

References

Australian Energy Market Commission, *National Energy Objectives*, aemc.gov.au/regulation/national-energy-objectives

Dahlgreen, W. (2017), 'Nationalise energy and rail companies, say public', *YouGov*, 4 November.

Energy Security Board (2017) 'Energy Security Board (ESB) advice on a retailer reliability, emissions guarantee and affordability', 13 October, coagenergycouncil.gov.au.

Green, R.J. and Newbery, D.M. (1992) 'Competition in the British electricity spot market', *Journal of Political Economy*, 100 (5): 929–953.

CIGRE Australia (1996) 'A Dictionary on Electricity: Contribution on Australia', International Council on Large Electric Systems, Australian National Committee.

Quiggin, J. (2003) 'Free market reform and the South Australian electricity supply industry', pp. 51–70 in Spoehr, J. (ed.) *Power Politics: the Electricity Crisis and You*. Kent Town, Wakefield Press.

——(2014) *Electricity Privatisation in Australia: A Record of Failure*, Report Commissioned by the Victorian Branch of the Electrical Trades Union, February 2014.

——(2017) 'Grid Renationalisation – a discussion paper', Australian Industrial Transformation Institute, Flinders University, February 2014. flinders.edu.au/fms/AITI/Documents/AITIQuiggin_Paper_Grid_Renationalisation.pdf

Rann, A. (1998) *Electricity Industry Restructuring – A Chronology*, Background Paper 21 1997–98, 30 June. Canberra, Australian Parliamentary Library.

Saddler, H. (2017) *National Energy Emmissions Audit – Electricity Update*, The Australia Institute, August.

Thompson, S., Macdonald, A. and Mouliakis, J. (2016) 'Ausgrid price explained; 1.41-times RAB', *Australian Financial Review*, 20 October.

CHAPTER 9

FAIR GO NO MORE: NEOLIBERALISM AND AUSTRALIAN LABOUR MARKET POLICY

JIM STANFORD

A fundamental reorientation of labour market and employment policy has been a centrepiece of neoliberal policy and political strategy virtually everywhere it has been implemented. Indeed, neoliberalism is defined in large part by a multidimensional, consistent effort to alter the landscape of work, and the balance of power between workers and employers (Cahill 2010). Neoliberalism engages numerous policy levers to consistently enhance the power and profit of employers: the abandonment of full-employment macro-economic strategy; sustained efforts to restructure institutions of labour market regulation and income distribution (including attacks on unions and collective bargaining); retrenchment of social and income support programs; and legal and regulatory changes that enhance the power of employers in workplaces.

The centrality of labour market reforms to the overall neoliberal project is particularly evident in the Australian case. This is partly because the distance travelled in labour market policy since the onset of neoliberalism has been greater here than in most other OECD countries. In the 1970s, Australia's economy ranked as one of the most egalitarian among industrialised countries. Now it ranks solidly among the more unequal, business-dominated countries in the OECD.

The importance of labour policy themes in the evolution of Australian neoliberalism also reflects the uniquely politicised, partisan nature of labour policy debates in Australia. Because of the polarised structure of Australian politics (with elections dominated by a contest between two major parties, one of which, the Australian Labor Party (ALP), is historically and institutionally connected to the trade union movement), labour and industrial relations issues have taken on particular importance. Attacks on unions and collective bargaining have fulfilled a dual role for the political right: directly, they undermine workers' power and enhance business freedom and profitability; indirectly, they function as a form of by proxy–attack on the Labor Party. So while Australian unions are now relatively weak compared to other OECD countries, the issue of labour relations features disproportionately in broader political and policy debates.

At the same time, the institutional connections between the union movement and one of the two major political parties has had a unique effect on the character of neoliberal labour market policy in Australia – some of the most ambitious neoliberal restructuring has in fact been undertaken by Labor governments, with at least nominal support from the unions themselves. All of this helps to explain both the dramatic effects of neoliberal labour market reforms in Australia, and their unique political context.

This chapter provides a historical synopsis of the evolution of neoliberal labour market policies in Australia since the 1980s. It shows that the neoliberal strategy cannot be described as a general process of deregulation or marketisation: while some aspects of employment relationships have been deregulated, others are intensely regulated and controlled, but always with the goal of enhancing employer power. I catalogue the impacts and consequences of neoliberal labour policy, including labour market, macro-economic, and distributional indicators. Finally, I review the interaction between the changing stance of labour policy during the neoliberal era, and the still-evolving, longer-term balance of power between the major combatants in that struggle.

The History of Neoliberal Labour Market Policy in Australia

Australia has a unique and in many ways inspiring history of innovative labour policy activism. Important labour struggles, including the Eureka Rebellion (1854), the campaign for an eight-hour working day (1856), and the famous 1891 shearer's strike, were influential in pre-Federation economic and political developments. Soon after Federation in 1901, a Commonwealth Conciliation and Arbitration Court was established to settle labour disputes on the basis of the 'rule of law'. The idea was to avoid frequently violent strikes and other industrial confrontations in favour of a process of reasoned argument, akin to the peaceful settlement of other legal and contractual disputes through the court system. The court's famous *Harvester* decision in 1907 established a minimum wage that was tied to the cost of living for workers and their families, thus introducing the concept of a 'living wage' as a benchmark for fair compensation. From that starting point, a national industrial relations system based on judicial conciliation and arbitration developed, eventually covering most workers in the economy. Unions were given official standing to represent workers' interests across entire sectors. Backed by strong union security provisions (including closed shops, preferential hiring rules, and dues check-off systems (see Weeks 1995; Fenwick and Howe 2009)), union membership expanded rapidly, reaching over 60 per cent of the workforce by the mid-1950s (ABS Year Book, Catalogue 1301.0).[1] In the later years of the postwar expansion, stronger unions were even able to negotiate 'over-award' terms in agreements with particular businesses, which they then campaigned to have extended across the entire sector through improvements in the award. Real wages grew rapidly and the share of total GDP allocated to labour compensation grew steadily, rising from 45 per cent of GDP in 1950, to 57 per cent in 1975 (see Figure 1). Reinforced by the postwar expansion of social welfare and income support programs, this established a foundation for major advances in income equality: by 1980, the share of personal income going to the richest one per cent of the population fell to just above 4 per cent (see Figure 2), which was among the lowest of any industrialised country.

However, opposition to this labour-friendly policy regime from businesses and their major owners intensified as the postwar era drew to a close, and Australian capitalism, like that in other OECD countries, confronted financial and political instability. The stage was set for a powerful attack on Australia's labour relations system, located within a broader package of market- and business-oriented reforms (including a flexible exchange rate, international trade liberalisation and the privatisation of

Figure 1. Labour share of GDP[2]

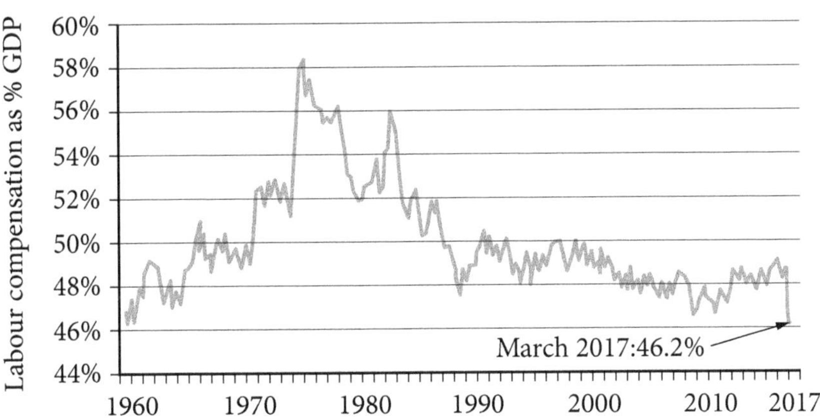

Source: Author's calculations from ABS catalogue 5206.0, seasonally adjusted

Figure 2. Top income share

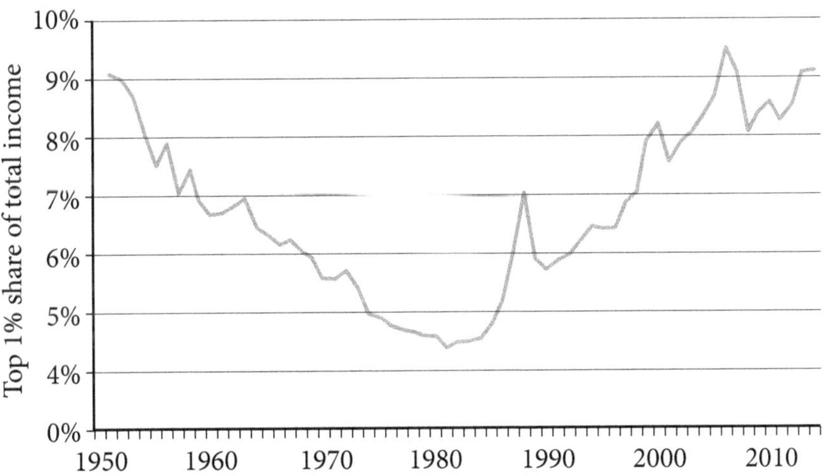

Source: World Inequality Database (2018)

public assets). As in other OECD countries, the purported rationale for this restructuring of employment relations focused on the alleged dangers arising from inflation, declining profitability and capital flight. But the implementation of neoliberal labour market reforms also reflected Australia's unique labour relations history and political context.[2]

There are a number of key moments in the ongoing evolution of neoliberal labour market policy:

The Prices and Incomes Accords

In the wake of the labour militancy and inflation that characterised the 1970s, a resurgent Labor party under Bob Hawke, himself a former union leader, wanted to assure voters that a Labor government could manage its union allies. The party and the union movement together signed a public accord in 1983 that pledged to restrain wage increases in return for improvements in social programs, including the introduction of compulsory superannuation[3] and universal healthcare benefits. The accord was successful in reassuring voters, and Labor was elected soon afterward. A series of follow-up Accords then shaped labour relations and employment policy during Labor's subsequent thirteen-year period in office. The willingness and ability of unions to cap wage demands did restrain wage growth during this period (Kenyon 1990) – in fact, average real wages fell slightly under the Hawke government (with wage increases falling slightly behind inflation) (Stanford 2016: 12). But by restraining union activity and wages, the Accords damaged the credibility of the awards system and were eventually associated with an erosion of union membership and activism. Wage increases were tied to the elimination of 'restrictive' practices and other measures to boost productivity (Stewart 2004); the Accords were implemented alongside other business-oriented policy shifts, including a floating exchange rate and trade liberalisation. The Accord and its associated policies thus represented a form of 'constrained neoliberalism' (Peetz and Baily 2011). While the strategy was initially intended as a grand compromise (trading off wage restraint for social welfare enhancements), the constraints it imposed on collective bargaining and union power were sharpened by later Coalition governments, which also tried to jettison the social dimension of the whole package.

Enterprise Bargaining

The *Industrial Relations Reform Act 1993*, passed under the Keating Labor government, reduced the power of sector-wide awards, and created a new system in which wages and working conditions were determined by collective bargaining at the enterprise level. The union movement supported this shift through the seventh – and final – accord signed with the Labor Party in 1991 (Forsyth and Holbrook, 2017). They hoped it would create an avenue for more generous wage increases, at least in some workplaces, and inspire greater local participation by members. This latter hope was not widely realised (Ewar et al. 1991), and union membership began to decline quickly. Industry-wide awards were reconstituted as a second tier or 'fall back' minimum (with the leading edge of industrial relations set by stronger unions through enterprise bargaining with particular firms); the direct standing of unions as a party to those awards was eventually removed.[4] The ability of the Industrial Relations Commission to arbitrate industrial disputes was constrained. The 1993 Act explicitly recognised, for the first time in Australia, the right of workers to strike, protected from civil action by employers (McCrystal 2010), but it also established strict boundaries around that right. The Act also ratified the practice of enterprise agreements being implemented without the participation of a union.

Initial Howard Reforms

After thirteen years of Labor rule, the new Coalition government in 1996 introduced numerous employer-friendly reforms to labour law, culminating in its *Workplace Relations Act 1996* (Fenwick and Howe 2009; Riley and Sheldon 2008). This Act further diminished the arbitration powers of the Industrial Relations Commission. It included prohibitions on union security measures (like closed shop agreements or preferential hiring systems in unionised workplaces); it required the provisions of enterprise agreements to be made equally available to all workers in a workplace, whether they were union members or not. The Act also extended the scope for non-union enterprise agreements, opening space for employers to implement very weak collective agreements. The Act also allowed enterprise bargaining to establish terms lower than minimum standards in some sectors, so long as workers were compensated by above minimum provisions in other facets of their employment. This dilution of the impact of minimum standards was justified by the supposed need for greater flexibility for individual businesses (Mitchell, Campbell and Barnes 2005).[5]

The conditions under which union officials were allowed to enter workplaces were now specified in legislation – and these terms were incrementally tightened in coming years.

Work Choices

Having gained voting control in both houses of parliament, the Howard government brought in more aggressive proposals during its last term in power, bundled in the *Work Choices Act 2005*.[6] Work Choices strengthened the reach of the federal industrial relations system, and included the takeover of what had formerly been state powers. New provisions allowing for individual contracts (even in workplaces covered by enterprise agreements) significantly weakened the practice of collective bargaining. Work Choices established five minimum pay and conditions standards that would, supposedly, underpin individual contracts, although those standards were not always recognised in practice. The new legislation also established strict rules regarding what matters could legitimately be discussed during collective bargaining, narrowing the scope of negotiations to core matters directly tied to the employment relationship, while excluding a wide range of other workplace issues such as technology, training, and relationships with outside firms (Stewart and Riley 2007). Work Choices enhanced the rights of employers to dismiss workers, especially in smaller businesses. Other labour policies enacted during the last term of the Howard government included the creation of the Australian Building and Construction Comission (ABCC) to police labour relations and curb union activity in the construction sector. These dramatic changes provoked a focused and effective opposition movement led by the Australian Council of Trade Unions (ACTU), which contributed to the electoral defeat of the Howard government in 2007 (Wilson and Spies-Butcher 2011).

Fair Work Act

The electoral victory of the Labor Party in 2007 owed much to the upsurge in labour activism against Work Choices, and so at that point hopes were high for a major shift in labour market and industrial relations policy. Ultimately those hopes were largely dashed. Labor's first major initiative was to begin streamlining and consolidating the system of industry wage awards from over 1500 separate awards to just 122 so-called 'modern awards'. This process reaffirmed that awards would now function solely as a safety net, setting minimum standards and benchmarks, including industry-specific minimum pay rates, for various industries – as opposed to leading the advancement of wages and conditions for the broader workforce.

More comprehensive, the *Fair Work Act 2009* created a new Fair Work Commission with the power to determine awards and minimum wages, but not to conciliate or arbitrate collective bargaining outcomes, except in very limited circumstances. This Act also established ten National Employment Standards (NES), expanding on the five previously proclaimed under the Howard government. Other provisions included: continued restrictions on union activity, including limits on right of entry, preferences for union members, and industrial action; a wide list of unlawful terms that were prohibited from enterprise agreements;[7] and a new low-paid bargaining stream that allowed multi-enterprise bargaining for specified low-wage sectors.[8] For the first time, a national employment standards enforcement agency – the Fair Work Ombudsman (FWO) – was created and charged with policing compliance with minimum wages, the NES and other employer obligations. However, the FWO's relatively weak 'persuasive compliance' model of enforcement (Goodwin and Maconachie 2011) has proved inadequate, as evidenced by the widespread non-enforcement of many minimum standards.[9]

The Abbott and Turnbull Governments

The Liberal–National Coalition returned to power in 2013. Its anti-union rhetoric has been as aggressive as ever; however, in part because of its minority status in the Senate, its industrial relations legislative agenda has been relatively incremental compared with previous conservative governments.

As one of its first acts, it established a royal commission into alleged union corruption. This set the stage for new initiatives to police union activity, including a resuscitated ABCC, and a Registered Organisations Commission (ROC) with new powers to investigate and surveil unions. Additional initiatives (that are still being debated at the time of writing) include proposals to limit unions' ability to establish welfare and insurance funds, and to reduce their role in the governance of industry-based superannuation funds. For the most part, these initiatives will have a limited material effect on a labour market in which unions and collective bargaining have already been marginalised; nonetheless, labour relations remain central to the Coalition's overall policy narrative, and its continuing efforts to damage its Labor opponents.

The general trajectory of labour policy in Australia under neoliberalism has thus followed a 'ratchet' pattern. Labor governments set the initial, important neoliberal reforms in motion, including the erosion of industry-wide regulation, its partial replacement with decentralised enterprise bargaining and the introduction of broad restrictions on union activity. When given the chance, Coalition governments enhanced those restrictions on unions with more intrusive and punitive measures – making the undermining of the long-run institutional, financial and social foundations of unions their special focus. Subsequent Labor governments eased off on some of those measures, but they have never been fully reversed. Regardless of which party was in power, the trend of de-unionisation, the erosion of the arbitration and awards system, and the individualisation of employment relations has been sustained (Buchanan and Considine 2007; Fenwick and Howe 2009; Bray and Stewart 2013). Overall, neoliberal labour policy should be understood as an integrated, multidimensional strategy to enhance the power of employers over work and employment. And such a strategy has in turn been central to the restoration of business power in all areas of life.

Deregulation or Micro-Management?

Neoliberalism is often equated with a process of downsising or rolling back the size and influence of the state. The simple assumption that a neoliberal state is a smaller, disempowered state has been widely criticised (Harvey 2005; Cahill and Konings 2017). There are many dimensions along which the modern neoliberal state retains an enormous capacity to intervene in and manage economic and social life in order to protect and promote the interests of capital. Providing the necessary physical and social infrastructure, policing labour relations and property rights, regulating the overall temperature of the macroeconomy and bailing out major players in times of crisis are some examples.

The issue is not whether the state is strong or weak, but rather in whose interests the state exercises its power. Under neoliberalism the overwhelming and consistent goal of policy is to stabilise, protect, and promote the accumulation of private capital. Where state-organised activities and services empower other interests, neoliberalism may indeed roll them back, when necessary invoking mantras of deficit reduction or tax competitiveness. But for state functions aligned with the interests of private investment, there is no downsising imperative – and money is never a barrier to their provision.

The descriptor 'labour market deregulation' is often applied to the process of dismantling postwar labour institutions, protections and standards, facilitating a less restricted interaction between employers and workers. In some ways, neoliberal labour market policy has indeed exhibited this deregulatory bent: the erosion of the scope and effectiveness of the modern sector awards is one example. In other ways, however, neoliberal labour market policy in Australia has exhibited an aggressive, interventionist and intrusive character, aimed quite explicitly at controlling and disciplining the activities and power of trade unions. The actual non-equivalence of neoliberalism and deregulation is especially evident in the case of labour market policy in Australia.

A particularly clear example of neoliberal interventionism is the limits that have been imposed on union activity in Australia. There are broad restrictions on union access to workplaces to inspect conditions or meet with workers. There are very elaborate restrictions on unions' ability to take protected industrial action, including requirements regarding the timing and wording of strike ballots of members, requirements that unions disclose their plans in advance (with no matching requirement for strategic transparency on the part of employers), and prohibitions on secondary boycotts and other actions.[10] There are even detailed restrictions on what union activists and officials can say and do in the workplace: right down to the use of profane language, the display of union signs and symbols, and the encouragement of participation in union actions.

A potent symbol of the restrictions on industrial relations practices is provided by the immense prescriptive detail of the Fair Work Act: 800 sections described in 652 pages of legislation, and much larger volumes of accompanying regulations and jurisprudence. And this does not include other state bodies (like the ABCC or the ROC) established to extend the surveillance and policing of union activity. It would thus be highly misleading to describe labour policy in Australia as deregulated. To the contrary, the close regulation of labour markets and industrial relations in Australia is unique.

Outcomes of Neoliberal Labour Policy

The cumulative impact of neoliberal labour policy in Australia has been a profound shift in power in favour of employers. There are a number of empirical indicators of this shift. Institutionally, one of the most dramatic indicators has been the erosion of trade union membership measured as a share of total employment – from sixty per cent in the mid-1950s to just 13 per cent in the most recent data (see Figure 3). The decline reflects the crumbling of union membership among traditional permanent paid employees alongside the growth of non-standard employment in recent years (including self-employment, casual work and independent contracting).[11] The fall in union density has been more dramatic in Australia than almost any other OECD country.[12]

Naturally, if union membership has declined, then the activities of unions have also declined – in some cases, even more dramatically. For example, industrial action has become infrequent (see Figure 4), declining by over 95 per cent from peak levels experienced in the 1970s and 1980s.[13] The almost complete disappearance of strike activity reflects declining union membership, restrictions on industrial action, and fear among workers that striking could jeopardise their jobs.

The erosion of collective bargaining coverage is another indicator of declining union power. Curiously, many more Australian workers are covered under enterprise agreements than are members of unions. This reflects the legally protected practice of 'free-riding', where workers can attain the benefits of a union-negotiated agreement without belonging to the union or contributing to negotiating and maintaining that agreement (Peetz 2005; Orr 2001). Recent data indicate that around thirty per cent of workers are covered by an enterprise agreement, more than twice the proportion of workers who belong to a union.[14] Hence, most workers covered by an agreement do not contribute to its negotiation or maintenance (a state of

Figure 3. Australian union density

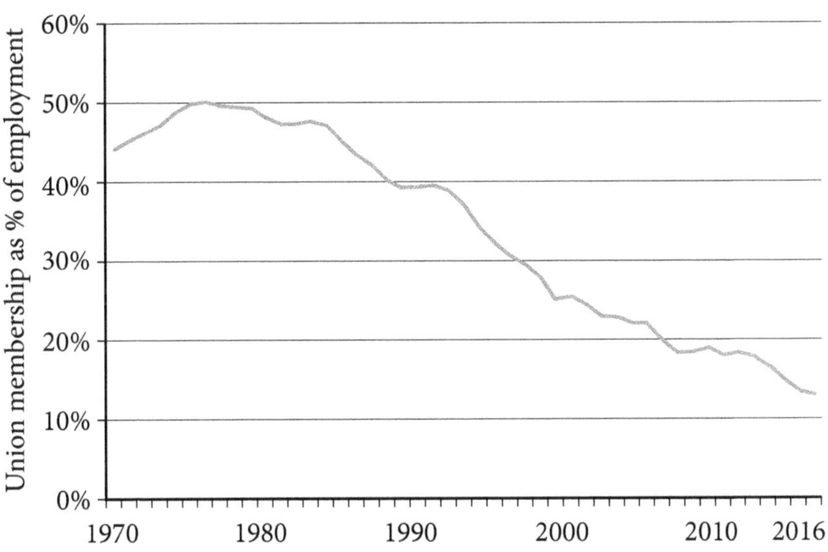

Source: Author's calculations from ABS Catalogues 6310.0 and 6333.0

Figure 4. Industrial action

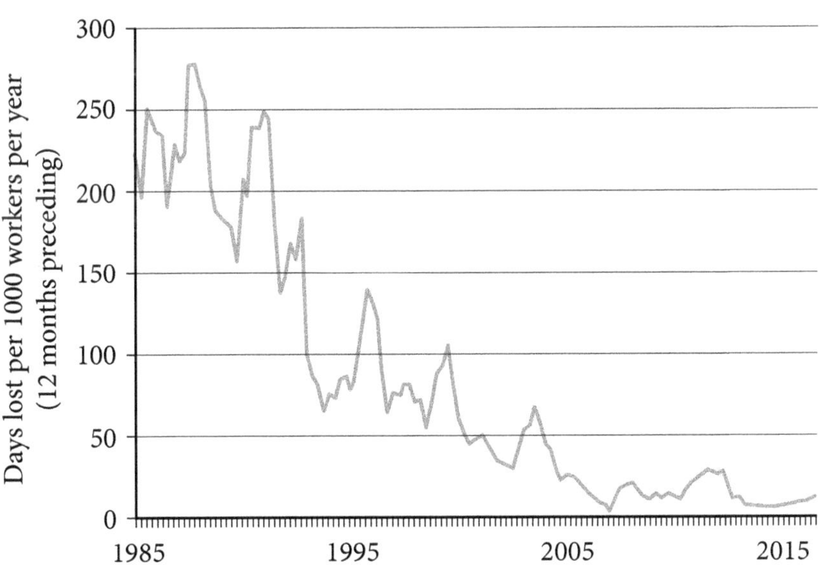

Source: Author's calculations from ABS Catalogues 1301.0, 6321.0, and Reserve Bank of Australia data.

affairs that hardly seems sustainable).[15] It is likely due to the widespread and unsustainable free-riding that the number of workers covered by enterprise agreements in the private sector began falling rapidly after 2013: it has now declined down by one-quarter or over 500,000 workers (see Figure 5).

A further measure of the pro-employer shift in labour market regulation has been the erosion of the minimum wage measured as a proportion of prevailing median wages. While Australia's minimum wage is still relatively high by international standards, its influence has declined under neoliberal policy: the minimum wage has lagged consistently behind general labour market compensation trends, and hence has declined relative to overall median wages (see Figure 6).

In these contexts it is worth noting that Australia's statutory labour protections remain relatively strong compared to other industrial countries, despite the employer-friendly direction of labour policy overall. Minimum wages are still relatively high despite their having been eroded, and other statutory protections include unique measures like extra pay for casual workers and penalty rates for working weekends and evenings. These instruments of labour regulation reflect the continuing influence of the previous quasi-judicial mechanisms that once governed Australian labour policy. Their ongoing relevance has supported wage levels and workers' incomes, even as collective bargaining has declined.

Nevertheless, the impact of neoliberal labour policy on income distribution in Australia has been substantial. As Figure 1 shows, the share of labour compensation in total GDP began to decline in the late 1970s and by early 2017 it had reached the lowest share since the ABS began publishing quarterly national income data – down to 46 per cent from a peak of 58 per cent in the late 1970s (Stanford 2017). The steady gains in relative labour compensation achieved in the postwar expansion have now been mostly reversed. Roughly simultaneously, the distribution of personal income in Australia also began to polarise: the richest segment of society has regained the same disproportionate share of total income it captured in 1950 (see Figure 2). Since the ownership of wealth – particularly business and financial wealth – is concentrated among the richest segments of society, the falling labour share of GDP and the rising share of income going to capital is automatically reflected in an increase in the share of personal income enjoyed by the richest households in society.

Figure 5. EBA coverage: Private sector

Source: Jobs and Small Business, 'Trends in Federal Enterprise Bargaining'.

Figure 6. Minimum wage 'bite'

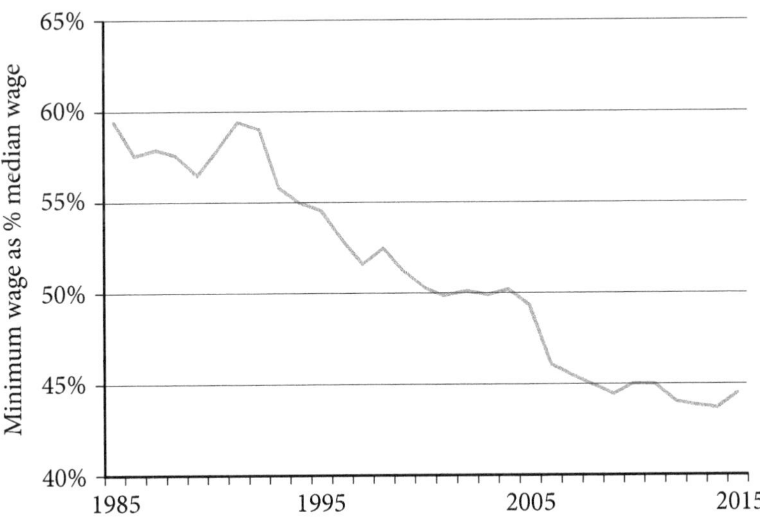

Source: Organisation for Economic Cooperation and Development, 'Employment and Labour Market Statistics'.

Conclusion

Neoliberal labour policy in Australia has fundamentally shifted the balance of power in employment relations in favour of employers. This has produced a redistribution of income from labour to capital, and from working households to those with significant wealth. Australia has descended from one of the most egalitarian countries in the advanced capitalist world to a country with relatively severe and worsening inequality, and a country where the terms of employment are determined overwhelmingly by private relations between individual workers and their employers.

Despite this overall trend, Australia's present labour market institutions and policies reflect a contradictory and unstable compromise. Regulatory instruments wielded directly by the state (including minimum wages, national employment standards and what remains of the awards system) continue to exert an important positive influence in the shaping of employment norms and the moderation of income distribution. But they are under sustained attack from employers, and the rules governing trade unions and collective bargaining are uniquely hostile. Without an empowered countervailing force to defend positive statutory standards (a force presumably led by unions), those standards will almost certainly be further eroded over time. It is very clear that the coexistence of strong universal standards and weak unions is not ultimately sustainable.

This relationship between the particular stance of policy at any point in time, and the longer-run balance of power between competing forces in society, also helps to explain the unique political character of neoliberal labour policy in Australia. The first big steps in the neoliberal restructuring of Australia's labour market were taken by Labor governments, with support from union allies. At the time of the Accords, many unionists concluded that this constrained form of neoliberalism was preferable to the more hard-nosed versions playing out in other countries, including the United States and the United Kingdom. That judgement will continue to be debated, but what is more obvious, in hindsight, is that the erosion of the institutional power and social legitimacy of workers' organisations that occurred in the wake of those initial neoliberal policies has had bigger consequences for the subsequent direction of labour market and employment policy. Unions accepted the shorter-run trade-offs embodied in the Accords in the hope that the worst excesses of neoliberal policies being implemented in other countries could be avoided; in so doing, they neglected the longer-run imperative of preserving their institutional base and social legitimacy. With a much smaller institutional status, falling membership and restrictions on their activities, unions' capacity to resist the further ratcheting-down of labour conditions was heavily undermined.

What are the prospects for change in this state of affairs? Australian unions have been weakened by years of government harassment, declining membership and free-riding. Yet the movement continues to mobilise against the worst abuses of the current regime, both economically and politically. New leadership at the ACTU has promised a sustained and focused campaign to rebuild unions' public profile and support, by linking the ongoing attacks against unions to the rise in inequality and the stagnation of wages and opportunity for millions of Australian workers. The objective economic conditions faced by Australian workers – widespread underemployment and casualisation, ubiquitous insecurity, unprecedented wage stagnation – create an environment in which unions' demands could, once again, resonate powerfully.

For the balance of power in employment relations to be shifted noticeably in workers' favour, the entire system of industrial relations will require wholesale revitalisation – not piecemeal, incremental reforms to existing practices. These wholesale changes would need to include greater freedom and protection for union activity, an effective enforcement and arbitration system, and provisions that allow unions to fund their activities fairly and sustainably, including remedies for the current epidemic of free-riding. The prospects for these changes to the world of work may be uncertain. But given the centrality of work to economic activity, and the centrality of labour policy to the overall neoliberal project, there is no doubt that debates and struggles in this realm will remain a core determinant of the broader evolution of neoliberalism in Australia.

Endnotes

1 *ABS Year Book Australia*, Catalogue 1301.0, various issues. Cooper and Ellem (2017) emphasise the importance of the formalised arbitration system to the foundation and growth of the Australian union movement.

2 Employee compensation includes wages, salaries, and employer super contributions

3 In particular, Humphrys and Cahill (2017) cite the unique and active role played by the Australian labour movement and the Labor Party in the implementation of neoliberalism.

4 Superannuation was originally conceived as a method of channelling labour compensation into a non-spendable pool of assets, in order to reduce the assumed inflationary effects of wage increases (Philips 2013).

5 Unions could of course make submissions and appeals regarding changes to the awards (like any other 'interest group'), but no longer held standing as full partners in their negotiation and arbitration.

6 This change also opened the door to widespread trading off of minimum standards in many collective agreements which has undermined the legitimacy of those agreements in the eyes of some workers (such as in the modern retail sector).

7 Fenwick and Howe (2009) point out, however, that the 1996 Act was the source of the more far-reaching restrictions on union security and union activity (including its prohibitions of union preference and membership clauses, and strong restrictions on union right of entry to workplaces). See also Riley and Sheldon (2008) and Forsyth (2006).

8 To be lawful, a term of an agreement must relate directly to the employment relationship. This prohibits a wide range of contract terms dealing with other issues including the actions of third-party firms (such as labour hire agencies), the general management of the business (including issues related to technological change), and others.

9 Initial applications of this stream have met with only limited success. See Cooper (2011).

10 Especially concerning have been repeated findings of underpayment and wage theft in numerous retail, hospitality, and agricultural workplaces, including underpayment of temporary foreign workers; see, for example, Berg and Farbenblum (2017) and Thornthwaite (2017).

11 Some experts have suggested Australia's restrictions on industrial action are among the most severe of any OECD economy (Long 2017).

12 Carney and Stanford (2018) review numerous dimensions of the growth of insecure work in Australia, which has been especially visible since the end of the mining investment boom after 2012.

13 Only Turkey and New Zealand experienced a greater decline in union membership as a proportion of employment since 1990; author's calculations from OECD (2017).

14 In 1974, the ABS reported a total of 6.3 million work days lost to industrial disputes, at a time when total employment in the economy was under 6 million. In 2016, the ABS reported only 125,000 lost days from total employment of over 11 million.

15 Author's calculations from ABS Catalogue 6333.0.

16 In fact the preponderance of free-riding is even greater than this, since many union members are not covered by an enterprise agreement.

REFERENCES

ABS (various) *Year Book Australia*, Catalogue 1301.0, Canberra.

——(2013) *Employee Earnings, Benefits and Trade Union Membership, Australia*, Catalogue 6310.0, Canberra.

——(2017) *Characteristics of Employment, Australia*, Catalogue 6333.0, Canberra.

——(2018a) *Australian National Accounts: National Income, Expenditure and Product*, Catalogue 5206.0, Canberra.

——(2018b) *Industrial Disputes, Australia*, Catalogue 6321.0, Canberra.

Berg, L. and Farbenblum, B. (2017) *Wage Theft in Australia: Findings of the National Temporary Migrant Work Survey*, 20 November. Sydney: Migrant Workers Justice Initiative.

Bray, M. and Stewart, A. (2013) 'From the arbitration system to the Fair Work Act: the changing approach in Australia to voice and representation at work', *Adelaide Law Review*, 34: 21–41.

Buchanan, J. and Considine, G. (2007) *The Evolution of Australian Workplace IR 1987–2007: Making Sense of Recent Policy and Practice*, Workplace Research Centre. Camperdown, University of Sydney.

Cahill, D. (2010) '"Actually Existing Neoliberalism" and the Global Economic Crisis', *Labour and Industry*, 20 (3): 298–316.

Cahill, D. and Konings, M. (2017) *Neoliberalism*. Hoboken, Wiley.

Carney, Shaun (1988) *Australia in Accord: Politics and Industrial Relations Under the Hawke Government*. Melbourne, Macmillan.

Carney, T. and Stanford, J. (2018) *The Dimensions of Insecure Work: A Factbook*. Sydney, Centre for Future Work.

Cooper, R. (2011) 'Can collective bargaining really lift workers out of low wages?' *The Conversation*, 24 May.

Cooper, R. and Ellem, B. (2017) 'Cold climate: Australian unions, policy, and the state', *Comparative Labour Law and Policy Journal*, 38 (415): 415–436.

Department of Jobs and Small Business, Australia (2018) *Trends in Federal Enterprise Bargaining*, Canberra.

Ewar, P., et al. (1992) *Politics and the Accord*. Leichhardt: Pluto Press.

Fenwick, C. and Howe, J. (2009) 'Union security after work choices' in Stewart, A. and Forsyth, A. (eds), *Fair Work: The New Workplace Laws and the Work Choices Legacy*. Sydney, Federation Press: 164–185.

Forsyth, A. (2006) 'Arbitration extinguished: the impact of the Work Choices legislation on the Australian Industrial Relations Commission', *Australian Bulletin of Labour*, 32 (1): 27–44.

Forsyth, A. and Holbrook, C. (2017) 'The prices and incomes accord', *The Conversation*, 24 April.

Goodwin, M. and Maconachie, G. (2011) 'Minimum labour standards enforcement in Australia: caught in the crossfire?', *The Economic and Labour Relations Review*, 22 (2): 55–80.

Harvey, D. (2005) *A Brief History of Neoliberalism*. Oxford, Oxford University Press.

Humphrys, E. and Cahill, D. (2017) 'How labour made neoliberalism', *Critical Sociology*, 43 (4–5): 669–684.

Kenyon, P. (1990) 'Insiders, outsiders and corporatism: an interpretation of the empirical evidence of the effects of the accord', Economics Programme Working Paper #45. Murdoch, Murdoch University.

Long, S. (2017) 'Have Australia's right to strike laws gone too far?' *ABC News Online*, 21 March.

McCrystal, S. (2010) *The Right to Strike in Australia*. Sydney, Federation Press.

Mitchell, R., Campbell, R. and Barnes, A. (2005) 'What's going on with the "no disadvantage test"? An analysis of outcomes and processes under the Workplace Relations Act', *Journal of Industrial Relations*, 47 (4): 393–423.

OECD (2017) 'Trade Union and Collective Bargaining Statistics', oecd.org/employment/collective-bargaining.htm

——(2018) *Employment and Labour Market Statistics*, Paris.

Orr, G.D. (2001) 'Agency shops in Australia? Compulsory bargaining fees, union security and the rights of the free rider,' *Australian Journal of Labour Law*, 14 (1): 1–27.

Peetz, D. (2005) 'Co-operative values, institutions and free riding in Australia: can it learn from Canada?', *Relations Industrielles/Industrial Relations*, 60(4): 709–736.

Peetz, D. and Baily, J. (2011) 'Neo-liberal evolution and union responses in Australia' in Gall, G., Wilkinson, A. and Hurd, R. (eds), *The International Handbook of Labour Unions: Responses to Neo-Liberalism*. Cheltenham, Edward Elgar.

Philips, K. (2013) 'Australia's strange history of superannuation', *Rear Vision*, ABC News, 23 April.

Reserve Bank of Australia Data (various) *Australian Economic Statistics 1949–1950 to 1996–1997, Occasional Paper No. 8*, Sydney.

Riley, J. and Sheldon, P. (eds) (2008) *Remaking Australian Industrial Relations*. Sydney, CCH Australia Limited.

Stanford, J. (2016) *Jobs and Growth … And a Few Hard Numbers: A Scorecard on Economic Policy and Economic Performance*. Sydney, Centre for Future Work.

——(2017) *Labour Share of Australian GDP Hits All-Time Record Low*. Sydney, Centre for Future Work.

Stewart, A. (2004) 'The AIRC's evolving role in policing bargaining', *Australian Journal of Labour Law*, 17 (3): 247–275.

Stewart, A. and Riley, J. (2007) 'Working around WorkChoices: collective bargaining and the common law', *Melbourne University Law Review*, 31 (3): 903–937.

Thornthwaite, L. (2017) 'The government needs to better enforce the laws it creates, to protect franchise workers', *The Conversation*, 2 March.

Weeks, P. (1995) *Trade Union Security Law: A Study of Preference and Compulsory Unionism*. Sydney, Federation Press.

Wilson, S. and Spies-Butcher, B. (2011) 'When labour makes a difference: union mobilization and the 2007 federal election in Australia', *British Journal of Industrial Relations*, 49 (s2): s306–s331.

World Inequality Database (2018) *Top 1% National Income Share, Australia, 1921–2015*, World Inequality Database, https://wid.world/.

CHAPTER 10

FINANCIAL DEREGULATION EXPOSES BANKING'S ANTISOCIAL CHARACTER

EVAN JONES

Financial deregulation has facilitated a banking sector prone to malpractice against customers. Regulatory authorities have been complicit, and self-regulation has been chimerical. Successive governments have avoided confronting the character of this ongoing malaise.

There is cause for mild optimism in some recent developments: bolstered by media exposure, the sheer scale of misconduct has generated a royal commission into the sector.

The 1981 Campbell Committee Report provided the bible for the ensuing and near-comprehensive deregulation of the finance sector. The ideological purity of the report's claims is both astounding and depressing. The otherwise extensive Committee inquiry failed to examine the historic reasons for the significant regulatory structure established in the sector after 1945. Times have changed, the report claimed: the current regulatory structure is dysfunctional. It was correct on both counts, but its erasure of the past coupled with its 'free market' preconceptions set the scene for a new structure whose dysfunctionality became immediately apparent.

A Special Sector

There is an implicit assumption in the Campbell Report's analysis and recommendations that banking is comparable to any other industry – to be treated by broad but hands-off regulatory principles. But banking is self-evidently unique. Banks lubricate economic exchange. Most fundamentally, bank credit creation expands societal purchasing power and business development. Banks are thus intrinsically public institutions.

In June 1991, the American investment banker Albert Wojnilower contributed to a Reserve Bank (RBA) conference on financial deregulation in Australia (see Wojnilower 1991). He argued that national financial systems inevitably serve a public purpose but are largely constituted by profit-oriented institutions. Sector-specific regulation is therefore inevitable, but there is no natural equilibrium. The system is innately unstable because the pursuit of profit, in tandem with innovation, undermines extant regulatory structures. Appropriate regulation has to be perennially refashioned to ensure that the public interest continues to be served. As Wojnilower claimed: the mere abolition of constraints will not automatically give birth to desirable new structures. Wojnilower's commonsense insights continue to be ignored.

The Campbell Report's *weltanshauung* was a Spencerian 'anarchy plus the constable' (Campbell 1981: 12). A government's role was merely to provide the background rule of law, and the enforcement of competition. The sole concession to sector specificity was the requirement for prudential regulation. Prudential regulation means that all covered financial institutions must hold as capital a percentage of its risk-weighted loans. The insistence on capital adequacy quanta exposes an implicit recognition that the finance sector, centred on banking, is unique – that the nature of this sector is that it is intrinsically capable of antisocial practices. But that implication has not been sufficiently thought through. That prudential regulation per se has not delivered the promises is evident, but the response of authorities has been a mere tweaking on the margins.

The False Promise of 'Competition'

The Campbell Report expressed a simple view of the merits of deregulation: that competition between providers would be sufficient to ensure that the facilities and terms desired by customers were made available. 'The Committee starts from the view', reads the Report's opening paragraph, 'that the most efficient way to organise economic activity is through a competitive market system which is subject to a minimum of regulation and government intervention' (1). The Committee, however, declined to outline its conception of 'competition'. While consumers may imagine that competition means 'the more banks the better' or, at worst, survival of the fittest, what has transpired has been the survival of the most powerful.

The banks took pre-emptive action. The Australia and New Zealand Banking Group Limited (ANZ) had been three distinct banks – the ANZ, the ES&A and Adelaide – a decade previously. In 1981, the Melbourne-based National Australia Bank (NAB) acquired the Commercial Banking Company of Sydney, and the Bank of New South Wales (renamed Westpac) acquired the Melbourne-based Commercial Bank of Australia. Both takeovers were facilitated because the mergers provision of the *Trade Practices Act* (section 50) had been significantly weakened by then Minister for Business and Consumer Affairs John Howard in 1978.

In 1985, Treasurer Paul Keating issued sixteen licenses for bank entry into Australia. The entrants found entry into retail and small business banking near impossible due to the expense of duplicating the extensive branch network. Bank numbers also swelled because of the conversion of building societies and the Colonial Mutual Life Assurance Society into banks, but the Trade Practices Commission (TPC), which became the Australian Competition and Consumer Commission (ACCC) in 1995, facilitated these successive takeovers and consolidation in the sector. By 2008, with the takeover of St George by Westpac and Bankwest by the Commonwealth Bank of Australia (CBA), the sector had returned to the previous model of Big Four–dominance, leavened only by a handful of marginal copycat banks.

Banks operate as de facto cartels. The sector's collective interest is funnelled through its powerful lobby, the Australian Banking Association (ABA). The banks don't compete on what matters – appropriate facilities and service. No bank has bothered to differentiate itself in terms of competence and integrity.

Competition was pursued in one particular arena – the uncontrolled expansion of housing loans to enhance market share, partly through gimmicks like discounted rates to new borrowers, and partly through other dubious means, like lowering the standards of borrower acceptability – whether corporate, small business, farm, or home mortgagor – or, at worst, fraudulently manipulating the process by using brokers to distance the bank from potential liability of adverse outcomes. For fear of pushing additional numbers of mortgagors into non-affordable repayment schedules and, consequently, into default, the RBA is now constrained in its discretionary ability to raise the cash rate for broad macro-economic purposes.

Banking Culture Before and After

The Campbell Report declined to contemplate the importance of banking culture. Several facets of the pre-deregulation age are relevant. Banking employment was essentially a lifetime career, with senior management conventionally promoted internally. This fostered a workforce culture of procedural familiarity, company loyalty and integrity. There was considerable training. Lending criteria were strict and tightly controlled.

During the 1970s, discretion was offered to loan managers in the form of 'delegated lending authorities' (DLAs). DLAs facilitated abuse, especially borrower asset valuation manipulations. Following deregulation in the 1980s, DLA limits were increased dramatically, with instructions to managers to 'lend, lend, lend.' 'Bottom line' (i.e. profit) imperatives led to a disinclination to engage in the expense of training lending staff to properly gauge prospective borrower viability. Front-line staff were forced into status and remuneration structures that pressured them into expanding their loan books and cross-selling on any terms. This pressure has led to the practice of bank staff themselves filling in important detail in a loan application, and knowingly including inaccurate information (with or without the knowledge of the borrower). Signatures have even been forged. Initially, these practices were done to enhance the prospect of a loan application approval at a more senior level, but such approvals have now been systematised, as I shall discuss further. Banking culture went from being relatively incorruptible to a world in which corruption has become an integral dimension of banking practices.

The Bank–Borrower Relationship

The sector-specific character of banking is most distinguished when we consider the structured relationship between parties. The relationship between bank lender and borrower is probably the most asymmetrical of all first-world commercial relationships. The bank essentially has the power of life and death over the borrower. Given the structural inability to raise equity capital, small and medium-sized enterprises (SMEs) are reliant upon borrowing. The sums involved are significant, frequently in the millions. Such debt portends an ongoing relationship involving prerogatives on the part of the lender. Legal academics have called such relationships 'incomplete contracts'.

For SMEs and farmers, a debt relationship involves a significant risk quotient. SMEs and farmers lack market power – indeed, they are the strategic target of exploitation by corporate business (see Jones 2011). Farmers also face the vicissitudes of weather. Loans are almost always based on security rather than on business prospects. The SME/farmer residence is the primary asset taken by the lender as security. Through its demand for such guarantees, the bank will take as much security as possible over borrower assets (effectively 'all money' guarantees), and over the borrower's family assets. If a bank initially holds security over SME business premises, bank staff will frequently engage in a ruse to tie the proprietor's residence to the business loan. If the bank decides to default the SME business, the bank appropriates the proprietor's residence as a 'bonus'.

This stratagem is a means by which the attendant risks of the lender-bank relationship are taken on as much as possible by the borrower. Lending on business prospects requires considerable investment in personnel training, which banks now seek to avoid in the interests of their bottom line. Post-deregulation, banks have become 'money lenders', with the lack of scruples that such a label implies. The asymmetry is multi-layered: the contract unequally binds parties whose relationship is rooted in asymmetry; the terms of the typical contract are all in the bank lender's favour; the complexity of the contract ensures that it will never be properly understood by the borrower, whatever external advice the latter pursues. In any event, the borrower has little choice, because the banks make comparable offerings.

Certain models of lender–borrower contracts are unconscionable per se. The prime example is the overdraft, that basic facility that is payable at call. Another example is the 'suspension clause' in the conventional contract, which dictates that all debt claimed by the lender must be repaid before a counterclaim by the borrower against bank malpractice can be pursued. Finally, the bank, as the most powerful party, can choose to break the terms of a contract at will, with myriad means at its disposal (Jones 2017b). The sanctity of the contract turns out to apply only for the weaker party. Most egregious has been the insertion by banks of 'non-monetary default clauses' into contracts, which allow the bank lender to trigger a default in cases even when the borrower has met the repayment schedules set out in their contract. For example, the bank may decide that the borrower's industry is facing more difficult trading conditions. Non-monetary default clauses are a means through which a bank's self-initiated discretion to default a borrower at will can be endowed with legitimacy, although such a clause further entrenches a relationship rooted in profound asymmetry.

From a policy perspective, the small business sector has long had an ambiguous status. When national consumer protection legislation was being mooted in 2008 by the Labor government, 'unfair contract' provisions relating to small-business contracts were being considered. Lobbying by corporate business prevailed, and the *National Consumer Protection Act* was legislated in 2009 without incorporating small business protection.

Bank attempts to maintain total control over lending to small business has a long history. Following the late 1980s, successive Hawke–Keating governments decreed that, save for the prudential arena, the banking sector would henceforth regulate itself. This was to be embodied in a banking ombudsman, established in 1989, and a code of banking practice first mooted in the early 1990s, but not established until 1996 and then largely under bank control. A parliamentary inquiry into banking recommended in November 1992 that 'an extension of the code to cover small business and rural customers also will be essential in rectifying damaged relationships in these areas' (Jones 2013). Small business coverage was omitted from both the ombudsman and the code. Small business and farmers were only belatedly included in the code in 2003. But the banks immediately set about neutering the code via duplicitous means (see Jones 2013).

A Code Compliance Monitoring Committee (CCMC) was established and given its own constitution in 2004; and a new code was subsequently established in May 2004. However, the committee's constitution hobbled both the committee and the code. Only when the committee itself complained of these constraints was the ruse publicly exposed and that situation righted. The code is now formally part of the loan contract, but banks continue to default borrowers in defiance of procedures contained in the revised code.

The asymmetry of power between bank lender and small business/farmer borrower is deeply entrenched and regularly reinforced due to a lack of assertive regulation of the sector. This asymmetry has an unexpected dimension. Banks will pursue the foreclosure of SME/farmer borrowers in situations where it would have been more profitable for the lender to maintain the relationship. This is especially the case when borrower assets are sold beneath their market value – a regular feature of bank foreclosures. Banks treat SME and farmers borrowers brutally, simply because they can.

Borrower Facilities

The conventional loan facilities offered to SMEs and farmers are not fit for purpose.

The SME borrower needs medium- to long-term finance, support in rocky times, and informed advice. These needs are enhanced in the case of family farmer borrowers (see Jones 2002). The bank lender, heavily dependent on short-term deposits and short-term borrowings, prefers short-term loans. The banking sector's operations are a legacy of the core institutions now underpinning the broader finance sector – trading banks, for whom short-term liabilities (deposits) match short-term assets (the overdraft facility) for short-term commercial needs. Previously distinct savings banks and building societies, structured for (long-term) housing mortgages, have been absorbed or transformed into all-purpose banks still dominated by trading bank culture. The *allfinanz* institutions that now dominate the entire economy through mergers and financialisation are themselves not fit for purpose.

The bill facility – the bank's preferred facility for the last several decades – has been pushed as an amenity that gives the borrower greater control over their borrowings. On the contrary: a bill facility is a short-term debt instrument for which the interest is paid up-front. Few SME/farmer borrowers understand them, and the necessity for their perennial renewal gives the lender the opportunity to make the terms more onerous upon turnover so as to default the customer at will.

In the case of home mortgages, problems are minimised if the facility is properly structured. But the bank preoccupation with market share (reinforced by bank officer remuneration structures being tied closely to the amount of business done) combined with the borrower's desperation for access to home ownership creates the potential for both formally decent facilities being pressed on unsuitable borrowers and structurally dysfunctional facilities being created. A tied sector of mortgage brokers has a self-interest in expanding the market beyond healthy limits.

Bank securitisation of home mortgages (the income stream, not the titles) has facilitated the dramatic escalation in mortgage loan finance. Securitisation involves the sale of a pool of mortgage-based cash flows as a security in return for immediate receipt of funds from the security investor. Mortgage securitisation took off in the late 1990s, reaching a peak in 2007, and fluctuating around $100 billion in total since then (RBA, 'Securitisation Vehicles').

New facilities have contributed to a 'permanent bubble' atmosphere – in particular, interest-only home mortgage loans and the 'low doc' loan. The latter is sold to households whose low income has previously denied them access to home finance.

In addition, some customers are targeted with sub-prime interest-only mortgages now pushed throughout the banking sector and on a large scale; these have become an integral dimension of corporate strategy. The 'asset rich income poor' (ARIPs) – home owners with low or no debt and low-income streams, typically elderly people – have been prime targets for these financial products. An expert in this sphere is Denise Brailey, of the Banking & Finance Consumers Support Association. Brailey notes that the process has long been regularised – applicants are permanently denied access to key sections of the documentation, borrower data is systematically fabricated, 'approval' is 'robo'-processed (without human input), loan-to-valuation ratios are dangerously extended, with an additional 'buffer' loan component hiding temporarily borrower inability to finance payments (Brailey 2017).

Such loans are set up to fail. According to Brailey, they make up a significant percentage of securitised mortgage packages. The banks do not release these details, and the authorities display no concern for the dangerous implications of the sub-prime component in securitised mortgage packages. How then is significant mortgage default consistent with relatively low 'impaired assets' ratios reported by the Australian Prudential Regulation Authority (APRA)? Many ARIPs are in limbo, in default but yet to be foreclosed. More generally, APRA relies on figures constructed and supplied by the lenders themselves, at their discretion. Such figures cannot be taken as legitimate.

Government Banks

The Campbell Report's approach to government-owned banks is shocking in its ignorance and prejudice (Campbell 1981: Ch.26). The report implied that no market gaps would exist if the existing regulatory structure was swept away and private institutions were not shackled from pursuing their natural instincts. Moreover, government-owned banks must seek and obtain commercial rates of return, ensuring 'competitive neutrality'. The report also made the claim that fiscal measures, achieved through the budget, were a preferable, non-market-distorting means of catering to social objectives – a ludicrous proposition.

Regarding the needs of particular sectors, of significance is the Commonwealth Development Bank (CDB), formed in 1959 from the merging of two Labor government initiatives – a rural bank created in 1943 and a small business bank created in 1945. The CDB lent more on business prospects than on customer asset security and employed specialist trained staff who took a hands-on approach to their clientele. Until the fateful late 1980s recession, its operations were generally profitable although the bank, because of its specialist orientation, did not earn a 'commercial' rate of return. The CDB was set up to fill a yawning 'market gap', but the private banks cried foul. It was dismantled in 1996, when the last tranche of the parent Commonwealth Bank of Australia was privatised, with the full support of the Liberal, National and Labor political parties (Jones 2001).

Private banks have never catered properly to SME or family farmer needs. Since the dismantling of the CDB and other farmer-specific institutions, private banks have readily proffered loans to these vulnerable sectors on the banks' own dysfunctional terms, defaulting many of them at will.

Legal Culture and the Courts

SMEs, farmers and home mortgagors defaulted and foreclosed by their bank lenders have the formal option to sue the lender in court. However, the foreclosed customer has often been stripped of assets and possibly bankrupted, and possesses a pittance at best. Law firms have no compunction in acting as ethics-free agents for banks.

The judiciary itself, steeped in contract law, is deeply prejudiced against the borrower's claims (see Jones 2017a): the borrower signed a contract to borrow a certain sum under certain conditions; the borrower is indebted to the bank; the bank wants the debt repaid; and the court rules in the bank's favour. Rarely does a judge inquire into the nature of the bank lender–borrower relationship.

There is a presumption that all parties to commercial relationships are in full command of relevant information and act rationally to pursue their own self-interest. But a peculiar inconsistency prevails. One the one hand, the parties are presumed to be of equal standing in the relationship. On the other hand, a party with an advantage over the other has a right to exploit that advantage to the full. The law of the jungle applies. A key banking law text claims that the lender–borrower relationship 'is based on contract and the parties deal at arm's length, with no obligation on either party to act with any higher duty to each other than that required by the law of the marketplace' (Tyree & Weaver 2006: 488). The courts have the equitable concept of 'duty of care' available, but the conditions of application of that concept have been dramatically narrowed into virtual irrelevance.

Deregulation Dissonance

The Campbell Report claimed that 'the Committee is satisfied that the financial system is fundamentally sound and stable' (1981: 12). From the earliest days of deregulation, the performance of the system diverged from that promise. The banks initiated loans in foreign currencies to SMEs and farmers, creating a toxic product with disastrous losses for borrowers, leading to a decade of court litigation. The banks rushed to lend intemperately to corporate mavericks. Some state-based savings banks, long regulated for prudence but now forcibly unleashed, were now bankrupt. By the late 1980s, bad debts and losses had put individual banks and the system itself at risk.

The Labor government responded to dissent by initiating a large-scale banking inquiry. However, the resulting report (Martin 1991) was a whitewash, ignoring myriad structural flaws associated with comprehensive deregulation. As noted, the government opted to reinforce a flawed system that operated via self-regulation.

Upon assuming office in mid-1996, the Howard government initiated another financial inquiry. The Wallis inquiry (1997) centred on the overlapping of previously separate sectors (notably banking and insurance) and the desirability of accommodating this development by fashioning inclusive regulatory structures. The inquiry was instructed to do a 'deregulation stocktake'. It asserted that 'deregulation has been beneficial for the financial system and its participants and for the wider economy' (Wallis 1997: 561), claiming spuriously that the disasters of the 1980s were the product of a system in transition.

However, no one on the Committee cared about the system 'under the hood'. A culture had been established in the banking sector in which senior management could be confident that incompetence and/or corruption had very minor chance of redress from either authorities or the courts. The much-vaunted reshaping of prudential regulation by the creation of APRA would prove ineffectual.

The Wallis Committee did recommend the centralisation and beefing up of retail consumer protection. Thus, in 1998 the Australian Securities Commission (ASC) was transformed into the Australian Securities and Investments Commission (ASIC), and given the brief of consumer protection in financial services. Simultaneously the House of Representatives Industry Committee was inquiring into the exploitation of small business through the imbalance of power in the marketplace. The bipartisan Reid Report, *Finding a Balance* (1997: ch. 5), contained evidence of the systematic failure of the deregulated and privatised finance sector to cater to SME needs. The Howard government legislated on several Reid Report recommendations, including the incorporation into the *Trade Practices Act* of a 'business unconscionability against business' clause, s51AC. After the passage of the *Financial Services Reform Act* in 2001, a copy of s51AC was incorporated into the ASIC Act as s12CC. Thus, ASIC now had formal oversight of business-to-business unconscionability in financial services.

In the ensuing years, bank malpractice has escalated. Courtesy of Fairfax Media coverage, we have been privy to a cascade of large-scale fraudulent practices by the CBA including:

- The underpinning then undermining of the Storm Financial scammers leading up to and following the global financial crisis (GFC);
- The foreclosure of hundreds of Bankwest-funded borrowers (mostly developers and hoteliers) after CBA's takeover of Bankwest in December 2008;
- The theft of investor nest eggs by the CBA's 'wealth management' arm Colonial First State and its subsidiary Commonwealth Financial Planning Ltd;
- The denial of legitimate claims by sick and dying clients against the CBA's insurance arm Comminsure; and
- The facilitation of large-scale money laundering via its strategically permissive ATM facilities.

The unconscionable or fraudulent default of SMEs and farmers has continued apace, but remains poorly reported. CBA senior management has shed crocodile tears and promised to do better. In some disclosures the bank steadfastly denies wrongdoing (the Bankwest foreclosures) and in others where failings are admitted (the Colonial First State scandal) the amount of compensation paid has been trivial. The CBA evidently plans to carry on with business as usual. In essence, the self-regulation mechanisms have been neutered, and the regulatory apparatus is indifferent or complicit.

Regulatory Failure

The banking ombudsman is now known as the Financial Services Ombudsman (FOS). FOS may resolve minor disputes for retail customers, but for SMEs/farmers it presents a bureaucratic nightmare. FOS's terms of reference regarding businesses are restrictive, and those limits are used in a discretionary fashion. FOS is funded by the banks, and the cases to which I have been privy show indisputably that FOS regularly acts in complicity with its funders.

The Code of Banking Practice has long been window dressing, with no tangible effect. However, when the National Australia Bank attempted to enforce a guarantee that had been improperly obtained, a judge decided for the respondent in the landmark case of *NAB v Rice* (2015), ordering that the code, as part of the loan contract, had legal status. The NAB claimed that the code was discretionary in its application and appealed the judgement, but the judgement was upheld in July 2016. Yet the *Rice* judgement appears to have had little impact in giving substance to the code's formal intent.

When the banking system itself was in crisis during the early 1990s and following the GFC in 2008, regulatory authorities choose to prop up the banks in the interests of system stability, without questioning structural flaws or responsibility. Customer victims are ignored as the price to pay for this 'higher goal'. ASIC has been complicit with the banks. ASIC has perennially responded to victim complaints with claims that their story is not significant enough to warrant a test case, or with the assertion that they are not empowered to treat their case. I have seen examples of such correspondence. ASIC has not taken a single case against a bank lender under s12 of its Act. In a Senate Impairment of Customer Loans Inquiry hearing on 23 November 2015, ASIC senior personnel admitted inaction, but claimed that it lacked the capacity to so act. On the Colonial First State 'wealth management' scandal, ASIC belatedly barred a handful of financial advisers, but whistleblower evidence highlighted ASIC's direct complicity with CBA management in failing to pursue this scandal to the root of the problem.

In the face of such disclosures and myriad personal complaints from victims to their parliamentary representatives, parliament (not the government) initiated a series of inquiries into the sectoral malaise. However, the typical report is overly generalised and abstract, avoids the details of victims' submissions, and makes some mild recommendations, which in turn are ignored or watered down by reigning governments.

For example, the Senate Economics Committee initiated an inquiry into ASIC's failings in 2014. Atypically, its sizeable report (Senate Economics References Committee 2014), was hard-hitting in its condemnation of ASIC's failings, albeit limited in scope to the wealth management scandal. But the official response to the report was oriented to ASIC's supposedly inadequate resources or to its inadequate powers to effectively intervene in matters of product suitability. The root problem – ASIC's dysfunctional culture – remains off the policy table.

A separate – and supposedly comprehensive – inquiry into the financial sector was initiated by the Abbott government (Murray Committee 2014). However, its treatment of 'consumer protection' (ch. 4) is risible. The report opines that alternative dispute resolution schemes are working well (on the contrary), that self-regulation is often superior to government regulation (it isn't), and that product providers need to lift their game in terms of accountability (they won't do this of their own accord). The small business and farmer borrower segments were, as usual, ignored.

The Murray Committee and Advisory Panel comprised bankers or business people. The Chair himself, David Murray, is personally culpable for the deterioration of the integrity and functionality of the banking system. Murray was appointed CBA CEO in 1992, during the Labor government's staged privatisation of the bank (1991/1993/1996), Murray presided over the destruction of the CBA's public role and its replacement by commercial imperatives, meaning profit maximisation on any terms.

Promising Signs and Appropriate Directions

Increasing dissatisfaction – indeed outrage – has led to a royal commission into the banking sector. The big four banks themselves induced Prime Minister Turnbull to establish the Commission, announced on 30 November 2017, but with terms satisfactory to the banks. One of the Turnbull government's diversionary moves has backfired. The Coalition beefed up a recently established federal small business unit into the Australian Small Business and Family Enterprise Ombudsman (ASBFEO), and installed Liberal Party functionary Kate Carnell as its head. Exposed to a myriad horror stories, Carnell has come out as a strong supporter of her supplicants.

After perennial victim complaints, 'unfair contracts' legislation was passed in November 2016 that forbade the use of non-monetary default clauses in loan contracts. The banks ignored the legislation, putting the lender–borrower asymmetry on full display. ASBFEO and (atypically) ASIC pressured the banks on this matter and, in August 2017, they belatedly agreed to remove such clauses from their loan contracts (Koehn 2017). The regulatory authorities will need to keep a permanent watch to ensure the banks adhere to the law.

The banks continue to treat the Code of Banking Practice as without substance, but judicial precedent provides hope that they will increasingly be bound by its constraints. FOS will soon be incorporated into a composite Australian Financial Complaints Authority; however, such an incorporation will change nothing unless the dysfunctionality regarding bank disputes mediation is consciously addressed.

ASIC has the legislative empowerment to pursue bank unconscionability. The new chairman, James Shipton, is a former Goldman Sachs banker. If Shipton decides to use this power, he will be breaking precedent. ASIC's charter needs to be complemented by the establishment of a specialist unit, possibly within the Australian Federal Police, devoted to the investigation of fraud within the financial sector, an area that currently is scandalously ignored.

Another positive step is the issuance of a parliamentary report into the penalties for white-collar crime (Senate Economics References Committee 2017). Although general in its coverage and recommendations, it ups the ante for the authorities to legislate so that penalties in this arena fit the seriousness of the crimes perpetrated.

Hearings of the Royal Commission since February 2018 have confirmed the malaise in the Australian finance sector. Over 6500 submissions have been received. Further appalling stories of the maltreatment of those seeking investment advice have been aired. Parents who have given guarantees for loans to a child's business have seen their own residences appropriated when the business has been foreclosed. The Commission has been unprepared for the scale and brutality of bank treatment of small business and farmer borrowers. The limited time conferred by the government to the hearings is a major factor inhibiting the Commission's capacity in these sectors. In all likelihood, the ongoing clamour from such victims will lead to the government acceding to the renewal of the Commission's mandate in 2019, even if it does so reluctantly.

References

Brailey, D. (2017) personal communication, 17–28 November.

Campbell (1981) Committee of Inquiry, *Australian Financial System, Final Report*, September.

Jones, E. (2001) 'A sorry saga of reform off the rails', *The Canberra Times*, 6 August.

——(2002) 'Rural finance in Australia: a troubled history', *Rural Society* 12 (2): 160–181.

——(2011) 'The Market Mechanism in Reality and Myth: Corporate Overlordship of Small Business', *Journal of Australian Political Economy*, 68, December.

——(2013) 'The NAB, Small Business and the Wilful Ignorance of Judges', *Independent Australia*, 16 June.

——(2017a) 'Chief Justice Kiefel and the Banks', *bankvictims.com.au*, 18 February.

——(2017b) *Submission, consumer protection in the banking, insurance and financial sector inquiry*, Senate Economics Committee, No. 87, 7 March.

Koehn, E. (2017) 'Fairer terms for small business loans locked in as the big four banks sign off on contract changes', *smartcompany.com.au*, 23 August.

Martin (1991) Committee, *A Pocket Full of Change: Banking and Deregulation*, November.

Murray (2014) Committee, *Financial System Inquiry Final Report*, November.

National Australia Bank v Rice (2015), Victorian Supreme Court, VSC 10, 26 March.

Reserve Bank of Australia (ongoing), 'Securitisation Vehicles', Table B19, column B.

Reid (1997) Committee, *Finding a Balance: towards fair trading in Australia*, May.

Senate Economics References Committee (2014), *Performance of the Australian Securities and Investments Commission*, June.

——(2017) *Lifting the Fear and Suppressing the Greed: Penalties for White-Collar Crime and Corporate and Financial Misconduct in Australia*, March.

Tyree, A. and Weaver, P. (2006), *Weerasooria's Banking Law and the Financial System in Australia*, 6th edn. Chatswood, Lexis Nexis.

Wallis (1997) Committee, *Financial System Inquiry Final Report*, March.

Wojnilower, A. (1991) 'Some principles of financial deregulation: lessons from the United States', in Ian Macfarlane (ed.), *The Deregulation of Financial Intermediaries*, Reserve Bank of Australia.

CHAPTER 11

HOUSING IN AUSTRALIA: THE GAME OF HOMES

PETER PHIBBS AND NICOLE GURRAN

You would have to be living on another planet not to have heard about the housing price rises in Australia over the decade to 2017. This asset price bubble has particularly affected the major east coast capital cities and nearby regional centres (see Figure 1).

Australian governments at all levels have responded to public anxiety about the issue with expressions of concern and the release of policies targeting housing affordability.[1] Many Australian politicians describe it as a simple problem of demand and supply, with the solution being to unlock supply. This usually involves calls to reform – and especially liberalise – the planning system to reduce pressure on prices.

This chapter finds that the inadequate supply argument misdiagnoses the causes of the current housing price bubble and that politicians and other groups are, in fact, strongly motivated to favour high and rising house prices. Seen from this perspective, the inadequate supply argument can be viewed primarily as a means to delay and avoid addressing the prime causes of the price bubble. The losers in this process are low-income groups and younger generations who are struggling to achieve the great Australian dream of home ownership. This situation amounts to a cruel 'game of homes' that has made large amounts of money for the privileged housing 'insiders' while delivering a bleak future for outsiders. It creates a precarious economic future for younger people, hardship for many Australian households on low and moderate incomes, increasing levels of homelessness, and has the potential to shift costs from housing insiders to taxpayers, given the likely rise in demand for public housing and public subsidies for private rental accommodation in the future.

FIGURE 1.

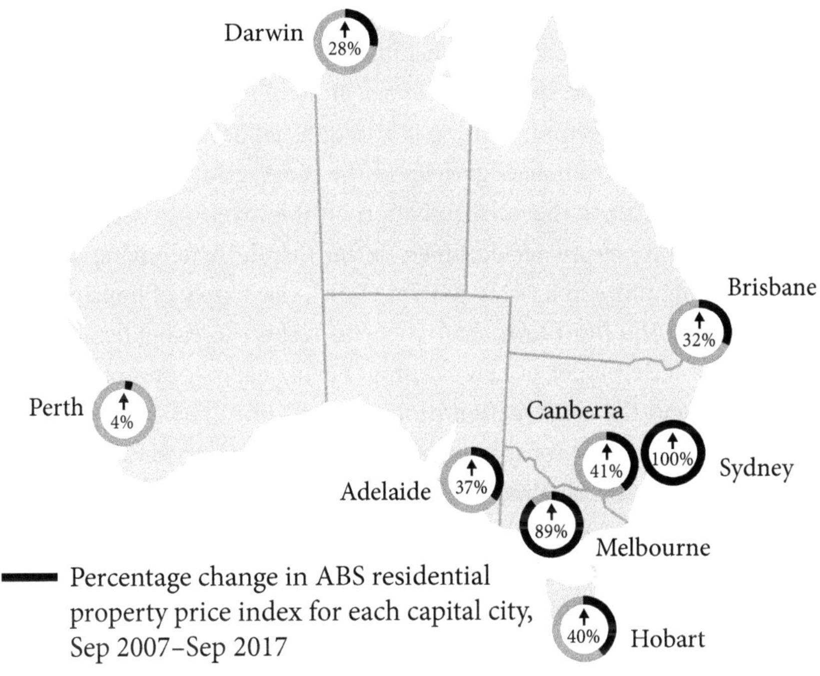

Source: ABS 2017a

Housing as an Unusual Economic Commodity

Housing is an essential commodity like food, health services and education. What makes it essential is that minimum supply is necessary for survival. Again, like other essential commodities there are markets for housing that determine supply and prices; but there is also some degree of government involvement in housing provision, as is the case with other essentials, like food, health and education. In the case of health services and education, government supply dominates, while in the case of food, the government regulates quality and indirectly supports demand through the welfare safety net.

The market for housing and the potential means that government may intervene in it are different to these other essential services and commodities in some important respects. First, housing is a long-term durable commodity; but, especially since the deregulation of the financial system in the 1980s and the enactment of other neoliberal policies, it is also a distinct asset class generating both income and capital gains. Like other asset classes such as shares, speculation and sentiment are key drivers of capital gains and losses. Second, housing is also unusual because, as the price of the existing stock of houses goes up in the short term, demand also goes up. This reflects the role of speculation on the investor market and, for upgraders and new owner-occupiers, a fear that delay in buying now will mean paying more in a rising market. Third, the supply of housing stock is, at least in the short term, inelastic with respect to rising demand and prices. For a developer of new housing, raising capital, gaining planning approvals and the construction process takes time, particularly as more housing stock consists of apartments, which are much slower to construct. The flip side to this is that, due to developers' ebullient expectations of future demand, the 'pipeline' of housing supply can overshoot actual medium-term demand, leading to boom and bust cycles, particularly in the new apartment market and in commercial property.

Players in the Game of Homes

Winners and Losers

It is useful to reflect on the main stakeholders operating in the housing space and how their position in the housing market shapes their view on house affordability. Table 1 summarises the various players and their motivation for favouring rises or falls in the housing property market.

Because Australia has historically been a nation of homeowners, most Australian adults have a vested interest in a rising housing market because it creates the perception that their wealth is increasing. This perception among 'middle Australia' (those whose wealth and income falls above the

Table 1. Property bubbles: who's for, who's against, and why

Players favouring higher prices	Motivation
Homeowners	• Increased wealth • Housing security • Financial security • Intergenerational wealth transfer
'Mum and dad' investors	• Secure investment • Intergenerational wealth transfer • Tax benefits
Property developers and commercial investors	• Reduced development risk with strong capital gains • Increased profits
Property lobby groups	• Encourages reduced controls on property development
Banks	• Reduced lending risk by capital gains on loan collateral • Increased size of individual loans and growth in the number of investors
Federal politicians	• Creates the perception of a strong economy which improves the mood of the electorate • Financially benefits 'middle Australia', most of whom are homeowners
State politicians	• Increased revenue through stamp duty
Newspapers with real estate advertising	• Increased sales • Provides a buffer against declining revenue from print media
Real estate agents/buyers' agents	• Increased commission and turnover

bottom 20 per cent, and below the top 20 per cent), favours incumbent governments because it creates the impression in a key section of the electorate that public policy is well managed.

Table 1. cont.

Players favouring lower prices	Motivation
Non-homeowners and people on low to moderate incomes	• Increased opportunity to enter the housing market • Reduced risk of remaining in the sub-optimal rental market • Increased opportunity to benefit from government housing subsidies • Possibility of reduced taxes if capital gains concessions are eliminated • Reduced risk of higher work commute travel costs
Parents of non-homeowners	• Increased opportunities for offspring to become financially independent • Reduced risk of higher travel costs to visit offspring (and their children)

Why Politicians Blame Inadequate Supply

The most common explanation of rapidly rising housing prices cited by our federal politicians is inadequate supply. Michael Sukkar (2017) an assistant minister in the Turnbull Coalition government, expressed a representative view:

> While the Government is examining all of the causes of Australia's housing affordability problems, it's widely accepted by all levels of government that the lack of housing supply has been a primary driver of these issues. So, addressing the endemic supply side issues that are inhibiting people from entering the market must be the key policy objective.

For a federal politician, lack of supply is an attractive diagnosis because it has a number of benefits. First, it sounds logical and a bit technical, and therefore carries some authority. Second, housing supply, especially as it is influenced by factors such as land availability and planning regulations, is primarily a state government issue, so federal politicians can shift responsibility onto the states. This is especially useful if most of the political parties in power in the states are from a different political party (which they often are). Third, framing inadequate supply as a planning problem lets federal politicians off the hook for not having any coherent national housing policy, and reduces pressure to fund social housing provision. Fourth, increasing supply is consistent with the dominant neoliberal ideology as it suggests a market-based solution is optimal to the problem of housing affordability. Also, framing the problem in his way allows neoliberal politicians to advocate for reduced planning red tape, without needing to dismantle property and investment settings, which are favoured by wealth developers and business interests, as discussed further below. Finally, identifying the problem as one of supply aligns politicians with the development lobby and business interests who are therefore more likely to support their party, including through political donations.

The Supply-Side Argument

There are two main supply-side explanations of the house price bubble: inadequate dwelling construction and planning red tape that constrains supply. Both of these explanations are wrong.

The Problem is a Housing Shortage

Establishing that there is a shortage of homes in Australia or an imbalance in the supply/demand relationship requires complex statistical analysis involving estimations of population growth, household size, and existing and projected dwelling numbers. Many commentators simply show graphs of population growth and compare it to dwelling completions and declare a shortage. However, the calculus is more complex than that; a key issue is what demand for new dwellings the population increase will generate. To accurately identify the adequacy of housing supply requires modelling of how projections of population growth will generate housing demand based on existing or forecast estimates of the living arrangements of the population, and estimates of household size; these estimates must then be compared with figures on the actual number of dwellings built over time. If new builds are less than the projections of demand, then a shortage of housing can be declared. Many of these models are based on the concept of 'underlying demand', where the demand for housing is separated from any notion of market conditions, including price.

This kind of modelling has been undertaken by the New South Wales Treasury (2016) and the National Housing Supply Council (2011), which both suggest that Australia does have a problem of housing supply. However, closer scrutiny reveals that these analyses missed three important factors: recent changes in household size; the impact of renovations on dwelling size; and a growth in student accommodation. When these factors are taken into account, a different picture emerges.

Changes in household size impact on the demand for housing, with larger households reducing demand and smaller households increasing it. Many factors influence household size, including the demographic profile of the population, immigration patterns, fertility patterns and changes in the financial capacity of families. In its modelling of housing demand, the National Supply Council used 2006 census data to estimate household sizes. Their dwelling projections, they explained, were

> not constrained by any supply-side factors such as availability of land, the number of vacant dwellings, construction of new dwellings and affordability. Our approach is to project housing demand on the basis of current and recent trends in demand inputs. (McDonald and Temple 2008: 3)

More recent census data shows there have been small but significant increases in household size, which means that dwelling demand estimates from both the National Supply Council and the NSW Treasury models are overestimates. The NSW Treasury model is particularly interesting. It used 2006 census data, with a small average household size generating a large demand for housing, since they considered the increase in household size was a temporary phenomenon associated with the global financial crisis (GFC). Accordingly, their model predicts a shortage of 100,000 dwellings in New South Wales. However, the results from the 2016 census reveal that for New South Wales, person per dwelling figures have actually increased. If the model had used the 2016 figures for persons per household, it would have in fact shown a small *surplus* in housing supply, rather than a shortage.

For Sydney itself household size changes have been even more marked. There was a significant increase in persons per household to 2.8 persons per household in 2016, compared with 2.7 in 2011 (ABS 2017b). Current dwelling targets in Sydney adopted by the NSW government assume that in the future the number of persons per household will decrease. For example, they assume that by 2021 the household size in Sydney will be 2.65.[2] If continuing affordability pressures increased the 2016 figure to 2.85 by 2021, this increase in household size in 2021 we could accommodate an additional 380,000 people in Sydney within the existing dwelling stock.

Second, Australian dwellings are able to accommodate an increase in household size because of the large size of Australian houses – we now have the second largest houses in the developed world (CommSec 2017). Between 1960 and 2010 the size of new homes in Australia more than doubled (Kearns 2012), although since then they have reduced by about 10 per cent as apartments have become more popular (CommSec 2017). In 1970, about 13 per cent of dwellings had four bedrooms compared to 30 per cent in the 2016 Census (ABS 2017b). This means that Australian dwellings can cope with the small increases in persons per dwelling we have seen over the last ten years in major cities – we are hardly generating massive overcrowding. For example, even with the small increase in household size, the 2016 census results for Sydney show that we still have on average no more than one person per bedroom.

Third, the modelling makes no allowance for the increasing size of dwellings as a result of renovations. The HIA (2017) estimates that the national market for home renovations is about $33 billion. In a market where transaction costs, especially stamp duties, are very high and owner-occupied housing is sheltered from tax (Yates 2016), many households have chosen to renovate rather than move as their circumstances change. When comparing population growth to dwelling completions in any year, we need to acknowledge additional housing capacity generated through additions to existing dwellings.

Fourth, population growth estimates include net overseas migration. This comprises both permanent migration and temporary migration. The largest contribution to net overseas migration in recent years has been from people on temporary visas – comprised mostly of international students and temporary skilled migrants (Phillips, Klapdor and Simon-Davies 2010: 1). The number of international higher education and VET enrolments in Australia rose from 128,768 in 2002 (in a period of lower net overseas migration) to 457,437 in 2018, with current growth in international student numbers sitting at about 15 per cent per annum (Department of Education and Training 2018). Although these numbers have a direct impact on housing demand, many international students live in purpose-built student accommodation, although such dwellings are not included in ABS counts of dwelling completions. This type of accommodation has been growing rapidly with property advisory firm Knight Frank (2018) estimating the total national supply to be 94,000 beds at the end of 2017, with a further 40,000 beds in the development pipeline (Savills 2017).

Changes in household size, the magnitude of housing additions and their impact on the size of dwellings, and the growth of student accommodation are confounding factors that should be taken into account in models comparing population growth and dwelling completions. But these are absent from these analyses. This failure seriously undermines claims that Australia faces a dwelling shortage.

A final reason to be sceptical of claims of long-run supply shortages is that, as noted earlier, there is an inherent disequilibrium in the relationship between demand and supply, with temporary periods of over and under supply. For example, Figure 2 shows that Sydney dwelling completions were very low in the period 2007 to 2012, but this followed a phase when the city was recovering from a surplus of dwellings from 2000 to 2006. In 2004, the total population growth in Sydney was about 21,000 people while the number of dwellings grew by 23,000. This oversupply was one of the reasons that, despite the substantial growth in population size from 2007, dwelling prices fell in 2008, related to the GFC, and then fell again in 2011.

FIGURE 2. POPULATION GROWTH AND DWELLING COMPLETIONS IN SYDNEY, 1982 TO 2016

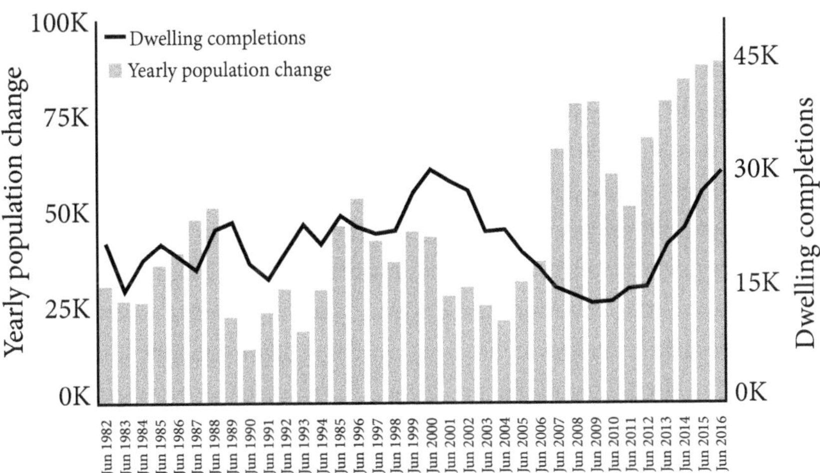

Source: planning.nsw.gov.au/Research-and-Demography/Research/Housing-Monitor-Reports/Metropolitan-Housing-Monitor-Sydney-Region

The Problem is Planning Red Tape

The argument that Australia's inflated housing market is the result of an undersupply of housing also supports efforts by corporate investors and property developers to reduce planning controls. Over the last ten years many voices have claimed that the main reason houses are expensive in Australia is because of the restrictions placed on supply by the planning system (Gurran and Phibbs 2015). Many orthodox economists think that planning and zoning controls are the last non-market bastion that neoliberalism hasn't been able to sweep away.

In this climate, the Council of Australian Governments (COAG) formed the Housing Supply and Affordability Reform (HSAR) Working Party to examine housing supply and government policy. The Working Party found that uncertainty, delays and costs in securing planning approval 'typically lower the overall supply and delivery of housing to the market, thereby reducing housing affordability' and that 'reforms that remove impediments to housing supply will remove unwarranted pressure on house prices' (COAG Reform Council 2012: 2–3).

The Property Council (2017: 12) mounted a very similar argument: So why is the average home in Melbourne just $566,000, but $785,000 in Sydney? The answer is supply. Put simply, Melbourne has been far better in planning for and delivering new housing than Sydney for nearly two decades.

The red-tape argument appeals to a development industry keen to enjoy a lower regulatory burden, and to state and federal treasury departments unwilling to commit increased funding to affordable housing provision, or to attempt politically unpopular tax reforms. It also takes the focus off other issues for government, like its abandonment of social housing.

There is little if any empirical evidence that the planning system is a supply bottleneck. In Sydney in 2016–17, dwelling approvals were 56,800 (ABS 2017a), but dwelling completions were around about 35,000 dwellings (see Figure 2). Other data shows that in New South Wales the quarterly number of dwellings approved but not yet commenced increased from an annual average of 43,480 for the period from 2008 to 2012, to a total of 80,308 in 2016–17 (ABS 2017c). These figures show that the planning system has responded to signs of rising house prices and delivered building approvals at record levels. Given these are annual figures, the stock of unused approvals in Sydney and Melbourne are likely to be in the order of more than 100,000 approvals in each city.[3] If there are some supply bottlenecks this suggests that it is not planning regulations that are the main problem. Nationally, the planning system has delivered in response to the surge in prices. Figure 3 shows that monthly private residential building approvals are at all-time highs. So, far from being a brake on housing supply, it seems that, under the right circumstances, the planning system can deliver planning approvals to support supply.

The limited role of reducing planning bottlenecks on dwelling prices was acknowledged by the Productivity Commission, who made the following observation about the price boom experienced at the turn of the new millennium:

> In the Commission's judgment, given the small size of net additions to housing in any year relative to the size of the stock, improvements to land release or planning approval procedures, while desirable, could not have greatly alleviated the price pressures of the past few years. (Productivity Commission 2004: 154)

Figure 3. Private residential building approvals, 1991 to 2017

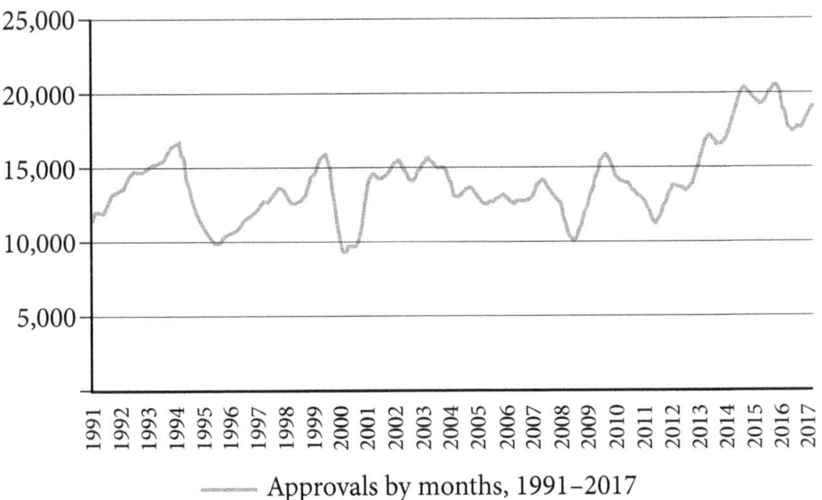

Source: ABS 2017c

The Real Causes of the Property Price Bubble

The Role of Interest Rates

When interest rates go down, the purchasing power of the buyer goes up. This has been a critical component of house price movements across the world since 2011. In Australia interest rates are currently at a forty-year low, producing rapid growth in real estate speculation, with the support of a very co-operative banking sector. The bank indicator rate for new owner-occupied homes fell from 11 per cent in 1996 to just over 5 per cent in 2017 (RBA 2017). Since the price of a mortgage is really the cost of repayments, this reduction in interest payments was equivalent to a sharp growth in demand. This has been the main driver of the most recent housing price boom.

This point was acknowledged by a previous RBA governor. Speaking to a parliamentary committee, Ian Macfarlane said:

> The first question is why have the prices of the eight million houses in Australia basically doubled over the last decade? The answer to

> that one, I think, is almost entirely on the demand side. Basically, because we returned to low inflation, interest rates were halved. People could now borrow, if they wished, twice as much. They did not have to borrow twice as much; they could have taken it in lower debt servicing if they had wanted to, but there were a whole lot of incentives in the system that meant they borrowed twice as much. The incentives were mainly tax incentives, plus a history of high inflation. So they borrowed the money and drove up house prices, so the whole stock of eight million houses basically doubled in price. (House of Representatives 2006)

Financial Deregulation and the Transformation of Banks into Building Societies

As providers of mortgages to those seeking to enter the housing market as investors or home owners, the banking sector plays a key role in shaping housing markets. Australian banks today have changed radically from their traditional role as all-purpose banks, to more closely resemble building societies.[4] This shift in focus away from lending to the business sector and towards the housing market began in the early 1990s and was the result of a number of factors (Debelle 2010). First, banks retreated from business lending during the savage recession of the early 1990s due to large losses, but losses on their housing loans were relatively mild. Second, demand for credit from the corporate sector declined as the sector underwent a period of deleveraging. Third, the introduction of the Basel Accord 1 in 1988 to regulate banking saw a change in the risk weighting in favour of housing assets. Prior to this, Australia used a capital-to-asset ratio for measuring the capital adequacy of banks, which gave banks an incentive to invest in riskier but higher yielding assets. Under the new risk-based approach, housing loans were given a risk weight of 50 per cent, whereas business and personal loans had a risk weight of 100 per cent. Banks were required to satisfy the new capital adequacy requirements by 1992, but as early as 1990 they had taken steps to increase their capital bases to the required levels.

As a result of these factors, banks focused on housing loans and decreased their activity in business lending: housing loans now account for over 63 per cent of the credit outstanding for major banks (APRA 2018) compared to 54 per cent in 2004.

The implications of unrestrained credit creation directed at finite assets are self-evident. Adair Turner (2015: 73), a previous chairman of the United Kingdom Financial Services Authority (FSA), described the issue in the following terms:

> Banks, unless constrained by policy, have an infinite capacity to create credit, money and purchasing power … But the supply of locationally desirable real estate (and ultimately land) is always somewhat inelastic and in some cities close to fixed. Potentially infinite nominal demand and finite supply combine to make the price of locationally specific real estate indeterminate and potentially volatile. The resulting credit and asset price cycles are not just part of the story of financial instability in modern economies, they are its very essence (2015: 73).

The Role of Taxation

In Australia, as in other comparable countries, the impact of low interest rates and readily available credit has been compounded by tax regimes that further stimulate demand for housing. Australia has a particularly favourable tax treatment of property investors through the combination of negative gearing and the 50 per cent capital gains discount introduced in 1999 (Yates 2016).

With capital gains taxed less than income, investors have preferred investments with strong capital returns. Many investors have been attracted to property despite its low annual returns from rental income because of their expectation of lighter taxes. The contribution of rapid growth in the investor market to housing price pressure is evident in Figure 4, which shows the ratio of investor loan approvals to owner-occupier approvals. Note that the two periods when the ratio approaches or exceeds one, corresponds with the two periods of strongest price growth.

FIGURE 4: THE RATIO OF INVESTOR AND OWNER-OCCUPIER LOAN APPROVALS IN AUSTRALIA, 1991–2017

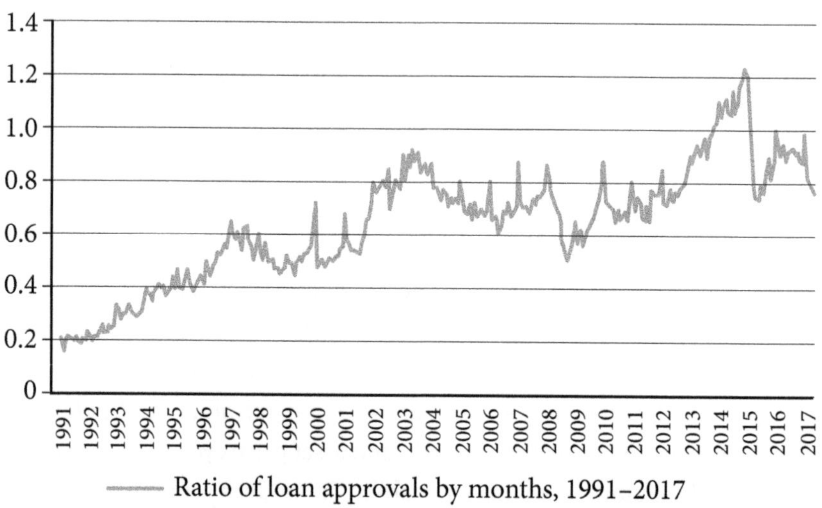

Source: Author's analysis of ABS (2017d)

Two periods of easing investor activity at the end of 2015 and in early 2017 coincided with action by the Australian Prudential Regulation Authority (APRA, the bank regulator) to reduce investor activity and the rate of dwelling price growth. Despite many economic commentators urging the federal government to change their taxation settings to moderate price growth, such taxation reforms have been resisted.

Changes in Social Housing

Neoliberal public policy has not only encouraged governments to frame the housing price bubble in terms of a planning problem, but also to cut its investment in public housing under the rationale that the market would fill this gap. While there has been a substantial increase in the total population and the total number of dwellings in the country, the stock of social housing – currently around 400,000 dwellings – has barely grown since the turn of the century. As a result, the proportion of dwellings in public rental has declined from 5.1 per cent of Australia's total housing stock in 2001 to just over 4 per cent today (Ong et al. 2017).

Left to its own devices, the market seems incapable of providing low-income housing stock. A recent report by The Australian Housing and Urban Research Institute (AHURI) analysed new housing supply constructed over the period from 2005 to 2014. It found that:

> Most of the growth in housing supply has been taking place in mid-to-high price segments, rather than low price segments. There seems to be structural impediments to the trickle-down of new housing supply. (Ong et al. 2017: 1)

AHURI's report concluded that policy interventions were needed in order to secure an adequate supply of affordable housing in the locations where it is most needed – the major capital cities – and in places were transport and employment are accessible.

Inadequate aggregate housing supply is not a major factor explaining the most recent housing price bubble. Rather, it is the outcome, directly and indirectly, of a number of mutually reinforcing neoliberal policies that, in combination, work to increase wealth inequality in Australia. These direct policies include the financial deregulation that has allowed banks access to vastly increase loanable funds and has permitted them to expand lending into speculative areas like housing, thereby creating system stability risks and increasing income and wealth inequity; the variety of tax concessions favouring speculation; and a dependence on monetary policy to stimulate the economy in times of economic downturn.

When governments exploit the 'inadequate housing supply' argument they obfuscate the real causes of the price bubble. This only benefits the winners in the game of homes, and does nothing for those locked out of the market. Reducing regulation – for example, permitting ever-smaller apartment floor plans – lowers the quality of accommodation without necessarily lowering prices or reducing rents. Allowing the development of housing in poorly serviced urban fringes means low-income workers and first home buyers are disadvantaged further by living far from employment centres. These strategies create large profits for developers and bankers, but generate large liabilities for taxpayers.

Measures to Improve the Australian Housing Market

If governments were serious about addressing these problems, there are a number of initiatives that could be taken to help slow price growth in Australian housing markets.

- Tax reform such as removing negative gearing and the 50 per cent capital gains tax concession on housing would eliminate the 'distortion' favouring investors over owner-occupiers. These could be replaced with specific tax incentives to create additional affordable housing supply, especially to overcome the current market failure in the supply of low-income homes.
- The planning system can increase affordable housing supply by requiring new developments to have a proportion of housing at lower price points for purchase or rent.
- Encourage institutional investment in housing, particularly from superannuation funds. These funds require stable, low-risk (but not necessarily high-return) asset options to cover pension annuity liabilities. This would be assisted by giving individuals in super funds an 'affordable housing' investment option.
- Use the prudential powers of the bank regulator to reduce investor exuberance when housing prices are climbing excessively.
- Increase government social housing and subsidies for housing construction by not-for profit entities, especially at the bottom of the housing cycle, when construction resources are in oversupply.
- Reduce the dependence on monetary policy in economic downturns to stimulate the economy.

Given the large number of players in the game of homes who are 'winning' from increasing house prices, we are not anticipating major policy change unless there is a effective coalition of those who are the losers in the game of homes.

Recent government responses to housing problems have come to resemble 'busy work': exhibiting and absorbing policy energy while at the same time constraining the suite of policy options and tools able to really address the housing affordability problems affecting low-income renters and aspiring owners in Australia.

Endnotes

1 The Victorian government released their package in March 2017 (www.vic.gov.au/affordablehousing.html), followed by the federal government, who announced a package as part of their May Budget (www.budget.gov.au/2017-18/content/glossies/factsheets/html/HA_11.htm). The New South Wales government announced a package in June 2017, focusing on first home buyers (www.nsw.gov.au/improving-nsw/projects-and-initiatives/first-home-buyers/).

2 See the Planning Region Households and Housing sheet at www.planning.nsw.gov.au/Research-and-Demography/Demography/~/media/14819B12DA0846238E8F8F63A3256701.ashx.

3 Development approvals remain valid for five years in New South Wales, and longer if substantial commencement of the project has occurred.

4 See Chapter 10 of this volume on financial deregulation and the culture of the banking sector by Evan Jones.

References

APRA (2018) *Quarterly Authorised Deposit Taking Institutions Performance Statistics* 21, June 2018. Canberra, Australian government.

Australian Bureau of Statistics (2017a) *Residential Property Price Indexes: Eight Capital Cities, Sep 2017, cat no. 6416.0*. Canberra, Australian Government.

——(2017b) *General Community Profile, Sydney Greater Capital City Statistical Area, 2016 Census Results*. Canberra, Australian Government.

——(2017c) *Building Activity, Australia, Jun 2017, cat. no. 8752.0*. Canberra, Australian Government.

——(2017d) *Housing Finance, Australia, Oct 2017 Cat no. 5609.0*. Canberra, Australian Government.

COAG Reform Council (2012) *Housing Supply and Affordability Reform*, COAG Housing Supply and Affordability Reform Working Party, 3 September. Canberra, Australian Government.

CommSec (2017) 'Australian home size hits 20-year low', *Economic Insights*, 17 November.

Debelle, G. (2010) *The State of the Mortgage Market*, address by Assistant Governor (Financial Markets), Reserve Bank of Australia, to the Mortgage Innovation Conference, Sydney, 30 March.

Department of Education and Training (2017) *International Student Data, 2017*. Canberra, Australian Government.

Gurran, N. and Phibbs, P. (2015) 'Are governments really interested in fixing the housing problem? Policy capture and busy work in Australia', *Housing Studies*, 30 (5): 711–729.

Housing Industry Association Limited (2017) *Home Renovations – Australia's Next Building Boom?* Media release, Housing Industry Association Limited, 23 March 2017. Canberra, Australian Government.

House of Representatives, Standing Committee on Economics, Finance and Public Administration (2006) *Hansard*, Canberra, Parliament of Australia, 18 August.

Kearns, J. (2012) 'The Outlook for Dwelling Investment', address by Head of Economic Analysis, Reserve Bank of Australia, to the Australian Business Economists' lunchtime briefing, Sydney, 13 November.

McDonald, P. and Temple, J. (2008) Projections of Housing Demand in Australia, 2006–2021, report prepared for the National Housing Supply Council, Australian Demographic and Social Research Institute. Canberra, Australian National University.

National Housing Supply Council (2011) *State of Supply Report 2011*, Department of Sustainability, Environment, Water, Population and Communities, Canberra, Australian Government, 1 December.

New South Wales Treasury (2016) *Intergenerational Report, Budget Paper No. 5, NSW Budget 2016–17*. Sydney, New South Wales Government.

Ong, R., Dalton, T., Gurran, N., Phelps, C., Rowley, S. and Wood, G. (2017) *Housing supply responsiveness in Australia: distribution, drivers and institutional settings*, Inquiry into Housing Policies, Labour Force Participation and Economic Growth for the Australian Housing and Urban Research Institute, *Australian Housing and Urban Research Institute Final Report*, no. 281, May, Melbourne, Australian Housing and Urban Research Institute Limited.

Phillips, J., Klapdor, M. and Simon-Davies, J. (2010) *Migration to Australia Since Federation: A Guide to the Statistics*, background note, Parliamentary Library. Canberra, Parliament of Australia.

Productivity Commission (2004) *First Home Ownership*, Productivity Commission Inquiry Report, no. 28. Canberra, Commonwealth of Australia.

Property Council of Australia (2017) *Fixing Housing Affordability*, 2 May. Sydney, Property Council of Australia.

Reserve Bank of Australia (2017) *Chart Pack: Graphs on the Australian Economy and Financial Markets*, Melbourne, Reserve Bank of Australia, 6 June.

Savills (2017) *Market Report 2017: Australian Student Accommodation*. Sydney, Savills.

Sukkar, M. (2017) 'Supply is the key to unlocking housing affordability', blog, *The Huffington Post*, 8 March 2017.

The Australian Housing and Urban Research Institute (2017) 'What is the right level of social housing?' *AHURI Brief 2017*, 7 April.

Turner, A. (2015) *Between Debt and the Devil: Money, Credit, and Fixing Global Finance*. Princeton, Princeton University Press.

Yates, J. (2016) 'Why does Australia have an affordable housing problem and what can be done about it?' *The Australian Economic Review*, 49 (3): 328–339.

CHAPTER 12

THE NBN AND 'THE MARKET': FAITH OR BLIND FAITH?

LEE RIDGE

At first glance the National Broadband Network, or NBN, might seem far removed from processes of privatisation and economic reform. After all, the NBN is a state-owned, monopoly provider of broadband infrastructure and was originally conceived as a 'nation-building project'. Ostensibly it exhibits the hallmarks of 'big government' – the antithesis of neoliberal 'economic reform'. However, as this chapter argues, both the original NBN model as conceived by the Rudd Labor government in 2009, and especially the subsequent, hybridised, slower, lower-capacity model now being rolled out by the Liberal–National Coalition, can only be understood in the context of the privatisation of Telstra, and a fundamentalist adherence to economic reform ideology.

This chapter examines the development of the NBN with a particular focus on how it was transformed from the Rudd government model – described by Vince Cerf, one of the founders of the internet, as the 'envy' of the world (Swan 2009) – to the current Coalition government's model, which, with respect to internet speed and connectivity, exposes Australia to falling behind the world. First, I outline the history of the NBN. I argue that the Rudd government's decision to build the NBN was itself proof of the failure of more than two decades of economic reform, especially the privatisation of Telstra and the unfounded faith that 'the market' could be trusted to provide essential social and economic goods – in this case, accessible high-speed broadband services. Despite privatisation's promise of increased competition and the adoption of the latest technologies, Telstra's market dominance looms large over the shaping of the NBN: the former government-owned telecommunications provider, now Australia's largest listed non-bank company, maintained its dominant market position after its privatization, and had little incentive to invest in national infrastructure, thus prompting Labor to develop the NBN. This chapter charts the transformation of Labor's original formulation of the NBN into a lower-capacity, potentially more expensive infrastructure network through a process of electoral opportunism by the Tony Abbott–led Liberal–National Coalition, describing the way that process benefitted Telstra, and its deployment of market fundamentalist rhetoric and assumptions. Finally, I examine the cost-benefit analysis commissioned by the Coalition government, which, I argue, was intended to provide a rationale for its preferred NBN model.

A Brief History of the NBN

The NBN as conceived in 2009 by the Rudd Labor government, was to be a new, national fibre-to-the-premises (FTTP) network, using optical fibre technologies that would not rely on the existing networks owned by Telstra, Australia's dominant telecommunications network owner and service provider. Such a network is called a fixed-line broadband network, and is essential for connectivity. According to the latest figures from the Australian Bureau of Statistics (ABS), more than 97 per cent of data downloaded – which has increased at more than 50 per cent per year since 2012 – used fixed-line broadband (ABS 2017).

From 2010, successive Labor governments oversaw the construction of the FTTP NBN until the Liberal National Party (LNP) took victory at the 2013 federal election. The LNP government is currently implementing a fibre-to-the node (FTTN) network using the existing copper network infrastructure belonging to Telstra, Optus and other network owners. This FTTN network will be significantly slower and will have less capacity than the FTTP network. According to Professor Rod Tucker (2017), the former

Director of the Institute for a Broadband-Enabled Society (IBES), Australia is heading in the opposite direction to the rest of the world in terms of network technology. A recent report by Ovum Ltd, an independent analyst specialising in global coverage of telecommunications, media and technology industries, stated that the year 2016 represented a worldwide 'tipping point', when FTTP connections surpassed digital subscriber line (DSL) connections using copper-based technologies. Ovum's study found that 'globally, FTTP connections increased by 77 per cent in 2016 and copper connections (including FTTN) decreased by 11 per cent of total deployments' (Tucker 2017). Further evidence that Australia is going backwards on this front was provided in Akamai's authoritative *State of the Internet Report* in 2017. Compared to the fourth quarter of 2015, when Australia ranked forty-eighth globally for average connection speed and sixtieth for its average peak connection speed, in the first quarter of 2017 Australia ranked, respectively, fiftieth and sixty-fourth. During the same period, the global ranking of New Zealand, where a FTTP network is being constructed, has improved from forty-first to twenty-seventh in average connection speed and from fifty-third to thirty-fifth for average peak connection speed (Akamai 2015; 2017). To understand how this situation eventuated, it is first necessary to appreciate the position of Telstra within Australia's telecommunications market, beginning with its privatisation.

A centrepiece of the LNP's 1996 federal election policy was the partial privatisation of Telstra. Privatisation would, the party asserted, 'necessarily benefit Telstra [and] the Australian public [would] also profit through increased investment opportunities, a more competitive and efficient telecommunications sector resulting in benefits for consumers, and the use of sale proceeds to retire debt' (Liberal Party of Australia 1996). No clear prescription was offered for how these benefits were to be achieved, especially given the competing interests of shareholders and consumers.

The option of breaking Telstra up – to structurally separate its wholesale network from its retail operations and therefore limit its market power – which was supported by the Labor party – was rejected by the LNP. This maximised Telstra's sale price, to the advantage of the company, its investors and the government. On this basis, 83 per cent of Telstra was privatised by successive Howard LNP governments between 1997 and 2006, over three tranches known as T1, T2 and T3, raising $45.4 billion. Prior to T3, the public still owned and 'controlled' 50.1 per cent of the company. However, Telstra exerted its market power by increasing prices for some services, delaying price reductions (as mandated by regulators) regardless of the rapid technological changes in communications, while failing to upgrade its fixed-line broadband infrastructure. In 2002, the Labor Party called for Telstra's structural separation to reduce its market dominance and increase competition in the sector. Labor communications spokesperson Lindsay Tanner wrote that 'in 2001, Telstra occupies approximately 75 per cent of the Australian telecommunications market and earned over 90 per cent of the profits in that market (Tanner 2002: 3). In 2004, while the public still owned and controlled 50.1 per cent of Telstra's shares, Prime Minister Howard argued that Telstra's price increases were 'beyond his control, and that Telstra would be more accountable if privatised' (Rossi 2004). Contrary to the promises of economic reform, competition had failed to bring about investment in network infrastructure. Telstra confirmed this before a committee of the Senate ironically inquiring into 'competition in broadband services': 'it is probably the last sweating, if you like, of the old copper network assets. In copper years, if you like, we are at a sort of transition – we are at five minutes to midnight' (Australian Senate 2003: 74).

However, not all Coalition government members were true believers in economic reform and the market. National Party members Barnaby Joyce and Fiona Nash co-authored *Future-Proofing Telecommunications in Non-Metropolitan Australia* in 2005, a position paper supporting a fast, optical fibre–based network to non-metropolitan communities. While confirming 'that competition is the most efficient way to ensure service delivery to non-metropolitan Australia at parity to metropolitan areas', the position paper recognised 'that government has a social obligation to ensure services to non-metropolitan areas where competition fails' (The Page Research Centre Limited 2005: 4). They recognised that a faith in the market providing 'future-proof technologies' was one thing, but that the market actually providing such technologies was another. In addition to Labor and National party critiques, the neoliberal think tank, the Institute for Public Affairs (IPA), considered the failure of privatisation in the sector as the result of the lack of regulatory reform, which 'held back investment'

(Berg 2007: 8). The business world also provided critics of the poor state of broadband infrastructure, commonly referred to as 'fraudband'. According to David Kirk, CEO of Fairfax Media, broadband in Australia was 'too expensive and slow and ... the problem was not government policy but the state of the market, dominated by one player – Telstra' (*Sydney Morning Herald* 2007). Telstra's management was aware of the poor state of the network. In 2005, a delegation from Telstra met with Prime Minister Howard, offering to build its own national broadband network in return for restricting competitors' access to such a network. The offer was rejected.

In March 2007, in the context of widespread discontent at more than a decade of economic reform, Australia's relative decline of broadband take-up among OECD countries and disgruntlement with Telstra's failure to invest in infrastructure, Labor launched its policy for a 'broadband future' for Australia, proposing to build a NBN estimated to cost $4.7 billion. This proved to be a key advantage for the ALP in its 2007 federal election victory.

After a false start on plans for this less ambitious NBN, on 7 April 2009, the incumbent Labor government announced that the NBN would deliver a FTTP network at a total cost of $43 billion, funded by a $21 billion government loan, and with the balance raised from private investors at no net cost to government. The NBN would connect '90 per cent of all Australian, homes, schools and workplaces with speeds up to 100 megabits per second and all other premises at speeds of up to 12 megabits per second using next generation wireless and satellite technologies' (Conroy 2009). The NBN would require the structural separation of Telstra, as the NBN was to provide the sole national infrastructure.

The rhetoric surrounding Labour's new NBN was partly positioned as a response to 'market failure' – a private monopoly (Telstra) 'owning the network infrastructure and dominating the retail sector' (Rudd 2009). The model placed faith in the assumption that by providing a single fast FTTP network, competition would increase in the provision of retail services to customers. Labor's NBN appeared to accept that the existence of a natural monopoly was a kind of market failure. (A natural monopoly exists where one provider, in this case due to the extent and cost of the network, can supply the market's entire demand for the service at a price lower than two or more providers can). It also appeared to be a response to the thirty-year dominance of privatisation policies – finally, an alternative to Thatcher's famous phrase 'there is no alternative' to neoliberalism.

Labor's NBN provoked extensive and sustained criticism. It was variously described as 'unnecessary', 'wasteful' and 'unaffordable'. Opposition leader Tony Abbott, questioned the need 'to spend $50 billion of hard earned taxpayers money in what is essentially a video entertainment system?' (2010). He later stated that taxpayers' money could be better spent on current infrastructure such as on 'our roads, our rail and our ports' (Le May 2012). The position of the LNP and its supporters was that because the market wasn't providing fast broadband, there was evidently little demand for it. The article of faith underlying such rhetoric was that markets are more efficient than government in delivering services. According to Abbott, it was 'common sense' that 'we can also be certain that this government will remain fundamentally incompetent at delivering services' (2010). This faith in the market ignored the complex reality of market failure and telecommunications as a natural monopoly in Australia, which had created the need for government to intervene to provide this national infrastructure.

Despite these criticisms, the NBN remained electorally popular. Former LNP minister Peter Reith's review of the LNP's 2010 federal election loss found that 'Labor's only real policy advantage was on the NBN' (2011: 17). While opposition to the NBN maintained a focus on the cost and the lack of a cost-benefit analysis, by political necessity, the LNP eventually recanted their policy of scrapping the NBN in favour of building an alternative NBN that was 'Fast. Affordable. Reliable.' This 'fast-affordable-reliable' NBN would comprise a 'multi-technology-mix, or 'MTM', that included fibre-to-the-node (FTTN), the existing copper-based network, and pay TV networks and satellite. For some time the NBN politically 'wedged' the LNP between an electorally popular policy that it would have to maintain if it won government, but to which it was ideologically opposed. LNP Communications spokesperson Malcolm Turnbull noted that for the past thirty years, governments had been 'getting out of telecommunications rather than getting back into it' (Turnbull 2013: 4). It stated that 'private ownership and an open, competitive market create more direct incentives for efficiency and lower prices for consumers', that the market delivered 'consumer choice and more rapid innovation in products and service', and that private investors are usually better placed to 'evaluate, fund and bear the risk of new investments in networks or technologies in an increasingly dynamic sector' (Turnbull 2013). The LNP's preferred MTM strategy, with its use of existing infrastructure, significantly advantaged Telstra and, to a lesser extent, Telstra's rival communications company Optus. The MTM strategy which is now being implemented under the Turnbull government, requires that Telstra be paid $11 billion valued in current dollars, for access to Telstra's infrastructure, such as underground pits and ducts where the network is to be laid. This was as previously agreed within the Rudd NBN model, but now Telstra would be paid to hand over its ageing copper and pay TV infrastructure, excluding Foxtel, as well as the burden of their maintenance to the NBN (Telstra 2014). Further, the NBN would pay Telstra an additional $1.6 billion to 'plan design, construct and manage' services within the existing Telstra pay TV network (Telstra 2016). This payment to Telstra had not existed under the Rudd NBN, in which pay TV was slated to be replaced by FTTP. The decades-long hope among Labor and the other telecommunications carriers apart from Telstra was that the structural separation of Telstra would solve the lack of competition problem. This proved illusory. Structural separation has not diminished Telstra's dominant market position – receiving revenue from the NBN of $1.25 billion alone in 2017 (Telstra 2017: 81) and will continue for thirty years as compensation for either access to or the purchase of previously funded public infrastructure that is past its 'end of life'.

A lack of support for Labor's FTTP NBN from big business was notable, given the opportunity that fast broadband would provide to deliver goods and services at lower cost. One explanation for this is that big businesses has the resources to invest in their own private high-speed internet, sourced from the wholesale internet sector. This sector is more competitive, with alternative providers to Telstra and Optus, such as M2, Pipe Networks, Vocus Communications and NextGen Networks. These providers own and operate their own fibre-based networks, unlike in the fixed-line retail internet sector, where only Telstra, Optus, Vodafone and, to a lesser extent, TPG have their own networks. As businesses have invested in connectivity, the $21 billion of government funds allocated to the NBN was regarded as being better spent elsewhere – on roads and ports, as suggested by Abbott. This view was understood and exploited by Abbott, who in his 2011 budget reply speech noted that 'speeds of up to 100 megabits are already potentially available to almost every *major* business and hospital, to most schools, and through high-speed cable already running past nearly a third of Australian households' (Abbott 2011, emphasis added). What the largest 100 companies, as represented by the Business Council of Australia, did want, however, was a cost-benefit analysis of the NBN (Business Council of Australia 2011: 6).

The Politics of Economics: The NBN Cost-Benefit Analysis

The Labor government's resistance to a cost-benefit analysis of the NBN provided a focal point for criticism of both the party and its NBN model. An analysis of newspaper articles and editorials in *The Age* and *The Australian* between 2008 and 2013 by Swinburne University researchers found that coverage of the NBN was 'overwhelmingly negative' and largely focused on potential impacts on Telstra, lack of a business plan and a sufficient cost-benefit analysis, problems with rollout, cost to the federal budget, and implications for business stakeholders (Wilken et al. 2015: 55).

Prior to the cost-benefit analysis of the NBN, communications minister Turnbull engineered the effective 'takeover' of NBN Co., the government-owned company tasked with building the NBN. Most of its board resigned and were replaced by Turnbull's former colleagues from Ozemail (a business he co-founded) and/or Telstra executives, or both. Dr Ziggy Switkowski, a former CEO of Optus and Telstra respectively, was appointed the Executive Chairman of NBN Co. and Justin Milne, who was formerly the CEO of OzEmail and Telstra BigPond, was appointed to the Board. In addition, Mr JB Rousselot, who worked with Turnbull at Turnbull and Partners and OzEmail, as well as having served as Executive Director of Digital Media and Internet Protocol Television (IPTV) at Telstra, (Le May 2013a) was appointed Head of Strategy and Transformation (NBN Co. 2013b), while Mr Greg Adcock, who spent twenty years with Telstra, was appointed Chief Operating Officer (NBN Co. 2013a).

Under its new hand-picked leadership, NBN Co. undertook a 'rapid' five-week strategic review which recommended scrapping the rollout of FTTP in favour of the MTM solution (NBN Co. 2013c: 18). NBN Co.'s strategy was now aligned with the LNP's MTM policy. Concurrent with the publication of their strategic review, Turnbull announced that there would be an independent cost-benefit analysis of the NBN by a panel of experts. However, there is strong evidence that this panel was far from independent: it was chaired by Dr Michael Vertigan, the former head of the Victorian Department of Premier and Cabinet during the period when Premier Jeff Kennett undertook Australia's most extensive privatisation of state government–owned assets. A 'controversial' appointment to the panel was economist Dr Henry Ergas (Le May 2013b; Swan 2013), who had been a member of Telstra's delegation to Prime Minister John Howard in 2005, and was a staunch and vocal critic of the NBN from its inception (Ergas and Ralph 2008; Ergas and Robson 2009; Ergas and Sloan 2013). Upon his appointment, Ergas stated that he could do the cost-benefit analyses 'in a matter of days' (Australian Senate 2015: 64). In 2009, Ergas, together with Dr Alex Robson (an economic adviser to Turnbull as well as being a member and contributor to neoliberal think tanks such as the IPA) published a cost-benefit analysis of the NBN which calculated that the NBN would have a net 'social loss in present value terms of between $13.9 billion and $20.4 billion, depending on the discount rate chosen' (Robson and Ergas 2010: 149). Other consultants appointed by the panel of experts had either published articles critical of the NBN, had previous or existing associations with Ergas or were avowedly pro-privatisation. The costing of the NBN scenarios, heavily redacted in the published NBN cost-benefit analysis, was reviewed by a long-time employee of Ergas (LinkedIn Inc. 2017). This financial and employer–employee relationship was not disclosed in the panel's reports or by the Australian Competition and Consumer Commission (ACCC). Turnbull had set the scene and, it seems, picked a team to facilitate a set of preferred findings in the NBN strategic review.

A cost-benefit analysis is regarded generally to be an objective process performed by independent economists, which combines mainstream or neoclassical economics, and mathematical modelling techniques in order to calculate a project's future benefits and costs; these are then adjusted using a discount rate to determine the net present value or value of a project in today's dollars. The NBN cost-benefit analysis concluded with '98 per cent certainty' that the Coalition government's MTM solution would cost a net $16 billion less than the FTTP solution. This finding was used by the Coalition as part of the justification for its low-capacity NBN model. Beneath the veneer of objectivity however, I argue the finding of 98 per cent certainty was misplaced, undermining the claim that the Coalition's FTTN NBN is 'future-proof'. Assumptions about the inherent superiority of market-based or private forms of service delivery were central to the justification of the NBN cost-benefit analysis, as were seemingly heroic assumptions regarding the costs and speed of the rollout of the Coalition's NBN.

'The Costs'

The panel of experts calculated that the net present value of the cost of the MTM option was $24.9 billion, $10.4 billion less than the cost of Labor's proposed FTTP option of $35.3 billion. At issue is whether the MTM costs were understated, or FTTP costs were overstated, or both. The accuracy of this estimate was soon thrown into doubt when the new NBN Co. announced in August 2015 that NBN peak funding had risen by $15 billion, in nominal dollars, from $41 billion to $56 billion (NBN Co. 2015: 39). Given only one year had elapsed between this significant cost revision and the publication of the NBN cost-benefit analyses in August 2014, which were both based on the strategic review's findings, one can conclude that the MTM costs were understated. The former CEO of NBN Co. Mike Quigley, argued that this $15 billion increase in costs was attributable to the MTM rollout alone, and due in particular to the costs of remediating Telstra's ageing copper network (Quigley 2015).

There is also evidence that the NBN cost-benefit analysis overstated the costs of Labor's FTTP option. Despite the redaction of the cost per FTTP connection in the NBN cost-benefit analysis, the amount of $4400 per connection has been widely reported (Quigley 2015; NBN Co. 2017c: 43). Critics of NBN Co.'s subsequent costing analysis have highlighted that costs per connection have decreased due to efficiencies gained during construction (Klan 2017; Quigley 2016). Moreover, in the broadly comparable case of New Zealand's broadband rollout, costs per FTTP connection declined by 44 per cent over a three-year period (Chorus 2016). Quigley also notes that Verizon in the United States reduced its cost per premise on FTTP by 38 per cent over three years (Quigley 2016). Estimated potential savings of this type on the FTTP network range between $1.6 billion and $3 billion, and are based on 8.1 million premises that remain to be connected (Gregory 2015). The panel of experts advised that their analysis did not include these potential efficiencies, arguing that international experience counted for little in the case of the Australian NBN (Australian Senate 2015: 69). The analysis therefore appears to have both significantly understated MTM costs and overstated FTTP costs.

The Importance of the Construction Period of the NBN

Using cost-benefit analysis, due to discounting future costs and benefits, the shorter the construction period of a project and hence the sooner a project's benefits start to flow, the higher a projects' calculated net benefits will be compared to a project of similar cost, but where the same, or even greater benefits, take longer to realise. The impact of a high discount rate is discussed in more detail later in this chapter. The shorter timeframe of the MTM rollout, and so the sooner benefits flowed was promoted as one of its great advantages. The NBN cost-benefit analysis modelled 10 million connected premises by the year 2018, compared to less than half this number for the FTTP rollout. (Department of Communications and the Arts 2014: 45) Once again, however, subsequent history would suggest that such calculations were optimistic. NBN Co.'s 2016 Corporate Plan revised its estimate of 'households ready for service' down to 9.1 million by the end of 2018 (NBN Co. 2015: 12) and further revised to 8 million 'activated premises' by 2020 (NBN Co. 2017b: 46). Moreover, the NBN cost-benefit analysis had estimated that Labor's FTTP plan would only reach this number of households by 2020, thus negating one of MTM's perceived advantages. In Figure 1, the relevant chart from the NBN cost-benefit analysis (Chart 4.3) (Department of Communications and the Arts 2014: 45), has been updated with information from NBN Co.'s corporate plans quoted above. Figure 1 shows that the MTM rollout, originally mooted as occurring more quickly, in practice has a nearly identical delivery date for the same number of households to the FTTP rollout. Consequently, the financial benefits of the MTM option as calculated in the NBN cost-benefit analysis and claimed by the LNP government seem overstated.

FIGURE 1. THE TIMING OF THE NBN ROLLOUT

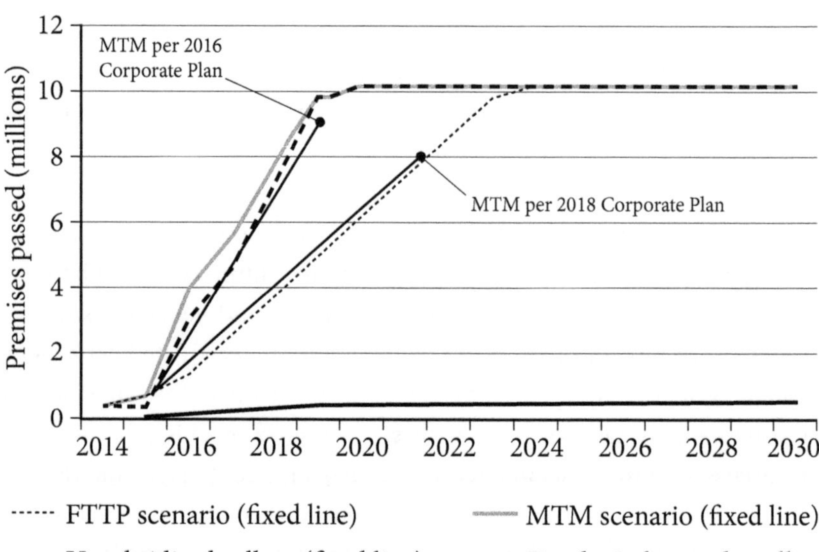

FTTP scenario (fixed line) — MTM scenario (fixed line)
Unsubsidised rollout (fixed line) — Fixed wireless and satellite

Sources: Department of Communications and the Arts (2014: 45); NBN Co. (2015: 12); NBN Co., (2017b: 46)

The sensitivity of NBN Co. and the Abbott government to the timing of the MTM rollout – and hence its estimated cost – can be gauged by their actions during the 2016 federal election campaign, when the coercive powers of the Australian Federal Police (AFP) were used to search for evidence of NBN Co.'s latest network costings in the parliamentary offices of Senator Stephen Conroy, the former Minister for Communications, as well as Labor's offices in Melbourne, and among NBN Co. staff (Lee and Massola 2016).

'The Benefits'

The economic modelling of the benefits of the NBN focused on calculating consumers' 'demand for speed', and their 'willingness to pay' for speed. Willingness-to-pay methodology does not consider consumers' *ability to pay*. The same consultants who advised the strategic review that there was not a high demand for speed, undertook this analysis for the NBN cost-benefit analysis. This modelling was based on a 'bottom up' approach, to determine the willingness-to-pay of representative households to access various apps such as Skype, Netflix and Facebook, as well as access to educational materials. These households were asked to state their preference based on current apps. With such a disruptive technology as fast broadband being proposed, and considering the iPhone only was launched as recently as 2007, the potential applications that will be developed in the next twenty to forty years are unknown. As Reimer noted, 'it is inherently impossible to undertake a cost-benefit analysis in any credible way that will do justice to such technologies. The problem is that, while we are well able to extrapolate the cost of building the NBN, the benefits it will unlock are fundamentally unknowable and unpredictable' (Reimer 2014). Further, the willingness-to-pay methodology does not consider the value consumers place on the network as a whole, and its future availability. The NBN cost-benefit analysis determined that the median Australian household would require bandwidth of 15 megabits per second (mbps) by the year 2023 (Department of Communications and the Arts 2014: 34). However, according to the ABS data on internet subscribers by advertised download speed, the majority of consumers were *actually* paying for more than 24 mbps already by early 2016, significantly sooner than predicted by the NBN cost-benefit analysis calculations, and Abbott's pronouncement that 'we are absolutely confident that 25 megs is going to be enough, more than enough, for the average household' (2013). Figure 2 shows the growth of internet subscribers paying for than 24 mbps, which suggests that consumers were far ahead of the panel of experts' economic modelling, upon which it based its findings in favour of the MTM solution.

Figure 2. Internet subscribers by sector by advertised download speed, for ISPs with more than 1000, June 2011 to June 2017

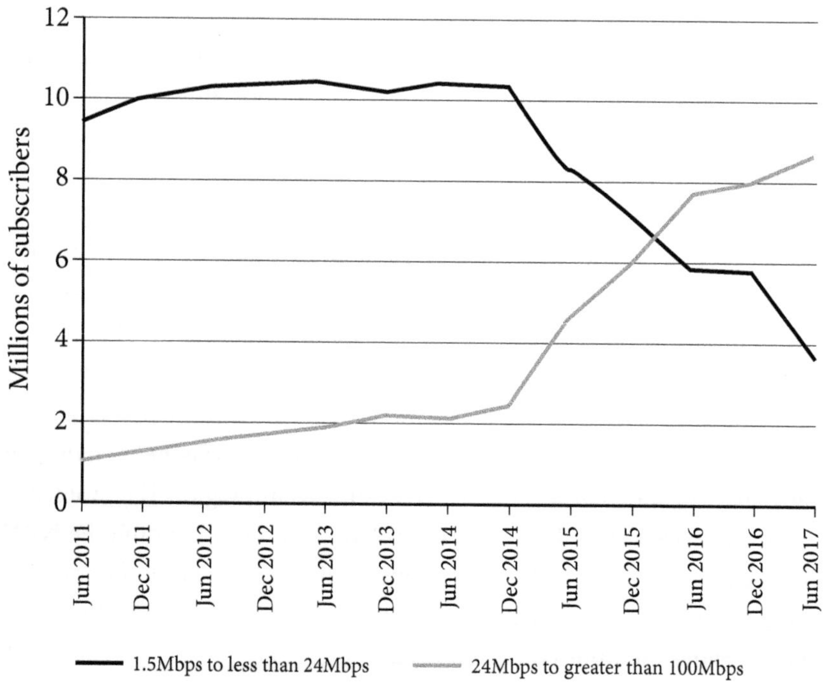

Source: ABS 8153.0: Internet Activity Australia, June 2017, released 29 Sep 2017

The Importance of the Discount Rate

The critical factor of any cost-benefit analysis is the discount rate. There has been significant debate in mainstream economics about the appropriate discount rate for long-term or intergenerational projects, such as those relating to the environment and, in this case, is also applicable to optical fibre infrastructure. As Quiggin notes 'one of the longest running controversies in welfare economics has concerned the appropriateness of applying different weights to people in different generations' (2008: 200). The Stern Review of the economic costs of global warming applied a rate of 1 per cent (Stern 2007) while the Garnaut Climate Change Review applied social discount rates of 1.35 per cent and 2.65 per cent (Scarborough 2011: 145).

Another measure of the discount rate is the 'risk free rate', which is equivalent to the rate on Australian government bonds, which at the time was 4 per cent. Discounting results in valuing the current generation more than future generations, which seems contrary to the very purpose of building long-term, national infrastructure.

The NBN cost-benefit analysis ignored the government's own recommended rate of 7 per cent, and broke new ground in economic analysis by using a 'high-speed broadband specific discount rate' of 8.3 per cent (Department of Communications and the Arts 2014: 40). Such a rate significantly reduces the expected benefits of the FTTP network, with its higher cost and extended construction period (but its potentially greater benefits for future generations). Applying a rate of 8.3 per cent is equivalent to arguing that someone born in 2000 will be seven times more valuable than someone born in 2025, and fifty times more valuable than someone born in 2050. Given the disruptive nature of the internet, the opposite would seem to be the case, and fast broadband seems likely to be *more* valuable in the future, not less. It is difficult not to conclude that the use of such a high, specific discount rate was biased against the FTTP NBN option. While the econometric model that calculated these values is not available for analysis, there is more than sufficient evidence to seriously question the '98 per cent confidence' expressed by the panel of experts in their favoured MTM solution. However, the NBN cost-benefit analysis served its purpose: it effectively ceased public debate on the economics of Labor's NBN.

Conclusion

The NBN emerged as a response to some of the negative consequences of economic reform in Australia, especially the creation of the privatised mega-corporation Telstra and its dominance of the telecommunications market. Yet the original model of the NBN has been transformed from one that looked forward to connecting 90 per cent or more Australians to an advanced, high-speed broadband network, to one that is very unlikely to be 'future-proof'. The explanation for this lies in a combination of political opportunism and partisanship on the part of the Coalition government and its intellectual fellow travellers, the mobilisation of market fundamentalist rhetoric to delegitimise the Labor government's NBN, and a re-shaping of the NBN in line with the interests of Telstra. Previously facing the loss of a significant part of its business, Telstra, in receipt of billions of dollars of government funding for its 'end of life' infrastructure, has emerged as the most significant beneficiary of the current NBN.

References

Abbott, T. (2010) Announcement of Coalition Shadow Ministry, Transcript of Joint Press Conference. Canberra, Australian Government.

Abbott, T. (2011) 'Full text of Tony Abbott's budget reply speech', *The Australian*, 12 May.

Abbott, T. (2013) Joint Press Conference with the Hon. Malcolm Turnbull MHR, Shadow Minister for Communications and Broadband. Transcript of the Hon. Tony Abbott MHR Joint Press Conference, Sydney.

Akamai (2015) *State of the Internet Report Q1 2017*. Cambridge, Akamai.

——(2017) *State of the Internet Report Q1 2017*. Cambridge, Akamai.

Australian Bureau of Statistics (2017) 8153.0 – *Internet Activity, Australia, June 2017*, 29 September. Canberra, Australian Government.

Australian Senate(2003) 'Competition in broadband services (Sen. Cherry – chair)', Environment, Communications, Information Technology and the Arts References Committee, 12 November 2003. Canberra, Commonwealth of Australia.

——(2015) Senate Select Committee on the National Broadband Network, Second Interim Report, Senate Select Committee on the National Broadband Network. Canberra, Commonwealth of Australia.

Berg, C. (2007) 'Regretting privatisation: broadband and the 2007 election', *Institute of Public Affairs Review: A Quarterly Review of Politics and Public Affairs*, 59: 5–8.

Business Council of Australia (2011) *BCA Budget Submission 2011–12*, bca.com.au/publications/bca-budget-submission-2011-12

Chorus (2016) *Introducing Chorus*. Macquarie Australia Conference, 6 May 2016.

Conroy, S. (2009) New National Broadband Network, http://parlinfo.aph.gov.au/parlInfo/search/display/display.w3p;query=Id%3A%22media%2Fpressrel%2FR R8T6%22

Department of Communications and the Arts 2014. *Volume II – The Costs and Benefits of High-Speed Broadband.*

Ergas, H. and Robson, A. (2009). 'The Social Losses from Inefficient Infrastructure Projects: Recent Australian Experience', *Productivity Commission Round Table: Strengthening Evidence-Based Policy in the Australian Federation.*

Ergas, H. and Ralph, E. (2008) 'A policy framework for a new broadband network', *Growth*, 60: 32–47.

Ergas, H. and Sloan, J. (2013) 'The $250bn cost of Kevin Rudd: a tale of waste and spending', *The Australian*, 3 August.

Gregory, M. (2015) 'How much do FTTP NBN connections really cost?' *The Australian*, 18 September.

Klan, A. (2017) 'NBN's connection costs are amomg the world's highest', *The Australian*, 6 July.

Le May, R. (2012) 'Australia doesn't need the NBN, says Abbott', *Delimiter*, 6 July.

——(2013a) 'Stacking the deck: NBN review filled with Turnbull cronies', *Delimiter*, 21 May.

——(2013b) 'Turnbull appoints Liberal supporter Ergas to NBN panel', *Delimiter*, 16 December.

Lee, J. and Massola, J. (2016) 'AFP raid ALP offices in Melbourne over NBN "leaks"', *The Sydney Morning Herald*, 20 May.

Liberal Party of Australia (1996) Privatization – Liberal and National Parties' Policy.

LinkedIn Inc. (2017) Emma Lanigan, https://au.linkedin.com/in/emma-lanigan-5baa0b12 (Membership of LinkedIn required)

NBN Co. (2013a) 'Greg Adcock named NBN Co Chief Operating Officer'. Sydney, NBN Co.

——(2013b) 'JB Rousselot appointed Head of Strategy and Transformation'. Sydney: NBN Co.

——(2013c) *Strategic Review December 2013*. Sydney, NBN Co.

——(2014) *NBN Co. Annual Report 2013–14*. Sydney, NBN Co.

——(2015) *Corporate Strategy 2016*. Sydney, NBN Co.

——(2017a) 'Board member biographies', nbnco.com.au/corporate-information/about-nbn-co/our-people/board-member-biographies.html

——(2017b) *Corporate Plan 2018*. Sydney, NBN Co.

——(2017c) *The Realities of Deploying FTTP in Australia*, 5 July, nbnco.com.au/blog/the-nbn-project/the-realities-of-deploying-fttp-in-australia.html

Quiggin, J. (2008) 'Stern and his critics on discounting and climate change: an editorial essay', *Climatic Change*, 89: 195–205.

Quigley, M. (2015) 'Exploding Malcolm Turnbull's Myths', September, abc.net.au/cm/lb/6907464/data/mike-quigley-article-data.pdf

——(2016) *The NBN: 2009 to 2016 and Beyond*, 22 June.

Reimer, K. (2014) 'NBN Cost-benefit analysis fails the "imagination" test', University of Sydney Business School, 11 September.

Reith, P. (2011) *Review of the 2010 Federal Election*, 25 May. Melbourne, Liberal Party of Australia.

Robson, A. and Ergas, H. (2010) 'Evaluating major infrastructure projects: how robust are our processes?' Chapter 6 – Conference Proceeding, Productivity Commission. Canberra, Australia.

Rossi, S. (2004) 'Privatization the solution to Telstra price hike: PM', *Computerworld*, 30 April.

Rudd, K. (2009) National Broadband Network, PM Transcripts, 16493, 7 April, http://pmtranscripts.pmc.gov.au/release/transcript-16493

Scarborough, H. (2011) 'Intergenerational equity and the social discount rate', *Australian Journal of Agricultural and Resource Economics*, 55: 145–158.

Stern, N.H. (2007) *The Economics of Climate Change: The Stern Review*. Cambridge, Cambridge University Press.

Swan, G. (2009) 'Broadband future: father of the internet praises NBN', *Computerworld*, 10 December.

Swan, J. (2013) 'Malcolm Turnbull to include Labor critic on NBN panel', *The Sydney Morning Herald*, 20 November.

Sydney Morning Herald (2007) 'Fairfax boss denounces fraudband', 8 March 2007.

Tanner, L. (2002) 'Reforming Telstra', Labor Discussion Paper, Australian Labor Party.

Telstra (2014) 'Telstra signs revised NBN Definitive Agreements – Announcement to the Australian Securities Exchange,' Telstra.

——(2016) 'Telstra and NBN announce HFC delivery agreement'. Telstra Corporation Limited.

——(2017) *Annual Report 2017*. Sydney, Telstra Corporation Limited.

The Page Research Centre Limited (2005) 'Future-proofing telecommunications in non-metropolitan Australia', The Page Research Centre Limited.

Tucker, R. (2017) 'The Tragedy of Australia's National Broadband Network', *Australian Journal of Telecommunications and the Digital Economy*, 5 (1) Article 94, March 2017.

Turnbull, M. (2013) 'The Coalition's Plan for Fast Broadband and an Affordable NBN', Background paper, April.

Wilken, R., et al. (2015) 'Framing the NBN: an analysis of newspaper representations', *Communication, Politics & Culture*, 47 (3): 55–69.

CHAPTER 13

UNIVERSITIES: A PARADOX OF PRIVATISATION

BEN SPIES-BUTCHER AND GARETH BRYANT

The experience of the Australian university sector over the last thirty years presents as a paradoxical case of market-oriented reform. Universities have been subject to wide-ranging corporate restructuring, marked by the rise of managerialism in decision-making, the casualisation of working conditions and the commercialisation of research. The composition of funding has also shifted from direct government grants to a range of tuition fee schemes for domestic and international students. This has led international comparative studies to classify the Australian university sector as highly privatised. Yet these changes, which are usually associated with forms of marketisation, privatisation and commodification, have occurred during a period of significant expansion of Australia's public universities, which support one of the highest participation rates in the world.

In this chapter we seek to explain the expansion of Australia's university sector within an environment of fiscal austerity imposed by federal governments. We nominate two key ways that federal governments have created notionally private sources of funding that have expanded university places while reducing budgetary pressures. The first is by encouraging full-fee paying international students to study in Australia, which provides a significant source of funding for universities as an export industry. The second – which is the main focus of this chapter – is Australia's system of income-contingent loans (ICLs) for domestic students, commonly known as HECS (the Higher Education Contribution Scheme). While international student fees are a genuinely private income stream, the imposition of fees via HECS has not been a case of straightforward privatisation. We argue that HECS is better understood as a policy hybrid that combines loan- and tax-like characteristics. The structure of HECS contains both the progressive and egalitarian principles of redistributive tax systems and the commodifying and privatising imperatives of market loans. Recognising the hybrid structure of HECS, we argue, helps to understand both the policy space available for further expansions in university funding and access, and the precise nature of recent threats to university students and graduates from a more privatised HECS system.

First, we outline the context, nature and outcomes of corporate internal restructuring in Australian universities and the shift in the external funding environment from direct government grants to student fees. Second, we reconceptualise HECS as a tax/loan policy hybrid, explaining how, in conjunction with new corporate and financial accounting practices, the scheme redefines ongoing public spending on universities as private spending from students. Third, we analyse emerging market imperatives to target the tax-like features of HECS and move the scheme closer to a private loan system by deregulating fees, charging real interest rates and reducing repayment thresholds. We conclude by reflecting on possible future pathways for HECS and the Australian university system.

Market Reforms in Australian Universities

Labor education minister John Dawkins' reforms (the 'Dawkins reforms') transformed the Australian university sector from the late 1980s. Since then, successive federal governments and university managements have driven a series of interlinked market reforms involving the corporatisation of university governance and a shift in funding from direct government grants to user payments. These reforms have involved an apparent paradox. On the one hand, free education was abandoned and fees reintroduced, and universities gradually became more focused on attracting full-fee paying international students. Yet, on the other, the simultaneous expansion of higher education has proven important in mitigating rising economic inequality (Bell and Keating 2018).

University restructuring has centred around corporatisation. Public sector managerialism has extended to university management structures, working conditions, relationships with the private sector and university cultures. In their study of the 'enterprise university', Marginson and Considine (2000) traced the rise of strong forms of executive control in Australian university management. They found increasingly direct ties between management and the private sector, and the adoption of 'new public management' models introduced elsewhere in the public sector. The impacts of corporate managerialism have been acute for working conditions at universities. Academic work has been casualised to the point that about half of university teaching loads are borne by casual staff on sessional contracts. This has created a bifurcated workforce where the share of university staff enjoying working conditions won for permanent staff is in decline (Ryan et al. 2013). The corporate transformation of internal university governance has coevolved alongside a transformed external research-funding environment for universities. Block grant funding of research has become increasingly performance-based and represents a declining share of research income for universities. A higher share of government research funding is instead now delivered through competitive grant schemes. This is linked to imperatives to secure funding and partnerships from the private sector for commercially oriented research (Watt 2015: 11–17).

The most significant restructuring of university finances has occurred in funding for teaching. As per-student government grants for teaching have declined, university finances have become reliant on two notionally private sources of revenue from students: fees from international full-fee paying students and domestic HECS students. The initial impulse for charging fees emerged from three related developments. First, globalisation meant that the government wanted to expand university participation to create a more skilled workforce. After remaining stable during the 1970s, high school retention rates doubled, from around 30 per cent to over 60 per cent, during the 1980s (Tunny 2006: chart 5). This meant a substantial increase in the proportion of school graduates looking to attend university, and pressure to significantly expand the number of undergraduate university places. Second, the government was committed to budget discipline in taxation, debt and spending levels. The Hawke government had pledged to very restrictive fiscal targets – known as the trilogy promise – which prevented a significant expansion of either taxation or government spending (Stilwell 1986: 15). Third, economic ideas on education as a 'private good' or 'human capital' and the potentially regressive incidence of public funding of universities held currency within the cabinet. Private contributions from students were justified on the basis that the middle class were more likely to attend university and gain private benefits in the form of higher wages (Chapman 1997).

Universities have become particularly reliant on income from full-fee paying international students, as well as full-fee paying domestic postgraduate students, who access HECS (known as FEE-HELP) (Lomax-Smith 2011: 4–5). Fees for these students are set by universities, rather than the federal government, and have delivered the most rapidly growing source of sector funding (Norton and Cakitaki 2016: 54). Competition for international students has brought the dynamics of the market into the university.

However, features of higher education constrain the implementation of abstract market ideals in universities, as Marginson (2013) argues. The 'public good' features of knowledge production and the presence of strong status hierarchies among universities changes the nature of competition in the sector. Among other factors, revenue from international student fees reflects the global status of universities, rather than the quality of education. As 'status maximising institutions', universities use this revenue to cross subsidise research in other parts of the university (rather than teaching international students), to boost international rankings and attract more students (Marginson 2013: 361, 2004: 195). Fees from international students have therefore been integral to the expansion of universities, but the associated framing of international students as consumers has excluded them from many of its benefits (Ramia, Marginson and Sawir 2013).

The introduction and subsequent increase in fees for domestic students has been the most politically significant aspect of the Dawkins reforms. The Hawke Labor government reintroduced undergraduate student fees for universities in 1989, only fifteen years after they had been abolished by the Whitlam Labor government. However, concerns over both the potential for fees to discourage low-income students from study and the unwillingness of private-sector banks to offer student loans prevented Labor from charging fees up-front. Instead, Australian National University economist Bruce Chapman was enlisted to design a system of income-contingent loans, then known as the Higher Education Contribution Scheme (HECS), and now officially called the Higher Education Loan Programme (HELP). HECS highlights the paradox of higher education reform in Australia. On the one hand it prevented the most pernicious aspects of market loans by allowing students to defer the repayment of their debts, which incurred no real interest rate until their incomes reached a certain minimum threshold (Chapman 1997). On the other, as Connell (2013: 102) argues, 'the re-introduction of university fees ... redefined higher education as a commodity not a citizen right.'

HECS as a Policy Hybrid

The various changes in higher education policy since the late 1980s have left Australia with what appears to be a highly privatised university system. According to the OECD, in 2014, 61.2 per cent of tertiary education spending came from private sources, a figure well above most comparable countries and only marginally below the United States (OECD 2017). Comparative scholars now place Australia's university system in the same privatised category as the United States (Ansell and Gingrich 2013; Willemse and de Beer 2012). Although there is clear evidence of the growing influence of managerialism and commodification within Australian universities, the description of Australia's tertiary sector as radically privatised along American lines sits uncomfortably with other evidence of the sector's organisation and operation.

Australian universities remain overwhelmingly public institutions (Department of Education and Training 2015: 5). Relatively few for-profit universities have been established in Australia, and those that do exist remain marginal, both in terms of the number of students they teach and their institutional status. International rankings suggest that Australia has a comparatively large number of high-performing universities, with approximately half of all Australian institutions ranked in the top 500 internationally, reflecting relatively egalitarian access to high-quality public institutions across the sector (Norton and Cakitaki 2016: 71–72). Australian students largely study close to home, rather than travelling to access 'elite' institutions.

Access to Australia's largely public university system has also grown over the period of privatisation. In absolute terms, domestic student numbers have more than doubled, from 420,000 in 1989 to over 1,026,000 in 2014. This translated to a large increase in the rate of university-level educational attainment. In 2014, 37.3 per cent of 25- to 34-year-olds had bachelor or higher degrees, compared to 12.3 per cent in 1989 (Department of Education and Training 2015: 28–29). Analysis of enrolment data shows that the reintroduction of university fees did not deter students from low-income families from going to university (Chapman and Ryan 2005). Following the introduction of HECS, the participation of students from disadvantaged backgrounds substantially increased, though that demographic remains underrepresented as a share of total enrolments. The proportion of low socio-economic status students remained largely stable following the introduction of HECS, but has improved slightly since 2010 (Bradley et al. 2008: 28; Department of Education and Training 2017), possibly reflecting policy efforts to reward universities enrolling non-traditional student cohorts.

Taken together, the evidence of rising private funding alongside the maintenance of a relatively egalitarian system of provision could be interpreted as demonstrating the success of privatisation. However, we suggest an alternative conclusion. Australia's funding model, we argue, is more 'public' than international comparisons suggest. This is the result of the unusual – and innovative – policy design of Australia's system of income-contingent loans. Understanding HECS as a system of loans exaggerates the private features of the policy. Rather than simply a partial privatisation, we argue that HECS is in fact a genuine policy hybrid that sits between a market-based 'loan' and a publicly financed 'tax and spend' system. As a policy hybrid then, HECS both advances privatisation and advances redistribution simultaneously, and in different ways. It is the 'tax-like' features of HECS that have enabled the university sector to expand along relatively egalitarian lines. Identifying these features can aid us to identify threats from more substantive forms of privatisation, such as those occurring in both Australian Vocational Education and Training (see Toner's analysis of the VET market in Chapter 3), or in the US student loan market.

Most economists consider systems like HECS to function as modified loans (see Chapman, Higgins and Stiglitz 2014). On closer inspection, these modifications almost all mimic aspects of government income tax or payments systems. The main example is that loan repayments are contingent on income, so those on low incomes do not have to make repayments. Thus, repayments resemble tax payments. Repayments are collected by the Australian Taxation Office (ATO) because only governments have the capactiy to properly determine how much you earn (Libich 2015: 112). Unlike a normal loan, if a student never earns enough to make sufficient repayments, then they are not required to pay off all of their debt. Loans are granted to all students, as a right, regardless of their income or credit history. Loans also do not incur a market interest rate; they are indexed to inflation, just as the benefit schemes Youth Allowance and Newstart are indexed. The net result is that HECS repayments are structured on a relatively progressive basis that is somewhat proportional to ability to pay (although the use of average rather than marginal repayment rates creates very high effective marginal tax rates for debtors when their income hits the initial threshold).

The design of the HECS system also shapes how students and universities interact. HECS fees are set by the government for undergraduate courses, and all universities charge the same fee for the same course. Differences in fee levels between courses do not reflect the cost of the course and prestige of the institution, but rather they reflect expectations of future earnings or social priorities. Thus, nursing students pay less than law students, even though it is cheaper to teach a law student (Norton and Cakitaki 2016: 57). Initially, the number of places in each type of program and at each institution were also set by government, reflecting predictions of future workforce needs. However, this has now changed. When the Gillard government deregulated the number of student places, universities began to behave more like you would expect in a private market, increasing the number of places they offered to meet as much demand as they could generate (Kemp and Norton 2014). The decision signals how the hybrid funding model allows for changes in the degree of public or market control, although recent efforts by the Coalition government to curb public funding for universities may see some restrictions reinstated.

As a hybrid system, HECS differs from conventional public grant funding of universities. Elements of a loan remain. Only those studying at universities pay, rather than distributing the cost across all taxpayers. The level of debt is linked to how much you study and what kind of course you study. Repayments are treated as repayments to the principal: once your repayments equal the fees you were charged, plus indexation, you stop making repayments, unlike with a normal tax.

It is the loan-like features than dominate the accounting treatment of HECS in government budgeting. Framing HECS as a student loan, rather than as a graduate tax, has allowed the public money given to universities to be shifted off federal budget balances. HECS funding is generally transferred from governments to universities, however, the spending is 'offset' by the creation of a financial asset in the budget representing the loan (Spies-Butcher and Bryant 2017). This accounting method reflects corporate accounting practices, and explains why Australia's higher education funding model appears so heavily privatised. A more recent implication is that policy changes that increase the total pool of HECS loans (either by increasing the size of individual loans or increasing the number of loans) allow governments to increase the total funding directed to universities without appearing to raise taxes or spending. Universities receive the increased funding straight away, while students make payments later, reducing political costs, with some of the money never being repaid. Thus, HECS can partly be understood as a political response to a context where governments recognised that expanding the university sector was important, but ideological attacks on the state made it difficult to raise taxes or ordinary forms of government spending for that purpose.

Potentially, the framing of HECS as a loan encourages more aggressive forms of privatisation. Some policy advocates have pointed to a growing gap between the size of the HECS loans issued by government (and paid to universities) and the relatively lower flow of repayments from students (Norton 2014). The proportion of this gap that will never be repaid has been called 'doubtful debt'. The doubtful debt analysis drives calls to reform HECS to bring the system more into line with market loans. Doubtful debt has no direct impact on the budget bottom line, as repayments are also removed from budget balances. The 'problem' of non-repayment is in fact integral to the tax-like properties of HECS, which have been central to the policy's success in enabling a relatively egalitarian expansion of access to universities. However, it is precisely these features that are now under threat. Proposed changes to HECS have the potential to privatise the sector much more radically, even though at face value they appear to be an extension of current policy settings.

The Privatisation of HECS

The hybrid construction of HECS is constantly evolving and always contested. Since the election of the Coalition government in 2013, public debate over the funding of universities has been dominated by proposals to dismantle elements of public control of HECS and create a more thoroughly marketised system. The conceptualisation of HECS as a tax/loan hybrid that we provide in this chapter offers a framework to identify the nature of the threats posed by these moves, and to understand the political possibilities for actors that support the public character of universities. Proposals put forward by conservatives and economic rationalists have targeted three key features of the tax-like elements of HECS. They advocate deregulating fee/debt setting arrangements; charging a real rate of interest; and reducing the thresholds at which repayments begin. Combined, these proposals threaten to move HECS from a hybrid instrument to something that is closer to a private loan. Whereas the previous section highlighted the way that accounting for HECS as a financial instrument creates fiscal space in the context of budget austerity, this section notes that the same corporate accounting practices construct new 'costs' resulting from 'doubtful debt'.

The deregulation of undergraduate fees, and thus debt levels, for domestic students, has been the most widely debated proposal for market reform to HECS. This would allow universities to set their own fee levels for different courses. The idea was initially proposed by the National

Commission of Audit established by the incoming Abbott Coalition government in 2013, and announced as part of the 2014 federal Budget. Under the proposal, decisions over fee levels would be devolved to individual universities, and direct government funding for undergraduate places would be reduced by 20 per cent. Universities would therefore have the power to determine the amount of HECS debt issued by the federal government to individual students. Under corporate accounting rules, this reduction in grant funding would deliver budget savings, while the cost of issuing larger HECS debts would be moved off the budget. The package also envisaged expanded access to HECS for private universities (Commonwealth of Australia 2014).

Deregulating decisions over fee increases represented a significant break to the hybrid structure of HECS. Rather than the current government-mandated fee structure, fees in a deregulated environment would more clearly operate as a 'price' for higher education. This would more intensely marketise the higher education sector, as price differentiation based on demand for degrees, costs of delivery and university status would be added to existing modes of competition. Because universities are subject to strong status hierarchies, this potentially creates divergent trends. High-status institutions would have incentives to reduce the number of places and increase their fees, while lower status institutions could move to create a larger number of 'low-cost' places, potentially leading to problems such as those experienced in the VET sector. The likely result is an expanded but more heavily stratified sector.

The second threat to the hybrid construction of HECS lies in efforts to charge real rates of interest on student debt. This was proposed as part of the same package as the deregulation of student fees but represented a more significant attempt to transform HECS in the image of a private loan product. The existing system of indexing interest rates to inflation ensures that the size of debts does not accumulate through the compounding of interest, as occurs in private credit markets. Instead, debts maintain their real value over time. This offers social protection to students and graduates that take longer to repay their debts due to extended periods of time below the income-repayment threshold, or because of further education, or precarious and/or low-paid employment, or time out of the workforce for such reasons as caring responsibilities. The exact proposal was to charge a rate of interest equivalent to the ten-year government bond rate, up to a maximum of 6 per cent per annum (Commonwealth of Australia 2014).

The imperative for charging real interest rates for HECS came from the construction of public debt interest costs from 'doubtful debt'. Because HECS is accounted for as a loan, the indexation of debts is treated as a concessional interest rate that must be financed through government borrowing. The public debt interest costs of financing HECS debts that will never be repaid have been projected to make up an increasing proportion of total public debt interest costs over time (Parliamentary Budget Office 2016). Two implicit assumptions underpin this thinking: (1) that HECS loans themselves require the government to incur a market debt (rather than funding spending from general revenue); and (2) that this market debt is then only repaid following private repayments by each individual student. Both are the constructions of the accounting system, rather than practical requirements. Nonetheless, the government exploited these assumptions to argue that a real interest rate was necessary to reflect the cost of government borrowing (Commonwealth of Australia 2014).

Proposals to deregulate fees and impose a real rate of interest were successfully blocked by Labor, Greens and crossbench senators on the back of campaigning by unions and students, and widespread public opposition (The Australia Institute 2015). The public debate was heavily shaped by widely-cited estimates of $100,000-plus degrees, which would be exacerbated by new interest charges (National Tertiary Education Union 2014). The success of political mobilisations in defence of the tax-like features of HECS against these changes indicates a durability in the hybrid construction of HECS. However, since abandoning the package in 2016, the government floated limited forms of fee deregulation for select 'flagship' courses (Knott and Cook 2016), and new proposals have emerged, such as charging a HECS initiation loan fee to recoup interest costs (Norton and Cherastidtham 2016). This suggests that imperatives for similar market reforms will be an ongoing feature of the funding landscape for Australian universities.

Indeed, the final proposal – reducing the threshold at which HECS debts begin to be repaid – has been the most consistently proposed market reform targeting the tax-like features of the HECS system. It is the element of the failed 2014 package relating to HECS that was both retained and extended in the 2017 federal Budget, which proposed to reduce the initial payment threshold from $55,874 to $42,000 (Commonwealth of Australia 2017). Reducing the income threshold to levels that are well below average earnings weakens the tax-like character of HECS by reducing the progressivity of repayments and thus the extent to which those repayments operate as income taxes. The lower the repayment threshold, the higher the proportion of debtors that make repayments, and the more closely the system mimics a private loan contract with regular minimum installments that are based on market considerations, rather than ability to pay.

As with the proposal to charge a real rate of interest, imperatives to enforce faster HECS repayments from lower-income earners come from the accounting consequences of 'doubtful debt'. The non-repayment of HECS debt reduces the 'fair value' of accumulated HECS debt, as a government-held financial asset, on the government's balance sheet of assets and liabilities. Fair value is essentially an estimate of the price an asset could be sold for to investors in the market. In 2015, non-repayment, combined with the concessional interest rate, reduced estimates of the fair value of accumulated HECS debt by $11.9 billion, compared to its nominal value of $52.2 billion (Parliamentary Budget Office 2016: 6–7). Moves to create a more loan-like system of HECS repayments, to increase the fair value of HECS as a financial asset, is an example of new pressures towards privatisation, not motivated by 'budget repair', but from the adoption of corporate accounting techniques in the public sector.

Conclusion

Market restructuring has transformed Australian universities. Corporatisation has reshaped university governance, undermining working conditions and tying research to private interests. Universities have become more dependent on fees from international students, reinforcing efforts to maximise status and respond to external ranking systems. However, the system has also grown rapidly, expanding access to an increasingly diverse student population. Much of that expansion has been driven by the introduction of HECS. HECS, we argue, looks like privatisation, but functions like a policy hybrid that simultaneously commodifies and redistributes educational opportunities. The tax-like features of HECS have protected students from the risks associated with privatisation, while its loan-like features enable governments to shift spending off their yearly budget balances to subvert the politically imposed fiscal constraints of economic rationalism. This hybrid construction, however, also generates new political pressures for privatisation evidenced in the Coalition's recent proposals.

For supporters of public education, HECS creates a paradox. When the relatively public nature of HECS is recognised, shifting to a system of free education becomes a less radical change. Governments would continue to fund universities, financed from tax revenue, as occurs with HECS. The main substantive change would be internal to the distributive design of the income tax system. However, the same accounting practices that allowed HECS to expand access to universities without increasing measures of taxation or spending, also exaggerate the cost of transitioning to 'free education'. Abolishing HECS would return these costs to yearly budget balances. Increasing the (measured) base funding of universities is necessary to improve the quality of teaching, the independence of research and working conditions. Our analysis points to a progressive policy agenda that extends the tax-like features already present in HECS. Changing HECS repayments from average to marginal rates and raising repayment thresholds would provide greater protection for students, without immediate budgetary cost. As the tax-like features of HECS expand, and the number of people attending universities and VET increases, efforts to privatise will meet greater resistance and free education may become more viable as a political solution to the accounting contradictions hybridity entails.

References

Ansell, B. and Gingrich, J. (2013) 'A tale of two trilemmas: varieties of higher education and the service economy' in Wren, A. (ed.), *Political Economy of the Service Transition*. Oxford, Oxford University Press: 214–243.

Bell, S. and Keating, M. (2018) *Fair Share: Competing Claims and Australia's Economic Future*. Carlton, Melbourne University Press.

Bradley, D. et al. (2008) *Review of Australian Higher Education: Final Report*. Canberra, Commonwealth of Australia, 12 December.

Chapman, B. (1997) 'Conceptual issues and the Australian experience with income contingent charges for higher education', *The Economic Journal*, 107 (442): 738–751.

Chapman, B., Higgins, T. and Stiglitz, J.E. (eds) (2014) *Income Contingent Loans: Theory, Practice and Prospects*. Basingstoke, Palgrave Macmillan.

Chapman, B. and Ryan, C. (2005) 'The access implications of income-contingent charges for higher education: lessons from Australia', *Economics of Education Review*, 24 (5): 491–512.

Commonwealth of Australia (2014) *Budget 2014–15: Higher Education*. Canberra, Commonwealth of Australia, 13 May.

——(2017) *The Higher Education Reform Package*. Canberra, Commonwealth of Australia, 1 May.

Connell, R. (2013) 'The neoliberal cascade and education: an essay on the market agenda and its consequences', *Critical Studies in Education*, 54 (2): 99–112.

Department of Education and Training (2015) *Higher Education in Australia: A Review of Reviews from Dawkins to Today*. Canberra, Commonwealth of Australia, 20 October.

——(2017) *2016 Appendix 2 - Equity groups*. Canberra, Commonwealth of Australia, 30 November.

Kemp, D. and Norton, A. (2014) *Review of the Demand Driven Funding System*. Canberra, Commonwealth of Australia, 16 April.

Knott, M. and Cook, H. (2016) 'The end of the one-size-fits-all university: Turnbull government considers big fee shake-up', *The Sydney Morning Herald*, 4 May.

Libich, J. (2015) *Real-World Economic Policy: Insights from Leading Australian Economists*. Southbank, Cengage Learning Australia.

Lomax-Smith, J. (2011) *Higher Education Base Funding Review: Final Report*, Department of Education, Employment and Workplace Relations, Canberra, Commonwealth of Australia, October.

Marginson, S. (2004) 'Competition and markets in higher education: a "glonacal" analysis', *Policy Futures in Education* 2 (2): 175–244.

——(2013) 'The impossibility of capitalist markets in higher education', *Journal of Education Policy* 28 (3): 353–370.

Marginson, S. and Considine, M. (2000) *The Enterprise University: Power, Governance and Reinvention in Australia*. New York, Cambridge University Press.

National Tertiary Education Union (2014) *A Degree Shouldn't Cost a Mortgage: NTEU Analysis of Higher Education Changes in the 2014 Federal Budget*. Melbourne, National Tertiary Education Union, 31 July.

Norton, A. (2014) *Doubtful Debt: The Rising Cost of Student Loans*. Melbourne, Grattan Institute.

Norton, A. and Cherastidtham, I. (2016) *Shared Interest: A Universal Loan Fee for HELP*. Melbourne, Grattan Institute.

Norton, A. and Cakitaki, B. (2016) *Mapping Australian Higher Education 2016.* Melbourne, Grattan Institute.

Organisation of Economic Cooperation and Development (2017), 'Spending on Tertiary Education', *Education at a Glance: Educational Finance Indicators*, database.

Parliamentary Budget Office (2016) *Higher Education Loan Programme: Impact on the Budget*, Report No. 02/2016. Canberra, Commonwealth of Australia.

Ramia, G., Marginson, S. and Sawir, E. (2013) *Regulating International Students' Wellbeing*. Bristol, Policy Press.

Ryan, S., et al. (2013) 'Casual academic staff in an Australian university: marginalised and excluded', *Tertiary Education and Management*, 19 (2): 161–175.

Spies-Butcher, B. and Bryant, G. (2017) 'Accounting for income contingent loans as a policy hybrid: politics of discretion and discipline in financialised welfare states', *New Political Economy*, 8 November: 1–18.

Stilwell, F. (1986) *The Accord – And Beyond: The Political Economy of the Labor Government*. Sydney, Pluto Press.

The Australia Institute (2015) *University Deregulation – Polling Brief*. Available from tai.org.au/content/university-deregulation-polling-brief

Tunny, G. (2006) 'Educational Attainment in Australia', *Economic Roundup*, Canberra, Commonwealth of Australia.

Watt, I. (2015) *Review of Research Policy and Funding Arrangements for Higher Education.* Canberra, Commonwealth of Australia.

Willemse, N. and de Beer, P. (2012) 'Three worlds of educational welfare states? A comparative study of higher education systems across welfare states', *Journal of European Social Policy* 22 (2): 105–117.

PART THREE

MACRO-ECONOMIC DIMENSIONS

CHAPTER 14

MONETARY POLICY AND UNEMPLOYMENT

MICHAEL BEGGS

1993 was year zero for reformed macro-economic policy in Australia. That was when the Reserve Bank adopted an inflation target – '2 to 3 per cent on average over a period of years' – and that is what central bankers keep looking back to in anniversary retrospectives (Stevens 1999; Stevens 2003; Debelle 2009). But 1993 was also the year of the *Industrial Relations Reform Act*, which confirmed the rise of enterprise bargaining and the decline of centralised bargaining – just as much a part of this story.[1]

Every ten years the Reserve Bank holds a conference looking back at the policy of the previous decade. Gruen and Stevens (2000) noted that the conference on the 1990s had a different format from the retrospective on the 1980s ten years prior. At the earlier conference there had been a paper on monetary policy (Milbourne 1990), and *another* paper on inflation (Carmichael 1990). This latter paper discussed inflation largely as a product of wage setting and, 'in this view of the world, the wages Accords of the 1980s … determined the rate of wage and price expectations'. The idea that 'wages outcomes were the proximate determinant of prices' was not just a 1980s fad – it was a 'long-standing tradition in Australian economic policy-making and many academic circles'. However, by the turn of the century, 'this view of the world' had come to look old-fashioned, due to 'the global intellectual shift towards inflation targeting' (Gruen and Stevens 2000: 52–53).

As evidence for this shift, Gruen and Stevens presented the Australian Industrial Relations Commission's 1997 review of award wages. The Commission decided for wage restraint on the grounds that:

> the Reserve Bank's intimations of the order of increase ... in its view, accords with its inflation target. Any increase greater than the amount which we grant carries a risk ... of leading to a rise in interest rates. In the current state of the economy, with a high and seemingly stationary unemployment rate and an inadequate growth rate, we are unwilling to take that risk (quoted in Gruen and Stevens 2000: 53)

This is telling indeed, but it hardly demonstrates the irrelevance of wage outcomes for inflation. It is, rather, a recognition that the central bank would now rule the roost, and any too-rapid growth in wages would have unfortunate consequences – not, mind you, because the central bank deliberately set out to *punish* workers with unemployment for the Commission's transgressions; it would just be over there, to one side of things, targeting inflation, and watching for hints of untoward price increases. It was up to the Industrial Relations Commission to make sure it would not be responsible for such hints.

Inflation was now established as a technocratic problem of demand management rather than one of conflicting income claims. In retrospect, we might see the 1970s stagflation and the Accord years as a tumultuous passage of responsibility through politics from one independent state institution – the arbitration system – to another – the central bank. But the arbitration system had a different kind of independence – judicial – and its mission required it to also consider factors besides macro-economics. During the long postwar boom, demand restraint always lurked in the background of wages policy – and sometimes came into play – but the notion of deliberately targeting less-than-full employment was politically poisonous.[2] In the 1990s, all was reversed: demand management became responsible for price stability; departure from full employment became the fault of labour market institutions.

Policymakers would not admit that the inflation-targeting regime involved turning away from full employment. They frame it differently.

'Inflation-targeting' does seem to identify the whole policy regime with a single-minded focus on inflation.[3] Monetary policy would be judged simply by its success in keeping consumer price inflation within the target range of '2 to 3 per cent on average over the cycle', as successive agreements between Governor and Treasurer have put it since 1996. On the face of it this seems to run against the Reserve Bank's statutory commitment to both 'the stability of the currency' *and* 'the maintenance of full employment'.[4] But, as Debelle (2009) argues, stipulating that the target need only be met 'on average over the cycle' leaves more room for the pursuit of growth and employment than would be the case were a stricter target set. In any case, there is no *long-run* trade-off between inflation and unemployment. To prioritise inflation is not to choose price stability over full employment, because there is no *sustainable* rate of unemployment below the rate compatible with stable inflation.

Figure 1: Unemployment and inflation

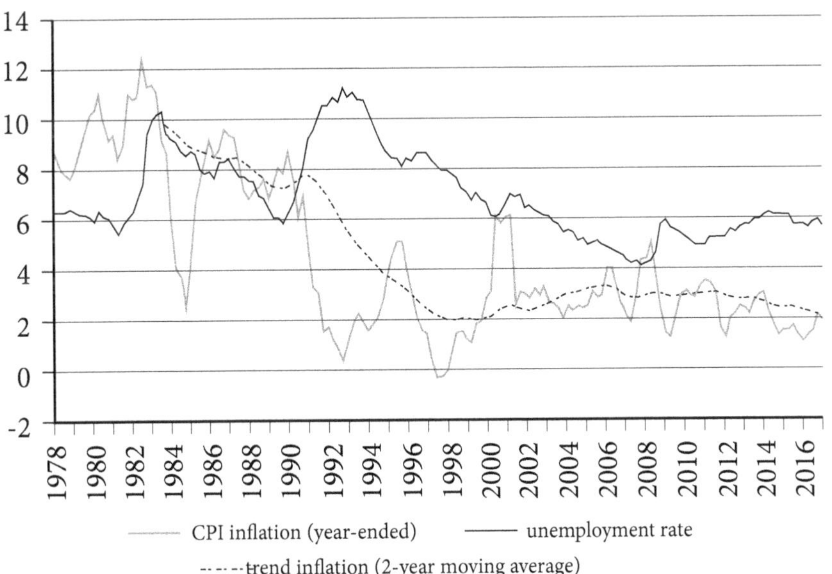

Source: ABS (2017a; 2917b)

In these terms, Australian macro-economic policy since 1993 has been a great success – at least compared with the previous two decades, as can be seen in Figure 1. We might wonder what there is to complain about. According to the Reserve Bank's clearly stated goals, Australian macro-economic policy has been successful. But we do not have to claim policy has been an unmitigated disaster to find fault. Some might raise the role of luck – and central bankers would be the first to admit that they share credit with exceptional economic weather (Stevens 2003: 24). This chapter presents a deeper critique – not of the implementation of policy, but of the framework itself. For those with higher aspirations to economic equality and security for all, the current regime falls short not judged by its own standards, but because it depends on the discipline of unemployment to meet them.

Diminished Expectations

Five per cent unemployment looks impressive against the background of the last quarter of the twentieth century, but not in relation to the postwar decades of 'full employment'. Why did macro-economics give up that goal? One popular answer was offered by the former governor of the Reserve Bank, Ian Macfarlane: policymakers once believed in a stable Phillips-curve trade-off between unemployment and inflation. But:

> to get unemployment below the level that was originally consistent with low inflation will take a series of increases in inflation with no apparent equilibrium end-point in sight ... This critique of the overly ambitious use of Keynesian demand management policy was mainly the work of Milton Friedman. For a decade or more it was hotly debated, but was ultimately proved right and is accepted today by economists of virtually all political persuasions (Macfarlane 2006: 21–24).

It is true that the 'natural-rate expectations-adjusted Phillips curve' associated with Friedman remains the basic framework for thinking about the relationship between unemployment and inflation. Economists speak of the 'non-accelerating inflation rate of unemployment', or NAIRU, rather than the 'natural rate', but the central idea remains. Because expectations adapt to inflation, for unemployment to remain below the NAIRU it is not enough for inflation to be high – it must keep getting higher.

The Reserve Bank does estimate a NAIRU for Australia (Cusbert 2017: 13). It does not rely on the NAIRU in a mechanical way, not least because of the level of uncertainty. But it plays a role in forecasts, and, perhaps more importantly, it justifies the moderation of expectations about what rate of employment it is reasonable to expect. How else could the governor speak of a 'strong labour market' in late 1994 while unemployment remained above 8 per cent (RBA 1994)? This is also why 5 per cent unemployment should now be considered a policy success: we might not know whether the NAIRU is 4 per cent or 6 per cent (the boundaries of the 70 per cent confidence intervals about the RBA's central estimate (Cusbert 2017: 15), but we know it is much higher than the 1.5 to 2 per cent once considered a decently tight labour market.

What is misleading about Macfarlane's story is the implication that it explains the stagflationary end to full employment in the 1970s. The casual listener would assume that policymakers had misguidedly believed in a stable trade-off, and had flown too close to the sun. In fact, the idea of a stable inflation-unemployment relation had always met with scepticism in Australia, both because of the role of the arbitration system in wage setting, and because of the importance of international commodities prices. Policymakers had often seen full employment and price stability as in tension, but their answer was not to make a trade-off in favour of the former; this was always seen as unsustainable. Instead, they tried to use the arbitration system to restrain wage inflation without the need for higher unemployment.

The postwar experience cannot have been the result of policy holding unemployment below the NAIRU. If it had, the model predicts that the period would have been one of ever-accelerating inflation, but inflation did not take off until the mid-1970s. In 1973, a monetarist made an early estimate of the 'natural rate of unemployment' in Australia, giving his 'best guess' that it was 'in the order of 1.7 per cent'! He recommended that 'a 2 per cent unemployment rate would bring inflation close to zero in something like five years' (Parkin 1973: 422–423). Rao (1977) estimated it at 2 per cent; and Nevile (1977), cautiously, estimated 2.3 per cent.

Estimates of the NAIRU followed actual unemployment up, and by the 1990s were in the range of 5 to 10 per cent (Borland and Kennedy 1998: 71). Australian economists had never been inclined to see the NAIRU as a *natural* rate, but one that depended on conditions that could evolve (this was the case even for Friedman).[5] The Treasury's TRYM model used a structural break to reflect that *something* had changed in the mid-1970s: it estimated the NAIRU at a constant 3 per cent or so before 1974, and a constant 7 per cent after (Johnson and Downes 1994: 8). Recursive estimation by Reserve Bank economists found the NAIRU to be around 2 per cent using data up to 1974, and 6 per cent using data all the way to 1997 (Gruen, Pagan and Thompson 1999: 17).[6] In the late 1990s, Reserve Bank economists pioneered estimates of a 'time-varying' NAIRU – that is, dropping the assumption that it was constant and allowing it to change over time – but a very rapid jump in the mid-1970s remained (Debelle and Vickery 1997; Gruen, Pagan and Thompson 1999: 22). Figure 2 shows Cusbert's (2017: 15) estimate of the NAIRU since 1980, using the same basic technique.[7]

These models generate estimates of the NAIRU while remaining agnostic about the reasons why it shifts. In the models, change in the rate of inflation (price or wage) depends on factors including – apart from the level of unemployment itself – *change* in unemployment, recent inflation, long-run expectations of inflation, and import prices. Movements in the NAIRU reflect shifts in the apparent unemployment-inflation relationship left unexplained by these factors. As Cusbert (2017: 18) acknowledges, if any relevant 'omitted variables change and cause inflation or wage growth to deviate from the model predictions, some of this deviation will be attributed to changes in the NAIRU'. Although it is not assumed by the estimation procedure, the estimated NAIRU usually moves slowly, which suggests that the missing variables usually move slowly (Cusbert 2017: 15–16). This is the basis for seeing the NAIRU as representing something real, though not directly observable.

Central bank economists themselves are tentative when it comes to the NAIRU. Given its large degree of uncertainty, it cannot be used as a well-calibrated gauge to guide policy in real time.[8] Rather than measuring the distance between actual unemployment and the central estimate of the NAIRU to make interest-rate decisions, central bankers watch for wage pressures, and the NAIRU estimate gives *one* indicator of labour market tightness. The real importance of the NAIRU is that it represents a presumed limit on what macro-economic policy can do.

Figure 2: Reserve Bank NAIRU estimate

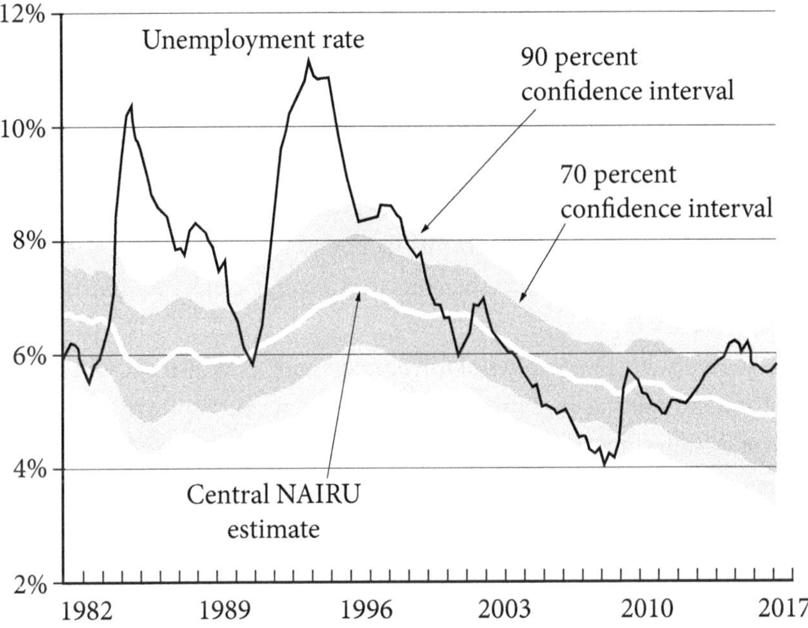

Source: Cusbert (2017: 5)

The NAIRU Story

We can distinguish, as Stockhammer (2008; 2011) does, between a 'NAIRU model' and the 'NAIRU story'. Any model in which the rate of change of inflation depends in part on the level of unemployment will have a NAIRU, whether it is explicit or implicit.[9] But there are different interpretations of the factors lying behind it. Marxian/post-Keynesian conflict models treat inflation as a result of incompatible nominal claims over real output (for example, Rowthorn 1977; Lavoie 2014: 541–573). Even among neoclassical interpretations there are wide variations: from Friedman's (1968) view of the 'natural rate' as arising from market imperfections and search costs, to Shapiro and Stiglitz's (1984) view of 'equilibrium unemployment as a worker discipline device'.[10]

The orthodox 'NAIRU story' that became conventional policy wisdom in the 1990s was one particular interpretation, reducing it to a question of labour market inflexibility. As the influential 1994 OECD *Jobs Study* put it, macro-economic policy could aim to counteract cyclical unemployment, which was a matter of demand, 'but it is relatively impotent in dealing with unemployment resulting from structural causes' (OECD 1994: 29). Reducing structural unemployment – and thus the NAIRU – was a job for labour market and micro-economic reform. The study called for getting rid as much as possible of regulations that caused wage inflexibility or protected 'insiders' from the competition of 'outsiders', and the tightening of unemployment benefits that lowered claimants' incentives to look for work.

In Australia, the decades of full employment were also decades of centralised bargaining in which full-time, long-term employment was the norm. Minimum wages were high relative to average wages. Nevertheless, versions of the story took hold within Australian policy debates, and it became a key argument motivating the Labor government to promote decentralised enterprise bargaining. The government's 1994 'Working Nation' white paper,[11] in the aftermath of the 1991 recession, explicitly framed employment policy in terms of reducing the NAIRU. It argued that 'the NAIRU has increased with the recent rise in the number of long term unemployed' and 'reversing this increase will reduce the economy's underlying inflationary pressures' (Keating 1994: 21). To be sure, actual unemployment was still above the elevated NAIRU (see Figure 2), so there was a role for monetary policy, but it was a limited one. Reducing the NAIRU itself called for labour market reform, including a shift towards enterprise bargaining, 'which lowers inflationary pressures by linking wage increases directly to productivity improvements in the workplace' (Keating 1994: 21).

The Logic of the Pre-Emptive Strike

Given uncertainty about the 'true' NAIRU, could policy not experiment by pushing unemployment lower – to see what would happen? The price of not doing so seems hefty, especially if, as many believe, the NAIRU is subject to hysteresis. (That is, the actual unemployment rate feeds back into the NAIRU: for example, long-term unemployment may lower the ability of the chronically jobless to compete for jobs.) But policymakers err on the side of caution for two reasons. First, they believe it is easier to feed inflation than to dampen it: sub-NAIRU unemployment increases inflation faster than above-NAIRU unemployment brings it down (Debelle and Vickery 1997: 26; Borland and McDonald 2000: 22). Given the importance of expectations, policy credibility is critical, but easily lost. Second, monetary policy cools demand only over a period of time. The long lag means the central bank cannot wait for actual untoward wage growth; it must get in ahead of it. Bryan (2000) tracks references to wage pressures in Reserve Bank statements accompanying decisions to raise interest rates, noting that even where wage growth had not happened yet, it was around the corner: 'wages growth has to date remained moderate, but some recent developments point to higher wage demands in the future' (RBA 2000). Similar language marks policy-tightening phases throughout the decade.[12] More recently, with annual wage growth below 2 per cent, Reserve Bank governor Lowe remarked that it was an unusual respite from 'the more standard challenge ... to keep wage growth in check'. Still he was scanning for threats: 'we could hit a point at which workers, having had only modest pay increases for a run of years, decide that it is time for a catch up. If such a tipping point were reached, inflation pressures could emerge quite quickly' (Lowe 2017).

The objective is nominal – not real – wage restraint. But given the need for pre-emption, is it any wonder that real wages have grown substantially slower than labour productivity during most of the period of inflation targeting? The commodity price boom absorbed some of the impact during the 2000s, allowing relatively strong real wage growth in terms of consumer prices even as unit labour costs for firms declined. As Figure 3 shows, the consumer real wage (against the consumer price index) grew substantially more than the producer real wage (against the GDP deflator) (Borland 2011: 180-181). More recently, this has reversed.

FIGURE 3: REAL WAGES AND PRODUCTIVITY (INDEX: 1995 = 100)

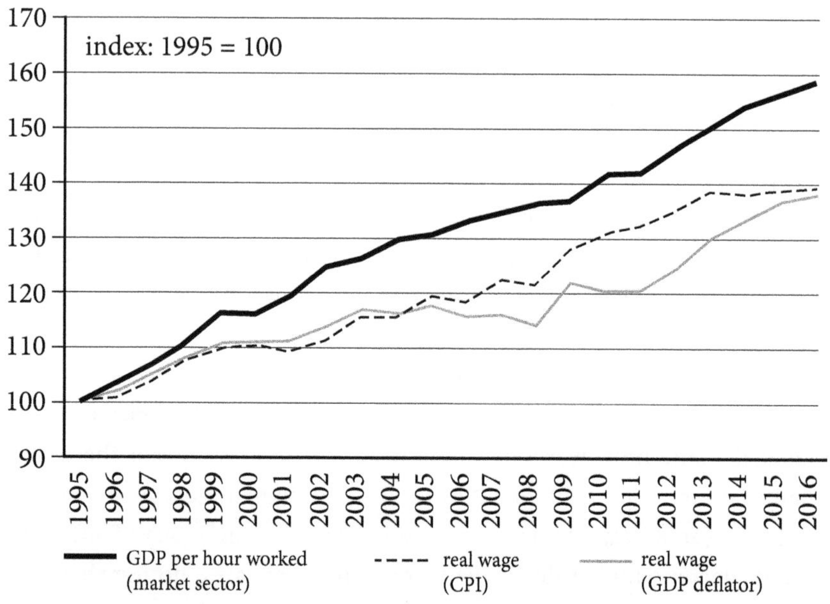

Source: ABS (2017c, 2017d, 2017e, 2017f).
Note: Real wage is represented by male full-time adult ordinary time weekly earnings. Data for all full-time adult ordinary earnings is not available for the whole period.

Restraint is also likely to have contributed to the rise in earnings inequality.[13] Some groups are much more at risk of unemployment than others. For example, the unemployment rate is more than twice as high among those with only a high school education than those with a university degree; it is three times as high among those who did not finish Year 12 or equivalent. As of August 2017, unemployment among managers (2.1 per cent) and professionals (1.7 per cent) is at full employment levels; for labourers it is 7.2 per cent. Unemployment is four times higher among Aboriginal and Torres Strait Islanders than among the population as a whole.[14]

Is Full Employment Possible?

What, then, is the alternative? The truth in the NAIRU is that there *are* limits to macro-economic policy; demand management alone at some point runs into an inflation barrier – a left-Keynesian idea before it was a neoclassical one (Robinson 1956; Stockhammer 2008). The open question is what determines the position of that barrier, and what might shift it. During the decades of full employment in Australia, most economists' answer to that question was that centralised wage bargaining insulated wage and price change from labour market conditions, at least to some extent. Centralised wage bargaining was seen as a way of making full employment compatible with price stability – so long as it kept money-wage growth in line with productivity growth.

This is what Gruen and Stevens (2000: 52–53) meant by the 'long-standing tradition in Australian economic policy-making and many academic circles that wages outcomes were the proximate determinant of prices, and that wages could be influenced independently of monetary policy.'[15] They implied that this tradition had been left behind by the framework of inflation-targeting, and based on a vision of macro-economics with the NAIRU at its core. But it is easier to estimate the NAIRU than explain it.

The orthodox 'NAIRU story' fills the void with the claim that the cure is labour market flexibility and tighter benefits. However, the evidence from cross-country studies was always mixed at best. Jackman, one of the pioneers of these studies, questions the degree to which they supported the deregulatory agenda. Employment protection regulation 'appears to have no strong effect on overall unemployment because its effects in reducing turnover offset its effects in increasing the duration of spells'. Union membership and coverage are linked to higher unemployment – but with a very interesting caveat: 'highly unionised economies where bargaining is centralised are able to sustain low unemployment rates over long periods of time' (Jackman 1998: 47).

In the 2000s, a number of studies called the NAIRU story into question (Stockhammer 2011: 306–307). Blanchard and Wolfers (2000), for example, show that 'explanations based solely on [labour market] institutions ... run ... into a major empirical problem: many of these institutions were already present when unemployment was low (and similar across countries), and … the movement since then has been mostly in the opposite direction' (Blanchard and Wolfers 2000: 2). Baker et al. (2005) find 'no empirical support for the OECD-IMF orthodoxy … [T]he strong cross-sectional relation between unemployment and institutions … is not robust to alternative definitions of the variables' (108). The strongest association they find between unemployment and labour market institutions is a *negative* link with bargaining coordination – that is, centralised bargaining 'has a very large effect in reducing unemployment' (106). Stockhammer and Klär find that once investment and interest rates are introduced into a model that includes all the labour market factors included in a standard OECD panel analysis, labour market institutional effects are 'only moderate and, for the most part, non-robust' (2011: 454).

In Australia, economists have often been cautious about the determinants of the NAIRU. Gruen, Pagan and Thompson (1999: 28–29) tested two popular candidates: the replacement ratio – the ratio of the unemployment benefit to average earnings – and the long-term unemployment rate, as a proxy for feedback channels of hysteresis that would lead above-NAIRU unemployment to increase the NAIRU. They found both to be 'neither statistically nor economically significant'. But they suggested that wage restraint under the Accord may explain the gradual decline in their estimated NAIRU in the 1980s, running against the standard story that centralised bargaining meant a higher NAIRU (21–22). Treasury economists similarly found that 'more centralised wage regimes have tended to reduce the sensitivity of wage inflation to pressure by insiders' (Johnson and Downes 1994: 7–8) – in other words, that the arbitration system had promoted wage restraint at any given level of unemployment. Cusbert (2017: 18) suggests that employee bargaining power could be an important influence on the estimated NAIRU – which is prominent in post-Keynesian conflict models – but it is 'unobservable' and difficult to find a proxy that could incorporate it into the model.

Borland and McDonald (2000) review the Australian literature, especially research trying to explain the sudden rise in the apparent NAIRU in the 1970s. In general, they suggest that increases in real unit labour costs in the 1970s reduced labour demand initially, while hysteresis explains why equilibrium unemployment did not return to 'normal' once that was reversed.[16] Labour market rigidities do not feature, though some suggest the rise in unemployment benefits relative to wages may also have played a role in the mid-1970s (Borland and McDonald 2000: 39). Overall, this is all more in line with the older view of the importance of wage-bargaining dynamics than with the orthodox 'NAIRU story'.

Might this tradition become relevant again? Could incomes policy be revived as the core of an alternative macroeconomic strategy in Australia? We have seen that policymakers have reason for caution in testing the potential for pushing unemployment lower. But if hysteresis effects are strong, the costs of not doing so are also high.[17] If centralised bargaining could help isolate wage movements from labour market pressure, could that free macro-economic policy to again pursue genuine full employment?

There is a long-standing left/labour tradition in Australian economics (with links to Cambridge post-Keynesianism) that supports incomes policy from the side of the labour movement (Harcourt 1997; 2001). It is now mostly forgotten, though it has been influential at times: informing labour arguments at the arbitration courts in the late 1950s and 1960s (Beggs 2015: 96–97; Millmow 2017: 135–136, 140–141), proposals for fighting inflation in the 1970s (Beggs 2015: 207), and, of course, feeding into the Accord in the 1980s.

Should it be revived? There are some concerns. First, the strategies had an existing institutional structure to work with. Even that was insufficient, but the once-mighty arbitration system is now vestigial. As Harcourt (1997) laments, the move to decentralised bargaining is a recipe not only for rising earnings inequality, but also for lower productivity. Tying wage increases to *local* rather than *general* productivity increases allows inefficient industries and firms to remain in business by repressing wages. But decentralised wage bargaining has also created winners who might resist egalitarian wage compression. Most people's wages have broken away from the 'safety net' Awards, though there has been a move in the other direction in the last few years (Jericho 2017). A macro-economically effective incomes policy needs to be able to impose ceilings on incomes, not just floors, but that is something the system at its height never did, and it would be doubly politically difficult today.

Another sting in the tail is that if incomes policy works to increase the compatibility of full employment with price stability, it does so by surrendering labour's *market* power to challenge the distribution of income. It works, after all, by restraining nominal income claims so that unemployment does not have to. Incomes policy proposals from the left have generally coupled wage control with controls on non-wage income. The original 1983 Statement of Accord proposed 'a substantial array of indirect measures' for controlling non-wage incomes, including dividends, capital gains, interest, and professional and trade incomes, and called for 'an equitable and clearly discernible *redistribution* of income' (reprinted in Wilson, Bradford and Fitzpatrick 2000: 290–291). But, in practice, this side of the Accord was given little else but lip service, so that it became mainly a device for wage restraint (Beggs 2015: 266–273).

The labour movement should learn from experience, be cautious about what it surrenders, and make sure that any incomes policy be part of a wider program of redistribution. The Accord was struck in a period of serious weakness for labour – with double-digit unemployment it had little market power. An incomes policy in full employment conditions would be different, leaving workers with other cards to play if necessary. I have argued elsewhere that full employment, backed by an incomes policy, is likely to be an unstable situation for capitalism, but worth pursuing nonetheless (Beggs 2016). It stabilises an economic problem only by politicising distribution. In an economic system dependent on profit-motivated investment, that will be vulnerable, but also potentially opens up new horizons.

ENDNOTES

1 On labour market policy, see Chapter 9 by Jim Stanford.

2 The history of inflation and Australian macro-economic policy from the postwar boom to the Accord is told in Beggs (2015).

3 It is interesting that the 'inflation-targeting' regime is named after its end rather than its means. Previous eras of monetary policy have been recalled for their means (for example, the postwar 'banking policy' period (Rowan 1980: 120–121)), theoretical framework (the 'Radcliffe period (Rowan 1980: 122–123)) or intermediate target (monetary targeting). The post-1993 regime might have been labelled for any of these features: it is also distinctive in means (an almost exclusive reliance on adjustment of the cash rate), theoretical framework, and intermediate target (estimated potential output).

4 There is also a third goal listed in the Reserve Bank Act 1959 – 'economic prosperity and welfare' – but it is vague.

5 With unemployment having peaked (for the moment) at 5 per cent in mid-1975, the Friedmanite Parkin adjusted his estimate upwards, confidently declaring the following year that '3.5 per cent seems like a safe topside estimate of the natural rate', but that 'around 2.5 per cent is rather likely'. He suggested 'improved unemployment compensation which makes unemployment more agreeable; revaluation and tariff cuts which raise labour turnover; the oil price rise … and massive about-turns in monetary and fiscal policy' were 'only the most obvious factors' behind the shift (Parkin 1976: 138–139).

6 The procedure for this estimation differs from estimates of a 'time-varying' NAIRU in that it involved estimating a *constant* NAIRU for each year using data up to the year in question. So, the estimates for early years use only a few years of data, while those for later years use data from many more years. We would naturally expect more stability in the estimates towards the end of the period, with their larger sample size – but it is notable that the NAIRU estimates up to 1974 are stable, with the exception of an outlier in 1972. The estimates then fluctuate wildly between −1.5 and 16.5 for years in the mid-1970s, and climb from around 4 per cent to 8 per cent from then to the early 1980s, before settling down at around 6 per cent.

7 The estimation uses data going back to 1968, but estimates for the years before 1980 are not reported on the chart.

8 As can be seen in Figure 2, the 90 per cent confidence interval extends at least 1.5 percentage points on either side of the central estimate. The RBA's estimate of the NAIRU at the end of 2016 places it somewhere between 3.5 and 6.5 per cent.

9 This does not mean the NAIRU will necessarily be unique or stable. Lavoie (2014: 541–543) presents post-Keynesian inflation theory as a 'rejection of the accelerationist hypothesis' – but is really objecting to the idea of a stable, exogenous NAIRU. It is clear from the 'reduced form' post-Keynesian Phillips curve presented in the conclusion that change in inflation depends in part on the level of unemployment (Lavoie 2014: 572). There is therefore an implicit NAIRU in the model – a rate of unemployment at which the rate of inflation will not change. It is not necessarily stable, because it depends on the other parameters in the model. But as we have seen, a variable NAIRU is now a common neoclassical proposition as well.

10 Pollin (1998) has even suggested that the concept of the NAIRU has brought neoclassical understandings of unemployment and inflation closer to radical views, recognising that 'the natural rate is really a social phenomenon measuring the class strength of working people, as indicated through their ability to organise effective unions and establish a liveable minimum wage' (Pollin 1998: 7).

11 See Olney and Gallet on the evolution of the employment services market in Chapter 7.

12 For example, in 2007–08: 'Growth in labour costs has been contained thus far … But growth in aggregate demand will, nonetheless, need to moderate if inflation is to be kept to 2–3 per cent in the medium term' (RBA 2007). And in 2010: while the

labour market is not as tight as in 2007 and 2008, some further strengthening would appear to be in prospect, judging by the trends in job vacancies' (RBA 2010).

13 See Stilwell on neoliberal economic reform and inequality in Chapter 19. The relationship is complicated because the wages of workers at the very bottom of the distribution have been protected from labour market slack by the Award 'safety net' in some periods. In the decade from 1993, the earnings of those in the bottom decile grew more rapidly than the earnings of those a little further up, though still less than those in the top half of the distribution. But during the take-off of the mining boom, 2003–08, the minimum wage was deliberately restrained, and earnings inequality widened across the board: those of higher deciles grew more than those of the middle, which themselves grew more than those at the bottom, which did not grow at all (Borland 2014: 2). From 2008 to 2013, growth improved at the bottom, and pulled back in the middle (and to some extent, further up), as the 'safety net' improved but many workers shifted onto enterprise agreements. Since then, these trends have reversed: there has been a widespread shift back from enterprise agreements to Awards – a major factor in recent wage stagnation (Jericho 2017).

14 Data is from ABS catalogue numbers 6227.0 and 6291.0.55.003 (August 2017) and 4714.0. Unemployed workers are classified by occupation based on their last job. See Borland and Kennedy (1998: 81–85) for comparable data from the 1990s.

15 Australian economists had generally been sceptical of the original Phillips curve: when Phillips himself visited in 1959 and estimated an unemployment-wage-inflation curve for Australia (Phillips 2000), 'it was so criticised and dissected ... that it never saw the light of day in the public domain' (Harcourt 2000: 304). The objections mainly came from the importance of the arbitration system in wage setting, which partially isolated wages from labour market conditions (Beggs 2015: 101–106).

16 Of course, hysteresis in the NAIRU itself calls for explanation – how exactly does unemployment feed back to change the NAIRU? Beveridge curve studies have looked at the relationship between job vacancies and unemployment to tackle the extent to which declines in job search efficiency, or regional or skill mismatches arising from structural change have been at work. Borland and McDonald (2000: 32–33) conclude that there is no evidence suggesting that structural change explains the apparent outward shift in the Beveridge curve in the 1970s (i.e. more vacancies for a given unemployment rate), but shifts in the regional pattern of production may have played a part.

17 Mitchell (1987) finds hysteresis strong enough in Australia that holding unemployment below the NAIRU would not mean ever-increasing inflation because the NAIRU would quickly catch up with the lower actual rare – a result that would encourage more ambitious macro-economic policy. In a tighter labour market apparent 'structural unemployment' would disappear.

References

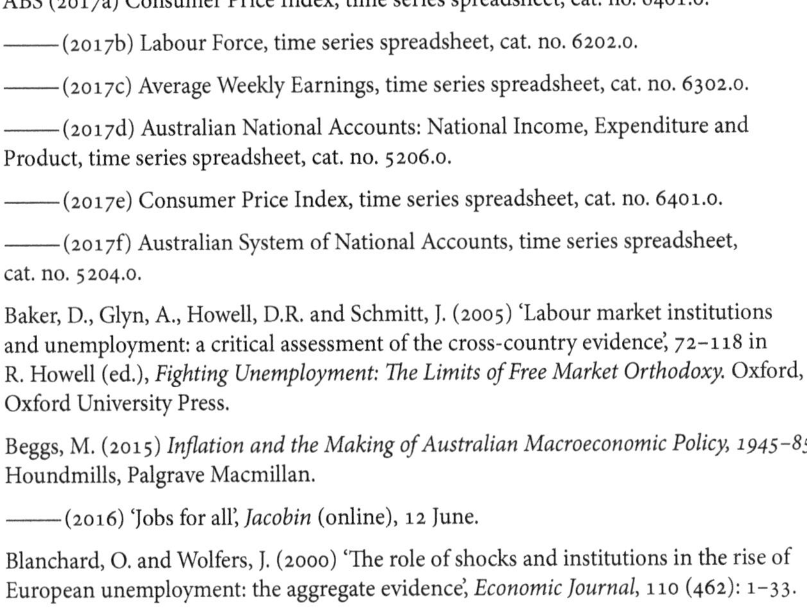

ABS (2017a) Consumer Price Index, time series spreadsheet, cat. no. 6401.0.

——(2017b) Labour Force, time series spreadsheet, cat. no. 6202.0.

——(2017c) Average Weekly Earnings, time series spreadsheet, cat. no. 6302.0.

——(2017d) Australian National Accounts: National Income, Expenditure and Product, time series spreadsheet, cat. no. 5206.0.

——(2017e) Consumer Price Index, time series spreadsheet, cat. no. 6401.0.

——(2017f) Australian System of National Accounts, time series spreadsheet, cat. no. 5204.0.

Baker, D., Glyn, A., Howell, D.R. and Schmitt, J. (2005) 'Labour market institutions and unemployment: a critical assessment of the cross-country evidence', 72–118 in R. Howell (ed.), *Fighting Unemployment: The Limits of Free Market Orthodoxy*. Oxford, Oxford University Press.

Beggs, M. (2015) *Inflation and the Making of Australian Macroeconomic Policy, 1945–85*. Houndmills, Palgrave Macmillan.

——(2016) 'Jobs for all', *Jacobin* (online), 12 June.

Blanchard, O. and Wolfers, J. (2000) 'The role of shocks and institutions in the rise of European unemployment: the aggregate evidence', *Economic Journal*, 110 (462): 1–33.

Borland, J. (2011) 'The Australian labour market in the 2000s: the quiet decade' in Gerard, H. and Kearns, J. (eds), *The Australian Economy in the 2000s*: 165–218. Reserve Bank of Australia, Sydney.

——(2014) 'Growing apart – earnings inequality in Australia from 1975 to 2013', *Labour Market Snapshot #9*, July, https://docs.google.com/file/d/0B_H1wGTm98W3SzE1MUJXQmtQWFU/edit

Borland, J. and Kennedy, S. (1998) 'Dimensions, structure and history of Australian unemployment', in Debelle, G. and Borland, J. (eds), *Unemployment and the Australian Labour Market*: 68–99. Sydney, Reserve Bank of Australia.

Borland, J. and McDonald, I. (2000) 'Labour market models of unemployment in Australia', Melbourne Institute Working Paper No. 15/00, September.

Bryan, D. (2000) 'A critical issue behind interest rates: how the Reserve Bank constitutes economic nationality', *Australian Review of Public Affairs Digest*, 14 July.

Carmichael, J. (1990) 'Inflation: performance and policy' in S. Grenville (ed.), *The Australian Macroeconomy in the 1980s*: 288–342. Sydney, Reserve Bank of Australia.

Cusbert, T. (2017) 'Estimating the NAIRU and the unemployment gap', *Reserve Bank of Australia Bulletin*, June: 13–22.

Debelle, G. (2009) 'The Australian experience with inflation targeting', speech delivered at Banco Central do Brasil XI Annual Seminar on Inflation Targeting, Rio de Janeiro, 15 May.

Debelle, G. and Vickery, J. (1997) *Is the Phillips Curve a Curve? Some Evidence and Implications for Australia*, RBA Research Discussion Paper 9706, October.

Friedman, M. (1968) 'The role of monetary policy', *American Economic Review*, 58 (1): 1–17.

Gruen, D., Pagan, A. and Thompson, C. (1999) *The Phillips Curve in Australia*, Reserve Bank of Australia Research Discussion Paper – RDP 1999-01, January.

Gruen, D. and Stevens, G. (2000) 'Australian macroeconomic performance and policies in the 1990s', in Gruen, D. and Shrestha, S. (eds), *The Australian Economy in the 1990s*: 32–72. Sydney, Reserve Bank of Australia.

Harcourt, G.C. (1997) 'Pay policy, accumulation and productivity', *Economic and Labour Relations Review*, 8 (1): 78–89.

——(2000) 'A left Keynesian view of the Phillips curve trade-off' in R. Leeson (ed.), *AWH Phillips: Collected Works in Contemporary Perspective*: 304–307. Cambridge, Cambridge University Press.

Jackman, R. (1998) 'European unemployment: why is it so high and what should be done about it?' in Debelle, G. and Borland, J. (eds), *Unemployment and the Australian Labour Market*: 39–63. Sydney, Reserve Bank of Australia.

Jericho, G. (2017) 'Is it time for Labor to end the hands-off approach to industrial relations?', *The Guardian*, 22 August.

Johnson, A. and Downes, P. (1994) 'The impact of a lower NAIRU on the Australian macroeconomy: responses in the Treasury macroeconomic (TRYM) model', paper presented to the 23rd Annual Conference of Economists, Economic Society of Australia. Canberra, Australian Government.

Keating, P.J. (1994) *Working Nation: The White Paper on Employment and Growth*. Canberra, Australian Government Publishing Service.

Lavoie, M. (2014) *Post-Keynesian Economics: New Foundations*. Cheltenham, Edward Elgar.

Lowe, P. (2017) 'The labour market and monetary policy', address to the Anika Foundation Luncheon, Sydney, 26 July.

Macfarlane, I. (2006) *The Search for Stability*. Sydney, ABC Books.

Milbourne, B. (1990) 'Money and finance' in S. Grenville (ed.), *The Australian Macroeconomy in the 1980s*: 222–271. Sydney, Reserve Bank of Australia.

Millmow, A. (2017) *A History of Australasian Economic Thought*. Milton Park, Routledge.

Mitchell, W.F. (1987) 'The NAIRU, structural imbalance and the macroequilibrium unemployment rate', *Australian Economic Papers*, 26 (48): 101–118.

Nevile, J.W. (1977) 'Domestic and overseas influences on inflation in Australia', *Australian Economic Papers*, 16 (28), 121–129.

Organisation for Economic Co-operation and Development (1994) *The OECD Jobs Study: Facts, Analysis, Strategies*. Paris, OECD Publishing.

Parkin, M. (1973) 'The short-run and long-run trade-offs between inflation and unemployment in Australia', *Australian Economic Papers*, 12 (21): 127–144.

——(1976) 'Yet another look at Australia's short-run and long-run trade-offs between inflation and unemployment', *Australian Economic Papers*, 15 (26): 128–139.

Phillips, A.W. (2000) 'Wage changes in Australia, 1947–1958' in Leeson, R. (ed.), *A.W.H. Phillips: Collected Works in Contemporary Perspective*: 269–281. Cambridge, Cambridge University Press.

Pollin, R. (1998) 'The "reserve army of labour" and the "natural rate of unemployment": Can Marx, Kalecki, Friedman and Wall Street all be wrong?', *Review of Radical Political Economics*, 30 (3): 1–13.

Rao, B.B. (1977) 'An analysis of the short and long-run trade-offs between unemployment and inflation and estimates of the equilibrium steady state unemployment rate in Australia', *Australian Economic Papers*, 16 (29): 273–284.

Reserve Bank of Australia (1994) 'Statement by the governor, Mr Bernie Fraser: monetary policy tightens', media release no. 1994-21, 14 December.

——(2000) 'Statement by the governor, Mr Ian Macfarlane: monetary policy', media release no. 2000-03, 2 February.

——(2007) 'Statement by Glenn Stevens, governor: monetary policy', media release no. 2007-20, 7 November.

——(2010) 'Statement by the Glenn Stevens, governor: monetary policy', media release no. 2010-26, 2 November.

Robinson, J. (1956) *The Accumulation of Capital*. London, Macmillan.

Rowan, D.C. (1980) *Australian Monetary Policy: 1950–1975*. Sydney, George Allen & Unwin.

Rowthorn, R. (1977) 'Conflict, inflation and money', *Cambridge Journal of Economics*, 1 (3): 215–239.

Shapiro, C. and Stiglitz, J.E. (1984) 'Equilibrium unemployment as a worker discipline device', *American Economic Review*, 74 (3): 433–444.

Stevens, G.R. (1999) 'Six years of inflation targeting', *Reserve Bank of Australia Bulletin*, May: 46–61.

——(2003) 'Inflation targeting: a decade of Australian experience', *Reserve Bank of Australia Bulletin*, April: 17–29.

Stockhammer, E. (2008) 'Is the NAIRU theory a monetarist, New Keynesian, post Keynesian or a Marxist theory?', *Metroeconomica*, 59 (3): 479–510.

——(2011) 'Wage norms, capital accumulation, and unemployment: a post-Keynesian view', *Oxford Review of Economic Policy*, 27 (2): 295–311.

Stockhammer, E. and Klär, E. (2011) 'Capital accumulation, labour market institutions and unemployment in the medium run', *Cambridge Journal of Economics*, 35: 437–457.

Wilson, K., Bradford, J. and Fitzpatrick, M. (eds) (2000) *Australia in Accord: An Evaluation of the Prices and Incomes Accord in the Hawke-Keating Years*. Melbourne, South Pacific Publishing.

CHAPTER 15

THE LOST GOLDEN AGE OF PRODUCTIVITY GROWTH?

JOHN QUIGGIN

Productivity was both the Holy Grail and the founding myth of economic reform in Australia. Established in 1989 at the peak of enthusiasm for micro-economic reform,[1] the government authority responsible for promoting reform is the Productivity Commission. From the 1980s to the global financial crisis (GFC) of 2008 and beyond, no discussion of Australian economic conditions was complete without an invocation of the need for Australians to 'increase their productivity', a phrase that rapidly became recognised as code for 'work harder for less pay'.[2]

The founding myth of micro-economic reform was the claim that the nation's economy experienced a surge in productivity in the mid-1990s following the round of reforms that began with the floating of the Australian dollar in 1983.[3] The putative surge was particularly welcomed by advocates of micro-economic reform given that the decade following the float was characterised by relatively weak productivity growth, macroeconomic performance that began well but ended in the deep recession of 1989–91, and the prolonged period of high unemployment that followed.

The case for the surge was based on estimates of multifactor productivity (MFP) calculated by the Australian Bureau of Statistics (ABS). The striking finding of the ABS estimates was that the rate of MFP growth had accelerated to more than 2 per cent per year. This was seen as proof that micro-economic reform was working, and that the economy had entered a new era of sustained productivity growth.

At the time I argued that the supposed surge in productivity reflected an increase in work intensity (Quiggin 2000), and predicted (Quiggin 2004) that:

> Much of the apparent productivity growth of the 1990s is likely to dissipate as workers find ways of winding back the increase in the hours and intensity of work extracted through the unilateral repudiation of implicit labour contracts in this period.

This prediction was borne out. The ABS estimate of quality-adjusted MFP declined over the period 2003–04 to 2007–08. For the entire period since 1998–99, the average annual rate of MFP growth has been 0.08 per cent, statistically indistinguishable from zero. Despite the accuracy of the predictions it generated, the view that measured changes in MFP growth rates are driven by changes in work intensity was ignored in the broader policy discussion around micro-economic reform.

The idea that the productivity miracle of the 1990s might instead have been a mirage is almost never raised. Instead, two contradictory accounts have emerged. Although they share an unquestioning acceptance of the measured productivity surge of the 1990s, they differ in their accounts of the 2000s.

The dominant view among economists is one of a 'lost golden age'. The disappearance of measured productivity growth in the 2000s is taken as a reflection of a real deterioration in economic performance, which is attributed to a slowdown or reversal of the process of micro-economic reform. In this analysis, the favourable terms of trade associated with globally high prices for minerals and strong demand from China are seen as have cushioned Australians from the harsh realities of the need for continued productivity growth.

An alternative view is that while the measured productivity surge of the 1990s was real, the reversal in measured productivity growth in the early 2000s was primarily attributable to special factors and measurement problems. This view was maintained vigorously by the Productivity

Commission during the early 2000s and is maintained to some extent in its ongoing discussions of this issue.

The conventional wisdom implicit in most discussions of the Australian economy is a somewhat incoherent mixture of these two ideas. On the one hand, in discussions of micro-economic issues, the 'lost golden age' view is dominant, and is reflected in calls for a new round of micro-economic reform. On the other hand, in discussions of Australia's strong macro-economic performance during the GFC, a considerable share of credit is commonly attributed to the flexibility derived from micro-economic reform.

Productivity: A Problematic Concept

Confusion about productivity growth is largely due to the problematic nature of productivity as a concept. At first sight, productivity seems like a simple generalisation of straightforward concepts such as crop yield (the output of a given crop per unit of land) or the number of units of a given good that a worker can produce in an hour. In national accounting, the single good in these examples is replaced by an aggregate output index such as gross domestic product (GDP). More importantly, aggregate measures of both labour and capital[4] are taken into account as inputs to production.

The starting point for the theory of productivity is the growth accounting framework developed by Solow (1956). In the standard model, the technology at time t is given by

(1) $Y(t) = AK(t)^{\alpha} L(t)^{1-\alpha}$

(2) $\log(Y(t)) = \alpha \log (K(t)) + (1- \alpha) \log (L(t)) + \log(A(t))$

where Y is output, K is capital input and L is (quality-adjusted) labour. The weighted average $K(t)^{\alpha} L(t)^{1-\alpha}$ is an aggregate measure of labour and capital inputs. The third term, A, is the ratio of output to this aggregate, and is therefore referred to as multi-factor productivity, or MFP. Since MFP appears as a residual in econometric estimates of growth equations, it is often called the Solow residual

Within this model increases in output per worker can be caused by:

(i) an increase in capital stock per worker (capital deepening);

(ii) an increase in the quality of labour input (education/experience);

(iii) an increase in effort per worker; or

(iv) an increase in multifactor productivity.

Except in the context of debates over micro-economic reform, the Solow residual is normally taken to reflect technological change or, more precisely, 'disembodied' technical change. To the extent that technological change takes the form of more powerful and efficient capital equipment, it should be represented by an increase in the capital stock – that is, by capital deepening.

When Solow models were first estimated in the 1950s the residual was found to be very large. However, the residual – that is, the estimated rate of MFP growth – has fallen over time. In part, this is because early estimates failed to take account of labour quality. More significantly, the mid-twentieth century was a period of steady technological progress for the economy as a whole. By contrast, recent decades have seen rapid technological change in information and communications technology (ICT), along with relative stagnation elsewhere. Improvements in ICT are embodied in faster, more powerful and cheaper devices, and therefore take the form of capital deepening. This means that, in an economy where technological progress is embodied in capital equipment and the effects of education on human capital are properly taken into account, these two factors should fully explain observed growth in output. That is, the rate of MFP growth should be zero.

The central claim of micro-economic reform is that the standard growth model fails to take account of inefficiencies caused by bad public policy. These inefficiencies mean that the actual level of output is below the potential level given by equations (1) and (2). If reforms remove these inefficiencies, productivity growth will be greater than can be accounted for by technological change alone. In particular, in the case where all technological change is embodied, so that the underlying rate of MFP growth is zero, micro-economic reform is the sole source of MFP growth. The converse is true. If the effect of public policy is to reduce technical efficiency, this will make a negative contribution to MFP growth.

Problems with the Growth Accounting Framework

Standard productivity measures fail to take account of the intensity with which capital and labour are used. To understand this problem, it is useful to consider the ways in which sustainable improvements in living standards can be generated. The most important improvement, by far, is technological progress – the introduction and adoption of technological innovations such as new products and improved production technologies. There is a much-cited statement from Krugman's (1997: 11) that 'productivity isn't everything, but in the long run it is *almost* everything. A country's ability to improve its standard of living over time depends almost entirely on its ability to raise its output per worker.' His assertion would be equally valid if the word 'productivity' were replaced by 'technological progress'.

For a small country like Australia, the rate of technological innovation is essentially exogenous. Furthermore, to the extent that innovation takes the form of a reduction in the cost of imported ICT equipment, it is measured as capital deepening. National policies can affect the rate of adoption of new technologies. In particular, new technologies are usually more skill-intensive and knowledge-intensive than old technologies, so rapid adoption of new technologies is feasible only with a skilled and educated workforce. Hence, investment in human capital can yield high returns.

The second potential source of improved living standards is a more efficient use of endowments of capital and labour. This may be achieved either as a result of good macro-economic outcomes (full/optimal employment of labour and capital) or through good micro-economic outcomes (output closer to the technological frontier for individual enterprises and industries).

Productivity measures, at least conceptually, exclude benefits arising from good macro-economic outcomes, but include the benefits of good micro-economic outcomes. In practice, however, the two are intertwined. Capital utilisation generally declines during recessions, while capital may be operated to yield unsustainably high service flows during booms. Standard productivity measures are based on the assumption that capital services are proportional to the capital stock. As the OECD (2001, Section 5.6) observes, attempts to include proxies for capital utilisation have proved problematic.

Measurement of labour input is even more problematic. On the one hand, labour hoarding during recessions tends to reduce productivity, producing a procyclical pattern of labour productivity. On the other hand, increased employment during expansions results in the recruitment of more marginal workers, producing anticyclical productivity. Historically, the first of these tendencies has predominated, producing procyclical productivity. But, as labour hoarding has declined, notably in the United States, productivity has become more anticyclical.

The use of a measure designed to include the benefits of good micro-economic outcomes and to exclude the benefits of good macro-economics is consistent with the thinking that has dominated Australian policy discussions since the 1980s, but it is deeply misleading. The primary reason for Australia's relatively strong growth in income per person since the early 1990s is the fact that, through a combination of good luck and good policy decisions, we have not experienced a recession.

ABS MFP Estimates

The ABS began reporting estimates of MFP growth in the 1990s, calculated back to the 1960s. The initial estimates of MFP growth for the mid-1990s were in excess of 2 per cent per year, a very high rate. These were subsequently revised downwards to 1.6 per cent. Unfortunately, the ABS currently reports MFP only for the period beginning 1998–99, although older estimates are given in Campbell and Withers (2017).

The issue is further clouded by the fact that the ABS reports MFP estimates in 'productivity cycles' that typically last about five years. The productivity cycle is a data-driven concept, with no explicit theoretical basis. In particular, productivity cycles do not necessarily correspond to business cycles, and productivity cycles in different industries are largely uncorrelated. Nevertheless, as I have shown elsewhere for the Australian economy as a whole, the MFP cycles reported by the ABS largely reflected the phases of the business cycle (Quiggin 2000). A typical business cycle contained two productivity cycles, with productivity growth being stronger in the cycle corresponding to the expansion phase and weaker in the cycle corresponding to the contraction phase (Dolman, Lu and Rahman 2006).

The productivity cycle plays a crucial role in the myth of the 1990s productivity surge, since it allows the years of strong productivity growth from 1993–94 to 1998–99 to be treated as a distinct period, while the weaker years at the beginning of the decade are discarded. The result is a widespread but false impression that the 1990s as a whole were a period of exceptionally strong measured MFP growth. In reality, the average rate of MFP growth for two ABS productivity cycles from 1988–89 to 1998–99 was 1.6 per cent – above average but not exceptional compared to preceding decades.

In summary, MFP growth over a productivity cycle is not a particularly useful measure of economic performance. Even when measured correctly, productivity estimates combine the effects of long-term technological growth with a subset of the factors that determine variations in short-term performance. In practice, accurate measurement is impossible. In the case of Australia's supposed productivity surge, the crucial problem is the failure to take account of changes in work intensity.

Work Intensity and Productivity

Labour productivity is typically measured in terms of output per hour worked. However, this measure can be problematic. For example, enterprise agreements and individual contracts adopted in place of awards commonly eliminate breaks such as tea breaks, which were treated as working time under the award system. On the other hand, employees have always taken unauthorised and unrecorded breaks of various kinds. A notable example that has emerged in the last ten to fifteen years is the use of office computers to visit internet sites that aren't work-related. Of much longer standing is the practice of making private phone calls during paid time at work. Conversely, employers may demand unpaid overtime, or contact their employees with work requests outside paid hours.

Although these practices are regularly the subject of dispute, the normal situation is one of equilibrium, where some deviation from official hours is part of the wage bargain tacitly accepted by both parties. The hours of work reported to statistical agencies will reflect some, but not all, of the deviations from award-determined or contractually agreed hours. How should these features of the labour market be reflected in productivity measures? At least conceptually, it seems clear that the appropriate measure is actual hours worked, rather than paid hours.

Now consider the case where the number of hours worked remains unchanged, but the pace of work varies. In some industries, such changes can be observed directly, and are the subject of explicit wage bargaining. The archetypal case is that of production line work, where employers typically seek to increase the rate at which the line moves, while workers and unions try to slow it down. The development of the word processor in the 1980s provides another example. Since the number of keystrokes could be measured directly, employers demanded higher rates, thus precipitating an epidemic of repetitive strain injury, a problem that had existed previously but was typically diagnosed as an individual pathology rather than a more broadly occupational hazard.

There is, in principle, no difference between an increase in the number of hours worked and an increase in the pace of work. In both cases, standard economic logic implies that an equilibrium wage bargain will typically involve a commitment of hours and effort greater than the level that would be chosen by workers in the absence of a monetary incentive.

In particular instances, depending on labour market institutions, the bargained outcome may involve more or less hours and effort than would characterise a Pareto-optimal bargain. However, the general assumption is that at the margin, increased hours and increased effort are equally costly to workers when they are normalised by the payment required to elicit them. It follows that, to the extent that increases in output are derived either from unmeasured increases in hours of work, or from increased intensity of work, there is no corresponding increase in productivity. If the hours or intensity of work were previously sub-optimal (or above the optimal level), there will be a net welfare gain (or loss), but this will be of second-order magnitude relative to the change in output.

Australian economic policymakers have shown considerable confusion on this point. Some have explicitly asserted that working harder is a genuine source of productivity gains. For example, the Productivity Commission (1996: 24) asserted that productivity gains could be achieved not only through resource reallocation but through people 'working harder and working smarter'. More than a decade later, the chairman of the Productivity Commission repeated an almost identical formulation (Banks 2011: 20): 'whether productivity growth comes from working harder or working "smarter", people in workplaces are central to it'. The appearance of scare quotes around 'smarter' is revealing. Whereas in the 1990s this phrase was used in all seriousness, 'working smarter' is now understood as a piece of management jargon, typically decoded as 'we're giving you more work to do with less resources, and it's up to you to figure out how to do it'.

The association of reform with harder and less pleasant work is usually implicit. Standard discussions of micro-economic reform and workplace reform are full of references to 'cutting out fat', the 'chill winds of competition' and so forth. It is not hard for workers to discern where there is fat to be cut, or to observe that CEOs are usually equipped with well-padded windbreakers, even in cases where their mismanagement leads to an early (but generously compensated) departure. By contrast, in debates over the validity of MFP statistics, most mainstream economists – particularly those associated with the Productivity Commission – have denied that changes in work intensity are an important source of changes in measured productivity.

The mid-1990s saw an upsurge in public concern about the pace of work, work–life balance, stress and related issues, which persisted into the early 2000s, leading to John Howard's description of the topic at an electorate dinner in Melbourne in 2002 as a 'barbecue-stopper'. In the context of a strengthening labour market, from about 2000 onwards community resistance to work intensification and to employer demands for longer hours of work became increasingly successful.

While the intensity of work is difficult to measure, there is sufficient evidence to support the general perception of an increase in work intensity in the 1990s. First, as discussed above, increases in work hours and in work intensity are substitutes both as inputs to production and as sources of disutility for workers. It follows that, when the equilibrium wage bargain involves an increase (or decrease) in hours, it will also involve an increase (decrease) in work intensity. The data on working hours is unequivocal and exactly consistent with the idea that fluctuations in MFP growth may be explained largely in terms of work intensity. As the ABS (2010) notes, the proportion of full-time workers working more than 50 hours per week increased from 13 per cent in 1978 to 19 per cent in late 1999 and early 2000, before falling to around 15 per cent in 2010.

There is some direct evidence on work intensity. The Australian Workplace Industrial Relations Survey undertaken in 1995 (Morehead et al. 1997) found that a majority of employees reported increases in stress, work effort and pace of work over the previous year, while less than 10 per cent reported reductions in any of these variables. This is consistent with evidence from the United Kingdom and some, though not all, other European countries (Green and McIntosh 2001). Moreover, Green and McIntosh observe that the increases in work intensity are associated with higher productivity (as would be expected) and are positively correlated with exposure to competition and with reductions in union density.

Defences of the Productivity Surge

As I have discussed elsewhere (Quiggin 2006), believers in the productivity surge produced a variety of 'stories' to explain the observed outcomes.

Asymmetric Measurement Error

During the 1990s, the Productivity Commission was the most prominent proponent of the claim that the strong growth in MFP reported by ABS reflected the emergence of a 'new economy' as a result of micro-economic reform (Parham 1999). Unsurprisingly, the Commission rejected claims that the apparent surge in MFP growth was due, in part or in whole, to measurement error or cyclical factors.

By contrast, as low rates of MFP growth emerged in the 2000s, the Commission became much more sympathetic to the idea that measurement error might be a problem. The poor productivity growth of the early 2000s was blamed on, among other factors, the Sydney Olympics, capital expenditure associated with the Y2K fiasco, the transitional effects of the introduction of the GST, and the drought that began in 2002 (Parham 2005). The drought persisted well into the decade, but these other factors should have been transitory.

As measured MFP performance deteriorated even further, attention has shifted to the mining sector. It seems clear that measurement problems associated with mining are significant. Investments in new or expanded mines count immediately as part of the capital stock, but contribute to output only with a delay of some years. Moreover, high mineral prices have led to the exploitation of less productive resources that would otherwise be uneconomic.

Since the quality of the resource is not measured as an input, this produces an illusory decline in productivity. Richardson and Denniss (2011) estimate that the measured growth rate of labour productivity over the first decade of the 2000s was reduced by one percentage point as a result of distortions in the mining sector. This is a significant effect, but not sufficient to explain the decline in measured MFP growth rates.

The view that the disappointing performance of measured MFP is primarily due to measurement error has lost favour over time, as disappointment has persisted. However, it frequently re-emerges in discussions of Australia's strong macro-economic performance during the GFC.

The idea that market-oriented micro-economic policies provide significant flexibility in response to macro-economic shocks has been influential in Australia since the beginnings of micro-economic reform in the 1980s. This idea contributed substantially to the policy misjudgements that produced the 1989–91 recession, when it was supposed that the economy was flexible enough to handle a 'short, sharp shock to interest rates' and then to bounce back rapidly from 'the recession we had to have'.

Counter examples to this idea abound, but the most striking is that of New Zealand, which has followed broadly similar micro-economic policies since the 1980s (though with more radical micro-economic reform until the mid-1990s, and a sharper reaction against some aspects of those policies subsequently), while adopting far more restrictionist macro-economic policies. From its initial position of approximate income parity with Australia in the early 1980s, New Zealand fell sharply behind, experiencing an even deeper recession from 1987 to 1991, and two subsequent recessions interspersed with periods of mostly sluggish growth. By 2000, income per person in New Zealand had fallen to around two-thirds of the Australian level, and has remained there. While it is unwise to attribute such a huge gap to any single factor (Hazledine and Quiggin 2006), poor macro-economic performance is an important part of the story.

The Lost Golden Age

The dominant interpretation of the MFP statistics today is of a 'lost golden age'. The surge in measured MFP growth is attributed to the micro-economic reform process that began in the 1980s, and the slowdown to 'reform fatigue' in the 2000s.

The major problem with this story is timing. It is difficult to see how a series of reforms undertaken over twenty years or more can have produced substantial productivity benefits confined to a single period of five years. It is even harder to see how the benefits of those reforms can have dissipated so rapidly, already on the wane when the reform process was still underway.

The beginning of the process of micro-economic reform is usually dated to the float of the Australian dollar in 1983. There is less agreement on the end of the process. As far as I can determine, I was the first to offer an explicit end date (Quiggin 2004) suggesting that the era of micro-economic reform in Australia 'began with a big bang – the floating of the dollar in 1983', and that it 'ended with another big bang – the package of tax reforms centred on the Goods and Services Tax (GST), which came into force in July 1999'. There have been retrospective attempts to backdate the end of micro-economic reform, sometimes as far as the election of the Howard government in 1996, but these do not stand up to scrutiny. Although it is true that the Howard government took a less consistent approach to reform than its Labor predecessors, it nevertheless introduced a number of major reforms in its first few years in office. Many of the reforms implemented under Howard were measures that had long been demanded by advocates of radical reform but resisted by the Labor government because of political sensitivities. These included the *Workplace Relations Act 1996*, the partial privatisation of Telstra in 1998 and 1999, waterfront reform in 1998, and, most notably, the 1999 GST.[5]

Moreover, many reforms introduced by the Hawke–Keating government did not begin to take effect until after the MFP surge. The most notable of these is National Competition Policy (NCP). Most states did not even complete their legislative reviews or set up their general regulatory bodies until the late 1990s, and the NCP process, with associated payments to the states, was not completed until 2005, when it was succeeded by the National Reform Agenda (NRA). Even after 2005, the push for micro-economic reform was continued through a proliferation of 'free trade' agreements, which were less focused on trade than on constraining government intervention in the domestic economy, as addressed by Pat Ranald (see Chapter 17).

The timing issue becomes more acute when we consider that the measured productivity surge did not begin until a decade after the float of the dollar. In fact, the years during which 'even the resident galah in the pet shop' was talking about micro-economic reform were characterised by the lowest productivity growth of the entire period for which data is available. And so, the story of the lost golden age relies on long-delayed benefits of the reforms of the early 1980s, combined with an instant (indeed, in some cases, retrospective) benefit from the reforms of the late 1990s. Even if we were to accept the story of the lost golden age, the whole rationale of micro-economic reform is called into question. Far from generating sustained growth, the golden age myth suggests that the decade or more of micro-economic reform that began with the floating of the dollar in 1983 produced only five years of above average productivity growth before requiring a renewed burst of reform merely to sustain past gains.

Conclusion

In the economy of the twenty-first century, increases in productivity arise almost entirely from capital deepening and improvements in education. Economic theory therefore predicts that the rate of MFP growth, properly calculated to take account of labour quality, should be close to zero. This prediction is borne out by the data. Nevertheless, the mythical productivity surge of the mid-1990s continues to dominate the thinking of policy-makers, leading to incessant demands for more micro-economic reform to generate higher productivity.

The correlation between demand for higher productivity and increases in work intensity is so evident to most Australians that we take it for granted. What is striking in this context is the failure of (most) Australian economists and economic commentators to accept the evidence on this point. Unlike virtually everyone else in Australia, economists have resolutely denied that the higher measured labour productivity growth evident in the mid-1990s was largely due to increased work intensity, and that the reversal of those measured gains in the 2000 was due to the fact that this intensification could not be sustained.

A belief that large increases in annual productivity growth rates can and should be achieved through micro-economic reform is not supported by the data and can lead to bad public policy decisions. Most notably, the belief lends support to the idea that 'Australians must work harder'. On the contrary, evidence from the labour market is that the work intensification of the 1990s was undesired and unsustainable. Genuine improvements in productivity should permit *reductions* in working hours and work effort, rather than demanding more and harder work.

ENDNOTES

1 Treasurer Paul Keating, the politician most responsible for micro-economic reform, declared at the time: 'I guarantee if you walk into any pet shop in Australia, the resident galah will be talking about microeconomic policy.' (ABC Radio National PM 1989)

2 A striking illustration of this took place in 2011, when then Treasury secretary Martin Parkinson gave a speech on productivity. Although Parkinson did not mention work intensity, his speech was reported on by two different news organisations under the headline 'Australians must work harder'.

3 The Whitlam government's tariff reforms, and its replacement of the old Tariff Board with the Industries Assistance Commission, the precursor of the Productivity Commission, are generally seen as a 'false start', largely reversed by subsequent protectionist measures.

4 The question of whether, and how, heterogeneous items of equipment could be aggregated into a single capital input was the subject of the famous 'Cambridge capital controversy' in the mid-twentieth century. Felipe and Fisher (2003) provide a summary of the issues.

5 Following the surprising achievement of a Senate majority in 2004, the last term of the Howard government included the passage of a package of labour market reforms, called WorkChoices. These reforms were mostly repealed by the Rudd Labor government, and cannot be regarded as a successful renewal of micro-economic reform.

REFERENCES

Australian Bureau of Statistics (2010) '6105.0 – Australian Labour Market Statistics, Oct 2010'.

Banks, G. (2011) 'Successful Reform: Past Lessons, Future Challenges', Report based on paper presented at Annual Forecasting Conference of the Australian Business Economists, 8 December 2010, Productivity Commission, Canberra.

Campbell, H. and Withers, S. (2017) 'Australian productivity trends and the effect of structural change', Australia Treasury Economic Roundup, 28 August.

Dolman, B., Lu, L. and Rahman, J. (2006) 'Understanding productivity trends', *Treasury Economic Roundup*, Summer, 35–52.

Felipe, J. and Fisher, F. (2003) 'Aggregation in production functions: what applied economists should know', *Metroeconomica*, 54 (2 & 3): 208–62.

Green, F. and McIntosh, S. (2001) 'The intensification of work in Europe', *Labour Economics*, 8 (2): 291–308.

Hazledine, T. and Quiggin, J. (2006) 'No more free beer tomorrow? Economic policy and outcomes in Australia and New Zealand since 1984', *Australian Journal of Political Science*, 41 (2): 145–59.

Krugman, P. (1997) *The Age of Diminished Expectations, Third Edition: U.S. Economic Policy in the 1990s*, MIT Press, Cambridge Massachusetts.

ABC Radio National PM (1989) 'The Treasurer, Paul Keating, has dismissed the call for a tax break on savings and the suggestion of a tax on luxuries', broadcast 21 June.

Morehead, A., Steele, M., Alexander, M., Stephen, K. and Duffin, L. (1997) *Changes at Work: The 1995 Australian Workplace Industrial Relations Survey*, Addison Wesley Longman Australia, Melbourne.

Organisation for Economic Co-operation and Development (2001) 'Measuring Productivity: Measurement of Aggregate and Industry-Level Productivity Growth – OECD Manual', OECD, Paris.

Parham, D. (1999) 'The new economy: A new look at Australia's productivity performance', Productivity Commission Staff Research Paper, Ausinfo,

——(2005) 'Is Australia's productivity surge over?', *Agenda*, 12 (3): 252–266.

Parkinson, M. (2011) 'Sustaining Growth in Living Standards in the Asian Century', Paper presented at Melbourne Institute Economic and Social Outlook Conference, 31 June 2011.

Productivity Commission (1996) 'Stocktake of Progress in Microeconomic Reform', Australian Government Publishing Service, Canberra.

Quiggin, J. (2000) 'Microeconomic Policies and Structural Change-Comments', Gruen, D. and Shrestha, S. (eds.) in *The Australian Economy in the 1990s*, Reserve Bank of Australia, Sydney, 268–270.

——(2004) 'Looking back on microeconomic reform: a skeptical viewpoint', *Economic and Labour Relations Review*, 15 (1): 1–25.

——(2006) 'Stories about productivity', *Australian Bulletin of Labour*, 32 (1): 18–26.

Richardson, D. and Denniss, R. (2011) 'Mining Australia's productivity: The role of the mining industry in driving down Australia's productivity growth', Policy Brief No. 31, The Australia Institute, Canberra.

Solow, R.M. (1956) 'A contribution to the theory of economic growth', *Quarterly Journal of Economics*, 69 (1): 65–94.

CHAPTER 16

HOW ORTHODOX ECONOMIC MODELS JUSTIFY DEREGULATION, INEQUALITY AND UNEMPLOYMENT

PETER BRAIN

Our main interest in economics lies in its potential to guide good government. While we can accept that all parties in a democracy have a right to advocate for their point of view, we need to resist powerful interests' use of economic theories and models to justify policies that advantage them solely. The chief bulwark against such subversion is the scientific method. Since the 1970s, vested interests have succeeded in subverting the scientific method in important branches of economics – particularly in macro-economics as it is practised in Anglophone countries. This has inflicted large economic and social costs and will continue to do so; ultimately, it will threaten to undermine capitalism itself.

In the first half of the nineteenth century, economics was called 'political economy' and concentrated on advocacy for the capitalist economic system that was then emerging. The discipline identified the structural changes required for capitalism to flourish fully, and was aimed at the creation of a political consensus to underpin these new structures. Scientific support for this advocacy was limited at the time due to the paltry collection of statistical data, and because no existing capitalist states had developed sufficiently to permit valid comparisons with political economists' predictions.

While early political economy was therefore largely a type of ideological advocacy, it also offered profound insights and methods of analysis.

For these early economists, capitalism is a highly dynamic system with an inherent tendency towards growth, but also towards instability in the growth path. The key forces propelling growth are capital investment and technical change, both of which are determined by the decisions of capitalists, who, driven by competition, seek to revolutionise methods of production and distribution by developing and deploying science and new methods of work organisation. These market forces drive productivity and profits; however, the unplanned nature of capitalism – its tendency towards over-capacity and over-production – inevitably leads to the instability of boom-and-bust cycles. The distribution of economic surplus (output minus the value of inputs into production) is determined by class conflict between those who own capital and those with only their labour to sell on the open market.

It hardly needs saying that this clear-eyed, and to some degree unflattering, analysis of capitalist society was hardly welcomed by capitalists. In the latter part of the nineteenth century, there emerged an intellectual counter-revolution against political economy called 'neoclassical economics'. Though it retained the former's zeal for the capitalist system, the new neoclassical school displaced the older school of political economics known as classical economics. Rather than looking at capitalism empirically, neoclassical economics constructed a theoretically optimal model based on a priori principles, arguing that all policy must be evaluated on the basis of its contribution to achieving this ideal system. Shorn of all impediments to the free flow of capital, labour and production, the so-called 'invisible hand' of the market would ensure full employment, optimally efficient production and consumption, and the fair distribution of income between capital and workers. The strong philosophical inference of the neoclassical model was that, once the economic system achieved the ideal model, market forces alone would balance supply and demand, both at an individual firm level and economy-wide. The role of government would be limited to enforcing the rule of law and providing national security.

The Great Depression of the 1930s, a massive expansion of state intervention during World War II and its continued role in the postwar boom clearly falsified the neoclassical hypotheses that the market was self-equilibrating, with no role for government. Another intellectual counter-revolution occurred in the 1930s, this time pitted again neoclassical economics. It was led by J.M. Keynes, who clarified the earlier political economist's analysis of the inherent instability in capitalist systems, but, crucially, identified a central role for the state in the regulation of business cycles, something that had been totally absent from early political economics. The combination of Keynes' insights, the experience of the Great Depression and subsequent economic history, and government investments in a vastly expanded collection of economic statistics unleashed the application of the scientific method to economics, and in particular to more effective forms of macro-economic theory and practice. In the 1950s and '60s, the econometrician Lawrence Klein incorporated economic statistics and Keynes' ideas into large mathematical models of the economy. These empirically based macroeconomic models were called Keynes-Klein or 'KK' models. In the postwar period, the power of rich elites – or in modern parlance, the top 1 per cent – was weakened and there was a substantial redistribution towards households in lower-income and wealth quintiles.

This transformed intellectual climate was not to the liking of established interests, especially financial markets. These forces seized on the opportunity of macro-economic instability caused by stagflation in the 1970s to launch a counter attack: neoliberalism. Neoliberalism incorporates the neoclassical economic system with a hard-edged political philosophy that government intervention in the economy is both unjustified and undesirable. Within a short period of time, in Anglosphere economies at least, the scientific approach was replaced by a reversion to pre-Keynesian ideas. KK models were displaced by so-called 'computerised general equilibrium' or CGE models incorporating neoclassical theory. These models harnessed the processing capability of newly emerging computer hardware and software, but they were deliberately designed so that the assumptions and theoretical conclusions of neoclassical theory overrode the input of economic data, ultimately driving the policy conclusion that government intervention in the economy was to be minimised at all costs.

The core objectives of this chapter are to show how the assumptions of CGE are falsified by economic data, how the predictions of CGE models generally run counter to effective policy, and how the use of CGE produces high and quantifiable costs within the context of 'economic reform'.

Economics, Models and the Scientific Method

The majority of economists would describe their discipline as a science. To qualify as a science the scientific method must form the backbone of research methodologies. The standard scientific method, developed by the philosopher Karl Popper (1935), relies on the theory of 'falsification'. Science proceeds by proposing hypotheses and developing predictions that are capable of being empirically tested. Crucially, hypotheses that survive initial empirical testing are always regarded as tentative – never proven 'true', but accepted only until they are not falsified by new observations.

Klein-Keynes Models

This standard scientific method was applied in the development of KK models from the 1950s to the 1970s. These models consisted of a wide range of hypotheses derived from data about how individuals and industries behave, and with results embodied in the empirically estimated coefficients of the structural equations of the model. The structural equations were determined by national accounts data and inter-industry input-output relationships. The general theories arising from the models were empirically validated by the ex-ante and ex-post forecasting abilities of the models. In the development of KK models, hypotheses were accepted so long as the data produced coefficients with the correct sign, were statistically significant, and made a useful contribution to the forecasting capabilities of the models. These models are described in Bodkin et al (1991). In Australia the leading KK-based model is that used in the National Institute of Economic and Industry Research (NIEIR).

The Theoretical Structure of CGE Models

The common theoretical structure of CGE models is straightforward, built as it is on neoclassical micro-economic foundations that guarantee long-run equilibrium and full employment. The model's key assumptions are:

(i) Producers are short- and long-run profit maximisers. They will only increase output if there is a prior increase in prices that increases profit and resource supply.

(ii) All industries have long-run constant returns to scale and decreasing short-run returns to scale. The rate of technological progress at the industry level is exogenous – that is, not determined by firms or workers. For a given industry, the rate of exogenous productivity growth is the same no matter what the location and scale of the business.

(iii) Labour markets with excess unemployment can only return to full employment if real wages fall. This is necessary to give short-run and long-run profit-maximising producers the incentive to expand production. Without a fall in real wages, demand expansion is ineffective in reducing unemployment, and unemployment therefore becomes 'voluntary' in the sense that workers are demanding excessive real wages. Simply put: economies are always in long-run full-employment equilibrium.

(iv) The level of investment is fixed by aggregate available savings and distributed to industry on the basis of relative profitability. In CGE models, investment is of minor importance compared to its centrality in KK models, where it is the key determinant of growth, the business cycle, the productive potential of the economy and the rate of technical change.

(v) If, due to some exogenous shock, an economy suffers excess capacity and unemployment, a fall in the price of capital and labour is required to match the fall in demand. This is the basic textbook mechanism. But as an economy expands towards the full employment of capital, labour unit costs and hence prices will rise.

In KK models, inter-industry demand relationships are dominant. CGE models also use input-output tables but primarily to determine imports into an economy, since industry output is fixed by real wage rates. In CGE models, demand impulses only impact on industry output to the extent that the real wage rate is impacted. The key assumptions and predictions of CGE models and KK models are compared in Table 1.

Table 1: CGE models compared to input-output (NIEIR) models

Key economic variable	CGE model claim	Keynesian/input-output/ demand-driven models
Private balance: investment and saving	Neoclassical investment: investment adjusts to savings, a function of income. Investment is savings-driven, following the standard neoclassical presumption that any funds available are channelled into productive investment. It is largely a residual in the system with full employment investment determined at the real wage rates consistent with full employment.	Keynesian investment: investment is endogenous. Investment is decided upon by the industry level and, following Keynesian theory, generates the savings necessary to finance itself from increased income, except at times of severe financial or capacity constraints. The key driver is the current level of capacity utilisation relative to the desired level one or two years ahead.
Public balance: government deficit and tax revenue	• Government deficits should not be a long-run problem. There is no long-run trade-off between government finances and economic growth. • As the long-run growth trajectory of the economy is independent of government expenditures, public sector financial stability should not be a problem as expenditure can be adjusted to revenue without long-run cost to growth.	• There can be a long-run trade-off between government deficits and economic growth. • In the short term, government expenditures can be an important driver of demand, as seen in the Asian and Australian responses to the GFC. In the longer term, the role of public sector infrastructure is an important determinant of productivity growth in the economy. There can be a trade-off between short-term and long-term requirements.

Productivity growth	Exogenous. That is, determined externally to the economic system at the industry level, and all industries have long-run constant returns to scale and short-run decreasing returns to scale. Prices will rise in the short term with any increase in demand.	• Productivity growth is significantly endogenous since many industries have both short-run and long-run increasing returns to scale (productivity growth is a function of demand growth), and technology is generally embodied in investment so the rate of investment will influence productivity growth. • In spatially disaggregated models productivity growth will be a function of: scale (the higher the scale the higher past and future productivity growth); the rate of growth of demand; the capital output ratio; and the scale of the labour market catchment.
Foreign balance: exchange rate and current account	• Elasticities adjust the balance of payments: the exchange rate adjusts to hold the current account in balance. • A constant current account corresponds to the idea of balanced trade; an exchange rate change combined with the 'right' elasticities ensures that an increase in the value of imports is met by an equivalent increase in the value of exports.	• Income or absorption adjust the balance of payments: the current account adjusts according to demand shifts, and the exchange rate is endogenous but can be driven by many other functions than the requirement for 'equilibrium' in the balance of payments. • In addition, the actual import and export elasticities may not allow for the exchange rate by itself to correct current account deficits.

Table 1 cont.

Key economic variable	CGE model claim	Keynesian/input-output/ demand-driven models
Government expenditure multipliers	Low multipliers assumed a priori and ex-post forecasting quantities not examined. Short-run multiplier around 0.5. Long-run multiplier 0. The medium and long-run trajectory of the economy is independent of government expenditures due to assumptions such as crowding out, and the tendency to full-employment of resources implies government business-cycle management is redundant and leads to inflation. One driver of crowding out is the Ricardian equivalence theorem in which agents increase savings rates in response to increases in government spending, anticipating higher tax rates. Second, there is a 'natural rate of unemployment' below which an increase in demand for labour simply increases inflation and not output (or output increase much less than the government stimulus). This is one factor underpinning the idea that government cannot influence the business cycle.	• Ex-post forecasting quantities are continually evaluated. • Short-run multiplier 1.3 to 1.6. • Long-run multipliers in excess of 2 and towards 3 for public infrastructure investments

Labour markets: employment and wages and population	• Neoclassical labour market: the level of employment is determined by the full employment wage rate. That is, total employment in the medium term is exogenous, with workforce and population fixed. • Producers maximise short- and long-run profits so will not respond to any increase in demand until prices increase, thereby reducing the real wage rate. Unemployment is caused by an elevated real wage rate. Government demand expansion policies are ineffective at reducing unemployment. Government demand expansion policies simply result in 'crowding out' or substitution of private for public spending and higher interest rates, which depresses private spending and therefore does not affect the aggregate employment level. If wages are flexible enough everybody will find work. Dynamic CGE models allow for a lagged adjustment from current disequilibrium. • At the regional level, since variations in real wage growth are essential to induce labour to shift to regions where the demand for labour is expanding and vice-versa, 'equilibrium' requires a convergence in real wages. Regions with high real wages should experience a fall in relative real wages as an influx of population and workers drives down real wages and vice-versa in regions losing workers. Population and workforce are fixed.	• 'Keynesian' labour market: employment is endogenous. Producers maximise long-run profits with the requirement for this being that all short-term increases in demand are met so as to maximise market share to reduce the risk of losing relative scale and therefore risk an uncompetitive cost structure (given that most industries have increasing returns to scale). Unemployment can persist into the long term because of deficiency of past investment, deficiency in demand or the failure of key drivers, such as the exchange rate, to take the required values. • The unemployment rate in Keynesian models is endogenous as is the participation rate. Real wages can continue to rise relatively in regions with previously high relative real wages because of endogenous productivity growth and returns to scale. Long-run unsatisfactory high unemployment rates are possible via "secular stagnation". • The workforce participation is positively correlated to the level of employment while population can be fixed or variable depending on whether or not migration is endogenous.

The Falsification of CGE Models

One way to falsify CGE models is to compare their structural equations (assumptions) and predictions with those in KK models and test both against the data. Brain (1986) did this and established that typically:

(i) Short- and long-run returns to scale exist in the majority of industries and not short-run decreasing returns to scale and constant long-run returns to scale as assumed by CGE models;

(ii) The elasticities of export and import prices with respect to the exchange rate are less than unity. They are not equal to unity as assumed by CGE models;

(iii) Investment at the industry level is driven by underlying demand via capacity utilisation rates and industry cash flow, and not by the relative profitability of industries across the whole economy, as assumed by CGE models;

(iv) Export supply elasticities are considerably less than those assumed by CGE models; and

(v) Most importantly, as output increases, with real wages remaining constant, prices fall rather than rise as assumed by CGE models. These falls originate in industries that are operating at less than peak capacity and they are due to short-run increasing returns to scale.

CGE model builders never responded to these criticisms. They have a logical self-contained theory of how the economy works and facts are irrelevant to them.

Testing CGE Predictions

This section empirically tests some of the CGE predictions in Table 1. (There was not space to cover them all.) The following uses mostly Australian data from NIEIR's local government area (LGA) database. The key CGE predictions tested include:

(i) The unemployment rate is inversely related to the real wage rate

At the core of CGE models is the micro-economic textbook assumption that producers, as profit maximisers, will only respond to an increase in demand if prices rise and, therefore, real wages fall. At the regional level this implies that areas with high unemployment will be regions where real wages are too high. Conversely, in regions with low unemployment, real wages will be low. There will be a positive relationship between the real wage rate and the unemployment rate.

Figure 1 shows that in 2016 there was strong inverse relationship between unemployment and the real wage rate for sixty-seven Australian regions. Further, Figure 2 shows that over time there is not even a positive relationship between the change in the unemployment rate and the change in real wages. The data suggests that between 1996 and 2016 the relationship was, on balance, negative. Poor regions have high unemployment because of demand-deficiency, at least as a proximate cause.

Figure 1. Australian major region – NIEIR unemployment rate versus $ per hour from work, 2016

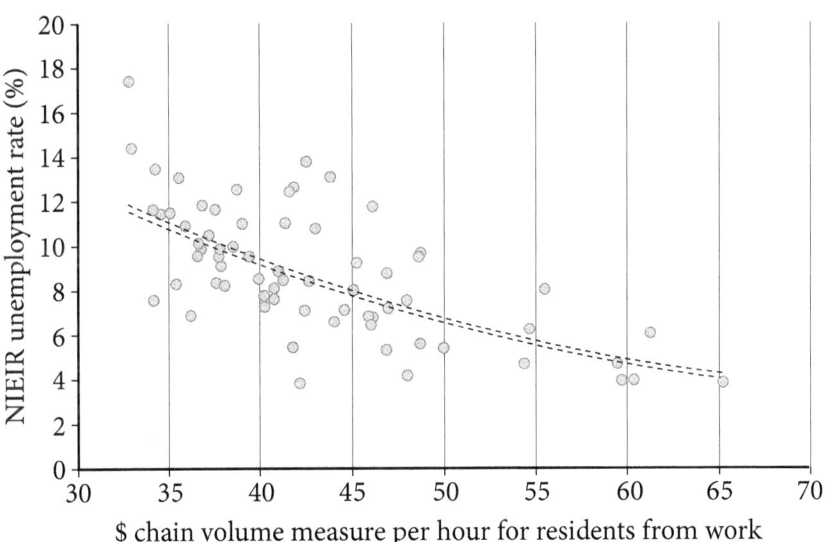

Source: NIER 2017

Figure 2. Australian major region – change in NIEIR unemployment rate 1996 versus change in $ per hour from work, 1996 to 2016

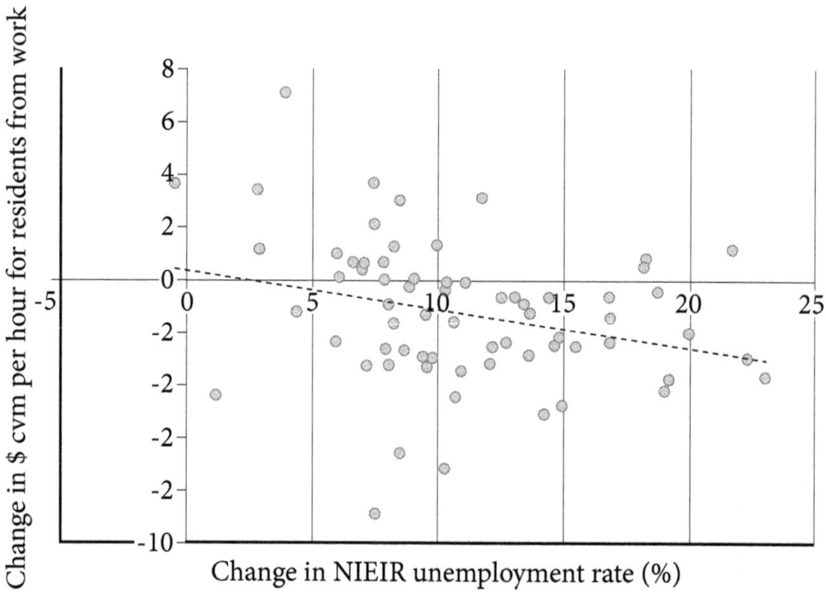

Source: NIER 2017

(ii) The short-run multiplier is significantly less than one

An alternative test of the role of real wages in CGE models is a test of the value of government expenditure fiscal multipliers. Dixon and Powell (1979) developed a seminal Australian multiplier estimate from a short-run CGE model. For the case of a 1 per cent increase in demand, aggregate employment increased by 0.6 per cent at the cost of a 1.7 per cent increase in inflation. Because of decreasing returns to scale, the GDP increase will be between third to two thirds of the employment increase, depending on the industry mix of the demand increase.

Unfortunately for CGE models the global financial crisis (GFC) provided a rich macro-economic dataset to test for government expenditure multipliers, thanks to the large-scale policy changes associated with the event. Up until 2011, the International Monetary Fund (IMF) adopted a fiscal multiplier of 0.5 in its forecasting assumptions. Expansionary government policy in response to the GFC from 2009 to 2010 demonstrated, however, that the fiscal multiplier lay between 0.9 and 1.8, which is within the range of crude textbook Keynesian multipliers. The IMF concluded that this had to be the case by examining their forecast errors (assuming a multiplier of 0.5) over the periods of stimulus, 2009 to 2010. This higher multiplier was also confirmed in the subsequent period of fiscal austerity (that is fiscal contraction) from 2011 to 2013. In its promotion of fiscal austerity, the IMF had argued for cuts in government expenditure to target a reduction in the public sector deficit, which, it believed, would have a powerful positive stimulus on the economy from confidence (via the Ricardian equivalence theorem), plus the CGE model inference that changes to the public sector deficit had little impact on the aggregate economy (IMF 2012). As Figure 3 shows, its expectations were not realised; and the IMF was honest enough to change its estimates of the fiscal multiplier to values closer to KK model estimates.

Figure 3. Growth versus austerity (degree of fiscal contraction)

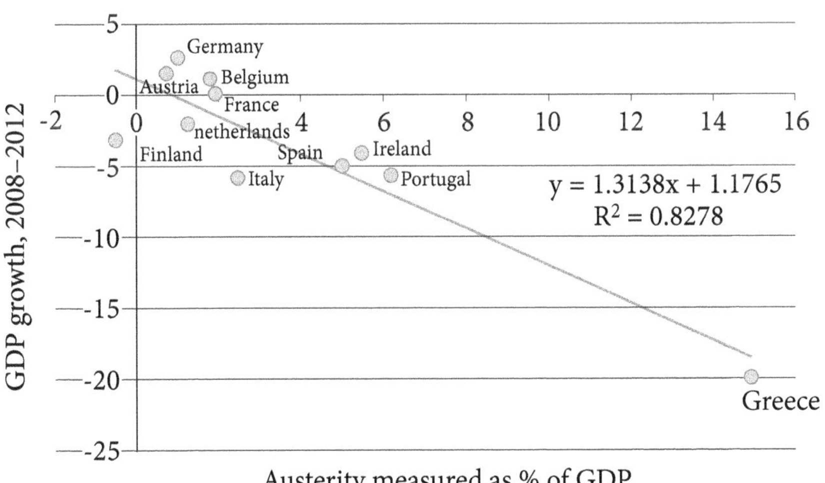

Source: Krugman 2013

This conclusion has been validated by others using different estimation methods.[4] On the basis of fiscal consolidation by the main nations in the European Union equal to 2.0 per cent of GDP in 2011 building to 3.9 per cent in 2013, GDP fell by 4.3 per cent in 2011, rising to 7.7 per cent in 2013. That is a multiplier of two.

The falsification of the low fiscal multiplier built into CGE models severely damages the hypotheses underlying these models.

(iii) A fixed labour supply

For fifty years KK models have incorporated labour-supply functions that allow for a variable participation rate inversely related to unemployment rate changes. Again, the GFC has provided a rich data base for testing this hypothesis – which is, consequently, again unfortunate for CGE models. In the United States, the participation rate fell from over 66 per cent in 2008 to less than 63 per cent by 2013. A key implication is that the unemployment rate is a poor guide to the extent of unutilised capacity in labour markets.

(iv) A fixed population

This is certainly not the case in Australia. For example, during the 2005 to 2011 mining boom, net immigration increased rapidly from around 150,000 to over 300,000 annually. Almost the entire extra workforce requirements stimulated by the boom were met by adjusting the level of net foreign immigration.

A key implication is that this supports the KK argument that economic growth is not constrained by the supply of factors of production; rather, labour supply responds to increasing aggregate demand.

(v) Constant returns to scale

There is no empirical evidence for universal constant returns to scale. Figure 4 shows how scale is related to productivity at the local government areas catchment level. ('Catchment' here refers to the value of total regional product (GRP) or output.) Economies of scale are indeed a factor in explaining regional economic performance.

Figure 4. Australian LGA catchments – productivity versus GRP, 2016

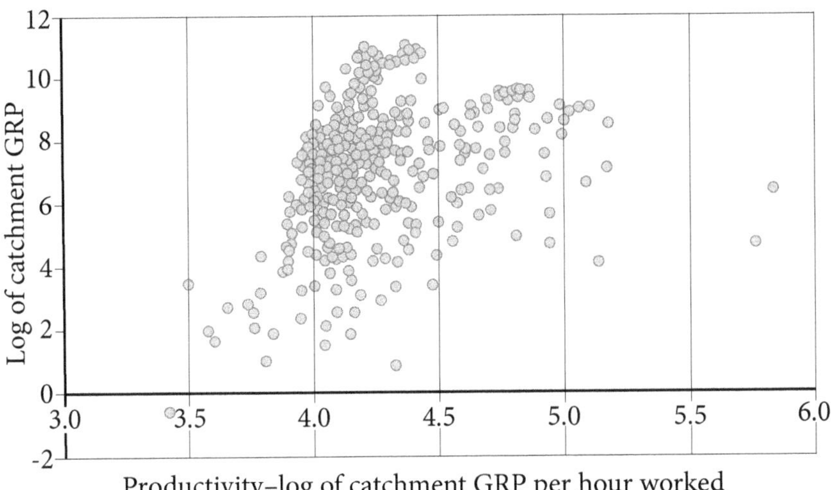

Source: NIER 2017

(vi) Productivity growth is largely exogenous

Scale is but one of a number of local factors driving local productivity. An analysis of the drivers in the Australian Local Government Association/ NIEIR's *State of the Regions Report 2017–18* using LGA catchment data found that productivity was also influenced, at similar elasticity, by non-dwelling capital stock installed, labour force skills, supply chain scale and density (supply-demand interaction between regional businesses), knowledge creation activity (employment in tertiary institutions, hospitals and advanced business services), and population growth. In weighted average terms, across the catchment areas for all 567 Australian LGAs, it was found that these factors explained a third of the total change in productivity (GRP per hour worked between 1996 and 2016).[5] In the policy context, the importance of local factors in driving productivity growth justifies a wide range of policy interventions to enhance local area economic development.

Figure 5. Australian LGA catchments – scale (1996) and growth in productivity (1996-2016)

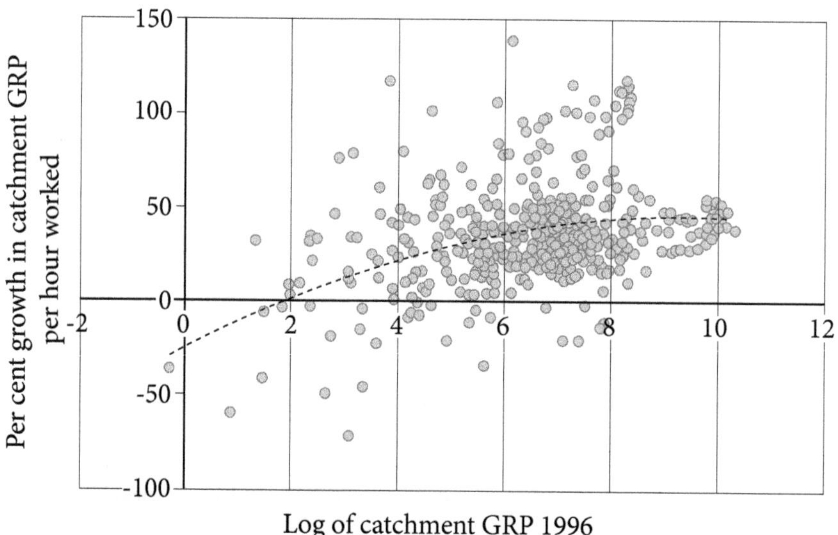

Source: NIER 2017

A flexible exchange rate maintains external and internal balance

For Australia it does not. In CGE models the main function of the exchange rate is to ensure the current account balance is sustainable. From the historical record, a current account deficit can be defined as sustainable when it is consistent with net foreign debt that is held at less than 50 per cent of GDP. Above the 50 per cent threshold, the probability of default on foreign debt increases sharply.

Since 2000, the Australian exchange rate has failed to maintain gross and net foreign debt at sustainable levels and, indeed, failed to slow down the rate of increase even after the 50 per cent threshold was passed. The reason for this is that the main drivers of the Australian exchange rate are:

- Commodity prices;
- Relative interest rates; and
- Sentiment towards Australia's major trading partners in general, and China in particular.

The outcome of these drivers has been exchange rates that are incompatible with the long-run stability of the Australian economy. From a KK perspective, the failure of the exchange rate to deliver sustainable current account deficits requires government to use fiscal and monetary policies to engineer a level of domestic demand compatible with the desired deficit and, in the long-run, employ industry policy to promote higher levels of export and import replacement.

An Example of CGE and Economic Policy: The Loss of the Australian Car Industry

Via its lobbying for the removal of tariff and other support to the Australian car industry, the Australian Productivity Commission (PC) exhibit a clear example of the pernicious real-world effects on public policy of the use of CGE modelling by neoliberal economists. Historically, there had been several rationales for tariff and budgetary support from government for the local car industry, Because it involves design, component manufacture and assembly, motor-vehicle production is R&D, technology- and capital-intensive. In 2017, when local car manufacture ceased in Australia, there were only thirteen nations globally that were capable of the complete process of car manufacturing, from design to showroom. There are significant forms of knowledge transfers or 'spillovers' to other industries of manufacturing technologies and work organisation practices, such as lean manufacturing techniques. These diversify the industrial base and reduce a dependence on unprocessed commodities, which may have a volatility-inducing effect on the aggregate economy. Assistance to the car industry was also justified to create technologies and skills for defence industries, population expansion and decentralisation. Local car production was also intended to lower persistently large import deficits in manufacturing, and, through a variety of Keynesian multiplier mechanisms, to lift employment and output above what would otherwise be the case.

In 2011–12 – the base year used by the PC for its modelling – the car-making and parts industry employed 50,000 workers directly, used around $15 billion of inputs from itself and other industries, such as engineering and computing consulting services for design and R&D, and generated combined profits and wages of $5.4billion (ABS 2013). Using various assumptions, the PC estimated the value of government assistance to the car industry to be $1.1 billion at that time. The PC argues that this support was a total waste of money: that there are no benefits whatsoever generated by such government support; worse, that output and employment would have been higher in the absence of a local car industry!

These results are generated by the PC's CGE (Monash Multi-Regional Forecasting–MMRF) model. Government support for the local car industry results in a 'misallocation' of resources and has two adverse effects: its raises costs and prices in other industries, reducing their competiveness; and it lowers GDP. This follows from the key assumptions that capital and labour are in fixed supply and fully employed. Government assistance simply crowds out other non-assisted industries given that 'overall resources are limited and one industry's expansion usually results in another's contraction' (PC 2012).

Removing assistance allows the market to allocate resources more efficiently with the PC assuming that the principle of comparative advantage ensures maximum welfare. The capital and labour 'liberated' from the car industry are quickly redeployed to, primarily, agriculture and mining. The PC assumes high internal labour mobility and high capital-labour substitution. Overseas demand for Australian commodities rises rapidly due to depreciation of the Australian dollar caused by a large increase in imports of cars. The large rise in commodity exports is driven by the model's very high commodity export price elasticity of demand of −10 (a 1 per cent fall in commodity prices leads to a 10 per cent increase in export demand) (PC 2014a).

Despite the contortions required to argue for the gains in shutting down the car industry, the PC has admitted that the modelled gains are 'small' and arguably even 'negative'. A negative result arises if labour and capital does not adjust as quickly and smoothly as projected: an expansion of commodity exports lowers their price (adverse terms of trade effect) and an expansion of predominately foreign-owned mining output means more profits accrue overseas (lifting GDP but lowering national income) (PC 2014b).

The Persistence of CGE Modelling

Why have falsified and pernicious economic ideas persisted and proven to exercise a remarkable grip on most of the economics profession and public policy? One answer is that they have helped preserve established interests by proposing 'plausible' reasons for blocking reform that could otherwise threaten these interests. For example, the CGE assumption of a fixed supply of resources means that they condemn any reform measures which increase demand or costs as likely to result in a range of macroeconomic woes, including inflation, a crowding out of existing productive activity, lower exchange rates which exacerbating the inflationary impact and, more likely than not, an (albeit small) long-run contraction in GDP. Any reform that involves redistributing income from capital to labour will result in a contraction in economic activity that is likely to be significant via the real wage impact. These outcomes stem directly from the fixed labour supply, long-run constant return to scale and short-run profit maximisation assumptions. CGE policy prescriptions are wonderfully attuned to the interests of financial capital, especially as perceived by selfish financial elites with constricted time, social and geographical horizons.

Conclusion

Until the practice of macro-economics is restored to a model accepted in scientific disciplines, economics will fail to provide policy guidance to maintain prosperity. Instead, it will justify policies that help to generate economic crises, particularly in the Anglosphere economies.

Endnotes

1 Gross of the net local area efficiency/inefficiency effect.

References

Australian Bureau of Statistics (2013) *Australian Industry, 2011–12, Cat. No. 8155.0*, 28 May. Canberra, Australian Government.

Brain, P.J. (1986) 'The Macroeconomic Structure of the Australian Economy', Croom Helm.

Bodkin, R.G., Klein, L.R. and Marwarh, K. (1991) *A History of Macroeconomic Model Building*. Cheltenham, Edward Elgar.

Dixon, P.B. and Powell, A.A. (1979) *Structural Adaptation in an Ailing Macroeconomy*: 20. Carlton, Melbourne University Press.

Forecast Error and Fiscal Multipliers, International Monetary Fund Working Paper, WP 13/1.

Gechert, S., Hallett, A. and Rannenberg, A. 'Fiscal multipliers in downturns and the effects of Eurozone consolidation', Centre for Economic Policy Research Policy, Insight no. 79, February 2015.

International Monetary Fund (2012), 'Are We Underestimating Short-Term Fiscal Multipliers?' *World Economic Outlook October 2012*: 41; Leigh, D. (2013), *Growth*

NIER's Regional Economic Database and Modelling Systems (2017)

P. Krugman (2013) 'How the case for Austerity has crumbled', *The New York Review of Books*, 6 June.

Productivity Commission (2012) *Annual Report 2011–12*, Productivity Commission Annual Report Series: 26. Canberra, Australian Government.

——(2014a) 'Economywide Modelling of Automotive Industry Change', Supplement to Australia's Automotive Manufacturing Industry: 39. Canberra, Australian Government.

——(2014b) 'Economywide Modelling of Automotive Industry Change', Supplement to Australia's Automotive Manufacturing Industry: 15. Canberra, Australian Government.

CHAPTER 17

THE REAL COSTS OF 'FREE' TRADE AGREEMENTS AND THE NEED FOR ALTERNATIVE TRADE POLICIES

PATRICIA RANALD

US President Donald Trump and Australian minor party One Nation have something in common: they have both tapped into widespread resentment of neoliberal trade policies, which have not delivered the jobs and growth they promised. But, their simplistic responses – placing high tariffs on imports, building walls and introducing discriminatory immigration policies – will not restore lost jobs, nor improve people's lives. An alternative is needed to both extreme nationalist and neoliberal trade policies. This chapter applies a critical political economy analysis to Australian neoliberal trade policy, measuring the benefits it has claimed against actual outcomes. It proposes alternative trade policies as part of a more equitable and environmentally sustainable economic policy.

Neoliberal trade theory argues that a reduction of tariffs and non-tariff trade barriers by all countries will increase trade and investment in a globalised competitive market and, eventually, will raise living standards for all. Each country should specialise in its most 'competitive' or lowest cost products or services, import everything else at the lowest possible prices, implement zero tariffs, impose no active industry policies and only minimal government regulation. This is a central component in the suite of neoliberal policies (Stiglitz and Charlton 2005: 2). Its actual results can be a race to the bottom on labour conditions and environmental standards.

Critics of neoliberal trade theory point to the limitations of the basic assumptions of early-nineteenth-century neoclassical comparative advantage theory (that all resources are used in production; that capital is immobile, for example), most of which does not apply to real-world, twenty-first-century economies (Dunkley 2004: 18–62; Stanford 2015: 304–311). Historical economic studies question whether the full implementation of neoliberal trade policies has actually delivered successful forms of economic development, or whether they have instead contributed to global inequality. Indeed, these historical studies argue that industrialised countries in fact achieved development through selective tariffs and active industry policies *before* agreeing to negotiate lower tariffs. The imposition of strict neoliberal policies on developing countries amounts to a 'kicking away of the ladder' to economic development (Chang 2002; Stiglitz and Charlton 2005). As for contemporary trade agreements, studies criticise their expansion into non-tariff areas of law and policy normally regulated through national democratic processes (Cox 1994; Stiglitz 2015; Ranald 2015).

Institutions at national and international levels are influenced – but not simply determined – by economic interests. Institutions also develop their own histories that, in turn, influence the development of policies, which can persist despite changes of government. State policies can reflect the outcomes of contests between social forces (Cox 1994). Neoliberal trade theory ignores both power relations and the development of historical institutions. This chapter examines trade institutions and government policies through a critical analysis of their social origins and histories, and of the power relationships between the social forces that influence them. These include powerful global corporations and business organisations on the one hand; and unions and community organisations that defend the interests of the less powerful on the other.

Transnational corporations pressure states for regulatory policies that suit their interests. The most powerful states like the United States use their national legal frameworks as a model for legally enforceable international regulation through trade agreements. Trade agreements, negotiated in secret, have expanded into many areas previously regarded as the domain of more transparent national parliamentary and regulatory processes. These include access to medicines, financial services, food regulation, government purchasing, labour and environmental policies. The transfer of laws and policies away from from national democratic scrutiny into secret trade negotiations can itself provoke resistance from a range of labour and social movements (Cox 1994: 52–53).

This chapter has four parts. The first deals with the transition from World Trade Organization (WTO) multilateral negotiations to preferential bilateral and regional agreements. The second analyses Australia's preferential agreements and compares the forecasts of the benefits predicted to flow from these agreements with the evidence from actual outcomes using the case study of the Australia–United States Free Trade Agreement (AUSFTA). The third part analyses the Trans-Pacific Partnership (TPP) as a new-generation trade agreement that attempts to limit national government regulation, and analyses the social movement resistance to this process. I conclude by outlining the elements of a progressive alternative trade policy.

From Multilateral to Preferential Agreements

From 1995, the WTO, which currently has 164 members, was the vehicle for multilateral trade negotiations. WTO agreements dealt with trade in goods, agriculture, services, trade-related intellectual property arrangements (TRIPS), and some regulatory issues like product labelling and quarantine. Following neoliberal trade theory, legally binding agreements could freeze and then reduce tariffs and other trade barriers in both industrialised and developing countries, with the aim of expanding global trade and prosperity. The WTO was dominated by the largest industrialised economies, and its agreements had only limited recognition of the specific needs of developing countries. Both the WTO and neoliberal trade theorists saw bilateral and regional agreements with more limited membership as preferential arrangements that discriminated against those who were excluded (Adams et al. 2003; Armstrong 2015).

But from 1996 the United States, the European Union and Japan began to support more rapid deregulation of trade in services, and new agreements on investment and government procurement, which suited their major export industries and corporations. Supported by community groups in many countries, developing country governments sought to retain more regulatory space for local industry development. These conflicts came to a head at the WTO 'Battle in Seattle' meeting in 1999, when thousands of protestors gathered in the streets surrounding the meeting and developing countries rejected the new agreements. These conflicts were only partially addressed by the launch of the Doha Development Round of negotiations, which commenced in 2001 (Stiglitz and Charlton 2005).

Developing country governments were also critical of the impacts of the WTO's TRIPS agreement, which had extended patent monopolies on medicines to 20 years, making them unaffordable for low-income countries. They rightly argued that stronger monopolies were contrary to the principles of free trade. WTO negotiations were slowed by years of debate to achieve some concessions on access to medicines for developing countries. The Doha negotiations halted in 2003 when the United States and the European Union refused to remove their subsidy payments to individual farmers, which reduced the price of their exports, undercutting the prices of local farmers in developing countries, with devastating impacts. Developing countries again refused new WTO agreements on investment and government procurement. These negotiations have essentially remained stalled until the time of writing (Stiglitz and Charlton 2005: 2–4, 141–146).

The United States, the European Union and Japan have since initiated preferential bilateral and regional agreements designed to maximise gains to their major industries, and which largely ignore the specific needs of developing countries. The United States, for example, has achieved stronger patent and copyright monopolies for its medicine, information technology and media industries than had been achieved in WTO agreements (Lopert and Gleeson 2013, Productivity Commission 2010). While WTO agreements are legally enforced through government-to-government dispute tribunals, preferential agreements have both government-to-government dispute processes and the investor-state dispute settlement (ISDS) process. ISDS gives individual foreign corporations the right to bypass national courts and sue governments for millions of dollars of compensation in a non-WTO international investment tribunal if a change in law or policy can be claimed to harm their investments, even if the change is in the public interest. This gives additional legal powers to already-powerful global corporations. The European Union and Japan have also supported ISDS (Tienhaara 2009).

Preferential agreements involving selected countries have also had another advantage for the United States and the European Union, which subsidise their domestic agriculture, effectively reducing their prices on global markets. These subsidies are paid to individual farm businesses at the national level in each country and so apply to all exports. This means they cannot be selectively reduced for exports to other particular countries through preferential agreements. They can only be reduced or removed through governments agreeing to do so in WTO multilateral negotiations applying to all WTO countries, to which the United States and EU have so far not agreed. Preferential agreements conveniently bypass this multilateral process and can achieve market access for other industries while leaving agricultural subsidies undisturbed (Ranald 2011: 86; Stiglitz and Charlton 2005: 50).

Preferential agreements can also be combined with security and other non-trade concerns to favour particular trading partners. For example, in the aftermath of the September 11 attacks, both the US Bush and Australian Howard governments confirmed that the AUSFTA was part of a broader strategic and military alliance (Ranald 2006: 35–36).

Australian Trade Policy

Prior to 2000, Australia's trade policy was shaped by neoliberal trade theory. Successive Australian governments from the 1970s onwards implemented unilateral reductions in tariffs on manufactured goods and participated in WTO multilateral negotiations. Australia was the leader of the WTO Cairns Group of agricultural exporting nations, who together lobbied for agricultural trade liberalisation, and against agricultural subsidies. The Australian policy contrasted with the US preferential bargaining chip approach to obtaining the largest possible gains from others while offering the smallest possible concessions (Quiggin 2010).

However, as successive Australian governments were advised that they were being disadvantaged by exclusion from preferential agreements, this policy changed from 2001. Australia negotiated preferential agreements with Singapore, the United States, Chile, Thailand, Malaysia, Japan, Korea, China and Peru. Currently, negotiations for preferential agreements with Hong Kong, India, Indonesia Mexico and Colombia are underway (DFAT 2017).

Australia also has a regional preferential agreement with the ten Association of Southeast Asian Nations (ASEAN) countries plus New Zealand through the ASEAN–Australia–New Zealand free trade agreement (AANZFTA), and is currently negotiating the Regional Comprehensive Economic Partnership (RCEP) with New Zealand, China, Japan, India, South Korea and the ten ASEAN countries. Other regional preferential agreements include the Pacific Agreement on Closer Economic Relationships (PACER-Plus) with New Zealand and nine Pacific Island countries, and the Trans-Pacific Partnership (TPP), which is explained in some detail below.

The specific objectives of Australian trade policy have been to obtain increased market access for agricultural and services exports. In practice, especially for Coalition governments, this has meant trading away tariffs and all other forms of support for manufacturing industry. This approach was summarised by Treasurer Joe Hockey's 2014 explanation of the government's decision to cut the remaining tariffs and domestic support to the vehicle industry, resulting in its closure in 2017, with the loss of thousands of jobs in South Australia and Victoria:

> Ending the age of entitlement for industry was a hard decision but it needed to be made because as a result of that decision we were able to get free-trade agreements with Korea, Japan and China. (Quoted in Maher 2014)

Economic Impacts of Trade Agreements: Economic Modelling Vs Real-World Outcomes

Australia's announcements of preferential trade negotiations have often been accompanied by predictive feasibility studies based on computable general equilibrium (CGE) econometric modelling. These build mathematical models of the economy based on neoclassical economic assumptions that bear no relation to real-world economies. They assume that all tariff and non-tariff barriers will be removed, that there will be full employment, perfect labour mobility, no income distribution effects and no trade balance effects. By assuming away negative effects, these models almost always produce results that predict future increases in economic growth, usually after ten to fifteen years. There is a substantial economic literature that has criticised GCE models and questioned their results (Taylor and von Anim 2006; see Chapter 16 by Peter Brain in this book). Studies of the impacts of preferential trade agreements after implementation, based on actual outcomes and more realistic assumptions, often show minimal change or negative impacts.

For example, the AUSFTA, negotiated by the Howard and Bush governments and implemented in 2005, provides the best example of the chasm between predictive studies and post-implementation studies. There was even a battle between different predictive feasibility studies while the agreement was being negotiated, which demonstrated the extent to which CGE modelling results depended on the assumptions of particular models. The Agreement included chapters on trade in goods, services, investment, government procurement, and an intellectual property chapter that applied US standards and resulted in longer copyright and medicine monopolies, to the detriment of Australian consumers. However, after a fierce public debate, the AUSFTA did not include an ISDS provision.

In 2001, the Howard government commissioned the Centre for International Economics (CIE) to conduct econometric modelling of the AUSFTA. This predictive study found that the immediate removal of all trade barriers would result in a 0.3 per cent increase in Australia's GDP after ten years (CIE 2001). Another study by ACIL consultants for the Rural Industries Research and Development Corporation (RIRDC) in 2002 assumed there would be only limited removal of US agricultural trade barriers. This study found that there would be net losses to the Australian economy (ACIL 2003).

The final text of the AUSFTA, published in 2004, showed that the United States gained more access to Australian markets than vice versa. The National Farmers' Federation (NFF) said it was 'not a free trade agreement', because there was no additional Australian access to the US sugar market, and increased access for other farm products was very limited with long lead times (NFF 2004). There was also limited access to the US market for Australian manufactured products, and for government procurement.

More econometric studies of the AUSFTA were conducted in 2004, based on these actual outcomes. A second CIE study showed gains for Australia resulting from agricultural and merchandise trade were marginal, but claimed huge gains from the reduced equity risk for US investors, resulting in an increased US investment in Australia and therefore a net economic gain (CIE 2004). The second study's assumptions about reduced equity risk were so far outside conventional econometric modelling norms that the Australian National University (ANU) Professor Ross Garnaut said that 'they did not pass the laugh test' (quoted in Armstrong 2015: 4). Other studies based on actual outcomes estimated the economic gains to be marginal or indeed negative for Australia (Dee 2004; National Institute for Economic and Industry Research 2004).

The AUSFTA's limited market access was criticised by the Australian Industry Group (Ai Group), the peak body for the local manufacturing industry, which surveyed its members in 2010. The survey found that 80 per cent of members agreed that the AUSFTA was not very effective in improving export opportunities, and 85 per cent said it had failed to help establish operations in the United States (Ai Group 2010).

A 2010 Productivity Commission report concluded that feasibility studies for bilateral and regional trade agreements had produced 'overly optimistic expectations of their likely economic effects'. The report used its own model to conclude that the actual economic effects of bilateral and regional trade agreements were 'modest' for the Australian economy as a whole and that there was 'little evidence to indicate that preferential agreements have provided significant commercial benefits' (Productivity Commission 2010: xxxvi, xxv and xxxv). The report also noted that AUSFTA increased the length of medicine monopolies, and increased payments to copyright holders. It concluded that, since Australia is a net importer of patented and copyright products, AUSFTA imposed net costs on consumers and the Australian economy, but these costs had not been included in the econometric modelling (Productivity Commission 2010: 259, 260, 263).

In 2015, ANU economist Shiro Armstrong applied an updated dataset to the Productivity Commission's model to measure the economic impact of the agreement (Armstrong 2015). This study measured the trade diversion effects of the actual outcomes of the AUSFTA. Trade diversion can occur because preferential treatment toward one trading partner may result in trade being diverted from more efficient and competitive suppliers in other countries. The study concluded that the agreement diverted trade away from other lower cost sources. Australia and the United States had by 2012 reduced their trade by US$53 billion with the rest of the world and were worse off than they would have been without the agreement. Although there was an increase in Australia's trade with East Asian economies during this period, this trade would have grown more in the absence of the trade diversionary effects of the AUSFTA. The study also concluded that there was no increase in the share of US investment relative to other foreign investment (Armstrong 2015: 10–13).

Only one post-agreement study was conducted on the impacts of the Japan, China and Korea FTAs, concluded in 2014–15. Even with the usual favourable assumptions, the study predicted very small economic gains of 0.05 per cent of GDP after twenty years, and net employment gains of only 5434 – a number described by *The Age* economics editor as 'hardly any jobs' (CIE 2015: 29; Martin 2015).

The debate about the assumptions of such studies, and their variable results, has doubtlessly contributed to the fact that they have fallen out of favour with government. For example, Andrew Stoler's minority report to the Productivity Commission in 2010 declared that 'the goal of successfully testing trade agreements to determine significant net economic benefit is unattainable' (Productivity Commission 2010: 317). Stoler claimed that statistical inadequacies, especially in assessing the positive impact of removal of barriers in services and investment, meant that economic benefits could not be measured accurately. This view seems to have been adopted by the Coalition government, which later refused to fund a study of the post-agreement economic outcomes of the TPP (Hutchens 2016).

The Trans-Pacific Partnership

The TPP between the United States, Australia and ten other countries in the Americas and the Asia Pacific[1] was negotiated from 2010, then finalised and published in November 2015. US President Obama (2011) claimed that the agreement would enable the United States rather than China to write the rules, and would be a twenty-first-century model for other agreements. The United States already had bilateral agreements in place with six of these countries, and was the driving force in the negotiations. As with the AUSFTA, the TPP had a strategic role – this time in US economic and military competition with China in the region. Australia already had free trade agreements with all but three of the TPP economies, meaning the TPP had limited impact on tariff levels and market access gains. The TPP negotiators stressed the gains from the establishment of common regulatory frameworks and seamless supply chains (DFAT 2015: 3–4).

Once the text became public, public debate centred on whether these regulatory frameworks, modelled on US law and heavily influenced by US pharmaceutical, media and other corporations, met the interests of Australia and other TPP countries. In addition to chapters dealing with trade in goods, agriculture, services, investment, quarantine, technical barriers to trade and government procurement, the TPP included financial services, telecommunications, electronic commerce, state-owned enterprises, regulatory coherence, competition policy, small and medium-sized enterprises, transparency, anticorruption, temporary workers, labour and environment. The TPP sought to intervene in an unprecedented number of areas, amounting to thirty chapters, compared with twenty in most previous agreements. Critics argued that many public policy areas that should normally be decided through open democratic parliamentary processes had instead been decided secretly through trade negotiations (Ranald 2015; Stiglitz 2015; Hirono et al. 2015).

Key critical issues in the text were longer monopolies on costly biologic medicines, which would delay the availability of cheaper versions of these medicines (PHAA 2016) and stronger copyright monopolies, which benefited copyright holders at the expense of consumers (Productivity Commission 2015). The labour and environment chapters were not as enforceable as the rest of the agreement. The agreement also contained ISDS, which enabled foreign corporations to bypass national courts and sue governments in international tribunals, which legal experts argued were not independent and lacked the legal safeguards of national systems. These international tribunals consist of investment trade law experts who can continue to be practising advocates, representing a corporation one month and sitting on a tribunal the next, and there are no precedents or appeals (French 2014; Kahale 2014). There are now 855 known ISDS cases, many against health, environment and other public interest legislation (UNCTAD 2018).

From the Productivity Commission (2010) to unions and community groups (AFTINET 2015), ISDS provoked a wide range of opposition; public opinion polls showed majority opposition (Essential Media 2015). The Labor Party opposed ISDS from 2011,[2] as did the Greens and the Nick Xenophon Team (Australian Labor Party 2015: 26; Senate Foreign Affairs, Defence and Trade References Committee 2016).

Critics also condemned the secrecy of the trade negotiation process and the failure to release the text until after it was agreed by Cabinet. This led to a Senate inquiry in 2015, which produced a report aptly titled *Blind Agreement*. The report recommended a more open process for the TPP and other trade agreements (Senate Foreign Affairs Defence and Trade References Committee 2015).

The government ignored these recommendations and the text of the TPP was not released until after it had been agreed. It was then reviewed by the government-dominated Joint Standing Committee on Treaties (JSCOT), which could not change the text, but only make recommendations for or against the implementing legislation. Parliament could only vote on implementing legislation, not the full text of the agreement. This means parliament could not vote on controversial provisions like ISDS.

As the government had refused to fund an independent study of the economic impacts of the TPP, the JSCOT inquiry instead relied on the National Interest Analysis produced by the Department of Foreign Affairs and Trade (DFAT), which had itself negotiated the agreement, and recommended its implementation (DFAT 2015). The government ignored requests for independent assessments of economic and other impacts from many community groups, the Productivity Commission and public health experts (Hutchens 2016; Productivity Commission 2015; Hirono et al 2015).

Resistance to the TPP came mainly from progressive groups including unions, churches, environment, public health and others in the United States and elsewhere (Public Citizen 2014; AFTINET 2015). US resistance from both Democrats and Republicans prevented Congressional approval of the TPP in 2016 and ensured that both Democrat and Republican presidential candidates opposed the TPP before the US elections (Reuters 2015). Donald Trump dealt the final blow by withdrawing in January 2017 (Baker 2017).

In Australia, critics succeeded in establishing a Senate inquiry into the TPP, on which Labor, Greens minor parties had a majority, as they did in the Senate itself. Its report, made after the US withdrawal, reflected many of the criticisms listed above and recommended a deferral of the implementing legislation (Senate Foreign Affairs, Defence and Trade References Committee 2016). The government did not present the legislation, so the original TPP deal was not endorsed by the Australian parliament.

The Japanese and Australian governments led attempts to resurrect the TPP without the US, arguing that a 'TPP-11' would preserve the claimed gains from the agreement and enable the United States to re-join if its policy changed (Ciobo 2017). However, other TPP governments had only reluctantly agreed to many of the US-initiated proposals on medicine and copyright monopolies to get access to the US market, and without such access many resisted these clauses (Nikkei Asia 2017). The eleven governments eventually agreed after a year of negotiations to rename the agreement the 'Comprehensive Progressive TPP' (CPTPP) and to suspend, but not delete, twenty-two of its most controversial clauses, mainly on medicines and copyright. These clauses could be reinstated if the US rejoins the deal (TPP Ministers 2017). However ISDS and other controversial clauses remain.

The CPTPP, now dubbed the TPP-11, was signed on 8 March 2018, but six TPP governments need to pass its implementing legislation before it can come into force. In Australia, the TPP-11 is being reviewed by the government-dominated Joint Standing Committee on Treaties, which is due to report in August 2018. Critics have also lobbied successfully for a Senate inquiry, due to report in September 2018 (JSCOT 2018; Senate References Committee 2018). It remains to be seen whether the majority in the Senate will pass the implementing legislation. Japan and Australia are also attempting to import TPP provisions on medicine monopolies, copyright and ISDS into the ongoing RCEP negotiations, but these are being resisted by India, China and most ASEAN governments, and negotiations continue in 2018 (Mathieson 2017).

Conclusion

Academic studies show that neoliberal trade policies of zero tariffs and zero other barriers to trade and investment have not delivered the economic growth and employment predicted by the neoliberal economic modelling applied to specific preferential trade agreements. This failure has generated both conservative and progressive resistance. Claiming that benefits still exist, but cannot be measured through economic modelling, the Australian Coalition government has abandoned such studies.

In the context of almost zero Australian tariffs, the TPP was an attempt by the US as the dominant state actor to establish US-style regional regulatory frameworks that suited its powerful export industries. ISDS also enables global corporations to restrain future regulation. But this secret negotiation of domestic regulation removed it from the democratic political process of public and parliamentary debate, delegitimising the agreement. The consequent resistance from a wide range of progressive community organisations pressured the Labor, Greens and minor party majority in the Senate to refuse to endorse the implementing legislation. The renamed TPP-11 without the United States has also faced resistance, and at the time of writing it remains to be seen if the Senate will endorse the implementing legislation.

The Trump administration continues to pursue its corporate agenda through even more selective bilateral agreements. There is less free-trade rhetoric and more blatant exercise of US economic power combined with discriminatory migration policies. This could result in trade wars, leading to contraction rather than expansion of trade.

A progressive alternative trade policy to both neoliberalism and Trump-style unilateralism is needed. Trade can improve people's lives if it is part of an economic policy that delivers employment and higher living standards in an environmentally sustainable society that rejects discrimination and respects human rights. This need not mean a return to high tariffs, but should enable expanded trade combined with active industry policies that deliver a range of jobs in manufacturing, services, agriculture and other sectors, supported by high quality education, health and other services. Trade rules should be negotiated openly and democratically in a system that includes all governments, and provides for the specific needs of developing countries. Trade agreements should not prevent governments from regulating in the public interest. They should not strengthen monopolies, nor give additional legal rights like ISDS to global corporations that already have enormous market power. Finally, trade agreements should be based on internationally agreed-upon and fully enforceable labour rights and environmental standards, to counter the global race to the bottom on these standards.

Endnotes

1 The twelve TPP countries were the United States, Canada, Mexico, Peru, Chile, Japan, Malaysia, Singapore, Brunei, Vietnam, Australia and New Zealand.

2 The Labor government commenced the TPP negotiations in 2010, but adopted policy against ISDS and stronger medicine monopolies, and for enforceable labour rights and environmental standards in 2011. The Coalition government, without these policies, completed negotiations from 2013 to 2015.

References

ACIL Consulting (2003) *A Bridge Too Far? An Australian Agricultural Perspective on the Australia/United States Free Trade Area Idea*, Report for the Rural Industries Research and Development Corporation, Canberra.

Adams, R., Dee, P., Gali, J. and McGuire, G. (2003) 'The Trade and Investment Effects of Preferential Trading Arrangements – Old and New Evidence', Staff Working Paper, Productivity Commission, Melbourne.

Armstrong, Shiro (2015) *The Economic Impact of the Australia-United States Free Trade Agreement, Australia-Japan Research Centre*, Working Paper, 1 January.

Australian Fair Trade and Investment Network (2015) 'Community groups tell Trade Minister TPP not in national interest'.

Australian Industry Group (2010) 'Business seeks better returns from trade agreements', media release, January.

Australian Labor Party (2015) *A Smart, Modern, Fair Australia*, National Platform, Canberra.

Baker, P. (2017) 'Trump abandons TPP', *The New York Times*, January 21.

Centre for International Economics (CIE) (2001) *Economic impacts of an Australia–United States Free Trade Area*, Canberra.

——(2004) *Economic analysis of the AUSFTA: impact of the bilateral free trade agreement with the United States*, prepared for the Department of Foreign Affairs and Trade, Canberra.

——(2015) *Economic benefits of Australia's North Asian FTAs*, prepared for the Department of Foreign Affairs and Trade, Canberra.

Chang, Ha-Joon (2002) *Kicking Away the Ladder: Development Strategy in Historical Perspective*, Anthem Press, London.

Ciobo, S. (2017) *Transcript of Bloomberg interview on the TPP-11*, 23 August.

Cox, R. (1994) 'Global Restructuring', in R. Stubbs and G. Underhill (eds), *Political Economy and the Changing Global Order*, Macmillan, London: 45-59.

Dee, P., (2004) *Submission to the Senate Inquiry on the Australia-US Free Trade Agreement*, June, Australian National University, Canberra.

Department of Foreign Affairs and Trade (2015) *National Interest Analysis of the Trans-Pacific Partnership*, Canberra.

——(2017) 'Free Trade Agreements', Canberra.

Dunkley, G. (2004) *Free Trade, Myth, Reality and Alternatives*, Zed Books, London and New York.

Essential Media (2015) 'Poll shows 61% of voters reject investor rights to sue governments', July 7, essentialvision.com.au/documents/essential_report_150707.pdf

French, R.F. Chief Justice (2014), 'Investor-State Dispute Settlement – a cut above the courts?', Paper delivered at the Supreme and Federal Courts Judges conference, July 9 2014, Darwin._

Hirono, K., Haigh, F., Gleeson, D., Harris, P., Thow., A. (2015) *A Health Impact Assessment of the proposed Trans-Pacific Partnership Agreement*, Centre for Health Equity Training Research and Evaluation, University of New South Wales, February.

Hutchens, G., (2016) 'Trade Minister Andrew Robb criticised for seeking TPP ratification without independent analysis', *The Sydney Morning Herald*, 9 February.

Kahale (2014) Keynote address, Eighth Juris Investment Arbitration Conference, Washington DC, 8 March.

Lopert, R. and Gleeson, D. (2013) 'The high price of 'free' trade: US trade agreements and access to medicines', *Journal of Law, Medicine and Ethics*, 41(1): 199–223.

Maher, S. (2014) 'Car industry cuts helped seal FTA deals', *The Australian*, 3 December.

Martin, P. (2015) 'How many jobs? The China FTA will create hardly any', *Sydney Morning Herald*, September 14.

Mathieson, R. (2017) 'Asia Trade Talks Chief Warns Against Turning Pact into New TPP', *Bloomberg*, March 22.

National Farmers Federation (2004), 'US disappoints in agriculture on trade deal', News Release, February 9, Canberra.

National Institute for *Economic and Industry Research (2004), An assessment of the direct impact of the Australian-United States Free Trade Agreement on Australian trade, economic activity and the costs of the loss of national sovereignty*, prepared for the Australian Manufacturing Workers Union, May, Melbourne.

Nikkei Asian Review (2017) '"TPP 11" talks set parameters for moving forward', September 23.

Obama, B. (2011) *Remarks by President Obama to the Australian Parliament,* The White House, 17 November.

Parliament of Australia, Joint Standing Committee on Treaties (2018) Inquiry into the TPP 11.

Productivity Commission (2010), *Bilateral and Regional Trade Agreements Final Report*, Canberra, 13 December.

——(2015) Trade and Assistance Review, 2013–14, June.

Public Citizen (2014) 'Letter from 600 civil society organisations to the US Senate', 10 September, www.citizen.org/documents/letter-wyden-fast-track-september-2014.pdf

Public Health Association of Australia (PHAA) (2016), Submission to the Joint Standing Committee on Treaties, March.

Quiggin, J., (2010) 'Lessons from the Australia-US Free Trade Agreement' in Kelsey, J., *No Ordinary Deal: Unmasking the Trans Pacific Partnership Free Trade Agreement,* Allen and Unwin, New South Wales: 98–108.

Ranald, P. (2006) 'The Australia-US Free Trade Agreement: A Contest of Interests', *Journal of Australian Political Economy,* June.

——(2011) 'The Trans-Pacific Partnership Agreement, contradictions in Australia and the Asia Pacific Region', *Economic and Labour Relations Review*, 22 (1), May.

——'The Trans-Pacific Partnership Agreement: Reaching behind the border, challenging democracy', *The Economic and Labour Relations Review*, 26 (2), April.

Reuters (2015), 'No point in TPP vote this year', 4 August.

Senate Foreign Affairs, Defence and Trade References Committee (2015), *Blind Agreement: Inquiry into the Commonwealth's Treaty-Making Process.*

——(2016) *Report on Proposed Trans-Pacific Partnership Agreement.*

——(2018) *Inquiry into the proposed TPP-11.*

Stanford, J. (2015) *Economics for Everyone* (second edition), Pluto Press, London.

Stiglitz, J. (2015) 'Don't trade away Health', *The New York Times*, 30 January.

Stiglitz, J. and Charlton A. (2005) *Fair Trade for All*, Oxford University Press, Oxford.

Taylor, L., and R. von Arnim (2006) *Computable General Equilibrium Models of Trade Liberalization: The Doha Debate,* New School for Social Research, Oxford.

Tienhaara, K. (2009) *The Expropriation of Environmental Governance: Protecting Foreign Investors at the Expense of Public Policy*, Cambridge University Press, Cambridge.

Trans-Pacific Ministers (2017), *Trans-Pacific Ministerial Statement,* 10 November.

United Nations Committee on Trade and Development (UNCTAD) (2018), UNCTAD *Investment Dispute Settlement Navigator.*

CHAPTER 18

FOREIGN INVESTMENT

DAVID RICHARDSON

In recent years there has been a backlash against the globalisation of the world economic system and the influence of big business in political and economic decision-making. Foreign investment is one of the chief channels of globalisation so it too should be the subject of debate. Instead, foreign investment in Australia only becomes an issue when particularly sensitive issues arise: Shell's attempted takeover of Woodside, the rejected takeover of GrainCorp, or when farmland and housing is purchased by foreigners, to note some examples. Despite public attitudes to globalisation there has been a radical shift in official attitudes, especially in Treasury, over the last forty years. Liberalisation of foreign investment has been part of the broader shift to neoliberalism.

This chapter charts the dramatic shift in government attitudes to foreign investment over the last forty years, and critically reviews the arguments favouring a policy of allowing virtually unfettered foreign investment in Australia. It describes the turn away from a long-standing determination in official economic thinking to control the scale and scope of foreign investment in the service of the 'national interest', towards the favouring of a liberalised flow of capital into and out of Australia. It also outlines the current scope of foreign investment. It then summarises the orthodox case for foreign investment and its criticisms, and briefly presents other common pragmatic arguments for and against foreign investment.

Finally, it argues for a more sceptical approach to foreign investment.

This chapter's focus is on public policy concerning the ownership or control of local 'investments', defined in national accounting terms as the purchase and/or construction of fixed durable assets, land, equipment and buildings that contribute to production and receive an income (profits) for capital services. It does not, in other words, consider short-term flows such as the overseas purchase of government or corporate bonds or currency and derivative trading.

The Revolution in Thinking about Foreign Investment in Australia

In 1972, Treasury reflected the intellectual mood when it declared that foreign ownership and control poses 'problems for Australian economic policy and, perhaps, for policy in fields going beyond the strictly economic'. It outlined these problems in a series of significant questions:

> Are the economic benefits of foreign capital sufficient to outweigh the gains it reaps from Australia? Will the growth of these gains impose, over time, a long-run burden on the balance of payments? Should we be content to have out natural resources developed by foreign companies? Are Australian exports being hindered by the policies of international corporations with affiliates in Australia? Do foreign-controlled enterprises in Australia behave in other ways contrary to our national interests? Do foreign takeovers of Australian enterprises raise special problems? Is there a general need for majority Australian ownership of investment projects? Could we finance more of our own development from local savings? (Treasury 1972)

These questions were never sufficiently answered and all remain valid.

In 1968, ALP Opposition leader Arthur Calwell, felt himself to be on sufficiently safe ground to criticise what had been held up as the exemplar of foreign investment success and icon of national pride – General Motors' investment in Holden car manufacturing. He contradicted the core assumption that the US corporation had augmented Australian savings so as to permit more investment than would otherwise occur. Calwell argued that none of GM's own money was involved; it was all borrowed within Australia (Calwell 1968). Rather than bringing new funds, GM used funds raised in Australia, but it nevertheless made very high profits which were repatriated overseas.

In the postwar decades, foreign investment had been severely proscribed. An example was mining, with general limits of 50 per cent foreign equity and 75 per cent Australian equity in the case of uranium. Special cases such as broadcasting, airlines, coastal shipping were off-limits altogether. There was concern around this time that Australia should be 'buying back the farm' – that is, using domestic savings to reduce the scale of foreign ownership. The Australian Industry Development Corporation was established in 1970 to oversee and administer domestic capital to free Australia from dependence on overseas investment.

The experience of the Depression and World War II had reinforced the importance of industrial and technological self-sufficiency and produced a wariness of business that was reflected in the enormous growth of direct state ownership of many economic activities. The regime of fixed exchange rates necessitated strict capital controls, as the dominant concern was to avoid current account deficits (CAD), the only remedy to which was to engineer a downturn in domestic demand. Foreign investment could provide an immediate boost to the capital account, which offsets the CAD, but in the longer term would produce a deficit due to continuing profit repatriation. The Report of the Vernon Committee of Economic Enquiry into the Australian economy in 1965 warned that:

> Once an economy has a substantial body of overseas investment, it is in a sense 'on the tiger's back' unless the trade balance is improving sufficiently to meet the additional income payable overseas. The continuation of capital inflow becomes seemingly more and more desirable as a means of offsetting the increasing payments on the latter account. As the annual amounts become larger, the immediate consequences for the economy of an interruption of the capital inflow, either contrived or occurring by reason of external

> circumstances, become more and more serious (Committee of Economic Enquiry 1965: 11.14).

By later in the 1970s, alongside the demise of the Bretton Woods system and the introduction of floating exchange rates and liberalised import and capital controls, official attitudes to foreign investment swung 180 degrees.[1] An excellent example of this revolution in economic thinking that made it conducive to liberalised foreign investment rules in Australia was the general abandonment of the concern about the CAD that so worried Vernon. Pitchford's (1990) influential thesis was that public policy should be indifferent to transactions between 'consenting adults' in Australia and overseas, even if the outcome was higher foreign debt and widening trade deficits. This was always controversial and, especially in light of the GFC, has been disproved with sustainability of the CAD again treated as a major policy concern.[2] There is remarkably little discussion of the merits or otherwise of foreign investment in contemporary public policy. It is just assumed to be 'good'.

In contrast to its earlier ambiguity, Treasury now believes that:

> foreign investment is integral to the Australian economy. As a resource rich country with a relatively high demand for capital and a small population, Australia has historically relied on foreign capital to finance the shortfall between national investment and national saving (McKissack and Xu 2016).

Present public policy is based on a notion that we should do nothing that might frighten foreign investment. In 1972, Treasury remarked on the fear in some policy circles that the imposition of controls or restrictions on one foreign investment may lead to 'frightening away other potential foreign investors'. It described this derisively as the 'startled fawn' approach to foreign investment. The startled fawn has reappeared as the foreign investor is now supposed to be so anxious that any hint of 'sovereign risk' is supposedly enough to scare it off. In 2017, the Coalition government Treasurer Scott Morrison invoked 'sovereign risk' multiple times, including in relation to increasing the renewable energy target. Playing around with that target would deter foreign investment in Australia according to the startled fawn view.

The Current Scope of Foreign Investment

We could argue that Australia now is in the position where foreign ownership and debt is so high that it cannot do without foreign investment. The total stock of foreign investment in Australia as at June 2017 was $3,238 billion, of which $1,148 billion, or 35 per cent, is equity investment; the rest is debt (ABS 2017). Foreign investment at these levels represents a large claim on Australia's income. The liabilities of the non-financial corporate sector (debt plus the equity in corporations based in Australia) are now 33 per cent owned by the 'rest of the world' (ABS 2018). More important than liabilities is the share of foreign ownership in the *equity* of corporations in Australia. Equity is important because it is the owners of the equity or shares in a company who determine the policy and practice of the company. Table 1 breaks down the shares of foreign ownership of the locally registered corporate sector by listed and unlisted companies and by financial and non-financial companies. The financial companies included here are financial corporations, banks and other depository corporations, insurance companies and other financial corporations.

TABLE 1: FOREIGN-OWNED EQUITY AS % OF ALL EQUITY.

	Selected financial corporations	Non-financial corporations	All corporations
Listed	35.6	35.7	35.7
Unlisted	55.9	32.3	36.5
Total	41.6	33.7	36.1

Source: ABS (2018).

Foreign investment in Australian corporations is now 36.1 per cent of total equity, and 35.7 per cent of listed corporations in Australia. We may imagine foreign investment to be concentrated in areas like manufacturing and mining, but there is a surprisingly high level of foreign investment in financial corporations (41.6 per cent) and that includes listed financial corporations – banks and insurance companies, for example.

Economic Arguments for Foreign Investment

The arguments for foreign investment can be usefully divided into orthodox and pragmatic varieties. These are briefly described below, as well as the main criticisms of each.

Orthodox Economic Arguments

The main orthodox argument favouring foreign investment is the perceived need to supplement inadequate domestic savings. This was the theme of Scott Morrison's recent speech at the Australasian Finance and Banking Conference (2016), in which he spoke about the historic and continuing importance of foreign investment for Australia's economic development and hence, in a classic non-sequitur, the need for tax cuts for continued foreign investment. 'As a large, resource rich country with relatively high demand for capital,' Morrison said, 'Australia has relied on foreign investment to meet the shortfall of domestic savings'. He continued:

> successive waves of foreign capital has allowed the Australian people – including our generation – to enjoy higher rates of economic growth and employment, and a higher standard of living than could have been achieved from domestic savings alone. Such capital is a necessity. It is a must have – not a nice to have.

A second argument involves neoclassical trade theory. The workhorse of the neoclassical trade theory is the Heckscher-Ohlin-Samuelson (HOS) model of international trade, which says that countries export goods and services that are intensive in the countries' abundant factors, capital or labour. The HOS model requires remarkably restrictive conditions – first, to establish the reasons why trade exists; and second, to ensure that 'free trade' is in aggregate 'welfare enhancing' for bilateral exchange between nations. (Even though it also allows some enterprise owners and some categories of labour to suffer income loss.) Importantly, however, HOS provides a simple, if not convincing, argument that 'free trade' is a 'good thing'.

Foreign investment and the transnational flow of capital, labour and knowledge, that tend to be transferred internationally as a package, are extremely awkward to reconcile with conventional theory of trade. As Hirsch argues, even relaxing two of the central pillars of HOS, international factor immobility and constant returns to scale, 'cannot explain international direct investment' (1976: 259). Hirsch argues that firm-specific intellectual property and high export transaction costs are the drivers of foreign investment.

But this is just one approach to explaining foreign investment. There are a multiplicity of other theories accounting for it, including the product cycle; vertical disintegration of production within a multinational firm across different locations each with specific advantages; absolute not comparative cost advantage; tariffs, non-tariff barriers; tax arbitrage; customising products to specific markets and sovereign wealth funds securing strategic assets such as raw materials, agricultural land and intellectual property. Importantly, 'no single theory fits the different types of direct investment or the investment made by a particular multinational corporation or country in any region' (Dinkar and Choudhury 2014).

Criticisms of Orthodoxy

The suggestion that Australia has inadequate domestic savings and must therefore use overseas savings to fund investment relies on the neoclassical argument that savings precede investment. By contrast, in a Keynesian model, savings will rise to match a higher level of investment given the higher output, consumption and savings generated by the initial investment. The simple neoclassical argument also ignores the role of banks in credit creation. A different, though recent form of credit creation is quantitative easing involving governments effectively printing money to buy public and private bonds.

The absence of a single, accepted orthodox explanation for foreign investment puts current advocates of more or less unfettered inward and capital flows in an interesting position.[3] At least orthodox trade theory provides a priori – though fanciful – reasons for the existence of trade and its mutual benefits.[4] No such omnibus theory exists for foreign investment. The key implication we can draw from this is that foreign investment, needs to be assessed on a case-by-case basis, with a careful empirical weighing of benefits and costs. Where is the national benefit in the simple transfer of ownership of local assets from domestic to overseas investors?

Even if it is assumed that overseas investment increases domestic production and employment, the question still arises about the balancing of possible losses on the part of some domestic residents with benefits to foreign investors. This is not a hypothetical question when we consider some large mining projects where revenues go abroad: there may be minimal local inputs to production or employment generated but environmental and other problems that destroy livelihoods and amenities for Australians. Policy has to balance the benefits to the foreign investors against losses to Australian residents. There is no guarantee that the net effect on Australians is actually beneficial. Quiggin (2012) has made the point that while foreign investment may well increase Australia's GDP it does not necessarily increase Australia's gross national income, which is the more appropriate measure of the actual 'benefit' to Australians.[5]

Pragmatic Arguments

The above complications mean that, from an orthodox/neoclassical perspective, there is no clear theoretical justification for free capital flows. As a result, those advocating laissez faire approaches to foreign investment typically adopt pragmatic arguments. These include claims for 'strong evidence that multinational firms have contributed to a geographical diffusion of technology and that active host countries can get access to modern technology via foreign direct investment' (Blomstrom 1991). Likewise, there may be access to consumer goods and services that are only available with the presence of the foreign supplier. Recently, the Productivity Commission (2017: 24) reported that 'foreign direct investment lifts productive capacity, generates new jobs, brings new technology into Australia, upgrades skills and strengthens competition, supporting productivity improvements and through that, national income growth'.

It does not follow that governments should simply allow foreign investment to take place exactly how the foreign investor would prefer. Yet that is the implication of the crude neoliberalism expressed in sentiments suggesting it is best to 'leave it to the market'. We might well argue that access to modern technology via foreign investment is a 'good thing' but there may be other mechanisms that deliver the same outcome. For example, the rapid development of the North Asian 'developmental states' showed how countries can use combinations of heavy investment in domestic science capacity, R&D incentives and industry policies as alternatives to foreign investment (Wade 1994). The Asian economic miracle also provides examples of countries bargaining with multinational corporations using access to the local market in return for explicit technology transfer, local equity participation and training. What we do not do well in Australia is question whether we are getting the best possible deal out of our relationships with foreign investors.

The important point is that while we can recognise the benefits of foreign investment there are many ways policymakers can maximise them. For example, the government allowed BHP to merge with Billiton provided that the head office and associated jobs remained in Australia. In the present neoliberal climate, we risk foregoing many of the benefits Australia should be deriving from foreign investment.

An interesting implication of high levels of foreign ownership of Australian business is that Australia's distribution of income and wealth appear more equal, or less unequal than they would be if the foreign owners were resident in Australia. The national accounts system (NAS) records the split of domestically produced national income between labour and capital, but local capital income flowing to foreign nationals is excluded.

Macro-economic Problems and Alternative Perspectives

A more convincing account of foreign investment and its costs and benefits can be told if we consider the macro-economic perspective. A separate issue is that an inflow of foreign capital can and does change the structure of the Australian economy. Unfettered capital inflows are not a substitute for intelligent industry policies through which democratically elected governments seek to encourage the development of industries that have desirable long-run characteristics. These characteristics include strong purchasing and supply linkages with other domestic industries, high productivity, high wages, innovation intensity and environmental sustainability. But, as will be argued below, unfettered capital flows, especially into an expansion of unprocessed commodities, can preclude the development of these features among industries.

Appreciation of the Australian dollar over the years of the resources boom has threatened Australian exporters and those industries that compete against imports. The recent resources boom has been fuelled by a foreign-owned resources sector, with the mining industry around 83 per cent foreign-owned (Richardson and Denniss 2011). The resources boom provides an interesting case study of how a surge in foreign investment affects the structure of industry and the macro-economy.

The resources boom involved an inflow of new money and thus encouraged a flow of goods and services in the same direction. For example, the appreciation of the Australian dollar as the boom progressed had the effect of increasing Australian imports, especially manufactured imports, and reducing local production. Between 2003–04 and 2008–09, manufacturing shrank from 9.1 to 7.8 per cent of GDP and by 2015–16 stood at just 6.0 per cent of GDP (ABS 2016). There was a loss of over 200,000 jobs in manufacturing, which more than offset the growth of employment in mining and associated industries (Richardson and Denniss 2011). In addition, due to the currency appreciation, more Australians holidayed abroad and fewer overseas tourists arrived in Australia.

The mechanisms underpinning those trends in Australia are referred to as the 'Gregory effect' (1976): rather than augmenting Australia's resources, the Gregory effect means that foreign capital tends to displace other domestic economic activity. The export phase of the boom, especially if accompanied by a large cyclical rise in commodity prices, will produce similar Gregory effects as export receipts increase and again keep the Australian dollar at a higher level. However, that effect may be offset somewhat given there is also a natural and large reverse flow of repatriated profits associated with most of Australia's resource exports. The key point is that a temporary resource boom causes a permanent and, arguably, adverse shift in the industrial structure. The combined effect of regular resource and other commodity booms in Australia, and the abandonment of industrial policies under neoliberalism imposes an excessively high-risk premium on private investment in manufacturing and other import-competing sectors (Brain 1999). The industrial structure will not revert to some 'equilibrium' state with a resurgence in the same industries that have declined once the large profits generated in the export phase are repatriated overseas and the value of the Australian dollar has dropped.[6]

The export phase causes other problems. For example, some of the gas projects may have very little impact on Australia if they generate huge profits accruing to foreign owners. In that case most of the revenue from operations would be sent abroad as payments to foreign suppliers and income for foreign owners. Indeed, to the extent that Asian buyers pay Chevron in California there need be very little by way of transactions involving Australian entities. Even depreciation and amortisation expenses booked in Australia are just notional items. Little more than modest government taxation revenue would remain in Australia.[7] The Australian Balance of Payments would show the export income but would also record payments going overseas again. Most of the money would never be seen in Australia. That is likely to be regarded by most people as unacceptable.

Without a mechanism to offset the monetary inflows associated with investment and export phases Australia's industrial structure will be distorted. The resources boom provides a good illustration of what the Vernon report meant by riding on the tiger's back: foreign capital inflows reduce activity in import competing and other export industries; eventually these investments imply the payment of income abroad to foreign owners, which can impose a burden on the domestic economy and hence it begins to look like we need to attract more foreign investment to cover the payment of income abroad.

The combined effect of an expanding resource and agricultural sector driven by overseas investment 'locks-in' an industrial structure focused on unprocessed commodities and low productivity services. For governments intent on pursuing economic growth there is, in effect, no alternative to expand these industries, given that active industrial policies are excluded from consideration. Again, as Peter Brain (1999) notes, resource industries oppose the development of local manufacturing and associated services if it means higher input costs and leads to the appreciation of the Australian dollar due perhaps to its import-replacement or export success. The adverse environmental effects of an excessive reliance on resource industries is another obvious cost.[8]

Finally, foreign investment encourages a different form of neoliberal policy 'lock-in' caused by competition for foreign investment between jurisdictions through lower corporate tax rates. In the speech already cited, Treasurer Morrison referred to 'the fight to attract the investment capital'. There is a mixture of cargo cultism and protectionism in this argument.[9]

The International Monetary Fund (IMF) has also long opposed the trend towards international tax competition to attract internally mobile capital. IMF Director Christine Lagarde stated in 2014 that 'there would be more revenue for all if countries resisted the temptation to compete with each other on taxes to attract business. By definition, a race to the bottom leaves everybody at the bottom'. Countries have cut corporate taxes throughout the world in order to attract foreign investment, but without success.

Conclusion

To some extent the problems identified here could be argued to relate not to the 'foreignness' of capital investment but to the problems caused by unfettered capital in general. Nevertheless, concerns remain over the CAD; macro-economic volatility induced by resource booms and fluctuating commodity prices; difficulty in crafting industry policies and democratically deciding on an appropriate industrial structure given the mostly unregulated inflow of overseas capital into the resource sector; enhanced scope for corporate tax avoidance on Australian earnings; pressure to lower corporate tax rates and asset price inflation in residential housing and other sectors. The latter is a zero sum game for domestic residents.

As Ranald notes in Chapter 17 on free trade agreements, Australia is almost unique among developed economies in having freely negotiated away the restrictions on foreign investment, known as 'exceptions' or 'reservations' that many developed economies retain under 'free trade' agreements. There is a case for being very wary of foreign investment that simply involves a transfer of local ownership to overseas owners with no clear local gain, except to the seller. There are conditions that might be imposed on foreign investors in order to leverage greater benefits for Australia. This would also require a much better compliance mechanism than governments have put in place to date.

The main lesson we need to learn from our history is that Australian policy should again reflect the view that foreign investment can have negative impacts and needs to be carefully assessed to ensure Australia gets the best deal.

Endnotes

1 See Cahill and Toner's introduction to this book for a brief account of the rise of neoliberalism and, relatedly, Evan Jones describes the thinking behind bank deregulation in Chapter 10.

2 The CA deficit does not matter school rely on a simple national accounting identity which, when manipulated, shows: foreign capital inflow = CAD = savings minus investment. The last term was interpreted as the savings gap implying that foreign investment responded to the savings gap (Richardson 1982). The direction of causation can be reversed to show that increased foreign investment creates repatriated profits that create an apparent savings deficit that drives the CAD. The assumption that foreign savings are invested is also invalid. Foreign monetary inflows can support consumption and asset bubbles, such as when banks borrow offshore to fund purchase of existing residential real estate. In addition, 'the global financial crisis and global recession has delivered a death blow to the Pitchford thesis by undermining the key assumptions of fiscal balance and rationality that underpins it' (Karunaratne 2010: 81). Peter Brain's chapter identifies persistent and high CA deficits as a problem for macro-economic stability.

3 Relaxing various neoclassical assumptions leads to the prediction that foreign investment should 'should flow from rich to poor countries'. This is due first, to the fact that the capital–labour ratio is much smaller in poor than in rich nations and, second, the assumption that scarce factors of production will achieve a higher return than abundant factors. One official study found that, using the United States and India as comparators, 'if the neoclassical model were true, the marginal product of capital in India should be about 58 times that of the U.S. In the face of such return differentials all capital should flow from U.S. to India. We do not observe such flows' (Alfaro et al. 2003: 1). Indeed, the reverse is often the case, with capital flowing from poor to rich nations.

4 That the conditions necessary for orthodox trade theory do not apply in the real world and that the actual gains from trade are decidedly mixed is dealt with in Ranald's chapter. A comprehensive analysis is provided by Dunkley (2016).

5 Benefit is put in inverted commas to emphasise that we do not regard any of the national accounting measures as good measures of the welfare of the people of Australia.

6 Now, it may be objected that a 'category mistake' has been made and these problems are not caused by the 'foreignness' of the capital investment but by the scale and industry characteristics of the investment. This is true, but the point can be made first that, for whatever reason, it is overseas capital that historically has driven resource booms, and second, it is the 'open door' nature of Australian foreign investment guideless that permits the scale and scope of these investments with their adverse effects.

7 Tax revenues associated with the company tax and petroleum resource rent tax will take a long time to ramp up given huge depreciation expenses and so on likely to be claimed by the companies concerned.

8 The proposed Adani mine, with its effects on water tables and the coastline, is an obvious example.

9 Public policy is also contradictory on this issue. The former Treasurer Keating justified the introduction of dividend imputation by saying it was all about giving Australian investors an advantage relative to foreign shareholders (Keating 2013).

References

ABS (2016) *5204.0 – Australian System of National Accounts*, 2015–16, 28 October.

——(2017) *5302.0 5 – Balance of Payments and International Investment Position, Australia, Jun 2017*, 4 September.

——(2018) *5232.0 – Australian National Accounts: Finance and Wealth, Dec 2017*, 29 March.

Alfaro, L., Kalemli-Ozcan, S. and Volosovych, V. (2003) 'Why Doesn't Capital Flow from Rich to Poor Countries? An Empirical Investigation', *IMF Seminar Paper*, December.

Blomstrom, M. (1991) 'Host country benefits of foreign investment', NBER Working Papers Series, 3615. Cambridge, National Bureau of Economics.

Brain, P. (1999) *Beyond Meltdown: The Global Battle for Sustained Growth*. Melbourne, Scribe Publications.

Calwell, A. (1968) 'Speech', *House of Representatives Hansard*, 4 April.

Committee of Economic Enquiry (1965) *Report of the Committee of Economic Enquiry, Vol. 1*. Canberra, Commonwealth of Australia, May.

Dinkar, N. and Choudhury, R.N. (2014). 'A selective review of foreign direct investment theories', ARTNeT Working Paper Series, 143, March 2014. Bangkok, ESCAP.

Dunkley, G. (2016) *One World Mania: A Critical Guide to Free Trade, Financialization and Over Globalization*. Zed Books, London.

Gregory, R.G. (1976) 'Some implications of the growth of the mineral sector', *Australian Journal of Agricultural Economics*, 20 (2), August: 71–91.

Hirsch, S. (1976) 'An international trade and investment theory of the firm', *Oxford Economic Papers*, 28 (2): 258–270.

Karunaratne, N.D. (2010) 'The sustainability of Australia's current account deficits – a reappraisal after the global financial crisis', *Journal of Policy Modeling*, 32: 81–97.

Keating P.J. (2013) 'Dividend imputation and superannuation are worth fighting for', *Cuffelinks*, 21 February.

Lagarde, C. (2014) 'The Caribbean and the IMF – building a partnership for the future', Speech to University of the West Indies at Mona, Jamaica, 27 June.

McKissack, A. and Xu, J. (2016) *Foreign Investment into Australia*, Treasury Working Paper, 2016-01, January.

Morrison, S. (2016) Speech to the Australasian Finance and Banking Conference, 14 December.

——(2017) 'Interview with Ray Hadley, 2GB', *Transcript*, 27 February.

Pitchford, J. (1990) *Australia's Foreign Debt: Myths and Realities*. Sydney, Allen & Unwin.

Productivity Commission (2017) *Rising Protectionism: Challenges, Threats and Opportunities for Australia*, Productivity Commission Research Paper. Canberra, Commonwealth of Australia.

Quiggin, J. (2012) 'The problem with GDP', *Business Spectator*, 26 June.

Richardson, D. (1982) 'Foreign investment: a host country perspective using Australian experience', *Journal of Post Keynesian Economics* IV (2): 240–252.

Richardson, D. and Denniss, R. (2011) 'Mining the truth: the rhetoric and reality of the commodities boom', Institute Paper No. 7, September.

Treasury (1972) *Overseas Investment in Australia*, Treasury Economic Paper No. 1. Canberra, Australian Government Publishing Services.

Wade, R.H. (1994) *Governing the Market*. Princeton, Princeton University Press

CHAPTER 19

INEQUALITY AND NEOLIBERAL ECONOMIC 'REFORMS' IN AUSTRALIA

FRANK STILWELL

Inequality has a major bearing on economic and social wellbeing. It is therefore an important lens through which to look at the effect of neoliberal economic 'reforms'. This is particularly so at present because of the widespread social disquiet about growing economic inequality in Australian society. Books like Piketty's blockbuster, *Capital in the Twenty-First Century* (2014), have helped to highlight the issues worldwide, while local studies by Leigh (2013), ACOSS (2015) and the Evatt Foundation (Sheil and Stilwell 2016) have helped put a spotlight on the Australian situation.

Have neoliberal economic reforms played a significant part in growing inequality? It is an obvious question to pose because privatisation, deregulation and other neoliberal policies are commonly said to create distinctive categories of winners and losers. For example, Ferguson (2009: 170) argues that, internationally, neoliberal policies 'have vastly enriched the holders of capital while leading to increased inequality, insecurity, loss of public services, and a general deterioration in the quality of life for the poor and working classes'. It is important to assess whether this is the case in Australia.

Proving a general causal connection between neoliberalism and inequality is difficult, however, because so many other processes have developed concurrently. Disentangling the effects of neoliberalism from the effects of globalisation, financialisation, rapid technological change, structural employment shifts and falling union membership is effectively impossible. These are all interconnected.

Yet we can make some progress in the inquiry on at least three fronts. First, we can clarify the relevant trends in economic inequality. Second, we can analyse the channels through which specific neoliberal policies have distributional impacts. Third, we can seek to understand how an embedded anti-egalitarianism becomes of the result of neoliberalism and inequality interacting in a process of circular and cumulative causation. This chapter proceeds in that order before offering some concluding reflections on both the current challenges and prospects for change.

Trends in Economics Inequality in Australia

The first task is to consider the evidence on inequality. This can be done briefly by highlighting three dimensions: (1) the household distribution of income; (2) the relative shares of capital and labour in the distribution of income; and (3) the distribution of household wealth. This constitutes a narrowly economic interpretation of inequality, setting aside its other social dimensions, such as those relating to gender, ethnicity and differences within the population constituted by health and educational standards. The economic data may be regarded as a ground-floor window onto that broader and more complex social scene.

The Distribution of Income

Income inequality is the conventional starting point for analysis because the income that households receive is the most direct influence on their material standard of living. Care must be taken in selecting appropriate and consistent information. Is it before or after tax? Is it adjusted to take account of how variations in household composition affect actual spending power? Taking the latter equivalised household incomes as the base, Table 1 presents the evidence for the period from 1995 to 2014. Two different measures of inequality are shown: (1) the Gini coefficient, a statistical measure of inequality in the overall distribution, ranging between zero (where all households have the same income) and unity (where one household has it all); and (2) the P90/P10 ratio, comparing the wealth of households at the ninetieth percentile of the distribution ('the quite rich') with households at the tenth percentile ('the quite poor').

TABLE 1: HOUSEHOLD INCOME INEQUALITY IN AUSTRALIA 1995–2014

	Gini coefficient	P90:/P10 ratio
1995–96	0.296	3.74
2000–01	0.311	3.97
2005–06	0.314	4.05
2011–12	0.320	4.10
2013–14	0.333	4.07

Source: Australian Bureau of Statistics, *Equivalised disposable household income, Australia, 1995–96 to 2013–14.*

By either measure, this evidence shows that inequality of incomes has been increasing. It would be useful to have a longer time series for the data, but this is difficult because earlier data is not necessarily consistent. However, we do have the results of a study by the National Centre for Economic and Social Modelling (NATSEM), which showed that, based on data from household expenditure surveys, the Gini coefficient of inequality rose between 1988–89 and 1998–99 (Harding and Greenwell 2002). So we may reasonably infer that inequality has been growing over a longer twenty-five year period, although we should remain wary of splicing the two sets of data together.

A third measure of income inequality looks at the evidence on the share of total income going to the richest 1 per cent of households (see Figure 2 on page 169 in Chapter 9 by Jim Stanford on labour market policy). This shows a particularly striking dimension of the distributional changes occurring over recent decades: as is the case in the United States, a fabulously wealthy elite has evidently been the major beneficiary of the distributional shifts.

To probe deeper into the political economic forces that have produced this growing income inequality, it is useful to consider how the relative shares of capital and labour in the national income have changed over the same period.

Capital-Labour Shares

Income to labour comes primarily as wages and salaries. Income to capital comes as profit, rent and interest – together comprising a 'gross operating surplus'. The relationship between these two types of income is called the 'functional distribution' because it classifies income by economic function (contrasting with the 'household distribution' shown in Table 1). It points to a class perspective because it shows the relative size of incomes from work and incomes from the ownership of capital. 'Factor shares' don't unambiguously align with class positions because some households receive income from both capital and labour: indeed, that is quite commonly the case. However, studying the changes in the relative capital-labour income shares is a useful first step to understanding why household distribution income has become more unequal.

The relevant data appears as Figure 1 in Chapter 9 (see page 169). It clearly shows the general decline in labour's share of the national income since the late 1970s. There was a small peak in the early 1980s around the time of the election of the Hawke government, but a quite rapid decline subsequently, continuing quite steadily through to 2008. As is usually the case with an economic recession, the immediate impact of the global financial crisis (GFC) hit capital incomes harder than labour incomes, but labour's share plunged again to a record low in the first half of 2017. Analysing the causes of these changing factor shares is complex (see Parham 2013) because contributory factors can include technological change and structural shifts among industries, as well as the effects of policies such as neoliberal reform. Yet the general observation remains: that labour's share in national income, relative to capital's, has declined over the period that neoliberalism has been the dominant policy model. Because the spread of capital incomes across households is invariably more concentrated than labour incomes, these income disparities tend, over time, to lead to even greater concentration of wealth.

The Distribution of Wealth

Whereas income is a flow, wealth is a stock. This distinction is important because, in common parlance, people with high incomes are often described as wealthy. Formally though, wealth relates only to the ownership of assets. These may be either physical (land, housing, business premises, cars, jewellery, and so on) or financial (cash, bank deposits, shares, bonds, derivatives, foreign currency, et cetera). They commonly are a mix of both.

Unfortunately, the wealth distribution data that we have in Australia is of poorer quality than the income distribution data. This is partly because, in the absence of a comprehensive wealth tax, evidence does not come directly as a by-product of taxation. However, some surveys and other indirect estimates enable us to see the general character of the shifts that have occurred in the last couple of decades. Looking at Australian households categorised by quintiles according to their wealth, we can see that the biggest percentage growth of net worth between 2003–04 and 2014–15 was in the top quintile (Sheil and Stilwell 2016). In other words, the biggest gains during this century have been made among the households that were already the wealthiest.

Time-series data for earlier periods is less readily available, although one study undertaken for the ABS (Northwood, Rawnsley and Chen 2002) made experimental estimates of the distribution of household wealth during the 1990s. It showed that the top decile of households increased its share relative to the next decile – that is, the distribution has become somewhat more 'stretched' towards the top end. Research of a rather different type, looking at the very top wealth-holders, as shown on the *Business Review Weekly*'s annual 'rich 200' lists, confirms this tendency to increased concentration in the hands of the 'super rich' (Katic and Leigh 2013).

This situation is not surprising because income inequality and wealth inequalities tend to be mutually reinforcing. Over time, businesses and households with high incomes can use that income to purchase and accumulate capital assets, while having substantial assets usually generates higher income (from dividends, rents and capital gains, for example). Concentrations of accumulated wealth also convey economic power. Vicious and virtuous cycles operate to perpetuate and more sharply differentiate losers and winners. So, as well as having mutually reinforcing effects, it is not surprising that inequality of wealth is almost invariably greater than inequality of incomes.

An interim conclusion is that both income and wealth inequalities have increased during the period when neoliberalism has been in vogue.

That it has occurred in wealth as well as incomes is indicative of its becoming more deep-seated within the social fabric and more resilient to potential future redistribution. This is of deep concern because of the growing volume of social science research that shows income inequality tends to compound social and environmental problems (Stilwell 2017; Wilkinson and Pickett 2009, 2018; Dorling 2017), and have adverse effects on macro-economic outcomes (OECD 2016; Ostry, Berg and Tsangaridis 2014; Stockhammer 2012).

The Impact of Neoliberal Reforms on Inequality

While a general correlation exists between growing inequality and neoliberal reform in Australia, both having occurred broadly over a similar time period, the question of causal connection is much more complex. However, some progress can be made by drilling down to look at particular policies and trying to infer their distributional effects. The most straightforward examples are fiscal policy, labour market policy, deregulation and privatisation.

Fiscal Policies

An explicitly neoliberal approach to fiscal policy began in Australia in 1984 when Prime Minister Bob Hawke announced the adoption of the 'Trilogy'. This was a self-imposed fiscal straightjacket, committing the federal Labour government to not increasing tax revenue, government expenditure or the budget deficit as a percentage of GDP. The prime minister had evidently felt the need to reassure financial markets and conservative critics that the government's progressive social agenda would be compatible with fiscal restraint. That set the tone for what has happened since, even after the Hawke government's progressive social agenda became a fading memory. Government ministers responsible for fiscal policy for the last three decades have generally sought to: (1) balance the budget, or, if possible, generate a budget surplus; (2) reduce tax rates for profits and personal incomes, particularly at the higher levels; and (3) cut expenditures, particularly by placing more restrictions on households' access to welfare payments.

Although this trifecta has featured regularly in political rhetoric, there have been many policy failures, even on neoliberals' own terms. Budget deficits rather than balanced budgets have been the norm, bracket creep has tended to push middle-income households into higher marginal income tax brackets, and cuts to expenditure frequently have not been achieved. As one would expect of a neoliberal program, welfare cuts have seldom been applied to corporate welfare with the same severity as they have been applied to low-income households.

It is also notable that significant differences in fiscal policy have existed between Australian Labour Party (ALP) and Liberal–National Coalition governments, notwithstanding some elements of continuity. In the 1980s, for example, during the years of the Hawke government, an Accord with the labour movement created a basis for greater capital-labour cooperation, while increases in the 'social wage' (particularly relating to health and education) compensated for agreements to wage restraint (Stilwell 1986). This gave the fiscal policy of the federal government a more progressive appearance, although neoliberalism was already starting to be implemented through policies such as privatisation and financial deregulation (Humphrys and Cahill 2017).

Subsequently, in the 1990s and 2000s, the mining boom and the growing demand for Australian exports resulting from rapid economic growth in China and India contributed significantly to an economic surplus. The Coalition government led by John Howard, with Peter Costello as Treasurer, used fiscal policy to ensure that business interests and upper-income households were the principal beneficiaries. The reductions in the progressivity of the income tax scale, the introduction of a 50 per cent discount for capital gains tax and the removal of income tax from superannuation embodied these biases. The introduction of the GST also created a regressive element in the overall tax mix.

With the ALP back in government in 2007 under Kevin Rudd's leadership, the radically different macro-economic conditions during the GFC required fiscal policy to play a dramatically different role, keeping the national economy relatively buoyant at a time when international capitalism was faltering. Keynesian-style pump priming, together with bank guarantees, helped to do the trick. This was an interregnum, however. With lower economic growth rates, and especially after the return of the Coalition government led by Tony Abbott in 2013, fiscal neoliberalism became resurgent with a more strikingly austere face. The notorious 2014 Budget prepared by Treasurer Joe Hockey proposed dramatic cuts in expenditures for welfare, health and education, while business remained favoured by various concessions. The capital gains tax discount was retained, as was the 'negative gearing' tax concession for investors in the housing market that has primarily benefitted upper-income groups and continues to exacerbate the difficulties facing first home buyers.

The ousting of Abbott and Hockey did not produce marked change in policy stance. Indeed, looking at the longer-term picture, elements of continuity dominate over short-run changes of style and emphasis. One such element is the use of fiscal policy to set the incentives for 'trickle-down economics'. The latter term is pejorative, of course, and neoliberals have usually preferred to talk of 'incentivisation' (during the Howard era) or generating 'jobs and growth' (during the more recent period of Malcolm Turnbull's prime ministership). The underlying element is the belief that economic inequality 'works' for Australian capitalism even though it may sit uncomfortably with concerns about social justice. Hence the drive to provide more investment incentives for the owners of capital by cutting their taxes and keeping wage costs down, while providing more incentives to the poor to get work by restricting welfare and keeping Newstart unemployment benefits below the poverty line. As the political economist J.K. Galbraith Snr once wryly remarked, the underlying presumption is that the rich will work harder if their incomes are raised, while the poor will work harder if their incomes are lowered (quoted in Davidson 1987).

Labour Policies

Seeking to undermine what little economic power remains in the hands of organised labour has been a second major element in the neoliberal program. Therein lies a particularly revealing feature of neoliberalism in practice because, taken at face value, neoliberals should be even-handed between capital and labour, seeking to promote competition in all markets and being equally tough on all impediments, including monopoly, monopsony, oligopoly, and restrictive trade practices of all types. Singling out trade unions for special attention shows the class-based – rather than market-based – priorities that dominate in practice. This is consistent with the interpretation of neoliberalism as a class project developed by Cahill (2014) and other political economists, revealing its 'reform' program as one that is at the service of corporate capital behind a veneer of free market ideology.

The emphasis on confronting unions has been particularly strident during periods of Liberal government. As prime minster for eleven years, John Howard was renowned for his anti-union inclinations. His government sought to undermine collective bargaining and shift the industrial relations regime towards a much stronger emphasis on individual contracts. It was an industrial relations policy that culminated ultimately in overreach because, after unexpectedly getting a parliamentary majority in the Senate, Howard and his colleagues decided to take the opportunity to push through the WorkChoices program of reforms, creating public disquiet that was a major factor in unseating his government at the 2007 election. However, the pressure on unions has been maintained and was ramped up again during the period of the Abbott and Turnbull governments.

The nature and effects of these industrial relations policies are explored more fully in Jim Stanford's chapter in this book (Chapter 9). As he points out, the shift in income shares from labour to capital may be regarded as evidence of the anti-labour effects of public policy, although the broader influence of structural changes in the economy, including workforce casualisation and the income squeeze on lower paid workers, have played their part. The declining union coverage of the workforce has also surely been a contributory factor (Leigh 2013: 71–74), while the shift towards more emphasis on enterprise agreements and less 'across the board' wage determination has tended to produce a less class-solidaristic basis for organised labour.

Deregulation

Deregulation is a third theme in the neoliberal policy program. Cutting government regulation of business features prominently in the rhetoric, although it does not always align with the policy practice. The deeper class agenda, rather than market freedoms per se, is evident in this aspect of policy too.

Financial deregulation provides an illustration. Starting in the 1980s, when Paul Keating was Treasurer in the government led by Bob Hawke, major initiatives were taken to reduce or remove regulations on financial institutions. Requirements for special reserve deposits were relaxed, the dollar was floated and the entry of foreign banks to the Australian economy was opened. Yet, to this day, the Big Four banks remain notably protected by government, evidently being deemed 'too big to fail'. Numerous consequences follow from this hybrid of deregulation and selective protection, including soaring bank profits. A notable slice of this bounty has taken the form of senior executive remuneration. The CEOs of the big banks now feature regularly among the most handsomely rewarded Australian executives. More generally, average CEO remuneration in large companies (relative to average workers' earnings) has climbed from a ratio of 18:1 in the late 1980s (Shields 2005) to around ten times that multiple today (Schofield-Georgeson 2018).

Asset-price inflation is a further consequence of reducing the regulation of the sources and uses of corporate capital. One channel through which this occurs is foreign investment, as analysed by Dave Richardson in Chapter 18. Foreign capital flowing into housing markets in Australian capital cities has tended to compound inflation in asset prices. The beneficiaries are all existing property owners, while low- and middle-income households face ever more difficulties of housing affordability. The outcome is greater accumulation and concentration of wealth. Combined with the tax-advantaged treatment of capital changes, particularly the reduction of the effective capital gains tax rate, financial deregulation has thereby compounded economic inequality.

It has also created conditions for increased economic volatility in the economy. The growth in real estate prices, as noted in Chapter 11 by Peter Phibbs and Nicole Gurran, has led to a rapidly growing volume of mortgage debt. Middle-income households drawn into the process by historically low interest rates in recent years may well default in large numbers as interest rates increase. The combination of inequality, housing stress, a widespread but ill-founded expectation of continuous growth in land and house values, together with inadequate regulation of finance, has eerie echoes of the situation leading up the global financial crash of 2008.

Privatisation

The privatisation of public enterprises is a fourth set of neoliberal reforms where a similarly direct association with increased inequality may be inferred. Privatisation has been a particularly prominent feature of the neoliberal project in Australia, as various chapters of this book identify. In relation to inequality, two pervasive effects may be noted. One is the direct effect of the sale of shares in privatised companies to already wealthy people and institutions. This need not necessarily always happen. In the case of the privatisation of Telstra, for example, many middle-income households were buyers, especially of the first tranche of shares that was offered to the public at an initial price well below their likely market value. Most financial commentators interpreted this 'bargain basement' sale of public assets as a sign of the government's aim to make privatisation widely popular with new 'mum and dad' shareholders. Over the longer term, however, the purchase of shares has more typically been by institutional shareholders and already wealthy players in the markets. One would hardly expect otherwise, because those with the most capital are best placed to take advantage of opportunities for further capital accumulation.

The sale of formerly publicly owned land and buildings is an obvious case in point. In the case of the New South Wales state government, for example, it has been calculated that, over the six years to 1917, $9.4 billion of real property assets were sold or leased by government agencies (Robertson 2017). The purchasers of large, valuable urban properties such as these are invariably substantial private wealth holders. This process has the characteristics of 'accumulation by dispossession' (Harvey 2005), as property rights over formerly public assets are transferred to already wealthy private interests.

The other principal effect of privatisations is longer-term, depending on how the new private owners run the formerly public enterprises. A principal reason for originally having natural monopolies – particularly essential services – in public ownership was to allow the application of public interest criteria to policies such as price setting. Privatised businesses tend to be less sensitive to the situation of poorer customers who are not directly profitable to serve. After the partial privatisation of the Commonwealth Bank of Australia (CBA), for example, the bank's management spoke openly about needing to shrug off the 'competitive disadvantage' that existed because many low- to middle-income households had 'unprofitable' small savings accounts with the bank. The subsequent record of the privatised CBA, revealed in the proceedings of the royal commission into banking, finance and superannuation, shows what disdain its senior executives have had for community service obligations and the broader public interest.

We should not be surprised by the tendency to monopoly or collusive oligopoly pricing by privatised entities unless increased regulation is introduced to prevent it. Therein lies a significant tension in neoliberal reforms, however, because the free market rhetoric sits awkwardly with the concentration of economic power that results. It can be generally inferred that public interest criteria, including distributional equity, are relegated to secondary status by these processes.

Embedded Anti-Egalitarianism

Each of these four policy areas have incubated processes through which greater economic inequalities are both reinforced and accentuated. A more extended analysis could consider other aspects of the neoliberal agenda, such as the demise of systematic industry policy and the trade liberalisation that Pat Ranald discusses in Chapter 17 on free trade agreements. Yet the preceding examples suffice to indicate how neoliberalism articulates with the capitalist economy's systemic tendency to reproduce polarity of poverty and wealth.

The Australian experience also points to a second type of connection between neoliberal 'reforms' and economic inequality, whereby inequality fuels neoliberalism. Increased inequality is not only a consequence of neoliberal reform: it acts as a driver for more of the same. For the elite, the appetite evidently grows the more it is fed. Indeed, it would be surprising, from a political economic perspective, if there were not mutually reinforcing processes operating. Thus, the relationship of neoliberal reforms to inequality exhibits features of circular and cumulative causation.

In effect, the neoliberal reforms change public perceptions of what is the norm. Because they have long-term effects on structures of economic power and prevailing social values and expectations, they make the institutions of civic society more marginal in relation to the concentrated centres of economic power. This political dynamic is arguably the most damaging long-term consequence of the neoliberal reform era. It creates a political constituency with a strong stake in the further centralisation of power. It is a 'winner-takes-all' situation, as Hacker and Pierson (2010) have shown in the case of the United States – a situation where an increasingly wealthy elite has a strong stake in ensuring continuity, irrespective of the damaging social consequences of growing inequality.

These are the more indirect political economic effects beyond the direct effects on income and wealth redistribution through fiscal policy, labour policies, deregulation and privatisation. They intensify the inherent tensions between capitalism and democracy. It is in the more anti-egalitarian nations that the political process is most corrupted by the capture of political institutions to serve the interests of major wealth-holders (see Stiglitz 2013; McCain 2017). Propelled by neoliberal 'reforms', Australia is in the process of joining this club.

Contradictions are ever-present, however. The policies can overreach, if they push too hard against prevailing values and social judgements about what is desirable and acceptable. It ain't all over …

Prospects

What are the lessons of more than three decades of neoliberal reforms, from the perspective of a concern with economic inequality? First, neoliberalism evidently 'works' as a means of serving the immediate interests of the wealthy.

Second, it works much less well in creating conditions for overall prosperity. This is evident in the increasing fragility of the Australian economy (Schroeder 2017) and the increased inequality that intensifies the problem of macro-economic demand-deficiency. Even from a capitalist perspective this is problematic, as is evident in public statements by the Governor of the Reserve Bank that identify the relative stagnation of wage incomes over the last decade as the principal impediment to economic growth. Post-Keynesians have long recognised this adverse macro-economic consequence of economic inequality: it now appears to be at the heart of the problem of demand-deficiency and secular stagnation post-GFC. Mike Beggs' chapter on monetary policy and unemployment in this volume develops this argument more fully (see Chapter 14).

Third, to the extent that neoliberalism reduces the relative size of the public sector in the economy, it makes the social stresses arising from economic inequality more acute. Having a low income would be less problematic if a strong public sector provided free or inexpensive public transport, public housing, public health, public education and public child care. Neoliberalism in general, and privatisation in particular, has taken Australia in the opposite direction. It has increased the social stresses arising from inequalities in private income and wealth.

Fourth, these processes create conflicts and contradictions that open up possibilities for changing direction. Policies that increase inequality tend to concurrently increase claimants for government transfer payments, unless more restrictions can be put into eligibility criteria. Increased inequality, compounded by the effects of an ageing population, also threatens to generate a growing welfare and health bill for governments. Attempts to restrain expenditure through austerity policies predictably create political trouble, obvious examples of which were the Abbott–Hockey budget of 2014 and the 'robo-debt' fiasco of 2017 when the Turnbull government sought to claw back payments previously made to welfare recipients. Neoliberalism morphing into the politics of austerity (albeit not with the intensity experienced in some European nations) is, for many people, a thoroughly unwelcome prospect.

So are we coming to the end of the line for the neoliberal reform agenda? My crystal ball clouds over at this point. Suffice to say that there are deepening tensions. The interests of the wealthy elite in perpetuating embedded anti-egalitarianism diverge from a broader public interest in having more economic equality, greater social cohesion and better public services. The opponents of neoliberalism, as ever, have to engage at all levels: material, ideological and organisational. The challenge is to develop an agenda for radical reforms in which egalitarian aims are at the forefront, along with strategies for achieving a more secure and sustainable socio-economic future.

REFERENCES

ACOSS (2015) *Inequality in Australia: A Nation Divided.* Sydney, Australian Council of Social Service.

Cahill, D. (2014) *The End of Laissez Faire: On the Durability of Embedded Neoliberalism.* Cheltenham, Edward Elgar.

Davidson, K. (1987) 'J.K. Galbraith and the new economics', *Sydney Morning Herald*, 24 February.

Dorling, D. (2017) *The Equality Effect: Improving Life for Everyone.* Oxford, New Internationalist Publications.

Ferguson, J. (2009) 'The Uses of Neoliberalism', *Antipode*, 41 (S1): 168–184.

Hacker, J.S. and Pierson, P. (2010) *Winner-Take-All Politics.* New York, Simon and Schuster.

Harding, A. and Greenwell, H. (2002) *Trends in Income and Expenditure Inequality in the 1980s and 1990s*, Discussion Paper No. 57, National Centre for Social and Economic Modelling. Canberra, Commonwealth of Australia.

Harvey, D.M. (2005) *A Brief History of Neoliberalism.* Oxford, Oxford University Press.

Humphrys, E. and Cahill, D. (2017), 'How Labour made neoliberalism', *Critical Sociology*, 43 (4–5): 669–684.

Katic, P. and Leigh, A. (2015) 'Top wealth shares in Australia 1915–2012', *Income and Wealth*, 62 (2), 20 January: 209–222.

Leigh, A. (2013) *Battlers and Billionaires: The Story of Inequality in Australia.* Carlton, Redback.

McCain, R.A. (2017) *Approaching Inequality: What Can Be Done About Wealth Inequality?* Cheltenham, Edward Elgar.

Northwood, K., Rawnsley, T. and Chen, L. (2002) *Experimental Estimates of the Distribution of Household Wealth in Australia 1994–2000*, Working Paper in Econometrics and Applied Statistics. Canberra, Australian Bureau of Statistics.

OECD (2016) *The Productivity–Inclusiveness Nexus*, Meeting of the OECD Council at Ministerial Level, Paris, 1–2 June.

Ostry, J.D., Berg, A. and Tsangaridis, N. (2014) *Redistribution, Inequality and Growth*, IMF Staff Discussion Note SDN/14/02, February.

Parham, D. (2013) *Labour's Share of Growth in Income and Prosperity*, Visiting Researcher Paper. Canberra, Productivity Commission.

Piketty, T. (2014) *Capital in the Twenty-First Century.* Cambridge, Harvard University Press.

Robertson, J. (2017), 'Property sales hit $9 b. in privatisation push', *The Sydney Morning Herald*, 5 September.

Schofield-Georgeson, E. (2018) 'Regulating executive salaries and reducing pay disparities: is pay disclosure the answer?' *Journal of Australian Political Economy*, 81, Winter: 95–120.

Schroeder, S. (2017) 'Just how fragile is the Australian economy?' *Australian Options*, 87, March: 18–22.

Sheil, C. and Stilwell, F. (2016), *The Wealth of the Nation*, report prepared for The Evatt Foundation, Sydney.

Shields, J. (2005) 'Setting the double standard: setting CEO pay the BCA way', *Journal of Australian Political Economy*, 56, December: 299–324.

Stiglitz, J. (2013) *The Price of Inequality: How Today's Divided Society Endangers Our Future.* New York, Norton.

Stilwell, F. (1986) *The Accord and Beyond: The Political Economy of the Labor Government.* Sydney, Pluto Press.

——(2017) 'Reducing economic inequality: a key element in the transition', in Washington, H. (ed.) *Positive Steps to a Steady State Economy*. Sydney, CASSE.

Stockhammer, E. (2012) *Rising Inequality as a Root Cause of the Present Crisis, Working Paper*, Political Economy Research Institute. Amherst, University of Massachusetts.

Wilkinson, R. and Pickett. K. (2009) *The Spirit Level: Why More Equal Societies Almost Always Do Better*. London, Allen Lane.

——(2018) *The Inner Level: How More Equal Societies Reduce Stress, Restore Sanity and Improve Everyone's Wellbeing*. London, Allen Lane.

ABOUT THE AUTHORS

Edited by:

Damien Cahill is an associate professor in political economy at the University of Sydney. His research examines the theory and practice of neoliberalism as well as the institutional foundations of capitalist economies. He has published widely on neoliberalism, including the books *The End of Laissez-Faire? On the Durability of Embedded Neoliberalism* and *Neoliberalism* (with Martijn Konings).

Phillip Toner is an honorary senior research fellow in the department of political economy at the University of Sydney. His research includes industrial structure analysis and industry policy, the economics of technical change and international vocational skills formation systems, and he has conducted projects on these topics for the OECD, the EU, the World Bank, Industry Canada, the South African Human Sciences Research Council, APEC, the Australian Research Council, the Department of Innovation, Science and Research and the National Centre for Vocational Education Research among others. Phillip is the author of *Main Currents in Cumulative Causation: The Dynamics of Growth and Development.* Previously he worked in economic and labour market analysis including for federal Treasury.

With Contributions from:

Jane Andrew is an associate professor of accounting at the University of Sydney Business School. Much of her work considers the way accounting information enables and obscures particular policy pathways. Jane holds a PhD from the University of Wollongong and is a member of the Sydney Institute of Criminology and the Imprisonment Observatory.

Max Baker is a senior lecturer of accounting at the University of Sydney Business School. Max researches the accountability practices of companies and governments in their efforts to provide social goods. He is a chief investigator of a nationwide investigation into the costs, performance and accountability of Australian private prisons.

Michael Beggs is a senior lecturer in political economy at the University of Sydney, where he works on the history of monetary theory and policy. He is the author of *Inflation and the Making of Australian Macroeconomic Policy, 1945-85*.

Peter Brain is the executive director and co-founder of the National Institute of Economic and Industry Research (NIEIR), and the founding author of the *State of the Regions* report. His work includes analysis of regional economics, infrastructure, major projects and events; environmental impacts, employment and education, international and regional trade, industry policy and the implications of these on social and economic development in Australia. Peter has participated in over 1500 economic consulting projects in Australia, South Africa and New Zealand, and spent many years developing NIEIR's IMP model of the Australian economy. A well-known commentator on economic matters, he has written widely on the Australian economy, including five major books on its structure and performance.

Gareth Bryant is a lecturer in political economy at the University of Sydney. His research explores the marketisation of different areas of socio-ecological life, with a current focus on climate/energy and education policy. His forthcoming book, *Carbon Markets in a Climate-Changing Capitalism*, will be published by Cambridge University Press. Gareth was awarded the Global Network for Financial Geography dissertation prize.

Bob Davidson is a researcher and consultant who has had extensive senior experience in the government, community, and corporate sectors across a wide range of social, economic and environmental areas. He is currently an honorary fellow at Macquarie University and a director of Danett Associates. In recent years his work has focused on the economics and provision of human services from both theoretical and empirical perspectives.

Paul Davies has worked in senior strategic roles in trade unions across a variety of industries for more than twenty years. Most recently he was a director with Professionals Australia, representing engineers, scientists and managers. In 2009 Paul established the Australian National Engineering Taskforce to research and develop solutions for the structural problems besetting the engineering workforce. He is currently a director with the Media Arts and Entertainment Alliance.

Stephen Duckett is director of the health program at the Grattan Institute. He has a reputation for creativity, evidence-based innovation and reform in areas ranging from the introduction of activity-based funding for hospitals, to new systems of accountability for the safety of hospital care. An economist, he is a fellow of the Academy of the Social Sciences in Australia and of the Australian Academy of Health and Medical Sciences.

Wilma Gallet is a lecturer in social services at the University of Divinity. She has extensive experience in employment services, including twenty years with the Commonwealth Employment Service, and ten years with The Salvation Army in senior policy development roles. She was the CEO of Employment Plus, the largest community-based provider of government funded employment services from 1998 to 2003.

Nicole Gurran is a professor of urban and regional planning at the University of Sydney, where she is program chair, leads Urban Housing Lab@Sydney and directs the University's Australian Housing and Urban Research Institute research centre.

Elizabeth Hill is a senior lecturer in the department of political economy at the University of Sydney and co-convenor of the Australian Work + Family Policy Roundtable. Elizabeth's research focuses on the political economy of women's paid work, unpaid care and the care workforce in Australia and the Asia Pacific. Her latest publications include *Women, Work and Care in the Asia Pacific* and *Employment Policy in Emerging Economies: The Indian Case.*

Evan Jones has a Bachelor of Commerce (with honours) from the University of Melbourne and a PhD from Michigan State. He lectured at the University of Sydney from 1973 until he retired in 2006, first briefly in economics and then in political economy. Evan has written continuously on the Australian banking sector since 2000.

Sue Olney is a research fellow in the Public Service Research Group at the School of Business at the University of New South Wales, Canberra, and an honorary senior fellow at the University of Melbourne school of government, with experience on both sides of the process of outsourcing public services in government and the community sector.

Peter Phibbs is a professor of urban planning and policy at the University of Sydney as well as director of the Henry Halloran Trust, a philanthropically funded research trust at the same university.

John Quiggin is a vice-chancellor's senior fellow in economics at the University of Queensland. He is prominent both as a research economist and as a commentator on Australian and international economic policy. His latest book, *Economics in Two Lessons: Why Markets Work, and Why They Can Fail So Badly*, will be published in 2019 by Princeton University Press.

Patricia Ranald is an honorary research fellow in the department of political economy at the University of Sydney. She was formerly a senior research fellow at the University of New South Wales, and has published widely on the social impacts of trade agreements for over twenty years. She is the honorary convener of the Australian Fair Trade and Investment Network

(AFTINET), which advocates for fair trade policies based on human rights, labour rights and environmental sustainability.

Lee Ridge is a postgraduate research student at the University of Sydney researching the national broadband network. He is chartered accountant and has worked extensively in telecommunications and accounting.

David Richardson taught at the Universities of New England and Western Australia before moving to Canberra and working in the economics group of the Legislative Research Service (Parliamentary Library). During the Hawke/Keating years he worked for various cabinet ministers. For the last decade David has worked for the Australia Institute.

Ben Spies-Butcher is a senior lecturer in sociology at Macquarie University. His work centres on the political economy of social policy. His most recent co-authored book, *Market Society* (with Joy Paton and Damien Cahill) was published with Cambridge University Press. Ben is a research associate at the retirement policy and research centre at the University of Auckland and was awarded the Australian Association of Gerontology's Glenda Powell Travelling Fellowship.

Jim Stanford is an economist and director of the Centre for Future Work at the Australia Institute, based in Sydney. He is Harold Innis Industry Professor of Economics at McMaster University in Hamilton, Canada, and an honorary professor of political economy at the University of Sydney.

Frank Stilwell is professor emeritus in political economy at the University of Sydney, where he began teaching in 1970. He is a well-known critic of conventional economics and an advocate of alternative economic strategies for social justice and ecological sustainability. Frank has written a dozen books on political economic issues and co-edited half a dozen others. His next book is *The Political Economy of Inequality*. He is a fellow of the Academy of Social Sciences in Australia, the coordinating editor of the *Journal of Australian Political Economy*, vice president of the Evatt Foundation and executive member of the Council for Peace with Justice.

Matt Wade is a senior economics writer and columnist for the *Sydney Morning Herald* and *The Age*. He was previously a foreign correspondent for Fairfax based in India and worked in the Canberra press gallery as economics correspondent for *The Herald*.

Acknowledgements

The editors express their deep appreciation to the contributors who responded so enthusiastically to the call to share their specialised expertise in this collective effort to assess the results of 'economic reform' over the last three decades. It would be impossible for a single author – or even a small team of researchers alone – to have achieved the depth and quality of analysis evident in these nineteen chapters. The achievement is truly more than the sum of its parts.

Deep appreciation is also extended to the board of La Trobe University Press, the publisher Chris Feik, and the outstanding staff at Black Inc. who prepared the book in what must be record time.

INDEX

www.ingramcontent.com/pod-product-compliance
Ingram Content Group UK Ltd.
Pitfield, Milton Keynes, MK11 3LW, UK
UKHW020426250726
13967UKWH00007B/2827

9 781760 640385